WISDOM AND SIRACH

.

THE IGNATIUS CATHOLIC STUDY BIBLE

REVISED STANDARD VERSION
SECOND CATHOLIC EDITION

WISDOM AND SIRACH

The Wisdom of Solomon: Introduction, Commentary, and Notes
by Scott Hahn and Curtis Mitch
with Mark Giszczak

The Book of Sirach: Introduction, Commentary, and Notes
by André Villeneuve with Scott Hahn and Curtis Mitch

and with

Study Questions by Dennis Walters

IGNATIUS PRESS   SAN FRANCISCO

Published with ecclesiastical approval
Original Bible text: Revised Standard Version, Catholic Edition
Nihil Obstat: Thomas Hanlon, S.T.L., L.S.S., Ph.L.
Imprimatur: + Peter W. Bartholome, D.D.
Bishop of Saint Cloud, Minnesota
May 11, 1966

Introduction, commentaries and notes:
Nihil Obstat: Ruth Ohm Sutherland, Ph.D., Censor Deputatus
Imprimatur: + The Most Reverend Salvatore Cordileone
Archbishop of San Francisco
January 10, 2020

The *nihil obstat* and *imprimatur* are official declarations that a book or pamphlet is free of doctrinal or moral error. No implication is contained therein that those who have granted the *nihil obstat* and *imprimatur* agree with the contents, opinions, or statements expressed.

Second Catholic Edition approved by the
National Council of the Churches of Christ in the USA

Cover art: *Wisdom of the Lord*, Sirach 1:1–4
1852–1860 illustration by Julius Schnorr von Carolsfeld
Lebrecht Music & Arts / Alamy Stock Photo

Cover design by Riz Boncan Marsella

Published by Ignatius Press in 2020

Introductions, commentaries, notes, headings, and study questions
© 2020 by Ignatius Press, San Francisco
All rights reserved
ISBN 978-1-62164-184-1 (PB)
ISBN 978-1-64229-124-7 (eBook)
Printed in the United States of America ∞

CONTENTS

INTRODUCTION TO
THE IGNATIUS STUDY BIBLE
by Scott Hahn, Ph.D.

You are approaching the "word of God". This is the title Christians most commonly give to the Bible, and the expression is rich in meaning. It is also the title given to the Second Person of the Blessed Trinity, God the Son. For Jesus Christ became flesh for our salvation, and "the name by which he is called is The Word of God" (Rev 19:13; cf. Jn 1:14).

The word of God is Scripture. The Word of God is Jesus. This close association between God's *written* word and his *eternal* Word is intentional and has been the custom of the Church since the first generation. "All Sacred Scripture is but one book, and this one book is Christ, 'because all divine Scripture speaks of Christ, and all divine Scripture is fulfilled in Christ'[1]" (CCC 134). This does not mean that the Scriptures are divine in the same way that Jesus is divine. They are, rather, divinely inspired and, as such, are unique in world literature, just as the Incarnation of the eternal Word is unique in human history.

Yet we can say that the inspired word resembles the incarnate Word in several important ways. Jesus Christ is the Word of God incarnate. In his humanity, he is like us in all things, except for sin. As a work of man, the Bible is like any other book, except without error. Both Christ and Scripture, says the Second Vatican Council, are given "for the sake of our salvation" (*Dei Verbum* 11), and both give us God's definitive revelation of himself. We cannot, therefore, conceive of one without the other: the Bible without Jesus, or Jesus without the Bible. Each is the interpretive key to the other. And because Christ is the subject of all the Scriptures, St. Jerome insists, "Ignorance of the Scriptures is ignorance of Christ"[2] (CCC 133).

When we approach the Bible, then, we approach Jesus, the Word of God; and in order to encounter Jesus, we must approach him in a prayerful study of the inspired word of God, the Sacred Scriptures.

Inspiration and Inerrancy The Catholic Church makes mighty claims for the Bible, and our acceptance of those claims is essential if we are to read the Scriptures and apply them to our lives as the Church intends. So it is not enough merely to nod at words like "inspired", "unique", or "inerrant". We

have to understand what the Church means by these terms, and we have to make that understanding our own. After all, what we believe about the Bible will inevitably influence the way we read the Bible. The way we read the Bible, in turn, will determine what we "get out" of its sacred pages.

These principles hold true no matter what we read: a news report, a search warrant, an advertisement, a paycheck, a doctor's prescription, an eviction notice. How (or whether) we read these things depends largely upon our preconceived notions about the reliability and authority of their sources—and the potential they have for affecting our lives. In some cases, to misunderstand a document's authority can lead to dire consequences. In others, it can keep us from enjoying rewards that are rightfully ours. In the case of the Bible, both the rewards and the consequences involved take on an ultimate value.

What does the Church mean, then, when she affirms the words of St. Paul: "All Scripture is inspired by God" (2 Tim 3:16)? Since the term "inspired" in this passage could be translated "God-breathed", it follows that God breathed forth his word in the Scriptures as you and I breathe forth air when we speak. This means that God is the primary author of the Bible. He certainly employed human authors in this task as well, but he did not merely assist them while they wrote or subsequently approve what they had written. God the Holy Spirit is the *principal* author of Scripture, while the human writers are *instrumental* authors. These human authors freely wrote everything, and only those things, that God wanted: the word of God in the very words of God. This miracle of dual authorship extends to the whole of Scripture, and to every one of its parts, so that whatever the human authors affirm, God likewise affirms through their words.

The principle of biblical inerrancy follows logically from this principle of divine authorship. After all, God cannot lie, and he cannot make mistakes. Since the Bible is divinely inspired, it must be without error in everything that its divine and human authors affirm to be true. This means that biblical inerrancy is a mystery even broader in scope than infallibility, which guarantees for us that the Church will always teach the truth concerning faith and morals. Of course the mantle of inerrancy likewise covers faith and morals, but it extends even farther to ensure that all the facts and events of salvation history are accurately presented for us in

---

[1] Hugh of St. Victor, *De arca Noe* 2, 8: PL 176, 642: cf. ibid. 2, 9: PL 176, 642–43.

[2] *DV* 25; cf. Phil 3:8 and St. Jerome, *Commentariorum in Isaiam libri xviii*, prol.: PL 24, 17b.

the Scriptures. Inerrancy is our guarantee that the words and deeds of God found in the Bible are unified and true, declaring with one voice the wonders of his saving love.

The guarantee of inerrancy does not mean, however, that the Bible is an all-purpose encyclopedia of information covering every field of study. The Bible is not, for example, a textbook in the empirical sciences, and it should not be treated as one. When biblical authors relate facts of the natural order, we can be sure they are speaking in a purely descriptive and "phenomenological" way, according to the way things appeared to their senses.

Biblical Authority Implicit in these doctrines is God's desire to make himself known to the world and to enter a loving relationship with every man, woman, and child he has created. God gave us the Scriptures not just to inform or motivate us; more than anything he wants to save us. This higher purpose underlies every page of the Bible, indeed every word of it.

In order to reveal himself, God used what theologians call "accommodation". Sometimes the Lord stoops down to communicate by "condescension"— that is, he speaks as humans speak, as if he had the same passions and weakness that we do (for example, God says he was "sorry" that he made man in Genesis 6:6). Other times he communicates by "elevation"—that is, by endowing human words with divine power (for example, through the Prophets). The numerous examples of divine accommodation in the Bible are an expression of God's wise and fatherly ways. For a sensitive father can speak with his children either by condescension, as in baby talk, or by elevation, by bringing a child's understanding up to a more mature level.

God's word is thus saving, fatherly, and personal. Because it speaks directly to us, we must never be indifferent to its content; after all, the word of God is at once the object, cause, and support of our faith. It is, in fact, a test of our faith, since we see in the Scriptures only what faith disposes us to see. If we believe what the Church believes, we will see in Scripture the saving, inerrant, and divinely authored revelation of the Father. If we believe otherwise, we see another book altogether.

This test applies not only to rank-and-file believers but also to the Church's theologians and hierarchy, and even the Magisterium. Vatican II has stressed in recent times that Scripture must be "the very soul of sacred theology" (*Dei Verbum* 24). As Joseph Cardinal Ratzinger, Pope Benedict XVI echoed this powerful teaching with his own, insisting that "the *normative theologians* are the authors of Holy Scripture" (emphasis added). He reminded us that Scripture and the Church's dogmatic teaching are tied tightly together, to the point of being inseparable: "Dogma is by definition nothing other than an interpretation of Scripture." The defined dogmas of our faith, then, encapsulate the Church's infallible interpretation of Scripture, and theology is a further reflection upon that work.

The Senses of Scripture Because the Bible has both divine and human authors, we are required to master a different sort of reading than we are used to. First, we must read Scripture according to its *literal* sense, as we read any other human literature. At this initial stage, we strive to discover the meaning of the words and expressions used by the biblical writers as they were understood in their original setting and by their original recipients. This means, among other things, that we do not interpret everything we read "literalistically", as though Scripture never speaks in a figurative or symbolic way (it often does!). Rather, we read it according to the rules that govern its different literary forms of writing, depending on whether we are reading a narrative, a poem, a letter, a parable, or an apocalyptic vision. The Church calls us to read the divine books in this way to ensure that we understand what the human authors were laboring to explain to God's people.

The literal sense, however, is not the only sense of Scripture, since we interpret its sacred pages according to the *spiritual* senses as well. In this way, we search out what the Holy Spirit is trying to tell us, beyond even what the human authors have consciously asserted. Whereas the literal sense of Scripture describes a historical reality—a fact, precept, or event—the spiritual senses disclose deeper mysteries revealed through the historical realities. What the soul is to the body, the spiritual senses are to the literal. You can distinguish them; but if you try to separate them, death immediately follows. St. Paul was the first to insist upon this and warn of its consequences: "God ... has qualified us to be ministers of a new covenant, not in a written code but in the Spirit; for the written code kills, but the Spirit gives life" (2 Cor 3:5–6).

Catholic tradition recognizes three spiritual senses that stand upon the foundation of the literal sense of Scripture (see CCC 115). **(1)** The first is the *allegorical* sense, which unveils the spiritual and prophetic meaning of biblical history. Allegorical interpretations thus reveal how persons, events, and institutions of Scripture can point beyond themselves toward greater mysteries yet to come (OT) or display the fruits of mysteries already revealed (NT). Christians have often read the Old Testament in this way to discover how the mystery of Christ in the New Covenant was once hidden in the Old and how the full significance of the Old Covenant was finally made manifest in the New. Allegorical significance is likewise latent in the New Testament, especially in the life and deeds of Jesus recorded in the Gospels. Because Christ is the Head of the Church and the source of her spiritual life, what was accomplished in Christ the Head during his earthly life prefigures what he continually produces in his members through grace. The allegorical sense builds up the virtue of faith. **(2)** The second is the *tropological* or *moral* sense, which reveals how the actions of God's people in the Old Testament and the life of Jesus in the New Testament prompt us to form virtuous habits in our own lives. It therefore draws from Scripture warnings against sin and vice as well as inspirations to pursue holiness and purity. The moral sense is intended to build up the virtue of charity. **(3)** The third is the *anagogical* sense, which points upward to heavenly glory. It shows us how countless events in the Bible prefigure our final union with God in eternity and how things that are "seen" on earth are figures of things "unseen" in heaven. Because the anagogical sense leads us to contemplate our destiny, it is meant to build up the virtue of hope. Together with the literal sense, then, these spiritual senses draw out the fullness of what God wants to give us through his word and as such comprise what ancient tradition has called the "full sense" of Sacred Scripture.

All of this means that the deeds and events of the Bible are charged with meaning beyond what is immediately apparent to the reader. In essence, that meaning is Jesus Christ and the salvation he died to give us. This is especially true of the books of the New Testament, which proclaim Jesus explicitly; but it is also true of the Old Testament, which speaks of Jesus in more hidden and symbolic ways. The human authors of the Old Testament told us as much as they were able, but they could not clearly discern the shape of all future events standing at such a distance. It is the Bible's divine Author, the Holy Spirit, who could and did foretell the saving work of Christ, from the first page of the Book of Genesis onward.

The New Testament did not, therefore, abolish the Old. Rather, the New fulfilled the Old, and in doing so, it lifted the veil that kept hidden the face of the Lord's bride. Once the veil is removed, we suddenly see the world of the Old Covenant charged with grandeur. Water, fire, clouds, gardens, trees, hills, doves, lambs—all of these things are memorable details in the history and poetry of Israel. But now, seen in the light of Jesus Christ, they are much more. For the Christian with eyes to see, water symbolizes the saving power of Baptism; fire, the Holy Spirit; the spotless lamb, Christ crucified; Jerusalem, the city of heavenly glory.

The spiritual reading of Scripture is nothing new. Indeed, the very first Christians read the Bible this way. St. Paul describes Adam as a "type" that prefigured Jesus Christ (Rom 5:14). A "type" is a real person, place, thing, or event in the Old Testament that foreshadows something greater in the New. From this term we get the word "typology", referring to the study of how the Old Testament prefigures Christ (CCC 128–30). Elsewhere St. Paul draws deeper meanings out of the story of Abraham's sons, declaring, "This is an allegory" (Gal 4:24). He is not suggesting that these events of the distant past never really happened; he is saying that the events both happened *and* signified something more glorious yet to come.

The New Testament later describes the Tabernacle of ancient Israel as "a copy and shadow of the heavenly sanctuary" (Heb 8:5) and the Mosaic Law as a "shadow of the good things to come" (Heb 10:1). St. Peter, in turn, notes that Noah and his family were "saved through water" in a way that "corresponds" to sacramental Baptism, which "now saves you" (1 Pet 3:20–21). It is interesting to note that the expression translated as "corresponds" in this verse is a Greek term that denotes the fulfillment or counterpart of an ancient "type".

We need not look to the apostles, however, to justify a spiritual reading of the Bible. After all, Jesus himself read the Old Testament this way. He referred to Jonah (Mt 12:39), Solomon (Mt 12:42), the Temple (Jn 2:19), and the brazen serpent (Jn 3:14) as "signs" that pointed forward to him. We see in Luke's Gospel, as Christ comforted the disciples on the road to Emmaus, that "beginning with Moses and all the prophets, he interpreted to them in all the Scriptures the things concerning himself" (Lk 24:27). It was precisely this extensive spiritual interpretation of the Old Testament that made such an impact on these once-discouraged travelers, causing their hearts to "burn" within them (Lk 24:32).

Criteria for Biblical Interpretation We, too, must learn to discern the "full sense" of Scripture as it includes both the literal and spiritual senses together. Still, this does not mean we should "read into" the Bible meanings that are not really there. Spiritual exegesis is not an unrestrained flight of the imagination. Rather, it is a sacred science that proceeds according to certain principles and stands accountable to sacred tradition, the Magisterium, and the wider community of biblical interpreters (both living and deceased).

In searching out the full sense of a text, we should always avoid the extreme tendency to "over-spiritualize" in a way that minimizes or denies the Bible's literal truth. St. Thomas Aquinas was well aware of this danger and asserted that "all other senses of Sacred Scripture are based on the literal" (*STh* I, 1, 10, *ad* 1, quoted in CCC 116). On the other hand, we should never confine the meaning of a text to the literal, intended sense of its human author, as if the divine Author did not intend the passage to be read in the light of Christ's coming.

Fortunately the Church has given us guidelines in our study of Scripture. The unique character and divine authorship of the Bible call us to read it "in the Spirit" (*Dei Verbum* 12). Vatican II outlines this teaching in a practical way by directing us to read the Scriptures according to three specific criteria:

1. We must "[b]e especially attentive 'to the content and unity of the whole Scripture'" (CCC 112).

2. We must "[r]ead the Scripture within 'the living Tradition of the whole Church'" (CCC 113).

3. We must "[b]e attentive to the analogy of faith" (CCC 114; cf. Rom 12:6).

These criteria protect us from many of the dangers that ensnare readers of the Bible, from the newest inquirer to the most prestigious scholar. Reading Scripture out of context is one such pitfall, and probably the one most difficult to avoid. A memorable cartoon from the 1950s shows a young man poring over the pages of the Bible. He says to his sister: "Don't bother me now; I'm trying to find a Scripture verse to back up one of my preconceived notions." No doubt a biblical text pried from its context can be twisted to say something very different from what its author actually intended.

The Church's criteria guide us here by defining what constitutes the authentic "context" of a given biblical passage. The first criterion directs us to the literary context of every verse, including not only the words and paragraphs that surround it, but also the entire corpus of the biblical author's writings and, indeed, the span of the entire Bible. The *complete* literary context of any Scripture verse includes every text from Genesis to Revelation—because the Bible is a unified book, not just a library of different books. When the Church canonized the Book of Revelation, for example, she recognized it to be incomprehensible apart from the wider context of the entire Bible.

The second criterion places the Bible firmly within the context of a community that treasures a "living tradition". That community is the People of God down through the ages. Christians lived out their faith for well over a millennium before the printing press was invented. For centuries, few believers owned copies of the Gospels, and few people could read anyway. Yet they absorbed the gospel—through the sermons of their bishops and clergy, through prayer and meditation, through Christian art, through liturgical celebrations, and through oral tradition. These were expressions of the one "living tradition", a culture of living faith that stretches from ancient Israel to the contemporary Church. For the early Christians, the gospel could not be understood apart from that tradition. So it is with us. Reverence for the Church's tradition is what protects us from any sort of chronological or cultural provincialism, such as scholarly fads that arise and carry away a generation of interpreters before being dismissed by the next generation.

The third criterion places scriptural texts within the framework of faith. If we believe that the Scriptures are divinely inspired, we must also believe them to be internally coherent and consistent with all the doctrines that Christians believe. Remember, the Church's dogmas (such as the Real Presence, the papacy, the Immaculate Conception) are not something *added* to Scripture; rather, they are the Church's infallible interpretation *of* Scripture.

Using This Study Guide This volume is designed to lead the reader through Scripture according to the Church's guidelines—faithful to the canon, to the tradition, and to the creeds. The Church's interpretive principles have thus shaped the component parts of this book, and they are designed to make the reader's study as effective and rewarding as possible.

Introductions: We have introduced the biblical book with an essay covering issues such as authorship, date of composition, purpose, and leading themes. This background information will assist readers to approach and understand the text on its own terms.

Annotations: The basic notes at the bottom of every page help the user to read the Scriptures with understanding. They by no means exhaust the meaning of the sacred text but provide background material to help the reader make sense of what he reads. Often these notes make explicit what the sacred writers assumed or held to be implicit. They also provide a great deal of historical, cultural, geographical, and theological information pertinent to the inspired narratives—information that can help the reader bridge the distance between the biblical world and his own.

Cross-References: Between the biblical text at the top of each page and the annotations at the bottom, numerous references are listed to point readers to other scriptural passages related to the one being studied. This follow-up is an essential part of any serious study. It is also an excellent way to discover how the content of Scripture "hangs together" in a providential unity. Along with biblical cross-references, the annotations refer to select paragraphs from the *Catechism of the Catholic Church*. These are not doctrinal "proof texts" but are designed to help the reader interpret the Bible in accordance with the mind of the Church. The *Catechism* references listed either handle the biblical text directly or treat a broader doctrinal theme that sheds significant light on that text.

Topical Essays, Word Studies, Charts: These features bring readers to a deeper understanding of select details. The *topical essays* take up major themes and explain them more thoroughly and theologically than the annotations, often relating them to the doctrines of the Church. Occasionally the annotations are supplemented by *word studies* that put readers in touch with the ancient languages of Scripture. These should help readers to understand better and appreciate the inspired terminology that runs throughout the sacred books. Also included are various *charts* that summarize biblical information "at a glance".

Icon Annotations: Three distinctive icons are interspersed throughout the annotations, each one corresponding to one of the Church's three criteria for biblical interpretation. Bullets indicate the passage or passages to which these icons apply.

Notes marked by the book icon relate to the "content and unity" of Scripture, showing how particular passages of the Old Testament illuminate the mysteries of the New. Much of the information in these notes explains the original context of the citations and indicates how and why this has a direct bearing on Christ or the Church. Through these notes, the reader can develop a sensitivity to the beauty and unity of God's saving plan as it stretches across both Testaments.

Notes marked by the dove icon examine particular passages in light of the Church's "living tradition". Because the Holy Spirit both guides the Magisterium and inspires the spiritual senses of Scripture, these annotations supply information along both of these lines. On the one hand, they refer to the Church's doctrinal teaching as presented by various popes, creeds, and ecumenical councils; on the other, they draw from (and paraphrase) the spiritual interpretations of various Fathers, Doctors, and saints.

Notes marked by the keys icon pertain to the "analogy of faith". Here we spell out how the mysteries of our faith "unlock" and explain one another. This type of comparison between Christian beliefs displays the coherence and unity of defined dogmas, which are the Church's infallible interpretations of Scripture.

Putting It All in Perspective Perhaps the most important context of all we have saved for last: the interior life of the individual reader. What we get out of the Bible will largely depend on how we approach the Bible. Unless we are living a sustained and disciplined life of prayer, we will never have the reverence, the profound humility, or the grace we need to see the Scriptures for what they really are.

You are approaching the "word of God". But for thousands of years, since before he knit you in your mother's womb, the Word of God has been approaching you.

One Final Note. The volume you hold in your hands is only a small part of a much larger work still in production. Study helps similar to those printed in this booklet are being prepared for *all* the books of the Bible and will appear gradually as they are finished. Our ultimate goal is to publish a single, one-volume Study Bible that will include the entire text of Scripture, along with all the annotations, charts, cross-references, maps, and other features found in the following pages. Individual booklets will be published in the meantime, with the hope that God's people can begin to benefit from this labor before its full completion.

We have included a long list of Study Questions in the back to make this format as useful as possible, not only for individual study, but for group settings and discussions as well. The questions are designed to help readers both "understand" the Bible and "apply" it to their lives. We pray that God will make use of our efforts and yours to help renew the face of the earth! «

INTRODUCTION TO THE WISDOM OF SOLOMON

Author The Wisdom of Solomon does not reveal the identity of its author. In the history of interpretation, several candidates have been proposed for authorship, including Philo of Alexandria, Ben Sirach, or a member of one of the Jewish sects such as the Essenes or the Therapeutae, but none has met with widespread acceptance. Internal analysis suggests that the unnamed writer of the book was a Jewish intellectual who was both steeped in the writings of the Old Testament and conversant in Greek philosophical ideas that were popular in the Hellenistic period. His probable location was the port of Alexandria, Egypt. Not only was this city a towering cultural and educational center in the ancient Mediterranean world, and one with a large Jewish population, but Wisdom's author shows a marked interest in Egypt, its religious cults, and especially in the biblical story of the Exodus. A consistency of language and style throughout has convinced most commentators that a single author is responsible for the whole book.

Beginning in 6:9, Wisdom's author refers to himself in the first person (I, me, my) but does not disclose his name. Nevertheless, the writer's allusions to details from other parts of the Bible indicate that he writes *as if* he were King Solomon, the quintessential wise man of ancient Israel. In other words, the author appears to be engaged in a literary impersonation of Solomon that aims at situating his teaching within the biblical Wisdom tradition, much of which is traceable to Solomon or his enduring inspiration. Modern readers sometimes find this practice strange or even deceptive, but writing in the name, or adopting the persona, of an illustrious figure from the past was not unknown in the ancient world. In this instance, the writer presumably thought that utilizing Solomon's voice was an effective way of commending wisdom to "kings" (6:1) and other "rulers of the earth" (1:1). A few modern scholars have argued that Solomon himself authored the book and that an original Hebrew version of all or part of the book was later translated into Greek. The great majority, however, have accepted its anonymity as unproblematic. The early Church Fathers tend to cite the book under the name Solomon, and some even attribute it to the historical Solomon (e.g., Lactantius, *Divine Institutes* 4, 16), but the more common opinion accepts that its Solomonic voice is a rhetorical device employed by a later, anonymous writer (e.g., St. Augustine, *City of God* 17, 20; St. Jerome, *Prologue to the Books of Solomon* 17–18; Eusebius, *Preparation for the Gospel* 11, 7, 5). According to the Muratorian Canon, which gives a list of the New Testament books accepted by the Church in Rome in the late second century A.D., the Book of Wisdom was written "by Solomon's friends in his honor".

Date The Book of Wisdom was probably the last book of the Old Testament to be written. Most date its appearance between 100 B.C. and A.D. 40 at the latest. These parameters are determined by two main factors: (1) the author of Wisdom quotes the Greek LXX version of Job, Proverbs, and Isaiah, books that appeared in translation by at least 100 B.C., and (2) the book appears to be familiar to several writers of the New Testament (see *Christian Perspective* below). Attempts at fixing a more precise date have been made that would place Wisdom's composition during the early Roman Empire, e.g., during the reign of Caesar Augustus (27 B.C. to A.D. 14) or possibly Gaius Caligula (A.D. 37 to 41), but these dates remain difficult to prove.

Title The Greek LXX titles the work *Sophia Salōmōnos*, "Wisdom of Solomon", whereas the earliest Latin versions give the title *Liber Sapientiae*, "Book of Wisdom". Both headings are apt in their own way—the Greek title because it spells out the book's implied connection with Solomon, and the Latin title because the book advocates a form of Israelite wisdom without naming Solomon explicitly. Modern English translations generally adopt the heading preferred in the Greek LXX.

Place in the Canon The Wisdom of Solomon is included in Catholic and Eastern Orthodox canons of the Bible but not in Jewish and Protestant canons. It is possible that Wisdom was revered as scriptural by some Diaspora Jews who spoke Greek, since the book is preserved in surviving codices of the Septuagint, but rabbinic Judaism excluded the book from its Bible, perhaps because it was written in Greek rather than Hebrew. Christians gave the book a more favorable reception. Although some, like St. Jerome, questioned the canonicity of the book, the majority of Church Fathers, beginning with St. Clement of Rome and St. Irenaeus of Lyon, embraced the Wisdom of Solomon as inspired Scripture. The book was also deemed canonical by the regional Synods of Rome (A.D. 382), Hippo (A.D. 393), and Carthage (A.D. 397). For reasons that remain unclear, Wisdom was occasionally listed among the books of the New Testament (Muratorian Canon; Epiphanius of Salamis, *Panarion* 76, 5).

Structure The organizational structure of the Book of Wisdom is delineated differently by various scholars. Focusing on its leading themes, some propose a threefold outline in which 1:1—5:23 presents *immortality* as God's gift to the righteous; 6:1—9:18 presents *wisdom* as God's gift to those who seek it through prayer; and 10:1—19:22 presents *salvation* as God's gift to his chosen people. Focusing on the literary features of the book, others discern a symmetrical division of the work into two equal halves, 1:1—11:1 and 11:2—19:22, both of which are said to consist of exactly 251 poetic units. Subdivisions of these two halves are made on the basis of parallel, linear, and concentric structures observable in the original Greek.

Literary Background The Book of Wisdom is one of two books in the Old Testament that appears to have been written in Greek rather than Hebrew or Aramaic (the other being 2 Maccabees). A fair number of Hebraisms have been identified in the text, but these do not demand a translation from a Semitic precursor. More significant for deciding the question of original language are its multiple instances of literary artistry and ornamentation that seem to require an original composition in Greek. Also, the author makes use of technical terms of Greek philosophy for which there is no known Semitic equivalent.

In terms of genre, the book is usually considered an "exhortatory discourse" (known in Greek as a *logos protreptikos*). It is a sustained appeal to follow and embrace one way of life (Judaism) over against another (paganism). This is achieved through the use of classical rhetorical devices such as *inclusion*, in which a word or phrase announces the theme of a given section by standing at its beginning and end (e.g., 1:1 and 1:15); *diatribe*, in which a lively debate is conducted between the author and a hypothetical dialogue partner for the purpose of education or persuasion (chaps. 1–6); and *synkrisis*, in which competing ideas or claims are compared and contrasted (chaps. 11–19). No less prominent is the author's use of Hebrew literary forms, including poetic parallelism, formulas of prayer, and expressions of praise.

The most conspicuous influence on the Wisdom of Solomon is the Old Testament, particularly the Greek Septuagint (LXX) translation. Occasionally the author quotes directly from the Greek Scriptures, e.g., citing Is 3:10 (2:12), Job 9:12 (12:12), and Is 44:20 (15:10), but this is the exception rather than the rule. Far more often he borrows its words and images to write in the style of a Jewish *midrash*. This means that countless teachings and turns of phrase from the Bible are woven into the fabric of the book as a way of making Judaism's scriptural heritage relevant and attractive to his contemporary readers. The author likewise shows himself knowledgeable of Jewish interpretive traditions outside the Bible, especially those found in ancient works such as *Jubilees*, the *Testament of Solomon*, and the *Testament of Levi*.

Occasion and Purpose The Book of Wisdom was written to a community of Alexandrian Jews struggling over issues of religious allegiance. Its purpose was to galvanize a Jewish minority living in the midst of a non-Jewish and sometimes anti-Jewish society. Judging from the contents of the book, it seems likely that some of the author's fellow Jews were drawn away from their ancestral faith by the enticements of Hellenistic philosophy, the popular appeal of local pagan cults, and the moral distractions that invariably come with living in a cosmopolitan culture. Others may have apostatized from Judaism under the pressure of religious persecution. These are the kinds of threats to Jewish identity and commitment that appear to have called forth the Wisdom of Solomon.

The author's response to this situation in Alexandria is both creative and compelling. On the one hand, he shows by example his appreciation for Greek learning. Apparently, he wants to convince intellectually minded Jews that one can benefit from a Hellenistic education without leaving Judaism behind. Human reason and divine revelation need not be set in opposition. Even more, he tries to persuade readers that Israel, being entrusted with the Scriptures, already possesses a "wisdom" that is far superior to anything on offer in the Alexandrian schools. On the other hand, while the author implicitly endorses a limited appropriation of Greek philosophy, he shows an open disdain for pagan idolatry, especially Egyptian cults that venerate animals. This, he argues—not the Jewish faith, as Hellenistic intellectuals often charged—is the real superstition that plagues ancient society and bears witness to man's frightful capacity to act irrationally.

Content and Themes The Wisdom of Solomon is partly traditional and partly original. It shows the greatest respect for Israel's scriptural heritage and reaffirms its central teachings. Two major events of salvation history in particular—Solomon's quest for wisdom (chaps. 6–9) and Israel's exodus from Egypt (chaps. 11–19)—are mined for their lessons about God and his ways. At the same time, the author advances new insights into God's relationship with his people, so that the book stands in close continuity with the Old Testament, even as it moves toward the fullness of truth to come in the New Testament. Its main contributions to the Bible may be summarized under three major headings.

(1) The book is an exposition of *the wisdom of God*, which is a divine attribute as well as a divine gift. As an attribute of God, wisdom is ultimately the Lord's creative and governing intelligence and is thus closely connected with his "providence" (14:3). Building on the personification of Lady Wisdom in Prov 1–9, the author depicts her (Greek *sophia*, "wisdom", is grammatically feminine) almost as a distinct personality within the Godhead: wisdom lives with God (8:3); she sits by God's throne (9:4); and she reflects God's eternal light (7:26), even as her presence reaches throughout the cosmos (8:1). More ancient than creation itself, wisdom is God's coeternal companion (9:9) as well as God's collaborator in fashioning the universe (7:22). As a gift that comes from God, wisdom is a spiritual perception of reality that comes through prayer (7:7; 8:21; 9:1–18). It is a healing and enhancement of human reason made possible by the gift of divine revelation. Wisdom is thus considered a guide for living (9:9), a teacher of the cardinal virtues (8:7), and a voice of heavenly counsel (9:17). She is to be cherished as a beloved bride (8:2) who brings joy to those who embrace her (8:16). Although she imparts knowledge about the world and its mysteries (7:16–21), her greatest blessing is to make the wise "friends of God" (7:27) and to lead them to an immortal life in the kingdom of God (6:17–20; 8:13).

(2) The book offers the fullest teaching on *life after death* in the Old Testament. Death, the author insists, does not terminate human existence in a definitive way. Man, who was created in the image of God, was created for eternity with God (2:23). The implication is that death was never a part of man's creation (1:13); instead, it represents an abnormality that took hold in the world through the devil's envy (2:23). What, then, is the final state of man following bodily decease? On this question, the author assumes a basic compatibility between the Greek conception of man as an "embodied soul" and the Hebrew conception of man as "flesh infused with the breath of life" (15:11; cf. 1:4; 8:19–20; 9:15). Despite the dissolution of the body or flesh, the soul or spirit of a person lives on and reaches its destiny after passing through the judgment of God. The righteous who adhere faithfully to the Lord and his covenant will know his "peace" (3:3) and "salvation" (5:2) and ultimately "live for ever" (5:15). But the wicked, who live in defiance of the Lord and often persecute his people, are destined to be "punished" (3:10) and "suffer anguish" (4:19). It can therefore be said that Wisdom defines immortality in covenantal rather than philosophical terms, meaning that people find undying blessedness through seeking the Lord in "righteousness" (1:15). Belief in a bodily resurrection, though an emerging hope in Old Testament theology (Is 26:19; Dan 12:2; 2 Mac 7:14), is neither affirmed nor denied in the Book of Wisdom.

(3) The book deepens Old Testament teaching on *the goodness of God*, showing that the Lord's beneficence in the past tells us about his actions in the present. General statements appear that affirm the Lord's kindness and patience toward his people

(15:1; 16:2), his love for all created things (11:24–26), and his merciful forbearance toward sinners (11:23; 12:10, 18). Most of what is said about God is illustrated from early biblical history. From various examples in the Bible we see God protecting his people (10:12; 19:6–8), delivering them from evil (10:1, 13; 16:8), guiding them according to his purposes (10:10, 17; 18:3), healing their ailments (16:10, 12), prospering their way (10:10–11; 11:1), and correcting their misbehavior with loving discipline (11:9–10; 12:2, 22). Especially significant is the series of seven antitheses featured in chapters 11–19. These are framed by the author, on the basis of the Exodus story, to underscore the contrast between the Lord's stern punishments on Egypt and his generous provisions for Israel. While the Egyptians reeled under the punishment of plagues, in which creation itself was recruited to fight Israel's enemies (16:24), the Israelites were supplied with food and water in the wilderness (11:7; 16:2, 20), furnished with light in the midst of darkness (18:1), and given a path of escape through the sea (10:18; 19:7–8). These events, in which the Exodus generation of Israel is a type of the community of God's people in every age, teach that "in everything, O Lord, you have exalted and glorified your people; and you have not neglected to help them at all times and in all places" (19:22).

Christian Perspective The Wisdom of Solomon is never quoted in the New Testament, but signs of its influence are present. For instance, 2:17–20 appears to stand behind Matthew's description of the Crucifixion, where Jesus is taunted by onlookers who challenge his claim to be God's Son (Mt 27:39–43). Likewise, several points made in chapters 11–15 on the subject of natural theology and the connection between idolatry and immorality are reiterated by Paul (Rom 1:20–32); so too, one can detect the influence of 5:18–20 in Paul's exhortations on spiritual warfare (Eph 6:13–17). Perhaps most significant is Wisdom's influence on the New Testament portrayal of God. On the one hand, the book all but equates wisdom with the "holy Spirit" (9:17; cf. 7:22), by whom "men were taught what pleases" the Lord (9:18). This is close to Paul's vision of the Holy Spirit as an indwelling guide and teacher of wisdom (e.g., Rom 8:1–14; 1 Cor 2:6–13). On the other hand, significant terms and attributes ascribed to wisdom are also attributed to Jesus Christ: both are identified as the "wisdom" of God (8:21; 1 Cor 1:30); both are designated an "image" and "reflection" of God (7:26; Col 1:15; Heb 1:3); and both are preexistent mediators of creation, through whom all things were made (7:22; 9:9; Jn 1:1–3; Col 1:16–17). Finally, the depiction of God's word in 18:15–16 shows a marked resemblance to the portrayal of Jesus as the sword-bearing Word who brings judgment in the Book of Revelation (Rev 19:13–15).

OUTLINE OF THE WISDOM OF SOLOMON

1. The Divine Gift of Immortality (chaps. 1–5)
    A. Rulers and Loving Righteousness (1:1–15)
    B. Death and the Pursuits of the Wicked (1:16—2:24)
    C. Fate of the Righteous and the Wicked Contrasted (3:1—4:20)
    D. Judgment of the Righteous and the Wicked Recounted (5:1–23)

2. The Divine Gift of Wisdom (chaps. 6–9)
    A. Rulers and Instruction in Wisdom (6:1–25)
    B. Solomon and the Excellence of Wisdom (7:1—8:21)
    C. Solomon's Prayer for Wisdom (9:1–18)

3. The Divine Gift of Salvation (chaps. 10–19)
    A. Salvation by Wisdom: Adam to the Exodus (10:1—11:3)
    B. First Exodus Antithesis: Thirst and Water (11:4–14)
    C. Divine Judgment and Mercy (11:15—12:27)
    D. Foolishness of Idolatry (13:1—15:19)
    E. Second Exodus Antithesis: Frogs and Quail (16:1–4)
    F. Third Exodus Antithesis: Insects and Healing (16:5–14)
    G. Fourth Exodus Antithesis: Hail and Manna (16:15–29)
    H. Fifth Exodus Antithesis: Darkness and Light (17:1—18:4)
    I. Sixth Exodus Antithesis: Death and Atonement (18:5–25)
    J. Seventh Exodus Antithesis: Destruction and Deliverance at the Sea (19:1–22)

THE
WISDOM OF SOLOMON

Exhortation to Uprightness and Avoidance of Evil

1 Love righteousness, you rulers of the earth,
   think of the Lord with uprightness,
and seek him with sincerity of heart;
²because he is found by those who do not put him
   to the test,
and manifests himself to those who do not distrust
   him.
³For perverse thoughts separate men from God,
   and when his power is tested, it convicts the
   foolish;
⁴because wisdom will not enter a deceitful soul,
   nor dwell in a body enslaved to sin.

⁵For a holy and disciplined spirit* will flee from
   deceit,
and will rise and depart from foolish thoughts,
and will be ashamed at the approach of
   unrighteousness.

⁶For wisdom is a kindly spirit
and will not free a blasphemer from the guilt of
   his words;
because God is witness of his inmost
   feelings,
and a true observer of his heart, and a hearer
   of his tongue.

1:1—5:23 Immortality, the theme of Wis 1–5, is explored through a series of contrasts between the righteous and the wicked, who differ in their way of life, their way of thinking, and their final destiny. The belief that life divides into "two ways"—the paths of virtue and vice, the one leading to God and the other away from him—is a recurring motif in Scripture (CCC 1696). See notes on Ps 1 and Prov 1:15.

1:1–15 Wisdom's prologue begins and ends extolling "righteousness" (1:1, 15). The biblical meaning of the term (Gk., *dikaiosynē*) overlaps with the classical notion of "justice" but goes beyond it to include faithful adherence to God and his commandments (Deut 6:25; Lk 1:6). Indeed, the way of righteousness defined by the Mosaic Law is Israel's "wisdom" in the sight of the nations (Deut 4:6). Kings and political leaders are counseled to embrace this standard of righteousness that the Lord loves (Ps 45:7) and by which he rules the world (9:3).

1:1 Love righteousness: Similar to the Greek LXX translation of 1 Chron 29:17, where David says that God "loves righteousness". Also, because righteousness is "immortal" (1:15), those who practice it die in the hope of immortality (3:3). **rulers of the earth:** Here and in 6:1, the author adopts the perspective of King Solomon speaking to fellow monarchs. Another possibility is that he is speaking to all men and women, to whom God has given royal dominion over creation (Gen 1:26). **seek him:** I.e., through prayer, fasting, and obedience to the Lord's commandments (1 Chron 16:11; 22:19; 28:8; 2 Chron 20:3). Scripture offers assurance that one who seeks God and his wisdom with **sincerity** will find them (6:12; 1 Chron 28:9; Jer 29:13; Mt 7:7-8) (CCC 2566-67).

The book describes the part that Wisdom plays in the life and destiny of men and how we should acquire it, says much about the divine Wisdom, and, in the latter part of the book, relates how the chosen people were guided thereby throughout their history. At times the book proclaims truths not exactly in harmony with beliefs then current, e.g., that suffering is not necessarily the consequence of sin. The book was written in Greek, probably in the first century B.C. Its author is unknown. It is ascribed to Solomon according to a widespread practice of the time of adopting the name of a famous man in antiquity to "father" one's work. Thus David was known to have written psalms and hence many subsequent psalms were ascribed to him. Moses enacted laws and thus many subsequent laws were ascribed to him which at best could be said to be only indirectly connected with the great lawgiver. So here, Solomon was the "wise man"—and hence it was natural to attribute the book to him.

*1:5, a *holy and disciplined spirit*: Literally, "a holy spirit of discipline." Verse 6 seems to suggest here a personification of the Holy Spirit; cf. also verse 7: *the Spirit of the Lord.*

1:2 put him to the test: Echoes the prohibition in Deut 6:16, which recounts how Israel challenged the Lord to prove his goodness in the wilderness (Ex 17:1-7).

1:3 perverse thoughts: Even secret sins of the heart and mind distance us from God and are subject to his judgment (Rom 2:16; 1 Cor 4:5).

1:4 wisdom: Personified as an indwelling tutor from God, closely linked with his Spirit (1:6-7; 9:17). In biblical teaching, wisdom guides both intellect and will, our mind as well as our moral choices. Wisdom finds no home in one who is deceptive and dominated by sin. See introduction: *Content and Themes*. For the Hebrew concept of wisdom, see word study: *Wisdom* at 1 Kings 3:28. **Soul ... body:** Use of this language suggests the author found the ancient Greek view of man as a composite of matter (body) and spirit (soul) compatible with Israel's view of man as "flesh" or "dust" that is made alive by a divine infusion of "breath" or "spirit" (15:8, 11; Gen 2:7; Job 34:14-15; Eccles 12:7). This body-and-soul anthropology, which appears elsewhere in the book (8:19-20; 9:15), anticipates the NT view of the human person (Mt 10:28; 1 Thess 5:23; 1 Pet 2:11) (CCC 362-66). **enslaved to sin:** One whose actions and decisions are controlled by the appetites and urges of the flesh. A situation of debt slavery may be in view. • Jesus likewise warns about slavery to sin (Jn 8:34), as does Paul, who speaks specifically about moral enslavement to the passions of the body (Rom 6:6, 12). • The soul immersed in God does not delight in things that deceptively seem good. If it succumbs to the defilement of passion, it violates its covenant of spiritual marriage. For the good Spouse cannot live with a soul that is easily angered, malicious, or gives shelter to similar defects (St. Gregory of Nyssa, *On Virginity* 16, 1).

1:5 holy and disciplined spirit: Literally, "a holy spirit of discipline", which some take as a reference to the Holy Spirit (cf. 1:6-7; 9:17; Is 63:10).

1:6-11 An admonition on careful speech, warning that sins of the tongue (e.g., grumbling, slander, lying) will not go unnoticed or unpunished by the Lord. This subject is often touched upon in the Bible's wisdom literature (Prov 4:24; 10:18-19; Sir 20:24-27; 28:13-26) and in the NT (Mt 12:34-35; Eph 4:29; Col 4:6; Jas 3:1-12) (CCC 2477-87).

1:6 kindly spirit: A "humanity-loving" spirit. Philanthropy is later ascribed to God (15:1) and is expected of the righteous (12:19). **observer of his heart:** Knowledge of man's hidden thoughts and intentions is an exercise of God's omniscience (Gen 6:5; 1 Chron 28:9; Ps 139:2-4; Heb 4:12-13).

⁷Because the Spirit of the Lord has filled the world,
and that which holds all things together knows
what is said;
⁸therefore no one who utters unrighteous things
will escape notice,
and justice, when it punishes, will not pass him
by.
⁹For inquiry will be made into the counsels of an
ungodly man,
and a report of his words will come to the Lord,
to convict him of his lawless deeds;
¹⁰because a jealous ear hears all things,
and the sound of murmurings does not go
unheard.
¹¹Beware then of useless murmuring,
and keep your tongue from slander;
because no secret word is without result,ᵃ
and a lying mouth destroys the soul.

¹²Do not invite death by the error of your life,
nor bring on destruction by the works of your
hands;

¹³because God did not make death, and
he does not delight in the death of the living.
¹⁴For he created all things that they might exist,
and the creaturesᵇ of the world are wholesome,
and there is no destructive poison in them;
and the dominionᶜ of Hades is not on earth.
¹⁵For righteousness is immortal.

¹⁶But ungodly men by their words and deeds
summoned death;ᵈ
considering him a friend, they pined away,
and they made a covenant with him,
because they are fit to belong to his party.
2 For they reasoned unsoundly, saying to
themselves,
"Short and sorrowful is our life,
and there is no remedy when a man comes to his
end,
and no one has been known to return from Hades.
²Because we were born by mere chance,
and hereafter we shall be as though we had never
been;

1:7 filled the world: The Spirit of God is diffused throughout the universe (Ps 139:7-10), just as the wisdom of God "pervades and penetrates all things" in creation (7:24). The biblical teaching on divine omnipresence means that God is not subject to the limitations of space but is present everywhere (Jer 23:24) and thus near to everything he has made (Acts 17:27-28). **holds all things together:** Paul makes a similar statement about Jesus Christ as the mediator of creation, in whom "all things hold together" (Col 1:17).

1:10 jealous ear: Divine jealousy is the love of God that tolerates no disloyalty on the part of his chosen people (Ex 20:5; 34:14).

1:11 murmuring: Means "complaining" or "griping" against God and his servants. This was the besetting sin of the Exodus generation (Ex 15:24; 16:2-3; 17:3; Num 11:1; 14:27; 21:5).

1:12 death: The subject of a theological debate in the book. The wicked mistakenly suppose that human life ends in *physical* death without hope for an afterlife (2:1-5). Consequently, they indulge in the sensual pleasures of life (2:6-9) and even condemn the righteous man to a shameful death in order to prove that his trust in God is foolish (2:20). Being ignorant of the Lord's designs, they are unaware that bodily death can be a means of divine purification and sacrificial service (3:5-6) that conveys the souls of the righteous into the hands of God (3:1). Nor do they realize that an early death, instead of being the ultimate tragedy, can be a blessing whereby God rescues the righteous from the corruptive temptations of sin (4:7-14). For Wisdom's author, physical death is far less dreadful than *spiritual* death. By this he means separation from God (1:3) and the prospect of condemnation at the final Judgment (3:10, 16-19). Spiritual death—the death of our union with God—entered human history through the work of the devil (2:24) and comes to those whose words and deeds are evil (1:16). God, on the other hand, is not the cause of any form of human death, spiritual or physical (1:13-14) (CCC 1006-1009).

1:13 does not delight: Echoes the sayings in Ezek 18:32 and 33:11.

1:14 Hades: A Greek name for the realm of the dead. For the biblical concept, see word study *Sheol* at Num 16:30.

1:15 righteousness is immortal: Implies that God rewards the righteous with undying life and peace (3:1-3; 5:15). Righteousness is the antidote to sinfulness and mortality because it cements a relationship with God that endures beyond the grave. The Book of Wisdom neither affirms nor denies the immortality of the soul on philosophical grounds, i.e., by insisting that incorruptibility is an inherent property of the soul as a spiritual substance. The belief that a blessed immortality depends on moral uprightness is a fundamentally Jewish doctrine (Philo of Alexandria, *On the Confusion of Tongues* 149) that was carried over into the NT (Mt 25:46; Jn 5:28-29; Rom 2:7) (CCC 1038-1041).

1:16—2:24 Death is personified as an ally of the wicked. Evildoers show by their actions that they "belong to his party" (1:16; 2:24).

1:16 covenant with him: Recalls the "covenant with death" in Is 28:15, where the corrupt rulers of Jerusalem took steps to avoid war and thus to defer their death as long as possible.

2:1-20 The twisted thoughts and motives of the wicked revealed in their own words. They are *materialists* who deny that man has a spiritual soul and hold that reason and thought are produced by the body (2:2); *annihilationists* who deny the existence of life after death (2:3-5); *hedonists* who pursue life's pleasures without moral restraint (2:6-9); *extortionists* who take advantage of the poor and powerless (2:10-11); and *violent extremists* who subject the righteous to mockery, torture, and death (2:12-20). It appears likely from 2:12 and 3:10 that the wicked are apostate Jews.

2:1 Short and sorrowful: Recalls Job's statement that man lives "few days" that are "full of trouble" (Job 14:1). **no remedy:** A denial of the Jewish belief in a bodily resurrection (Is 26:19; Dan 12:2; 2 Mac 7:9, 11, 14). **no one ... from Hades:** I.e., no one comes back from the dead (2:5). See note on 1:14.

2:2 born by mere chance: A denial that life is part of God's providential plan for the world. Some think the wicked are influenced by Epicurean philosophy, which held that life begins and is pulled along by the blind forces of fate. **reason**

ᵃ Or *will go unpunished.*
ᵇ Or *the generative forces.*
ᶜ Or *palace.*
ᵈ Gk *him.*

because the breath in our nostrils is smoke,
   and reason is a spark kindled by the beating of
      our hearts.
³When it is extinguished, the body will turn to
      ashes,
   and the spirit will dissolve like empty air.
⁴Our name will be forgotten in time,
   and no one will remember our works;
   our life will pass away like the traces of a cloud,
   and be scattered like mist
   that is chased by the rays of the sun
   and overcome by its heat.
⁵For our allotted time is the passing of a shadow,
   and there is no return from our death,
   because it is sealed up and no one turns back.

⁶"Come, therefore, let us enjoy the good things that
      exist,
   and make use of the creation to the full as in youth.
⁷Let us take our fill of costly wine and perfumes,
   and let no flower of spring pass by us.
⁸Let us crown ourselves with rosebuds before they
      wither.
⁹Let none of us fail to share in our revelry,
   everywhere let us leave signs of enjoyment,
   because this is our portion, and this our lot.
¹⁰Let us oppress the righteous poor man;
   let us not spare the widow
   nor regard the gray hairs of the aged.
¹¹But let our might be our law of right,
   for what is weak proves itself to be useless.

¹²"Let us lie in wait for the righteous man,
   because he is inconvenient to us and opposes our
      actions;
   he reproaches us for sins against the law,
   and accuses us of sins against our training.
¹³He professes to have knowledge of God,
   and calls himself a child ᵉ of the Lord.
¹⁴He became to us a reproof of our thoughts;
¹⁵the very sight of him is a burden to us,
   because his manner of life is unlike that of others,
   and his ways are strange.
¹⁶We are considered by him as something base,
   and he avoids our ways as unclean;
   he calls the last end of the righteous happy,
   and boasts that God is his father.
¹⁷Let us see if his words are true,
   and let us test what will happen at the end of his
      life;
¹⁸for if the righteous man is God's son, he will help
      him,
   and will deliver him from the hand of his
      adversaries.
¹⁹Let us test him with insult and torture,
   that we may find out how gentle he is,
   and make trial of his forbearance.
²⁰Let us condemn him to a shameful death,
   for, according to what he says, he will be
      protected."

²¹Thus they reasoned, but they were led astray,
   for their wickedness blinded them,

---

is a spark: The wicked claim (1) that reason is simply a by-product of bodily operations, not the faculty of an immaterial soul, and (2) that it shines brightly during one's life and burns out at death. Some detect the influence of Stoic philosophy, which viewed the soul as an ethereal substance comparable to fire.

2:3 the spirit will dissolve: A denial of the Jewish belief that the human spirit lives on after bodily death in Sheol or Hades, the shadowy underworld of the dead (16:13).

2:4 forgotten in time: Considered a grievous misfortune (Ps 109:15).

2:6 enjoy the good things: Pursuit of maximal pleasure and minimal pain is an Epicurean philosophy of life that leaves God and his evaluation of our actions out of consideration. It is fueled by the looming prospect of death (Is 22:13; 1 Cor 15:32). This is not to say that feasting and fun times are themselves condemned as wickedness; within reasonable limits, these can be experienced as blessings from God. See note on Eccles 2:24.

2:10 Let us oppress: A life of self-indulgence may begin as a private pursuit that appears to harm no one (2:6–9), but it soon turns the hedonist against others, especially if they burden his conscience by opposing his actions as sinful (2:12).

2:11 might ... law of right: Ruthless men strain to justify their abuse of power by declaring weakness to be **useless** in the practical affairs of life. Adopting the view that "might makes right" amounts to a denial of human accountability to God for acts of injustice (CCC 1902–1904, 1932).

2:12–20 Hatred of the righteous, provoked by their opposition to evildoing, leads to their persecution and execution. • These verses are commonly read in connection with the Passion of Jesus. In particular 2:18–20, which details how the righteous man is made to suffer in order to test his claim to be God's son, closely parallels the account of the Crucifixion in Mt 27:39–44.

2:12 inconvenient to us: A borrowing from the Greek LXX translation of Is 3:10, part of which reads: "Let us bind the righteous man because he is inconvenient to us". **the law:** The Torah, which was the primary source of religious **training** in Israel. By implication, the wicked in view are Jews who have betrayed their spiritual heritage (cf. 3:10).

2:13 knowledge of God: The wisdom that comes from God (6:22; 7:7) and makes one a friend of God (7:14, 27). **child of the Lord:** Or "servant of the Lord". • The ridicule and rejection of the godly man recall the Suffering Servant of the Lord in Is 52:13—53:12.

2:16 something base: Or "counterfeit". **God is his father:** Kinship with God, understood as a father-and-son relationship, is the essence of Israel's covenant with the Lord (Deut 8:5; 14:1). In the OT, the Fatherhood of God is often expressed in relation to the nation of Israel collectively (Deut 32:6; Is 63:16) and sometimes to the Israelites individually (14:3; Sir 23:1) (CCC 239, 270).

2:17 let us test: The wicked not only test the faith of the righteous man; they also put God to the test to see if he "will help" his suffering servant (2:18). This is contrary to the counsel in 1:2. • The onlookers who reviled Jesus on the Cross likewise challenged God to deliver his faithful Son (Mt 27:43).

2:21 wickedness blinded them: See note on Rom 1:21.

ᵉ Or *servant.*

²²and they did not know the secret purposes of God,
nor hope for the wages of holiness,
nor discern the prize for blameless souls;
²³for God created man for incorruption,
and made him in the image of his own eternity, ᶠ
²⁴but through the devil's envy death entered the world,
and those who belong to his party experience it.

The Destiny of the Righteous Contrasted to the Ungodly

3 But the souls of the righteous are in the hand of God,
and no torment will ever touch them.

²In the eyes of the foolish they seemed to have died,
and their departure was thought to be an affliction,
³and their going from us to be their destruction;
but they are at peace.
⁴For though in the sight of men they were punished,
their hope is full of immortality.
⁵Having been disciplined a little, they will receive great good,
because God tested them and found them worthy of himself;

2:22 secret purposes: Mysteries concerning the afterlife that are known to the author and spelled out in 3:1–6. **wages of holiness:** A blessed immortality in the presence of God (5:15). Its opposite is spiritual death, which is paid to the evildoer as "the wages of sin" (Rom 6:23). The Greek *misthos* ("wage", "payment") appears also in 10:17 (translated "reward"), hinting that Israel's exodus from Egypt foreshadows the salvation that awaits the righteous.

2:23–24 An inspired interpretation of Gen 1–3. • It affirms that God **created** man and woman in his **image** (Gen 1:26–27) and further teaches that **death**, spiritual as well as physical, only **entered the world** when the **devil's** temptation successfully lured the original couple into disobedience (Gen 2:16–17; 3:1–19). This is the first time in Scripture that the serpent of Gen 3:1–15 is openly identified with the devil, or Satan, a teaching also found in the NT (Jn 8:44; Rom 16:20; Rev 12:9). Paul, who alludes to this verse in Rom 5:12, also traces the origin of spiritual death to the sin of Adam, as does the Hellenistic Jewish author Philo of Alexandria, *Allegorical Interpretation of Genesis* 1, 105–6 (CCC 391, 1008).

2:23 incorruption: An undying life of union with God (3:4) that wisdom offers to the wise (6:18–19). The point is that spiritual death and separation from God are a deviation from God's original plan. Likewise, physical death for man and woman was not part of creation in the beginning but originated as a penalty imposed on human sin (Gen 3:19). • The original divine intention is finally realized in Jesus (Rom 6:9), who reconciles sinners to God (Rom 5:11) and will raise our bodies to be immortal like his own (1 Cor 15:35–57; Phil 3:20–21; CCC 997–1001). • God created men to be incorruptible, making them in his image. But having gone astray, they were reduced to death and corruption since they are fashioned from earth. Through penance, the soul once controlled by unrighteousness can receive virtue and grace; for, being made in the likeness of God, it is capable of receiving every virtue (St. Ambrose, *On the Psalms* 1, 48).

3:1—4:19 Divine revelation concerning life after death puts perennial problems such as unjust suffering (3:1–13a), childlessness (3:13b–4:6), and premature death (4:7–19) in a whole new light. The discussion contrasts the perception of the wicked ("what evildoers think") with spiritual reality ("the way God judges the matter").

3:1–13a In the end, the righteous will enjoy the "peace" of God (3:3), but the ungodly will be "punished" by God (3:10) (CCC 1022–37). • Salvation and judgment are described in terms of the Exodus story. The author **(1)** speaks of the death of the faithful as a "departure" (Gk., *exodos*) from the afflictions of this life (3:2); **(2)** he calls faithful Jews "righteous" (3:1) and "holy" (3:9), just as he later describes the Exodus generation (10:15, 17; 11:13); and **(3)** he insists that the oppressors of God's people will be "punished" (3:10), just as the Egyptians made themselves targets of divine judgment (11:5, 8, 16).

3:1 the souls: The spiritual component of man that survives bodily death. The Book of Wisdom does not explicitly affirm the resurrection of the body, but neither does it deny the doctrine. See note on 1:4. **in the hand of God:** I.e., protected by the power of God, who, despite appearances, delivers the righteous from "the hand" of their persecutors (2:18). **no torment:** Describes the freedom from pain that the righteous will experience in heaven. • You do not know where the saints have gone, but wherever they are, they are with God. They went through suffering to a place without suffering. They arrived at a place of freedom by the narrow and constricted path. Those traveling to such a home should not lose heart if the way is difficult to follow (St. Augustine, *Sermons* 298, 3).

3:2 the foolish: The persons described in 2:1–22. **departure:** A biblical idiom for death (2 Pet 1:15).

3:3 at peace: Echoes the words of Is 57:1–2.

3:4 immortality: The reward for righteousness. See note on 1:15.

3:5 disciplined: The trials and ordeals of life are viewed as a form of divine training, i.e., as the actions of a loving Father

Word Study

Envy (2:24)

Phthonos (Gk.): translates "envy". The term appears twelve times in the Bible, three times in the Greek OT and nine times in the NT. Since classical times, envy has been defined as the inner pain or sadness one feels toward the good fortune of another (e.g., Aristotle, *Rhetoric* 2, 10). It is the opposite of "good will" (Phil 1:15) and is closely allied with "malice" (Tit 3:3). In the Book of Wisdom, envy is directly opposed to wisdom (Wis 6:23) and is exposed as the sinister force behind the devil's effort to strip the first man and woman of the gifts they received from God (Wis 2:24). Envy was also at work in the condemnation of Jesus, the new Adam: the leaders of Jerusalem were pained by the influence he was having with the crowds, and so they plotted his demise (Mt 27:18; Mk 15:10). Unlike jealousy, which seeks to emulate another or acquire a comparable good fortune, envy consists of wishing others harm and often engenders actions that would rob them of their blessings. In the moral teaching of the Church, envy is one of the seven capital sins (CCC 1866, 2538–40).

ᶠ Other ancient authorities read *nature.*

6like gold in the furnace he tried them,
   and like a sacrificial burnt offering he accepted
      them.
7In the time of their visitation they will shine forth,
   and will run like sparks through the stubble.
8They will govern nations and rule over peoples,
   and the Lord will reign over them for ever.
9Those who trust in him will understand truth,
   and the faithful will abide with him in love,
   because grace and mercy are upon his elect,
   and he watches over his holy ones.g
10But the ungodly will be punished as their
      reasoning deserves,
   who disregarded the righteous manh and rebelled
      against the Lord;
11for whoever despises wisdom and instruction is
      miserable.
   Their hope is vain, their labors are unprofitable,
   and their works are useless.
12Their wives are foolish, and their children evil;
13their offspring are accursed.
   For blessed is the barren woman who is
      undefiled,
   who has not entered into a sinful union;
   she will have fruit when God examines souls.

14Blessed also is the eunuch whose hands have
      done no lawless deed,
   and who has not devised wicked things against
      the Lord;
   for special favor will be shown him for his
      faithfulness,
   and a place of great delight in the temple of the
      Lord.
15For the fruit of good labors is renowned,
   and the root of understanding does not fail.
16But children of adulterers will not come to
      maturity,
   and the offspring of an unlawful union will
      perish.
17Even if they live long they will be held of no
      account,
   and finally their old age will be without honor.
18If they die young, they will have no hope
   and no consolation in the day of decision.
19For the end of an unrighteous generation is
      grievous.

The Reward of the Righteous

4 Better than this is childlessness with virtue,
   for in the memory of virtuei is immortality,
   because it is known both by God and by men.

---

who seeks to strengthen the faith and fidelity of his children by allowing them to undergo difficult circumstances in which reliance on him is necessary (Deut 8:5; Prov 3:11–12; Sir 2:1–5). Consequently, the suffering of the righteous is not necessarily a sign of God's punishment; where no personal fault is involved, it can be a form of divine education that promotes spiritual growth.

3:6 like gold in the furnace: Smelting precious metals to remove impurities is often a metaphor in the Bible for spiritual purification (Prov 17:3; Sir 2:5; Is 48:10; Zech 13:9; Mal 3:3; 1 Pet 1:1–7). **burnt offering:** Martyrdom of the righteous is likened to a sacrifice that ascends to God as smoke rising from an altar. • The NT similarly describes the death of Jesus and the earliest Christian martyrs in terms drawn from the sacrificial liturgies of the Temple (Eph 5:2; Phil 2:17; Heb 9:11–14; Rev 6:9–11).

3:7 visitation: The coming day of divine judgment (3:13), also called "the day of decision" (3:18). **they will shine:** The righteous, once vindicated and rewarded, will radiate with the brightness of heavenly glory (Ps 37:6; Dan 12:3; Mt 13:43). **sparks through the stubble:** Perhaps an image of God's people judging the wicked, as in Obad 18.

3:8 govern nations: Perhaps related to Daniel's vision of the saints sharing in the reign of the messianic Son of man (Dan 7:13–14, 22, 27; cf. Mt 19:28; 1 Cor 6:2).

3:9 trust ... truth: Faith in God and acceptance of his wisdom opens up a fuller understanding of reality.

3:10 their reasoning: The thoughts in 2:1–22. **rebelled:** Or "apostatized". This verse, along with 2:12, suggests the wicked are Jews who repudiated their ancestral religion.

3:11 wisdom and instruction: Despised by "fools", according to Prov 1:7.

3:12 Their wives ... children evil: The result of evildoers leading their families into habits of senseless thinking and sin.

It is also possible the author is accusing the wicked of consorting with sin (as a spouse) and so giving birth to further sin (as offspring). Note how the "fruit" of the barren woman in 3:13 and the eunuch in 3:15 is virtue, not biological descendants. This may suggest that sin and vice rather than actual wives and children are the primary targets of criticism.

3:13 their offspring: Or, better, "their origin".

3:13b—4:6 Bearing the "fruit" of spiritual and moral virtue—not simply bearing offspring—is an unmistakable indicator of blessing. After all, even persons burdened with infertility (the barren woman) or castrated by others (the eunuch) are able to lead godly lives. That said, it is true that having children can be a sign of God's blessing (Ps 127:3; 128:3–4; CCC 2373).

3:14 the eunuch: The emasculated man is unable to father children and was excluded from the worshiping assembly of Israel (Deut 23:1). • Acceptance of the faithful eunuch into the Lord's house of worship recalls Is 56:3–7. **temple of the Lord:** Not the visible sanctuary in Jerusalem, but the Lord's unseen Temple in heaven (Ps 11:4; Heb 8:5; Rev 11:19).

3:16 children of adulterers: Illegitimate children, who live with the bitter consequences of their parents' sins, despite being innocent themselves. Beyond this, the author may also have in mind the offspring of rebellion against the Lord (3:10), often described by the Prophets as spiritual "adultery" (Is 57:3; Ezek 16:32; Hos 2:2). On this reading, nothing born of apostasy will endure or afford consolation on the Day of Judgment.

3:18 day of decision: When God vindicates the faithful (Esther 10:10–12) and brings vengeance upon their enemies (Jud 16:17).

4:1 childlessness: Experienced as a burden and disappointment in biblical times (Gen 15:2; 30:1; 1 Sam 1:11), while having children was viewed as a blessing (Ps 127:3). Here, however, godliness is more highly esteemed than natural offspring. **virtue:** Translates the Greek *aretē* which is the strength of will for doing good. The author of Wisdom commends observance of the four cardinal virtues (8:7). See word study: *Excellence* at Phil 4:8.

---

g The text of this line is uncertain, and it is omitted here by some ancient authorities. Compare 4:15.
h Or *what is right*.
i Gk *it*.

²When it is present, men imitate[j] it,
and they long for it when it has gone;
and throughout all time it marches crowned in
triumph,
victor in the contest for prizes that are
undefiled.
³But the prolific brood of the ungodly will be
of no use,
and none of their illegitimate seedlings will
strike a deep root
or take a firm hold.
⁴For even if they put forth boughs for a while,
standing insecurely they will be shaken by the
wind,
and by the violence of the winds they will be
uprooted.
⁵The branches will be broken off before they
come to maturity,
and their fruit will be useless,
not ripe enough to eat, and good for nothing.
⁶For children born of unlawful unions
are witnesses of evil against their parents when
God examines them.[k]

⁷But the righteous man, though he die early, will
be at rest.
⁸For old age is not honored for length of time,
nor measured by number of years;
⁹but understanding is gray hair for men,
and a blameless life is ripe old age.

¹⁰There was one who pleased God and was loved
by him,
and while living among sinners he was taken
up.

¹¹He was caught up lest evil change his
understanding
or guile deceive his soul.
¹²For the fascination of wickedness obscures what
is good,
and roving desire perverts the innocent mind.
¹³Being perfected in a short time, he fulfilled long
years;
¹⁴for his soul was pleasing to the Lord,
therefore he took him quickly from the midst of
wickedness.
¹⁵Yet the peoples saw and did not understand,
nor take such a thing to heart,
that God's grace and mercy are with his elect,
and he watches over his holy ones.

¹⁶The righteous man who has died will condemn
the ungodly who are living,
and youth that is quickly perfected[l] will condemn
the prolonged old age of the unrighteous
man.
¹⁷For they will see the end of the wise man,
and will not understand what the Lord purposed
for him,
and for what he kept him safe.
¹⁸They will see, and will have contempt for him,
but the Lord will laugh them to scorn.
After this they will become dishonored corpses,
and an outrage among the dead for ever;
¹⁹because he will dash them speechless to the
ground,
and shake them from the foundations;
they will be left utterly dry and barren,
and they will suffer anguish,
and the memory of them will perish.

4:2 contest: The Greek *agōn* can indicate a battle (2 Tim 4:7) or an athletic competition such as a race (Heb 12:1) in which the winners are crowned (1 Cor 9:24–25).

4:3–6 Similar words about the offspring of sinners appear in Sir 23:22–25. See notes on 3:12 and 3:16.

4:7–19 Wisdom contests the view that an early death is always a sign of divine punishment. On the contrary, the author insists, a life pleasing to God is measured by wisdom and virtue, not necessarily by reaching old age (4:8–9; CCC 1308). Still, length of years can be a blessing (Deut 5:16), just as premature death can be a chastisement from God (Prov 10:27; 20:20).

4:7 will be at rest: Equivalent to being "at peace" with the Lord (3:3).

📖 **4:10–15** The author supports his claim in 4:7–9 by alluding to Enoch, the patriarch in Genesis whose short life was nevertheless a saintly life of walking with God (Gen 5:21–24). Enoch's translation into heaven, far from being a tragedy or curse, was an act of God's "grace and mercy" (4:15) that rescued him from the corruption of the world (4:11–12). The author of Wisdom often takes this approach of referring to persons and stories of the OT in order to provide living examples of his spiritual teaching. He does this, however, without citing their names, perhaps to invite readers to think deeply about his remarks and even to take delight in discovering the biblical connections.

4:10 one who pleased God: Enoch, as also stated in 4:14, Sir 44:16; Heb 11:5.

4:12 the fascination of wickedness: The glamour of evil. **roving desire:** The movements of an unsettled heart that wanders away from wisdom into covetousness and other sins (Eccles 6:9; Jas 1:14–15).

4:13 perfected: Means that Enoch had attained spiritual maturity.

4:14 took him quickly: By primeval standards, not by modern standards. Enoch is said to have lived to be 365 years old (Gen 5:23); yet most of the Patriarchs before the flood lived to be more than 800 years old (Gen 5:8, 11, 14, 17, etc.).

4:15 did not understand: Sinners misjudged the shortness of Enoch's life. **nor take ... to heart:** Reflects an ancient Jewish tradition that Enoch furnished "an example of repentance" for others (Sir 44:16). **Grace ... holy ones:** Repeats the final lines of 3:9.

4:16 youth ... old age: Overturns the notion that older is always wiser. Righteousness rather than age is the real sign of wisdom.

4:17 kept him safe: I.e., in the afterlife (3:1; 5:15).

📖 **4:18–19** These verses echo various passages of the OT, including Ps 2:4; 37:13; Is 13:6–16; 24:18–19; 66:24.

---

[j] Other ancient authorities read *honor*.
[k] Gk *at their examination*.
[l] Or *ended*.

²⁰They will come with dread when their sins are
reckoned up,
and their lawless deeds will convict them to their
face.

5 Then the righteous man will stand with great
confidence
in the presence of those who have afflicted him,
and those who make light of his labors.
²When they see him, they will be shaken with
dreadful fear,
and they will be amazed at his unexpected
salvation.
³They will speak to one another in repentance,
and in anguish of spirit they will groan, and
say,
⁴"This is the man whom we once held in derision
and made a byword of reproach—we fools!
We thought that his life was madness
and that his end was without honor.
⁵Why has he been numbered among the sons of
God?
And why is his lot among the saints?
⁶So it was we who strayed from the way of
truth,
and the light of righteousness did not shine
on us,
and the sun did not rise upon us.
⁷We took our fill of the paths of lawlessness and
destruction,
and we journeyed through trackless deserts,
but the way of the Lord we have not known.
⁸What has our arrogance profited us?
And what good has our boasted wealth brought
us?

⁹"All those things have vanished like a shadow,
and like a rumor that passes by;
¹⁰like a ship that sails through the billowy water,
and when it has passed no trace can be found,
nor track of its keel in the waves;
¹¹or as, when a bird flies through the air,
no evidence of its passage is found;
the light air, lashed by the beat of its pinions
and pierced by the force of its rushing flight,
is traversed by the movement of its wings,
and afterward no sign of its coming is found
there;
¹²or as, when an arrow is shot at a target,
the air, thus divided, comes together at once,
so that no one knows its pathway.
¹³So we also, as soon as we were born, ceased to be,
and we had no sign of virtue to show,
but were consumed in our wickedness."*
¹⁴Because the hope of the ungodly man is like
chaff^m carried by the wind,
and like a light hoarfrost^n driven away by a
storm;
it is dispersed like smoke before the wind,
and it passes like the remembrance of a guest
who stays but a day.

¹⁵But the righteous live for ever,
and their reward is with the Lord;
the Most High takes care of them.
¹⁶Therefore they will receive a glorious crown
and a beautiful diadem from the hand of the
Lord,
because with his right hand he will cover them,
and with his arm he will shield them.

4:20—5:23 At the final Judgment, the faithful departed will face their persecutors (5:1) and receive from the Lord a crown of everlasting glory (5:15–16). The wicked, by contrast, will come to see the error of their ways (5:4–14), only to be seized with panic and painful regret (5:2–3).

5:3 repentance: The wicked will finally gain moral clarity and acknowledge their sins, but it will be too late to change the course of their lives (cf. Mt 25:10–12; Lk 13:25).

5:4 his life was madness: Recalls the statement in 2:15 that the "ways" of the righteous man seem "strange" to the ungodly.

5:5 sons of God ... saints: These expressions are sometimes used of angels (Job 1:6; Zech 14:5) and sometimes of the faithful of Israel (Deut 14:1; Dan 7:27). Some scholars hold that Wisdom envisions the righteous dead joining the company of the angels in heaven, an idea that finds some support in Jewish tradition (e.g., *1 Enoch* 39, 5; Dead Sea Scroll 1QH 11, 20–23). This does not mean, however, that the saints *become* angels, since they will be reunited with their bodies in the general resurrection (CCC 997–1001).

5:7 journeyed ... trackless deserts: The same three terms describe Israel's Exodus journey through the wilderness in 11:2 (translated "journeyed", "untrodden", and "wilderness"). A typological connection is implied: then as now, rebels will be punished by God with death and disinheritance, but the righteous will receive the blessings the Lord has in store for them (Num 14:28–35).

5:9 vanished: Earthly wealth and power bring no lasting benefit to the deceased (Mt 6:19–20; Lk 12:13–21).

5:10–12 Illustrations based on the **ship**, the **bird**, and the **arrow**, which leave no evidence of their path in sea or sky. Some think that Prov 30:19 lies in the background.

5:14 carried ... dispersed: Biblical metaphors for God's judgment on evildoers (Ps 1:4; Hos 13:3; Mt 3:12).

5:15–23 At the final Judgment, vindication will come to the saints (5:15–16) and vengeance will fall hard on brazen sinners (5:17–23) (CCC 1038–1041).

5:15 live for ever: Undying life was God's intention for man and woman from the beginning (2:23), but fulfillment of this plan was delayed by sin (Gen 3:22).

5:16 glorious crown: Represents everlasting life, as in the NT (2 Tim 4:8; Jas 1:12; Rev 2:10). • The image of a "crown" or "diadem" in the Lord's "hand" comes from Is 62:3, where it symbolizes a faithful remnant of Israel restored in Zion. **from the hand ... right hand:** In biblical language, God's hand creates (Is 66:2), preserves (Job 12:10), punishes (Ex 15:6), and gives strength (1 Chron 29:12; Is 41:10).

---

^m Or *dust*.
^n Other authorities read *spider's web*.
*5:13: Vulgate adds (verse 14): "¹⁴Such things as these the sinners said in hell."

¹⁷The Lord° will take his zeal as his whole armor,
and will arm all creation to repel° his enemies;
¹⁸he will put on righteousness as a breastplate,
and wear impartial justice as a helmet;
¹⁹he will take holiness as an invincible shield,
²⁰and sharpen stern wrath for a sword,
and creation will join with him to fight against
the madmen.
²¹Shafts of lightning will fly with true aim,
and will leap to the target as from a well-drawn
bow of clouds,
²²and hailstones full of wrath will be hurled as
from a catapult;
the water of the sea will rage against them,
and rivers will relentlessly overwhelm them;
²³a mighty wind will rise against them,
and like a tempest it will winnow them away.
Lawlessness will lay waste the whole earth,
and evil-doing will overturn the thrones of
rulers.

Admonition to Rulers

6 Listen therefore, O kings, and understand;
learn, O judges of the ends of the earth.
²Give ear, you that rule over multitudes,
and boast of many nations.

³For your dominion was given you from the Lord,
and your sovereignty from the Most High,
who will search out your works and inquire into
your plans.
⁴Because as servants of his kingdom you did not
rule rightly,
nor keep the law,
nor walk according to the purpose of God,
⁵he will come upon you terribly and swiftly,
because severe judgment falls on those in high
places.
⁶For the lowliest man may be pardoned in mercy,
but mighty men will be mightily tested.*
⁷For the Lord of all will not stand in awe of any
one,
nor show deference to greatness;
because he himself made both small and great,
and he takes thought for all alike.
⁸But a strict inquiry is in store for the mighty.
⁹To you then, O monarchs, my words are directed,
that you may learn wisdom and not transgress.
¹⁰For they will be made holy who observe holy
things in holiness,
and those who have been taught them will find a
defense.

5:17 his whole armor: The image of God arming himself with his attributes is based on Is 59:17, where the Lord is a divine Warrior who suits up for battle with a breastplate, helmet, and military garments. • Paul draws from both Isaiah and Wisdom when he exhorts believers to prepare for spiritual warfare by putting on the "whole armor" of God (Eph 6:13-17).

5:21-23 God enlists the forces of creation in waging war against his enemies (16:16-29; Sir 39:28-31; Zech 9:14). • Several stories of the OT substantiate the claims of the author that the Lord brings judgment on the wicked by means of lightning (2 Kings 1:10), hailstones (Josh 10:11), the waters of the sea (Ex 14:27-28), and flooding rivers (Judg 5:19-21).

5:23 Lawlessness will lay waste: I.e., the divine wrath provoked by lawlessness will lead to the overthrow of evil nations and kingdoms.

6:1—9:18 The central part of the book, which focuses on the origin, nature, and benefits of divine wisdom. See introduction: *Outline*.

6:1-11 Reiterates the opening appeal to "rulers of the earth" (1:1-15), who are urged again to "learn wisdom" (6:9). See note on 1:1. • In line with centuries of Christian tradition, several modern popes have turned to this passage to reaffirm that God is the source of human power and the One to whom civil rulers stand accountable for their exercise of authority over others (Leo XIII, *Diuturnum* 9; Pius XII, *Mystici Corporis* 105; John XXIII, *Pacem in Terris* 83).

6:1 Listen: The Latin Vulgate begins this chapter with the words: "Better is wisdom than power, and better is a prudent man than a strong man." **the ends of the earth:** A biblical idiom for distant nations, meaning countries far from Israel's homeland (Ps 72:8; Zech 9:10; 1 Mac 8:4; Acts 1:8). Some scholars hold that the Roman Empire is in view, since it ruled over "many nations" throughout the Mediterranean world at this time (6:2).

6:3 dominion was given you: Political authority is a sacred stewardship entrusted to rulers and government officeholders by God (Jer 27:5-6; Dan 2:37-38; 4:31-32). Hence, they are held responsible by God for the just or unjust use of their power (6:4-8) (CCC 1899). For similar statements in the NT, see Jn 19:11-12 and Rom 13:1-7.

6:4 his kingdom: God's kingship over the world is a prominent theme in the OT, where several references are made to his everlasting "kingdom" (10:10; 1 Chron 17:14; 28:5; Tob 13:1; 2 Chron 13:8; Ps 103:19; 145:13; Dan 2:44; 4:34). Political rulers participate in God's government of the world as **servants** charged with the wise administration of society, which includes praising and pursuing the good as well as punishing evildoing (Rom 13:3-4; 1 Pet 2:13-14). • The "kingdom of God" is a theme that is deepened and expanded in the NT, which announces that God now rules over the world through Jesus, the risen Lord and Messiah (Mk 1:15; Lk 11:20; Jn 3:5; Acts 1:3; 28:23; Rom 14:17) (CCC 1042, 2816). **law:** Presumably the natural moral law, which coheres with the ethical "wisdom" given to Israel in the Mosaic Law (Deut 4:5-8; Sir 24:23-25).

6:6 mightily tested: Scrutinized with severity before God the Judge (6:8; cf. Jas 3:1). • No one lacks the gifts of God entirely. This one is inclined to more excellent virtues, and that person to humble and modest ones. God has given to each according to the measure of his faith. Therefore, the one entrusted with much will be examined more severely, since of him much will be required (St. John of Damascus, *Homily for Holy Saturday* 34).

6:7 nor show deference: God judges impartially, without showing favoritism to one over another (Deut 10:17; Rom 2:11).

6:10 observe holy things: Possibly a reference to keeping the laws and commandments of God, which are "holy" (2 Mac 6:28; Rom 7:12). **a defense:** An argument in one's favor at a time of divine judgment (Job 31:14) or possibly wisdom for a time of great need (Sir 8:9).

°Gk *He.*
°Or *punish.*
*6:6, *tested*: The meaning seems rather to be "tormented" and to refer to punishment.

¹¹Therefore set your desire on my words;
    long for them, and you will be instructed.
¹²Wisdom is radiant and unfading,
    and she is easily discerned by those who love her,
    and is found by those who seek her.
¹³She hastens to make herself known to those who
       desire her.
¹⁴He who rises early to seek her will have no
       difficulty,
    for he will find her sitting at his gates.
¹⁵To fix one's thought on her is perfect understanding,
    and he who is vigilant on her account will soon
       be free from care,
¹⁶because she goes about seeking those worthy of
       her,
    and she graciously appears to them in their paths,
    and meets them in every thought.

¹⁷The beginning of wisdom^q is the most sincere
       desire for instruction,
    and concern for instruction is love of her,
¹⁸and love of her is the keeping of her laws,
    and giving heed to her laws is assurance of
       immortality,
¹⁹and immortality brings one near to God;
²⁰so the desire for wisdom leads to a kingdom.

²¹Therefore if you delight in thrones and scepters,
    O monarchs over the peoples,
    honor wisdom, that you may reign for ever.

²²I will tell you what wisdom is and how she came
       to be,
    and I will hide no secrets from you,
    but I will trace her course from the beginning of
       creation,
    and make knowledge of her clear,
    and I will not pass by the truth;
²³neither will I travel in the company of sickly envy,
    for envy^r does not associate with wisdom.
²⁴A multitude of wise men is the salvation of the
       world,
    and a sensible king is the stability of his people.
²⁵Therefore be instructed by my words,
    and you will profit.

Solomon's Prayer for and Love of Wisdom

7 I also am mortal, like all men,
    a descendant of the first-formed child of earth;
    and in the womb of a mother I was molded into
       flesh,
²within the period of ten months, compacted with
       blood,
    from the seed of a man and the pleasure of
       marriage.
³And when I was born, I began to breathe the
       common air,
    and fell upon the kindred earth,
    and my first sound was a cry, like that of all.
⁴I was nursed with care in swaddling cloths.
⁵For no king has had a different beginning of
       existence;

6:12 Wisdom: Personified as an attractive woman, accessible to those who desire her (6:14) and pursuing those who are worthy of her gifts (6:16). Ultimately, she is a sure guide to the kingdom of God (6:18–20). Her depiction as a woman is based on the biblical terms for "wisdom", which in Greek as well as Hebrew are grammatically feminine. • The imagery in Wis 6–9 draws from and develops Prov 1–9, where wisdom appears as a woman who calls out at the city gates and offers peace and understanding to all who will accept her counsel (e.g., Prov 1:20–33; 8:1–21). **found by those who seek:** The same is said about the Lord himself in 1:1–2.

6:16 goes about seeking: Points to God's initiative in taking the first step to establish a relationship with humanity, known in later theology as "prevenient" or "antecedent" grace (CCC 2001, 2022).

6:17 desire for instruction: Presupposes humility of mind as well as fear of the Lord (Ps 111:10; Prov 1:7).

6:17–20 A chain of interlocking statements in which each successive line picks up a word from the preceding line and makes it the basis for another assertion. For other instances in the Bible, see Rom 5:3–5 and 2 Pet 1:5–7.

6:18 love: Biblical language for obedience to divine commandments (Ex 20:6; Deut 7:9; Sir 2:15; Jn 14:15).

6:20 leads to a kingdom: Desiring wisdom draws one toward God and his immortal life, called "the kingdom of God" in 10:10. This is the culmination of the author's appeal to the world's kings and judges (6:1). • The kingdom of God/heaven is the central focus of Jesus' preaching in the Gospels, e.g., in the parables that compare the kingdom to a growing seed (Mk 4:26), a mustard seed (Mk 4:31), a lump of leaven (Lk 13:21), a hidden treasure (Mt 13:44), and a pearl of great price (Mt 13:45). Christians pray for the full arrival of this kingdom in the Lord's Prayer (Mt 6:10; Lk 11:2).

6:21—9:18 An autobiographical praise of wisdom utilizing the voice of King Solomon. His name never appears in the text, but numerous allusions to his life and reign, as known from the OT, make it clear that Solomon is the person represented by the "I" who is speaking. On this literary technique, see introduction: *Author* and *Date*.

6:21 reign for ever: I.e., come to share in God's heavenly kingdom. See note on 3:8.

6:22 secrets: Or "mysteries". The author will reveal the hidden designs of God's wisdom.

6:23 envy: Directly opposed to wisdom. See word study: *Envy* at 2:24.

7:1–6 Even mighty Solomon shared the mortal condition common to all, as indicated by the humble circumstances of his conception, gestation, and birth. Some detect a polemic in this verse against royal ideologies of the ancient world that deified human kings.

7:1 like all men: Or "equal to all". **first-formed child of the earth:** Adam, the first human being, whose body was made from the dust of the ground (Gen 2:7; Sir 33:10; 1 Cor 15:47).

7:2 ten months: Ten lunar months equals 40 weeks. **blood … man … pleasure:** The natural circumstances of human generation and birth (Ezek 16:4–6; Jn 1:13).

7:4 swaddling cloths: Bands of cloth wrapped snugly around the arms and body of a newborn. • A possible allusion to this description of Solomon appears in Luke's account of the Nativity, which depicts the infant Jesus wrapped in "swaddling cloths" in Bethlehem, the hometown of King David (Lk 2:7).

---

^qGk *Her beginning.*
^rGk *this.*

⁶there is for all mankind one entrance into life, and
a common departure.

⁷Therefore I prayed, and understanding was given
me;
I called upon God, and the spirit of wisdom came
to me.
⁸I preferred her to scepters and thrones,
and I accounted wealth as nothing in comparison
with her.
⁹Neither did I liken to her any priceless gem,
because all gold is but a little sand in her sight,
and silver will be accounted as clay before her.
¹⁰I loved her more than health and beauty,
and I chose to have her rather than light,
because her radiance never ceases.
¹¹All good things came to me along with her,
and in her hands uncounted wealth.
¹²I rejoiced in them all, because wisdom leads
them;
but I did not know that she was their mother.
¹³I learned without guile and I impart without
grudging;
I do not hide her wealth,
¹⁴for it is an unfailing treasure for men;
those who get it obtain friendship with God,

commended for the gifts that come from
instruction.
¹⁵May God grant that I speak with judgment
and have thoughts worthy of what I have received,
for he is the guide even of wisdom
and the corrector of the wise.
¹⁶For both we and our words are in his hand,
as are all understanding and skill in crafts.
¹⁷For it is he who gave me unerring knowledge of
what exists,
to know the structure of the world and the
activity of the elements;
¹⁸the beginning and end and middle of times,
the alternations of the solstices and the changes
of the seasons,
¹⁹the cycles of the year and the constellations of the
stars,
²⁰the natures of animals and the tempers of wild
beasts,
the powers of spirits ᵃ and the reasonings of men,
the varieties of plants and the virtues of roots;
²¹I learned both what is secret and what is manifest,
²²for wisdom, the fashioner of all things, taught me.

For in her there is a spirit that is intelligent, holy,
unique, manifold, subtle,

7:7-21 Recollections based on Solomon's prayer for wisdom in 1 Kings 3:5-14. It illustrates **(1)** that wisdom is a gift that comes from God, **(2)** that wisdom is acquired through prayer, and **(3)** that wisdom is more valuable than any other blessing in life, including power, prosperity, and personal health.

7:7 I prayed: Divine wisdom is not something one can *earn* through effort, experience, or education. Rather, it can be received only as a gift from the Lord, who bestows understanding upon those who seek it (Prov 2:3-6; Sir 1:1; 51:13-22; Jas 1:5).

7:9 gem ... gold: Valuing wisdom over precious metals and gemstones (= wealth) is a classic motif in the Bible's wisdom literature (Job 28:12-19; Prov 3:13-15; 8:10-11).

7:10 health ... beauty ... light: Things that pass away with time.

7:11 along with her: Wisdom is a gift that bestows other gifts, as Solomon discovered in 1 Kings 3:11-13.

7:12 their mother: I.e., the source of all that brings life and happiness.

7:13 I learned ... I impart: Wisdom is not merely for private benefit but is a gift to be shared with others.

7:14 friendship with God: Associated especially with Abraham (2 Chron 20:7; Is 41:8; Jas 2:23; cf. Jn 15:15).

7:17 knowledge of what exists: Solomon, taught by divine wisdom, had an encyclopedic knowledge of the natural world and its operations that was unmatched in Semitic antiquity (1 Kings 4:29-34). The author seems to hint that Solomon's understanding of philosophical and scientific matters likewise exceeded that of the Hellenistic intellectuals of his own day. One implication of this verse is that divine revelation and human reason are complementary and harmonious, since both come from God (CCC 216, 283).

7:20 powers of spirits: Jewish tradition held that Solomon was an exorcist and practitioner of various healing arts (*Testament of Solomon* 1, 5-7). His understanding of the potency

of **roots** may point to a knowledge of herbal medicine; alternatively, ancient stories tell us that Jewish exorcists not only invoked Solomon's name to expel demons, but they did so with the help of exotic roots thought to be prescribed by him (Josephus, *Antiquities* 8, 45-49; *War* 7, 180-85). At least by NT times, the Messiah was expected to wield the same power over evil spirits as Solomon, the royal son of David (Mt 12:22-23; CCC 550, 1673).

7:22—8:1 A litany of wisdom's attributes and activities. It builds on earlier texts of the OT concerning the origin and activity of wisdom, especially Prov 8:22-31 and Sir 24:1-34, and makes use of terms drawn from Greek philosophy about the nature of deity. It is most striking that the figure of wisdom takes on a personal identity that is somehow *divine* and yet *distinguishable* from the Almighty (7:25). Wisdom proceeds from God (7:25) as "an image of his goodness" (7:26) and "an associate in his works" (8:4); at the same time, she shares the attributes of God, such as his omnipresence (7:24) and omnipotence (7:27), and her beauty surpasses the splendor of creation (7:29) (CCC 2500). • This poem is the nearest thing in the OT to a revelation of the interpersonal mystery of God, which is not fully disclosed until the NT proclamation of the Trinity (Mt 28:19; 2 Cor 13:14). • Characteristics here attributed to wisdom are attributed to the Son and the Spirit in the NT. Jesus Christ is the divine **wisdom** through whom **all things** were made (compare 7:22 with Jn 1:3; 1 Cor 1:30; Col 1:16) as well as the **image** of God and a **reflection** of divine glory (compare 7:26 with Col 1:15; Heb 1:3). At the same time, God's **holy** Spirit dwells in those who are sanctified as **holy** people and inspires **prophets** (compare 7:22, 27 with Jn 14:17; 1 Cor 6:11; 1 Pet 1:10-11).

7:22-23 Wisdom is praised for 21 outstanding qualities, this number being the product of two figures (7 x 3) that were held to represent "perfection" or "totality".

7:22 fashioner: Denotes a "technically skilled artisan" here and in 8:6. God himself is called a "craftsman" in 13:1. **unique:** The Greek is *monogenes*, a word used in the NT to describe Jesus as the "only-begotten" Son of the Father

---

ᵃ Or *winds*.

mobile, clear, unpolluted,
distinct, invulnerable, loving the good, keen,
irresistible, [23]beneficent, humane,
steadfast, sure, free from anxiety,
all-powerful, overseeing all,
and penetrating through all spirits
that are intelligent and pure and most subtle.
[24]For wisdom is more mobile than any motion;
because of her pureness she pervades and
penetrates all things.
[25]For she is a breath of the power of God,
and a pure emanation of the glory of the Almighty;
therefore nothing defiled gains entrance into her.
[26]For she is a reflection of eternal light,
a spotless mirror of the working of God,
and an image of his goodness.
[27]Though she is but one, she can do all things,
and while remaining in herself, she renews all
things;
in every generation she passes into holy souls
and makes them friends of God, and prophets;
[28]for God loves nothing so much as the man who
lives with wisdom.
[29]For she is more beautiful than the sun,
and excels every constellation of the stars.
Compared with the light she is found to be superior,
[30]for it is succeeded by the night,
but against wisdom evil does not prevail.

8 She reaches mightily from one end of the earth
to the other,
and she orders all things well.

[2]I loved her and sought her from my youth,
and I desired to take her for my bride,
and I became enamored of her beauty.

[3]She glorifies her noble birth by living with God,
and the Lord of all loves her.
[4]For she is an initiate in the knowledge of God,
and an associate in his works.
[5]If riches are a desirable possession in life,
what is richer than wisdom who effects all
things?
[6]And if understanding is effective,
who more than she is fashioner of what exists?
[7]And if any one loves righteousness,
her labors are virtues;
for she teaches self-control and prudence,
justice and courage;
nothing in life is more profitable for men than
these.
[8]And if any one longs for wide experience,
she knows the things of old, and infers the things
to come;
she understands turns of speech and the
solutions of riddles;
she has foreknowledge of signs and wonders
and of the outcome of seasons and times.
[9]Therefore I determined to take her to live with me,
knowing that she would give me good counsel
and encouragement in cares and grief.
[10]Because of her I shall have glory among the
multitudes
and honor in the presence of the elders, though I
am young.
[11]I shall be found keen in judgment,
and in the sight of rulers I shall be admired.
[12]When I am silent they will wait for me,
and when I speak they will give heed;
and when I speak at greater length
they will put their hands on their mouths.

(Jn 1:18). **mobile:** The attribute of a spiritual being who is not limited by a physical body (7:24).

7:23 humane: I.e., kind or loving toward human beings (1:6).

7:25 breath of the power of God: The divine breath is the power that creates the world (Ps 33:6), works mighty miracles (2 Sam 22:16), scatters the enemies of his people (11:20), and inspires the Scriptures (2 Tim 3:16).

7:29 more ... superior: Wisdom's beauty is said to outshine and outlast creation.

7:30 night ... does not prevail: Wisdom's association with divine glory (7:25) suggests that she is an eternal light that never gives way to darkness (Is 60:19–20; Rev 21:23–25).

8:2–21 Practical benefits of acquiring wisdom include possession of moral virtue, personal encouragement, public honor, and ruling authority.

8:2 my bride: Wisdom is likened to a desirable woman who is pursued and wedded to the righteous as a bride. She brings delight to the one who lives on intimate terms with her (8:18). A loving union with wisdom amounts to a loving friendship with God himself (7:14, 27). For similar depictions of wisdom as a feminine companion and helpmate in life, see Prov 4:5–9; 7:4–5; Sir 15:1–5.

8:5 what is richer: Wisdom's value exceeds the finest things on earth. See note on 7:9.

8:6 she is fashioner: A reference to wisdom's role in creation (Prov 3:19–20; 8:22–31; CCC 295).

8:7 virtues: Strengths of mind and will for reasoning rightly and living responsibly. Those specified are the "cardinal virtues" celebrated since classical antiquity (Plato, *Phaedo* 69c). Here they are claimed for the Jewish life of wisdom (see also *4 Maccabees* 1, 18). These four cornerstones of human formation are **self-control** (temperance in matters pertaining to the body), **prudence** (the ability to discern and to do the right thing at the right time), **justice** (giving to each person what is rightfully due), and **courage** (the fortitude to do what is right in spite of fear or other obstacles). Catholicism likewise commends the four cardinal virtues as essential to Christian morality (CCC 1805–9).

8:8 wide experience: Knowledge of the past and future can only be imparted by God, who transcends time and history. Only his wisdom "knows and understands all things" (9:11). **solutions of riddles:** Solving riddles was one of Solomon's more famous intellectual abilities (1 Kings 10:1–3). **signs and wonders:** Biblical terminology for miracles (Ex 7:3; Deut 6:22; Acts 5:12).

8:9 to live with me: Continues the depiction of wisdom as a "bride" (8:2).

8:11 keen in judgment: Demonstrated by Solomon's ingenious solution to the case of the two harlots in 1 Kings 3:16–28. Note that God's wisdom is described as "keen" in 7:22.

8:12 hands on their mouths: A gesture of silent deference before one who possesses superior wisdom (Job 29:9; 40:4).

¹³Because of her I shall have immortality,
  and leave an everlasting remembrance to those
    who come after me.
¹⁴I shall govern peoples,
  and nations will be subject to me;
¹⁵dread monarchs will be afraid of me when they
    hear of me;
  among the people I shall show myself capable,
    and courageous in war.
¹⁶When I enter my house, I shall find rest with her,
  for companionship with her has no bitterness,
  and life with her has no pain, but gladness and
    joy.
¹⁷When I considered these things inwardly,
  and thought upon them in my mind,
  that in kinship with wisdom there is immortality,
¹⁸and in friendship with her, pure delight,
  and in the labors of her hands, unfailing wealth,
  and in the experience of her company,
    understanding,
  and renown in sharing her words,
  I went about seeking how to get her for myself.
¹⁹As a child I was by nature well endowed,
  and a good soul fell to my lot;
²⁰or rather, being good, I entered an undefiled body.
²¹But I perceived that I would not possess wisdom
    unless God gave her to me—
  and it was a mark of insight to know whose gift
    she was—
  so I appealed to the Lord and implored him,
  and with my whole heart I said:

The Prayer of Solomon

9 "O God of my fathers and Lord of mercy,
  who have made all things by your word,
²and by your wisdom have formed man,
  to have dominion over the creatures you have
    made,
³and rule the world in holiness and righteousness,
  and pronounce judgment in uprightness of soul,
⁴give me the wisdom that sits by your throne,
  and do not reject me from among your servants.
⁵For I am your slave and the son of your
    maidservant,
  a man who is weak and short-lived,
  with little understanding of judgment and
    laws;
⁶for even if one is perfect among the sons of
    men,
  yet without the wisdom that comes from you he
    will be regarded as nothing.
⁷You have chosen me to be king of your people
  and to be judge over your sons and daughters.
⁸You have given command to build a temple on
    your holy mountain,
  and an altar in the city of your habitation,
  a copy of the holy tent which you prepared from
    the beginning.
⁹With you is wisdom, who knows your works
  and was present when you made the world,
  and who understands what is pleasing in your
    sight
  and what is right according to your commandments.

8:13 immortality: Has a double meaning in this context: it is **(1)** the undying legacy of one who lives on in the memory of later generations and **(2)** the gift of a blessed afterlife that God gives to the righteous who know him (1:15; 15:3).

8:14 govern peoples: Solomon's rule extended over several neighboring states bordering Israel (1 Kings 4:20–24).

8:15 courageous in war: One detail not attested in the life of Solomon (1 Chron 22:9).

8:16 I shall find rest: Peace of mind and soul are imparted by wisdom (Sir 6:28).

8:19–20 A brief reflection on the author's natural endowments. Already in his youth it was apparent that God had given him intellectual ability and moral sensitivity, which together fostered his awareness that wisdom must ultimately come from God (8:21). Some scholars read these verses to mean the author subscribed to the Platonic belief in the preexistence of souls that eventually became entrapped in bodies, but this is unlikely for two reasons. **(1)** It is clear from 8:20 that the author of Wisdom views the body in a positive way, quite unlike the classical Greek view, which likened the human body to a prison. **(2)** It is clear from 15:11 that he embraces the biblical understanding of man as a body infused with the breath of life from God (see Gen 2:7).

8:21 unless God gave her: Wisdom is a gift of grace that God imparts to those who ask for it in prayer. As such, it is not an endowment bestowed at birth along with natural talents and aptitudes (7:7; Prov 2:1–6; Jas 1:5).

📖 **9:1–18** Solomon's prayer for divine wisdom, based on his prayer for an "understanding mind" in 1 Kings 3:6–9 and 2 Chron 1:8–10. The king seeks wisdom for guidance in personal life (9:12) and for the exercise of his royal responsibilities (9:4–7). The prayer links God's wisdom with his "word"

(9:1) and with his "holy Spirit" (9:17). • The NT reveals the mystery of the Trinity in terms that recall these OT portraits of wisdom. Christ, like divine wisdom, is the Word who was "with" God at creation and through whom "all things" were made (9:1, 9; Jn 1:1–3). The Spirit, like divine wisdom, knows the hidden counsel of God and conveys it to others "from on high" (9:13, 17; Lk 24:49; 1 Cor 2:10–13). See also note on 7:22–8:1.

9:1 by your word: Creation came into being through the powerful utterances of God (Gen 1:3; Ps 33:6–9; Rom 4:17; Heb 11:3).

9:2 dominion: For the mandate given to man and woman as royal stewards of creation, see Gen 1:28; Ps 8:6; Sir 17:3–4.

9:4 your throne: The presence of God from which his word and his wisdom are sent forth into the world (9:10; 18:15).

9:7 chosen me: The Lord chose Solomon to sit on David's throne in preference to several older brothers, including Amnon, Absalom, and Adonijah.

📖 **9:8 build a temple:** The terms of the Davidic covenant specify that David's royal heir would construct a house of worship for the Lord (2 Sam 7:12–13). The task is accomplished by Solomon and is summarized in 1 Kings 6–7. **your holy mountain:** Mt. Moriah, one of the elevations of Jerusalem (2 Chron 3:1). **copy of the holy tent:** The sanctuaries of Israel were earthly replicas of an eternal reality in heaven. Its pattern was shown to Moses on Sinai for the making of the wilderness Tabernacle (Ex 25:9, 40) and later revealed to David as an inspired blueprint for the Jerusalem Temple (1 Chron 28:11–19). Both structures served as representations of the Lord's heavenly sanctuary (Ps 11:4; Heb 8:2–5; Rev 11:19; 15:5).

9:9 when you made the world: Also stated of wisdom in Prov 8:27–31.

¹⁰Send her forth from the holy heavens,
  and from the throne of your glory send her,
  that she may be with me and toil,
  and that I may learn what is pleasing to you.
¹¹For she knows and understands all things,
  and she will guide me wisely in my actions
  and guard me with her glory.
¹²Then my works will be acceptable,
  and I shall judge your people justly,
  and shall be worthy of the throne[t] of my father.
¹³For what man can learn the counsel of God?
  Or who can discern what the Lord wills?
¹⁴For the reasoning of mortals is worthless,
  and our designs are likely to fail,
¹⁵for a perishable body weighs down the soul,
  and this earthy tent burdens the thoughtful[u] mind.
¹⁶We can hardly guess at what is on earth,
  and what is at hand we find with labor;
  but who has traced out what is in the heavens?
¹⁷Who has learned your counsel, unless you have
    given wisdom
  and sent your holy Spirit from on high?
¹⁸And thus the paths of those on earth were set right,
  and men were taught what pleases you,
  and were saved by wisdom."

The Deeds of Wisdom

10 Wisdom[v] protected the first-formed father of
  the world,
  when he alone had been created;
  she delivered him from his transgression,
²and gave him strength to rule all things.

³But when an unrighteous man departed from her
    in his anger,
  he perished because in rage he slew his brother.
⁴When the earth was flooded because of him,
    wisdom again saved it,
  steering the righteous man by a paltry piece of
    wood.

⁵Wisdom[w] also, when the nations in wicked
    agreement had been confounded,
  recognized the righteous man and preserved him
    blameless before God,
  and kept him strong in the face of his compassion
    for his child.
⁶Wisdom[w] rescued a righteous man when the
    ungodly were perishing;
  he escaped the fire that descended on the Five
    Cities.[x]
⁷Evidence of their wickedness still remains:
  a continually smoking wasteland,
  plants bearing fruit that does not ripen,
  and a pillar of salt standing as a monument to an
    unbelieving soul.
⁸For because they passed wisdom by,
  they not only were hindered from recognizing the
    good,
  but also left for mankind a reminder of their folly,
  so that their failures could never go unnoticed.

⁹Wisdom rescued from troubles those who served
    her.

9:12 my father: King David.

9:13 what man can learn: Human ignorance of divine things made a deep impression on the author. Despite the degree to which Greek philosophy expanded the frontiers of rational discovery, man remains woefully uninformed about God and his ways. **the counsel of God:** Inaccessible apart from divine revelation.

9:15 weighs down the soul: Greek thinkers used this language to describe the trials of the human condition (e.g., Plato, *Phaedo* 81c). The same is true of the author, but from his Jewish perspective, the body is part of God's good creation, not something evil or fit to be discarded. Christianity likewise affirms the goodness of the body, despite the difficulties we face in our fallen condition (CCC 362–65). **earthly tent:** An image of the mortal human body, stressing its transitory nature (Is 38:12; 2 Cor 5:1–4).

9:17 your holy Spirit: Uniquely qualified to know the mind of God (7:22; 1 Cor 2:9–12).

9:18 saved by wisdom: Announces the theme of the following chapters.

10:1–21 Chapter 10 reviews the activity of wisdom in early biblical times. It examines the leading personalities in Genesis (Adam, Cain, Noah, Abraham, Lot, Jacob, Joseph) and Exodus (Moses, Israel), but without using their names. Allusions are also made to various expansions and interpretations of the biblical stories known from Jewish tradition. Salvation history is retold in this way to underscore that God revealed his ways over time and through concrete events. God's work in the world is described as his "wisdom" acting as a Savior and guide for the People of God.

10:1 the first-formed: Adam, the first man, whose body was fashioned by God from the ground (Gen 2:7). **father:** Genesis portrays Adam as the progenitor of the entire human race. **from his transgression:** Implies that Adam repented of his disobedience and received forgiveness from God, although this is not mentioned in Genesis.

10:3 unrighteous man: Cain, the first man to commit murder in the Bible (Gen 4:8).

10:4 flooded because of him: The waters of the flood came as divine judgment on the violence and corruption perpetrated by Cain and his wicked line of descendants (Gen 6:5, 11–13). See note on 3:12. **righteous man:** Noah, who alone was righteous in his generation (Gen 6:9). **piece of wood:** The ark, made of gopher wood (Gen 6:14).

10:5 confounded: God confused the builders of the Tower of Babel and scattered them over the face of the earth (Gen 11:6–9). **righteous man:** Abraham, pronounced righteous by God because of his faith (Gen 15:6). **kept him strong:** Abraham's willingness to sacrifice his son, Isaac, was made possible by the help of divine grace (Gen 22:1–15).

10:6 righteous man: Lot, the nephew of Abraham (Gen 11:27) who narrowly escaped the annihilation of Sodom (Gen 19:1–28). See note on 2 Pet 2:7. **the Five Cities:** The cities of the Jordan Valley that God destroyed with fire and brimstone from heaven (Gen 19:24, 29). Scripture names four of them: Sodom, Gomorrah, Admah, and Zeboiim (Deut 29:23).

10:7 smoking wasteland: A description suggested by the haze and lifeless landscape surrounding the Dead Sea. **pillar of salt:** Lot's wife (Gen 19:26).

---

[t] Gk *thrones.*
[u] Or *anxious.*
[v] Gk *She.*
[w] Gk *She.*
[x] Or *Pentapolis.*

¹⁰When a righteous man fled from his brother's
wrath,
she guided him on straight paths;
she showed him the kingdom of God,
and gave him knowledge of angels;ʸ
she prospered him in his labors,
and increased the fruit of his toil.
¹¹When his oppressors were covetous,
she stood by him and made him rich.
¹²She protected him from his enemies,
and kept him safe from those who lay in wait for
him;
in his arduous contest she gave him the victory,
so that he might learn that godliness is more
powerful than anything.

¹³When a righteous man was sold, wisdomᶻ did
not desert him,
but delivered him from sin.
She descended with him into the dungeon,
¹⁴and when he was in prison she did not leave him,
until she brought him the scepter of a kingdom
and authority over his masters.
Those who accused him she showed to be false,
and she gave him everlasting honor.

¹⁵A holy people and blameless race
wisdomᵃ delivered from a nation of oppressors.

¹⁶She entered the soul of a servant of the Lord,
and withstood dread kings with wonders and
signs.
¹⁷She gave to holy men the reward of their labors;
she guided them along a marvelous way,
and became a shelter to them by day,
and a starry flame through the night.
¹⁸She brought them over the Red Sea,
and led them through deep waters;
¹⁹but she drowned their enemies,
and cast them up from the depth of the sea.
²⁰Therefore the righteous plundered the ungodly;
they sang hymns, O Lord, to your holy name,
and praised with one accord your defending
hand,
²¹because wisdom opened the mouth of the mute,
and made the tongues of infants speak clearly.

11 Wisdomᵃ prospered their works by the hand
of a holy prophet.
²They journeyed through an uninhabited
wilderness,
and pitched their tents in untrodden places.
³They withstood their enemies and fought off
their foes.
⁴When they thirsted they called upon you,
and water was given them out of flinty rock,
and slaking of thirst from hard stone.

10:10 righteous man: Jacob, who fled from the murderous rage of his brother, Esau (Gen 27:41-45). **the kingdom of God:** The will and rule of God accomplished on earth as it is in heaven. Allusion is made to Jacob's dream at Bethel, where he saw a vision of **angels** ascending and descending on a mystical ladder that spanned heaven and earth (Gen 28:12-15). See notes on 6:4 and 6:20.

10:11 his oppressors: Laban and his kinsmen (Gen 30:35-36; 31:7, 22-23).

10:12 those who lay in wait: May reflect the Jewish tradition that Esau hired mercenaries to attack Jacob (*Jubilees* 37-38). **his arduous contest:** Refers to the night Jacob outwrestled God's angel on the banks of the Jabbok River (Gen 32:22-32).

10:13 righteous man: Joseph, whose envious brothers sold him to caravan merchants and into slavery in Egypt (Gen 37:1-28). **delivered him from sin:** By giving Joseph the moral strength needed to resist temptations to sexual impurity (Gen 39:7-12).

10:14 the scepter of a kingdom: Joseph, made wise by the Spirit, was also made prime minister of Egypt (Gen 41:37-45). **Those who accused him:** May reflect the Jewish tradition that not only Potiphar's wife but other female servants accused Joseph of making sexual advances (Philo of Alexandria, *On Joseph* 51).

10:15 holy people: Israel (Deut 7:6). **nation of oppressors:** Egypt (Ex 3:9).

10:16 servant of the Lord: Moses (Ex 14:31). **dread kings:** The mighty pharaohs of Egypt (Ps 105:30).

10:17 reward of their labors: The jewelry and clothing that Israel received from the Egyptians on Passover night

(Ex 12:35-36). **a shelter:** The pillar of cloud (Ex 13:21) formed a protective canopy over Israel in the wilderness (Ps 105:39).

10:18 over the Red Sea: The miracle of the sea crossing (Ex 14:21-29). For possible locations of the event, see note on Ex 13:18.

10:20 plundered: Reflects the Jewish tradition that Israel confiscated the weapons of the drowned Egyptian soldiers who washed up on the seashore (Josephus, *Antiquities of the Jews* 2, 349). **sang hymns:** The Song at the Sea (Ex 15:1-18) as well as the Song of Miriam (Ex 15:20-21).

11:1—19:22 The final chapters of Wisdom continue tracing the events of salvation history by reflecting on Israel's Exodus from Egypt. The Lord's mighty power in rescuing his people is emphasized, as are his justice and mercy. In the overall argument of the book, these saving actions of God in the past (chaps. 11-19) give hope for his saving intervention in the future, including the time of the author and his readers (chaps. 1-6). Many classify these chapters as an extended *midrash*, a Jewish homiletical genre that retells the stories of the Bible in ways that uncover deeper meanings and draw out practical applications. The author also makes use of a Greek rhetorical device known as *synkrisis*, or "comparison", to set in bold relief the contrast between the Lord's treatment of Egypt and Israel. Seven antitheses punctuate this part of the book (11:4-14; 16:1-4; 16:5-14; 16:15-29; 17:1–18:4; 18:5-25; 19:1-22).

11:1 holy prophet: Moses (Deut 34:10).

11:2 journeyed ... wilderness: See note on 5:7.

11:3 their enemies: E.g., the Amalekites (Ex 17:8-16) and the Midianites (Num 31:1-12).

11:4-14 The first Exodus antithesis: God brought thirst upon the Egyptians by turning their water into blood (Ex 7:14-24), while he quenched the thirst of the Israelites with fresh water from a desert rock (Ex 17:1-7). See note on 11:1—19:22.

11:4 called upon you: Also noted in Ps 107:4-6. **flinty rock:** The rock of Horeb (Ex 17:6).

ʸOr *of holy things.*
ᶻGk *she.*
ᵃGk *she.*

⁵For through the very things by which their
    enemies were punished,
they themselves received benefit in their need.
⁶Instead of the fountain of an ever-flowing river,
    stirred up and defiled with blood
⁷in rebuke for the decree to slay the infants,
    you gave them abundant water unexpectedly,
⁸showing by their thirst at that time
    how you punished their enemies.
⁹For when they were tried, though they were
    being disciplined in mercy,
they learned how the ungodly were tormented
    when judged in wrath.
¹⁰For you tested them as a father does in warning,
    but you examined the ungodly^b as a stern king
    does in condemnation.
¹¹Whether absent or present, they were equally
    distressed,
¹²for a twofold grief possessed them,
    and a groaning at the memory of what had occurred.
¹³For when they heard that through their own
    punishments
the righteous^c had received benefit, they
    perceived it was the Lord's doing.

¹⁴For though they had mockingly rejected him
    who long before had been cast out and
    exposed,
at the end of the events they marveled at him,
    for their thirst was not like that of the
    righteous.

¹⁵In return for their foolish and wicked thoughts,
    which led them astray to worship irrational
    serpents and worthless animals,
you sent upon them a multitude of irrational
    creatures to punish them,
¹⁶that they might learn that one is punished by the
    very things by which he sins.
¹⁷For your all-powerful hand,
    which created the world out of formless matter,
did not lack the means to send upon them a
    multitude of bears, or bold lions,
¹⁸or newly created unknown beasts full of rage,
    or such as breathe out fiery breath,
    or belch forth a thick pall of smoke,
    or flash terrible sparks from their eyes;
¹⁹not only could their damage exterminate men,^d
    but the mere sight of them could kill by fright.

11:5 through the very things: An overarching theme of chaps. 11–19. As several examples from the Exodus story illustrate, the divine judgments sent against Egypt proved to be divine blessings for Israel (11:13).

11:6 ever-flowing river: The Nile, rendered undrinkable by the first plague (Ex 7:24).

📖 **11:7 rebuke for the decree:** The first plague was punishment for Pharaoh's edict to drown all newborn Hebrew boys in the Nile (Ex 1:22). The same interpretation appears in later Jewish tradition (*Pirqe de Rabbi Eliezer* 19). See note on Ex 7:20.

11:8 their thirst: Suggests that Israel was given a taste of the hardship that God brings upon sinners as a warning against future rebellion.

11:9–10 Israel's testing in the wilderness was a time of moral and spiritual training (Deut 8:2–5). It was an exercise of the Father's **mercy**, lest Israel transgress his covenant and suffer his **wrath** like a criminal who is sentenced by a ruthless monarch. Whether preventative or corrective, divine discipline aims at steering people away from sin and strengthening their relationship with the Lord (12:2; Heb 12:5–11). See note on Prov 3:11–12.

11:11 absent or present: I.e., whether Israel was away in the wilderness or still captive in Egypt.

11:12 twofold grief: Egypt lamented the devastation of the ten plagues as well as Israel's release from compulsory service.

11:13 the righteous: The people of Israel.

11:14 rejected him: Moses. **exposed:** Set adrift on the Nile as an infant (Ex 2:3). **their thirst:** The Egyptians experienced a thirst during the first plague (Ex 7:24) that was more severe than Israel's thirst in the wilderness (Ex 17:1).

📖 **11:15 worship irrational serpents:** Egypt was famous in ancient times for its animal cults (12:24). Theirs was a form of idolatry in which gods and goddesses were venerated under the images of wild animals (jackal, falcon, lioness), farm animals (bull, cow, ram), reptiles (crocodile, cobra, frog), and insects (beetle, Ichneuman fly). Several of these cults continued into Roman times (*Letter of Aristeas* 138; Philo of Alexandria, *On the Decalogue* 76–80; Tacitus, *Histories* 5, 4). From a Jewish perspective, God opposes the worship of other gods as well as the representation of other gods under the forms of created things (Ex 20:3–4; Deut 4:15–18). • Paul views this and other forms of idolatry as evidence that wicked men have suppressed the truth about God and become futile in their thinking (Rom 1:18–23).

📖 **11:16 the very things:** Recalls the thesis statement in 11:5. Here it reveals the logic of God using animals to punish those who worshiped animals, e.g., by sending plagues of frogs (Ex 8:1–7), gnats (Ex 8:16–19), flies (Ex 8:20–24), and locusts (Ex 10:1–6) and by bringing death to flocks and herds (Ex 9:1–7). The idea is that God's judgment is more than mere punishment for wrongdoing; it is tailored to the nature of the crime and aims at redressing offenses in an appropriate way. In the case of the Egyptian plagues, God shows that worshiping animals is self-destructive. Beyond this, the suffering he imposes through the animal plagues is meant to break Egypt's attachment to animal cults. The author will return to this point in 12:27.

📖 **11:17 your all-powerful hand:** Both an anthropomorphism, a poetical description of God having bodily features, and an affirmation of divine omnipotence, the doctrine that God "can do all things" (11:23). On the former, see note on Gen 6:6. **formless matter:** The state of creation when the world was "without form and void" (Gen 1:2), i.e., before God conquered the primeval chaos by establishing the order and distinctions of the universe we know today (Gen 1:3— 2:3). Many commentators detect in this expression a reference to the Greek philosophical idea that matter is eternal. If such a reference is intended, it would seem the author is reworking it to express the biblical doctrine of "creation out of nothing" (2 Mac 7:28).

11:18 unknown beasts: The point is not that fire-breathing monsters were thought to exist, but that God could have created them to terrify the wicked if he had so wanted.

---

^b Gk *those*.
^c Gk *they*.
^d Gk *them*.

²⁰Even apart from these, men[e] could fall at a single breath
  when pursued by justice
  and scattered by the breath of your power.
  But you have arranged all things by measure and number and weight.

²¹For it is always in your power to show great strength,
  and who can withstand the might of your arm?
²²Because the whole world before you is like a speck that tips the scales,
  and like a drop of morning dew that falls upon the ground.
²³But you are merciful to all, for you can do all things,
  and you overlook men's sins, that they may repent.
²⁴For you love all things that exist,
  and you loathe none of the things which you have made,
  for you would not have made anything if you had hated it.
²⁵How would anything have endured if you had not willed it?
  Or how would anything not called forth by you have been preserved?
²⁶You spare all things, for they are yours, O Lord who love the living.*

12 For your immortal spirit is in all things.
  ²Therefore you correct little by little those who trespass,
  and remind and warn them of the things wherein they sin,
  that they may be freed from wickedness and put their trust in you, O Lord.

³Those who dwelt of old in your holy land
⁴you hated for their detestable practices,
  their works of sorcery and unholy rites,
⁵their merciless slaughter[f] of children,
  and their sacrificial feasting on human flesh and blood.
  These initiates from the midst of a heathen cult,[g]
⁶these parents who murder helpless lives,
  you wanted to destroy by the hands of our fathers,
⁷that the land most precious of all to you
  might receive a worthy colony of the servants[h] of God.
⁸But even these you spared, since they were but men,
  and sent wasps[i] as forerunners of your army,
  to destroy them little by little,
⁹though you were not unable to give the ungodly into the hands of the righteous in battle,
  or to destroy them at one blow by dread wild beasts or your stern word.
¹⁰But judging them little by little you gave them a chance to repent,
  though you were not unaware that their origin[j] was evil
  and their wickedness inborn,
  and that their way of thinking would never change.

11:20 the breath of your power: Here refers to a divine word of judgment. See note on 7:25. **measure and number and weight:** The cosmos is ordered according to laws of mathematical proportion and quantity. This biblical outlook stands in marked contrast to pagan world views that venerated the elements of the natural world as deities. The biblical conviction that a divine rationality is inscribed into creation would later inspire the research and discovery of the natural sciences (CCC 299). • Without exception, every creature was made through the Word, the smallest as well as the greatest, things above us as well as things below us, things spiritual as well as things corporeal. There is no form or harmony of parts, no substance that can be measured by weight, number, or height—nothing at all exists except through that Word (St. Augustine, *Tractates on John* 1, 13).

11:22 like a speck ... like a drop: Images of the nations suggested by Is 40:15.

11:23 overlook men's sins: Not a divine indifference toward sin but a divine forbearance that waits patiently for sinners to come to repentance (Rom 2:4; 2 Pet 3:9).

11:24–26 Divine love is the source and rationale behind the creation and preservation of all things. In view of this, God's judgments on the wicked must not be misunderstood as acts of divine hatred against creatures who owe their existence to his goodness (CCC 301).

11:26 O Lord who love the living: Or "O Lord, Lover of souls".

12:1 your immortal spirit: Not the "world soul" of Stoic philosophy, but the "breath of life" that comes from God (Eccles 12:7) and animates all living creatures (Gen 1:30; 2:7; 7:15).

12:2 little by little: The Exodus plagues were unleashed gradually and sequentially to afford the Egyptians time to repent of their idolatry (11:15–16; 12:10).

12:3–11 An aside on the conquest of Canaan, which illustrates the same point as the Exodus event: that God is merciful even in his judgments. The Canaanites were robbed of life and land as judgment for abominations that included child sacrifice (Lev 20:1–5), sexual impurity (Lev 18:6–25), and occultism (Deut 18:9–14). The Lord could have annihilated the Canaanites at a stroke for their crimes (12:9); instead, he parceled out punishments "little by little" with the aim of inducing repentance (12:8, 10).

12:3 holy land: Canaan, the land God promised to the descendants of Abraham (Gen 17:8).

12:5 feasting on human flesh: Cannibalism. This is the only ancient source to ascribe the practice to the Canaanites.

12:6 by the hands of our fathers: For some of the reasons behind the Israelite takeover of Canaan, see essay: *The Conquest of Canaan* at Josh 6.

12:7 the servants of God: The people of Israel.

12:8 wasps ... little by little: A reiteration of Ex 23:28–30. For additional reasons why the conquest of Canaan was a drawn-out process, see note on Judg 2:22.

12:10 a chance to repent: The ultimate reason that God tempers his judgment with mercy. See note on 11:23. **their origin was evil:** This does not mean the Canaanites were created evil or predestined for damnation, since the first part of the verse reveals the divine intention to bring them to repentance.

---

[e] Gk *they*.
[f] Cn: Gk *slaughterers*.
[g] The Greek text of this line is uncertain.
[h] Or *children*.
[i] Or *hornets*.
[j] Or *nature*.
*11:26, *Lord who love the living*: Vulgate has "souls" for "living." The Greek word could mean either.

[11]For they were an accursed race from the
beginning,
and it was not through fear of any one that you
left them unpunished for their sins.

[12]For who will say, "What have you done?"
Or who will resist your judgment?
Who will accuse you for the destruction of
nations which you made?
Or who will come before you to plead as an
advocate for unrighteous men?
[13]For neither is there any god besides you, whose
care is for all men,[k]
to whom you should prove that you have not
judged unjustly;
[14]nor can any king or monarch confront you about
those whom you have punished.
[15]You are righteous and rule all things righteously,
deeming it alien to your power
to condemn him who does not deserve to be
punished.
[16]For your strength is the source of righteousness,
and your sovereignty over all causes you to spare
all.
[17]For you show your strength when men doubt the
completeness of your power,
and rebuke any insolence among those who know
it.[1]
[18]You who are sovereign in strength judge with
mildness,
and with great forbearance you govern us;
for you have power to act whenever you
choose.

[19]Through such works you have taught your
people
that the righteous man must be kind,
and you have filled your sons with good hope,
because you give repentance for sins.
[20]For if you punished with such great care and
indulgence[m]
the enemies of your servants[n] and those
deserving of death,
granting them time and opportunity to give up
their wickedness,
[21]with what strictness you have judged your
sons,
to whose fathers you gave oaths and covenants
full of good promises!
[22]So while chastening us you scourge our enemies
ten thousand times more,
so that we may meditate upon your goodness
when we judge,
and when we are judged we may expect
mercy.
[23]Therefore those who in folly of life lived
unrighteously
you tormented through their own abominations.
[24]For they went far astray on the paths of error,
accepting as gods those animals which even their
enemies[o] despised;
they were deceived like foolish infants.
[25]Therefore, as to thoughtless children,
you sent your judgment to mock them.
[26]But those who have not heeded the warning of
light rebukes
will experience the deserved judgment of God.

The idea is that Canaanite iniquity had been culturally ingrained and institutionalized for centuries before their land was given to Israel (Gen 15:16). **inborn:** Or "implanted".

12:11 accursed race: A reference to Gen 9:25, where Noah pronounced a curse upon Canaan, the offspring of his wicked son Ham (Gen 10:6).

12:12–18 The author responds to critics of Israel's conquest of Canaan who accused God of injustice and abuse of power. He challenges these allegations by insisting **(1)** that the Creator has sovereign rights over the fate of all living creatures (12:16), **(2)** that God never condemns those who are undeserving of judgment (12:15), and **(3)** that critics have overlooked God's forbearance (12:18) toward those Canaanites who were left alive and thus "unpunished" for their crimes (12:11).

12:12 What have you done?: The words of one who questions the wisdom and justice of God's actions (cf. Job 9:12; Rom 9:19–23).

12:15 You are righteous: Here means that God judges all, the righteous and wicked alike, with impartial fairness (Gen 18:25). See word study: *Righteous* at Neh 9:8.

12:18 mildness: God shows himself merciful despite having the power to be merciless.

12:19 kind: Or "loving toward humanity", which is an attribute of eternal wisdom (1:6; 7:23). Insofar as the author considers God's kindness toward sinners, his words anticipate Jesus' teaching on loving all people, even enemies, in imitation of the Father (Mt 5:43–48). **your sons:** The children of Israel, who become the children of God by covenant (Deut 14:1). **you give repentance:** Means that God affords everyone "time and opportunity to give up their wickedness" (12:20). This is one of the subthemes of this section of Wisdom (see 11:23; 12:10, 26).

12:21 fathers: The Patriarchs. **oaths and covenants:** A hendiadys meaning "covenant oaths" (also in 18:22). In the biblical world, covenants were established by the swearing of oaths, which is why the terms "oath" and "covenant" are often juxtaposed in Scripture (Gen 26:28; Deut 4:31; Ps 89:3; Ezek 17:13; Hos 10:4; Lk 1:72–73). When God makes a promise on oath, he gives the strongest possible assurance regarding its fulfillment (Heb 6:17–18). See essay: *What Is a Covenant?* at Deut 5.

12:22 while chastening: A summary of the whole preceding section from 11:5—12:22.

12:23–27 Resumes the discussion of the Exodus from 11:1–20. Because the Egyptians refused to repent after **light rebukes** (the initial plagues, Ex 7–11), Pharaoh and his people suffered **the utmost condemnation** (death of every first-born, Ex 12:29–32; drowning of the army, Ex 14:26–28). The lesson is that God judges with dreadful severity when his leniency has been spurned.

12:24 gods ... animals: On the animal cults of Egypt, see note on 11:15.

---

[k] Or *all things*.
[1] The Greek text of this line is uncertain.
[m] Some ancient authorities omit *and indulgence*; others read *and entreaty*.
[n] Or *children*.
[o] Gk *they*.

²⁷For when in their suffering they became incensed
　at those creatures which they had thought to be
　　gods, being punished by means of them,
　they saw and recognized as the true God him
　　whom they had before refused to know.
　Therefore the utmost condemnation came upon
　　them.

The Foolishness of Idolatry

13 For all men who were ignorant of God were
　　foolish by nature;
　and they were unable from the good things that
　　are seen to know him who exists,
　nor did they recognize the craftsman while
　　paying heed to his works;
²but they supposed that either fire or wind or
　　swift air,
　or the circle of the stars, or turbulent water,
　or the luminaries of heaven were the gods that
　　rule the world.
³If through delight in the beauty of these things
　　menᵖ assumed them to be gods,
　let them know how much better than these is
　　their Lord,
　for the author of beauty created them.
⁴And if menᵖ were amazed at their power and
　　working,
　let them perceive from them
　how much more powerful is he who formed them.
⁵For from the greatness and beauty of created
　　things
　comes a corresponding perception of their
　　Creator.

⁶Yet these men are little to be blamed,
　for perhaps they go astray
　while seeking God and desiring to find him.
⁷For as they live among his works they keep
　　searching,
　and they trust in what they see, because the
　　things that are seen are beautiful.
⁸Yet again, not even they are to be excused;
⁹for if they had the power to know so much
　that they could investigate the world,
　how did they fail to find sooner the Lord of these
　　things?
¹⁰But miserable, with their hopes set on dead
　　things, are the men
　who give the name "gods" to the works of men's
　　hands,
　gold and silver fashioned with skill,
　and likenesses of animals,
　or a useless stone, the work of an ancient hand.
¹¹A skilled woodcutter may saw down a tree easy
　　to handle
　and skilfully strip off all its bark,
　and then with pleasing workmanship
　make a useful vessel that serves life's needs,
¹²and burn the castoff pieces of his work
　to prepare his food, and eat his fill.
¹³But a castoff piece from among them, useful for
　　nothing,
　a stick crooked and full of knots,
　he takes and carves with care in his leisure,
　and shapes it with skill gained in idleness;�q
　he forms it like the image of a man,

12:27 punished by means of them: See note on 11:16. **recognized as the true God:** May be a reference to Pharaoh's remorse in Ex 10:16–17.

📖 **13:1—15:17** An excursus on the foolishness of Gentile idolatry. It seeks to strengthen Jewish readers against conforming to the religious culture of Hellenistic Egypt. The author's approach is to mock pagan worship as irrational. See introduction: *Occasion and Purpose.* • At several points the author makes use of traditional OT satire to poke fun at idols and their devotees (Ps 135:15–18; Is 44:9–20; Jer 10:3–9). In the NT, Paul borrows insights from this section of the book to formulate his own polemic against idolatry. Notice how Wisdom and Paul **(1)** both define idolatry as worshiping creation rather than the Creator (13:1-4; Rom 1:25); **(2)** both contend that God's existence can be perceived from the world that God made (13:5; Rom 1:20); **(3)** both declare the failure to know the true God an inexcusable error (13:8; Rom 1:20); and **(4)** both single out idolatry as the root cause of social and sexual immorality (14:12, 22–31; Rom 1:24-32).

✿ **13:1-9** The author faults idolaters for deifying nature and not discerning the Supreme Deity whose beauty and might are revealed through nature. Instead of coming to know the Creator, they stopped at "the things that are seen" (13:7) and worshiped terrestrial elements (fire, air, water) as well as celestial luminaries (stars, sun, moon) (CCC 2112-14). In short, they failed to recognize that the world is a work of art pointing beyond itself to a divine Artist or "craftsman" (13:1)

(CCC 2129). • The Catholic Church upholds the teaching of Scripture in affirming that God's existence can be known with certainty by the light of human reason reflecting on created things (Vatican I, *Dei Filius* 2; Vatican II, *Dei Verbum* 3; CCC 31–36, 41, 1147).

📖 **13:1 by nature:** Here means "by upbringing". The natural constitution of man is not in view so much as the prevailing ways of thinking about the world in Gentile cultures. **him who exists:** Alludes to the name of God revealed to Moses in Ex 3:14, which the Greek LXX translates: "I AM HE WHO IS."

13:2 luminaries: The sun and moon (Gen 1:16).

13:5 a corresponding perception: A remarkably positive assessment of human reason. The author contends that, by an application of the philosophical principle of "analogy", the mind can rise from the observation of visible things to a perception of invisible things, even to a knowledge that all things originate from an intelligent Designer.

13:6 little to be blamed: Mitigated blame is assigned to worshipers of creation to the extent they desire to find God. The author delineates three categories of blame in this section: **(1)** Those who worship the natural world are guilty of an *inexcusable* error (13:8); **(2)** those who worship hand-made images are *miserable* to a greater degree (13:10-19); and **(3)** those who worship animals are the *most foolish* of all (15:14–16).

13:10 likenesses of animals: The idol images of Egyptian religion. See note on 11:15.

13:11 a useful vessel: A humble container made from wood is more profitable than an idol made from precious metal (13:10), stone (13:10), or a knotty stick (13:13).

13:13 image of a man: The idol images of Greek and Roman religion.

ᵖ Gk *they*.
q Other authorities read *with intelligent skill*.

¹⁴or makes it like some worthless animal,
  giving it a coat of red paint and coloring its surface red
  and covering every blemish in it with paint;
¹⁵then he makes for it a niche that befits it,
  and sets it in the wall, and fastens it there with iron.
¹⁶So he takes thought for it, that it may not fall,
  because he knows that it cannot help itself,
  for it is only an image and has need of help.
¹⁷When he prays about possessions and his marriage and children,
  he is not ashamed to address a lifeless thing.
¹⁸For health he appeals to a thing that is weak;
  for life he prays to a thing that is dead;
  for aid he entreats a thing that is utterly inexperienced;
  for a prosperous journey, a thing that cannot take a step;
¹⁹for money-making and work and success with his hands
  he asks strength of a thing whose hands have no strength.

14 Again, one preparing to sail and about to voyage over raging waves
calls upon a piece of wood more fragile than the ship which carries him.

²For it was desire for gain that planned that vessel,
  and wisdom was the craftsman who built it;
³but it is your providence, O Father, that steers its course,
  because you have given it a path in the sea,
  and a safe way through the waves,
⁴showing that you can save from every danger,
  so that even if a man lacks skill, he may put to sea.
⁵It is your will that works of your wisdom should not be without effect;
  therefore men trust their lives even to the smallest piece of wood,
  and passing through the billows on a raft they come safely to land.
⁶For even in the beginning, when arrogant giants were perishing,
  the hope of the world took refuge on a raft,
  and guided by your hand left to the world the seed of a new generation.
⁷For blessed is the wood by which righteousness comes.

⁸But the idol made with hands is accursed, and so is he who made it;
  because he did the work, and the perishable thing was named a god.

13:15 a niche: An inset in the wall where a cult statue was displayed in the home. **with iron:** I.e., with nails (Is 41:7; Jer 10:4).

13:16–19 In a series of contrasts, the author ridicules handcrafted idols for being helpless, lifeless, motionless, and powerless. Even though idolaters recognize this at some level, they cling to the vain hope that statues are capable of influencing human affairs.

14:1–2 A seaworthy vessel is more a product of God's wisdom and protection than that of a wooden idol fastened to the ship's prow and petitioned for a safe sea voyage.

14:2 desire for gain: Seafaring was often pursued as a business venture, not least by King Solomon (1 Kings 9:26–28; 10:22). The point is that maritime trade brings more practical benefit to people than manufactured idols do.

14:3 O Father: The language of prayer is rooted in the covenant, through which the people of Israel became God's adopted children (Deut 14:1). The Fatherhood of God is acknowledged several times in Scripture in relation to Israel (e.g., Sir 23:1, 4; Is 63:16; 64:8; Jer 3:19; 31:9; Mal 1:6). However, it takes on new meaning and prominence in the NT once Jesus reveals himself as God's eternal Son (Mt 11:25–27). Christians become adopted sons and daughters of God by their baptismal union with Christ and now invoke the Lord as "Abba! Father!" (Rom 8:15; Gal 4:6), just as Jesus did (Mk 14:36).

14:6 the beginning: The early history of the world. **giants:** The Nephilim, remembered as a people of mighty stature (Gen 6:4) who were swept away in the biblical flood (Gen 7:21–23; Bar 3:26–28). **a raft:** Noah's ark (Gen 7:7).

14:7 blessed is the wood: The ark, made of gopher wood, preserved the "righteous man" Noah (Gen 6:9). • The Fathers of the Church often applied this verse to the Cross, which the NT describes as the wood/tree (Gk., *xylon*, as in Acts 5:30) on which Jesus died to bring sinners the gift of righteousness (Rom 5:17).

14:8 made with hands: The biblical critique of idols in a nutshell (13:10; Deut 4:28; Ps 115:4; Bar 6:51).

Word Study

Providence (14:3)

Pronoia (Gk.): translates "providence" or "provision" and refers to the care one exercises in making arrangements to meet the foreseeable needs of another. The word first appears in the OT in the Book of Wisdom (Wis 14:3), where it designates the exercise of God's lordship over creation; in the NT, it is used for the political reforms of a human governor (Acts 24:2). In ancient Greek writings, *pronoia* denotes the divine governance of the world by wisdom (Plato, *Timaeus* 30b), extending to the lives and circumstances of individuals (Josephus, *Antiquities* 2, 60), to the needs of animals (Herodotus, *Histories* 3, 108), and even down to the conditions required for seeds and plants to grow (*1 Clement* 24, 5). Latin speakers designated this benevolent rule and wise ordering of the cosmos as the *providentia* of the gods (Cicero, *On the Nature of the Gods* 2, 75). Hebrew had no single word that expressed the idea of God's Providence, but numerous passages express the belief that the Lord cares for the well-being of his creatures and takes steps to address their needs (Gen 8:21–22; Job 10:12; Ps 145:15–20; Prov 20:24; Jer 5:24, etc.). Biblical teaching on divine Providence is often subsumed under the notion of divine wisdom, which "orders all things well" (Wis 8:1). In Catholic teaching, divine Providence leads creation to its perfection (CCC 302).

⁹For equally hateful to God are the ungodly man
　　and his ungodliness,
¹⁰for what was done will be punished together with
　　him who did it.
¹¹Therefore there will be a visitation also upon the
　　heathen idols,
　　because, though part of what God created, they
　　　became an abomination,
　　and became traps for the souls of men
　　and a snare to the feet of the foolish.

¹²For the idea of making idols was the beginning
　　of fornication,
　　and the invention of them was the corruption of
　　　life,
¹³for neither have they existed from the beginning
　　nor will they exist for ever.
¹⁴For through the vanity of men they entered the
　　world,
　　and therefore their speedy end has been
　　　planned.
¹⁵For a father, consumed with grief at an untimely
　　bereavement,
　　made an image of his child, who had been
　　　suddenly taken from him;
　　and he now honored as a god what was once a
　　　dead human being,
　　and handed on to his dependents secret rites and
　　　initiations.
¹⁶Then the ungodly custom, grown strong with
　　time, was kept as a law,
　　and at the command of monarchs graven images
　　　were worshiped.
¹⁷When men could not honor monarchs ͬ in their
　　presence, since they lived at a distance,
　　they imagined their appearance far away,
　　and made a visible image of the king whom they
　　　honored,
　　so that by their zeal they might flatter the absent
　　　one as though present.

¹⁸Then the ambition of the craftsman impelled
　　even those who did not know the king to
　　　intensify their worship.
¹⁹For he, perhaps wishing to please his ruler,
　　skilfully forced the likeness to take more beautiful
　　　form,
²⁰and the multitude, attracted by the charm of his
　　work,
　　now regarded as an object of worship the one
　　　whom shortly before they had honored as a
　　　man.
²¹And this became a hidden trap for mankind,
　　because men, in bondage to misfortune or to
　　　royal authority,
　　bestowed on objects of stone or wood the name
　　　that ought not to be shared.

²²Afterward it was not enough for them to err
　　about the knowledge of God,
　　but they live in great strife due to ignorance,
　　and they call such great evils peace.
²³For whether they kill children in their initiations,
　　or celebrate secret mysteries,
　　or hold frenzied revels with strange customs,
²⁴they no longer keep either their lives or their
　　marriages pure,
　　but they either treacherously kill one another, or
　　　grieve one another by adultery,
²⁵and all is a raging riot of blood and murder, theft
　　and deceit, corruption, faithlessness, tumult,
　　　perjury,
²⁶confusion over what is good, forgetfulness of
　　favors,
　　pollution of souls, sex perversion,
　　disorder in marriage, adultery, and debauchery.
²⁷For the worship of idols not to be named
　　is the beginning and cause and end of every evil.
²⁸For their worshipers ͬ either rave in exultation, or
　　prophesy lies,
　　or live unrighteously, or readily commit perjury;

---

accursed: Recalls the covenant curse in Deut 27:15. **perishable:** Not only fleeting (13:13) but doomed to destruction (13:14; Is 2:18; Mic 5:13).

14:11 visitation: A time of divine judgment (3:7).

14:12 beginning of fornication: The abandonment of God for idols is a form of spiritual harlotry (see Ex 34:15-16; Lev 17:7; Deut 31:16). This is more than just a metaphor, since pagan cults in the biblical world lured participants into ritual prostitution and other forms of sexual depravity.

14:13 neither ... from the beginning: A claim that monotheism, the worship of one God only, was the original form of religion that later degenerated into polytheism, the worship of many gods and goddesses. Idolatry first appeared in the patriarchal period, according to Scripture (Gen 31:19; Josh 24:2) and Jewish tradition (*Jubilees* 11, 4; *Sifre Deuteronomy* 43).

14:15-21 Idolatry is traced to ancient customs of the family (14:15) and the state (14:16-20). In one case, the consolation of a bereaved father transforms into the divinization of his deceased child (cult of the dead). In another, the admiration of royal statues degenerates into the deification of a human monarch (cult of the king). The ruler cult was widely practiced in Hellenistic Egypt and later by Imperial Rome.

14:21 not to be shared: The Lord shares neither his name nor his glory with graven images according to Is 42:8.

14:22-31 Idolatry triggers an eruption of immorality and impurity in human society. For a restatement of this thesis in the NT, see Rom 1:22-32.

14:23 frenzied revels: Sexual orgies linked to the worship of Dionysius and other mystery cults (cf. 2 Mac 6:4).

14:26 sex perversion: Literally, "an inversion of generation". This is probably a reference to homosexual acts, which are contrary to the order and purpose of human sexuality that God inscribed into nature (Rom 1:26; cf. Philo of Alexandria, *Special Laws* 3, 39; *Testament of Naphtali* 3, 4) (CCC 2357-59).

ͬ Gk *them*.
ͬ Gk *they*.

²⁹for because they trust in lifeless idols
  they swear wicked oaths and expect to suffer no
    harm.
³⁰But just penalties will overtake them on two
    counts:
  because they thought wickedly of God in
    devoting themselves to idols,
  and because in deceit they swore unrighteously
    through contempt for holiness.
³¹For it is not the power of the things by which
    men swear,ᵗ
  but the just penalty for those who sin,
  that always pursues the transgression of the
    unrighteous.

True Worship of God Contrasted to Idols

15 But you, our God, are kind and true,
    patient, and ruling all thingsᵘ in mercy.
²For even if we sin we are yours, knowing your
    power;
  but we will not sin, because we know that we are
    considered yours.
³For to know you is complete righteousness,
  and to know your power is the root of
    immortality.
⁴For neither has the evil intent of human art
    misled us,
  nor the fruitless toil of painters,
  a figure stained with varied colors,
⁵whose appearance arouses yearning in fools,
  so that they desireᵛ the lifeless form of a dead
    image.
⁶Lovers of evil things and fit for such objects of
    hopeʷ
  are those who either make or desire or worship
    them.

⁷For when a potter kneads the soft earth
  and laboriously molds each vessel for our service,

he fashions out of the same clay
  both the vessels that serve clean uses
  and those for contrary uses, making all in like
    manner;
  but which shall be the use of each of these
  the worker in clay decides.
⁸With misspent toil, he forms a futile god from the
    same clay—
  this man who was made of earth a short time
    before
  and after a little while goes to the earth from
    which he was taken,
  when he is required to return the soul that was
    lent him.
⁹But he is not concerned that he is destined to die
  or that his life is brief,
  but he competes with workers in gold and silver,
  and imitates workers in copper;
  and he counts it his glory that he molds
    counterfeit gods.
¹⁰His heart is ashes, his hope is cheaper than dirt,
  and his life is of less worth than clay,
¹¹because he failed to know the one who formed
    him
  and inspired him with an active soul
  and breathed into him a living spirit.
¹²But heˣ considered our existence an idle game,
  and life a festival held for profit,
  for he says one must get money however one can,
    even by base means.
¹³For this man, more than all others, knows that he
    sins
  when he makes from earthy matter fragile
    vessels and graven images.

¹⁴But most foolish, and more miserable than an
    infant,
  are all the enemies who oppressed your people.

14:29 wicked oaths: Sworn in the name of lifeless idols, perhaps with the intent to deceive others (14:30). Hence, the criminal charge of "perjury" also applies (14:28).

15:1 true ... patient ... mercy: Divine attributes made known to Moses in Ex 34:6. The Lord is true, not only in the sense of being faithful and reliable, but also in the sense of truly existing, unlike false gods (Jer 10:8–10).

15:2 we are yours: Israel, by divine election, belongs to the Lord (Deut 7:6). Far from being a license to sin, belonging to God constitutes a primary motive for his people to turn away from sin (Deut 7:7–11).

15:3 immortality: Everlasting life with God. See note on 1:15.

15:4 misled us: A claim, not that Israel never succumbed to idolatry, but that Israel learned from God's revelation that idolatry is evil and foolish.

15:7–13 Another exposé on the absurdity of making idols.

15:7 potter ... same clay ... vessels: Perhaps this passage inspired Paul's description of God as a divine Potter who fashions "out of the same lump one vessel for beauty and another for menial use" (Rom 9:21).

15:8 made of earth: Points out the irony that, according to Genesis, man himself is formed from the ground (Gen 2:7) and destined to return to the ground (Gen 3:19), just like the earthen figurines that the craftsman calls gods. **the soul that was lent him:** The "living spirit" (15:11) divinely infused in man was believed to return to God at death (Eccles 12:7). On man as a unity of body and soul in Wisdom, see note on 1:4.

15:10 His heart is ashes: Words drawn from the Greek LXX translation of Is 44:20.

15:11 the one who formed him: For the image of God as a potter, see Is 29:15–16; 45:9; Jer 18:6. **living spirit:** Designated "the breath of life" in Gen 2:7. See note on 8:19–20.

15:12 life a festival: An idea that also appears in Greco-Roman writings (Cicero, *Tusculan Disputations* 5, 3, 9). **profit:** The idol craftsman, with his heart set on income, is a mercenary more than a devout artist (cf. Acts 19:23–27).

15:14 the enemies: The Egyptians (Ex 3:9).

ᵗ Or *of the oaths men swear.*
ᵘ Or *ruling the universe.*
ᵛ Gk *and he desires.*
ʷ Gk *such hopes.*
ˣ Other authorities read *they.*

¹⁵For they thought that all their heathen idols were
   gods,
 though these have neither the use of their eyes to
   see with,
 nor nostrils with which to draw breath,
 nor ears with which to hear,
 nor fingers to feel with,
 and their feet are of no use for walking.
¹⁶For a man made them,
 and one whose spirit is borrowed formed them;
 for no man can form a god which is like himself.
¹⁷He is mortal, and what he makes with lawless
   hands is dead,
 for he is better than the objects he worships,
 since^y he has life, but they never have.

¹⁸The enemies of your people^z worship even the
   most hateful animals,
 which are worse than all others, when judged by
   their lack of intelligence;
¹⁹and even as animals they are not so beautiful in
   appearance that one would desire them,
 but they have escaped both the praise of God and
   his blessing.

16 Therefore those men were deservedly punished through such creatures,
 and were tormented by a multitude of animals.
²Instead of this punishment you showed kindness
   to your people,
 and you prepared quails to eat,
 a delicacy to satisfy the desire of appetite;
³in order that those men, when they desired food,
 might lose the least remnant of appetite^a
 because of the odious creatures sent to them,
 while your people,^b after suffering want a short
   time,
 might partake of delicacies.

⁴For it was necessary that upon those oppressors
   inexorable want should come,
 while to these it was merely shown how their
   enemies were being tormented.

⁵For when the terrible rage of wild beasts came
   upon your people^c
 and they were being destroyed by the bites of
   writhing serpents,
 your wrath did not continue to the end;
⁶they were troubled for a little while as a warning,
 and received a token of deliverance to remind
   them of your law's command.
⁷For he who turned toward it was saved, not by
   what he saw,
 but by you, the Savior of all.
⁸And by this also you convinced our enemies
 that it is you who deliver from every evil.
⁹For they were killed by the bites of locusts and
   flies,
 and no healing was found for them,
 because they deserved to be punished by such
   things;
¹⁰but your sons were not conquered even by the
   teeth of venomous serpents,
 for your mercy came to their help and healed
   them.
¹¹To remind them of your oracles they were bitten,
 and then were quickly delivered,
 lest they should fall into deep forgetfulness
 and become unresponsive^d to your kindness.
¹²For neither herb nor poultice cured them,
 but it was your word, O Lord, which heals all
   men.
¹³For you have power over life and death;
 you lead men down to the gates of Hades and
   back again.

15:17 he has life: Idols are more obviously subhuman than superhuman. An ancient Jewish philosopher similarly declared it absurd for persons with souls to worship soulless images (Philo of Alexandria, *On the Decalogue* 76).

15:18 animals: Egyptian deities were represented as reptiles, insects, livestock, beasts of prey, etc. See note on 11:15.

■ **16:1–4** The second Exodus antithesis: God plagued the Egyptians with animals and so destroyed their appetite (frogs, Ex 8:1-15), while God fed the Israelites with animals in order to satisfy their appetite (quail, Ex 16:12-13). See note on 11:1—19:22.

16:3 lose ... appetite: Presumably because the frogs infested ovens and kneading bowls (Ex 8:3). **suffering want:** God allowed the Israelites to feel the pangs of hunger in the wilderness in order to give them a taste of the affliction that he brings upon ungodliness (16:4).

■ **16:5–14** The third Exodus antithesis: God sent stinging insects to bring death to the Egyptians (locusts and flies,

Ex 8:20-32; 10:1-20), while he sent venomous snakes among the Israelites along with a remedy to save them from death (fiery serpents, Num 21:4-9). See note on 11:1—19:22.

■ **16:6 warning:** The serpent incident was meant to discipline Israel and turn the people back to God's Law (cf. Deut 8:5). **token of deliverance:** The bronze serpent crafted by Moses (Num 21:9). The author is careful to stress that this was merely a sign of the Lord's mercy and not an idol that possessed magical healing abilities (16:7) (CCC 2130). • Jesus appealed to the lifting of the bronze serpent as a foreshadowing of the Cross, which brings salvation and life to all who look to him for healing (Jn 3:14).

16:9 deserved to be punished: Reiterates the point made in 11:15-16, namely, that those who worship animals are fittingly menaced by animals.

16:10 your sons: The children of Israel (16:26; Deut 14:1; CCC 441).

16:12 your word: An instrument of divine healing (Ps 107:20; Mt 8:8).

■ **16:13 power over life and death:** All living things are in the hand of God and subject to his absolute Lordship (Deut 32:39). The point here is that the Lord can bring a man to the brink of death and back again to full health, if he so desires (1 Sam 2:6; 2 Kings 20:5-6; Tob 13:2). **the gates of Hades:** Also known as "the gates of death" (Ps 9:13) and

---

^y Other authorities read *of which.*
^z Gk *They.*
^a Gk *loathe the necessary appetite.*
^b Gk *they.*
^c Gk *them.*
^d The meaning of the Greek is obscure.

¹⁴A man in his wickedness kills another,
  but he cannot bring back the departed spirit,
  nor set free the imprisoned soul.
¹⁵To escape from your hand is impossible;
¹⁶for the ungodly, refusing to know you,
  were scourged by the strength of your arm,
  pursued by unusual rains and hail and relentless
    storms,
  and utterly consumed by fire.
¹⁷For—most incredible of all—in the water, which
    quenches all things,
  the fire had still greater effect,
  for the universe defends the righteous.
¹⁸At one time the flame was restrained,
  so that it might not consume the creatures sent
    against the ungodly,
  but that seeing this they might know
  that they were being pursued by the judgment of
    God;
¹⁹and at another time even in the midst of water it
    burned more intensely than fire,
  to destroy the crops of the unrighteous land.
²⁰Instead of these things you gave your people the
    food of angels,
  and without their toil you supplied them from
    heaven with bread ready to eat,
  providing every pleasure and suited to every taste.
²¹For your sustenance manifested your sweetness
    toward your children;
  and the bread, ministering*e* to the desire of the
    one who took it,
  was changed to suit every one's liking.
²²Snow and ice withstood fire without melting,
  so that they might know that the crops of their
    enemies

were being destroyed by the fire that blazed in
    the hail
  and flashed in the showers of rain;
²³whereas the fire,*f* in order that the righteous
    might be fed,
  even forgot its native power.

²⁴For creation, serving you who have made it,
  exerts itself to punish the unrighteous,
  and in kindness relaxes on behalf of those who
    trust in you.
²⁵Therefore at that time also, changed into all
    forms,
  it served your all-nourishing bounty,
  according to the desire of those who had need,*g*
²⁶so that your sons, whom you loved, O Lord,
    might learn
  that it is not the production of crops that feeds
    man,
  but that your word preserves those who trust in
    you.
²⁷For what was not destroyed by fire
  was melted when simply warmed by a fleeting
    ray of the sun,
²⁸to make it known that one must rise before the
    sun to give you thanks,
  and must pray to you at the dawning of the
    light;
²⁹for the hope of an ungrateful man will melt like
    wintry frost,
  and flow away like waste water.

The Plague of Darkness and Death

17 Great are your judgments and hard to describe;
  therefore uninstructed souls have gone
    astray.

"the gates of Sheol" (Is 38:10). The realm of the dead, known in Greek as Hades and in Hebrew as Sheol, is imagined as a gated city in the darkness of the underworld. Once a deceased "soul" passed within, it was "imprisoned" away from the upper world of the living (16:14) (CCC 633). See word study: Sheol at Num 16:30.

16:15–29 The fourth Exodus antithesis: God sent fire and hail from heaven to destroy the food supplies of Egypt (crop damage, Ex 9:22–26), while God rained bread from heaven to feed the Israelites (manna, Ex 16:4–21). See note on 11:1—19:22.

16:16 fire: Probably a reference to lightning, which "blazed in the hail" and "flashed in the showers of rain" (16:22) but was not extinguished amidst the precipitation (16:17, 19).

16:17 the righteous: Israel, which was sheltered from the plagues in Goshen (Ex 9:26).

16:20 the food of angels: The manna as described in the Greek LXX translation of Ps 78:25. **from heaven with bread:** The manna as described in Ex 16:4 and Ps 105:40. • Both expressions have been used in Catholic liturgy and hymnody as titles of the Eucharist, owing in part to the fact that Jesus called himself "the true bread from heaven" (Jn

6:32) (CCC 1094). **suited to every taste:** A detail not mentioned in the biblical accounts of the manna but also asserted in rabbinic writings.

16:21 your sweetness: The manna tasted like "wafers made with honey" (Ex 16:31). The author infers from this that Israel was given a taste of the goodness of God (cf. Ps 34:8).

16:22 Snow and ice: Manna had the appearance of frost (Ex 16:14 LXX) or crystal/ice (Num 11:7 LXX), and yet it could be baked and boiled without melting (Ex 16:23; Num 11:8).

16:24 creation, serving you: The natural world, far from being a realm that is full of deities, is subservient to the Lord, who employs its elements as instruments of blessing and cursing (5:17–23; Ps 148:7–8).

16:26 your sons: The children of Israel (16:10; Deut 14:1). **Not ... crops ... your word:** A saying based on Deut 8:3, where Moses interprets the manna as a lesson that man does not live "by bread alone" but "by everything that proceeds out of the mouth of the LORD".

16:27 melted: The manna disappeared each day when the sun grew hot (Ex 16:21).

16:28 before the sun: Prayer before dawn or at daybreak was a traditional Jewish custom (Ps 88:13; Sir 39:5; Mk 1:35).

17:1–18:4 The fifth Exodus antithesis: God shrouded Egypt in three days of darkness (Ex 10:21–29), while God provided Israel with various forms of light (Ex 10:23)—not only daylight (18:1), but a pillar of fire (18:3) and the guiding light of the Torah (18:4). The author gives a psychological

---

e Gk *and it, ministering.*
f Gk *this.*
g Or *who made supplication.*

²For when lawless men supposed that they held
the holy nation in their power,
they themselves lay as captives of darkness and
prisoners of long night,
shut in under their roofs, exiles from eternal
providence.
³For thinking that in their secret sins they were
unobserved
behind a dark curtain of forgetfulness,
they were scattered, terribly ʰ alarmed,
and appalled by specters.
⁴For not even the inner chamber that held them
protected them from fear,
but terrifying sounds rang out around them,
and dismal phantoms with gloomy faces appeared.
⁵And no power of fire was able to give light,
nor did the brilliant flames of the stars
avail to illumine that hateful night.
⁶Nothing was shining through to them
except a dreadful, self-kindled fire,
and in terror they deemed the things which they
saw
to be worse than that unseen appearance.
⁷The delusions of their magic art lay humbled,
and their boasted wisdom was scornfully
rebuked.
⁸For those who promised to drive off the fears and
disorders of a sick soul
were sick themselves with ridiculous fear.
⁹For even if nothing disturbing frightened them,
yet, scared by the passing of beasts and the
hissing of serpents,
¹⁰they perished in trembling fear,
refusing to look even at the air, though it
nowhere could be avoided.
¹¹For wickedness is a cowardly thing, condemned
by its own testimony; ᶦ
distressed by conscience, it has always
exaggerated ʲ the difficulties.

¹²For fear is nothing but surrender of the helps that
come from reason;
¹³and the inner expectation of help, being weak,
prefers ignorance of what causes the torment.
¹⁴But throughout the night, which was really
powerless,
and which beset them from the recesses of
powerless Hades,
they all slept the same sleep,
¹⁵and now were driven by monstrous specters,
and now were paralyzed by their souls' surrender,
for sudden and unexpected fear overwhelmed
them.
¹⁶And whoever was there fell down,
and thus was kept shut up in a prison not made
of iron;
¹⁷for whether he was a farmer or a shepherd
or a workman who toiled in the wilderness,
he was seized, and endured the inescapable fate;
for with one chain of darkness they all were
bound.
¹⁸Whether there came a whistling wind,
or a melodious sound of birds in wide-spreading
branches,
or the rhythm of violently rushing water,
¹⁹or the harsh crash of rocks hurled down,
or the unseen running of leaping animals,
or the sound of the most savage roaring beasts,
or an echo thrown back from a hollow of the
mountains,
it paralyzed them with terror.
²⁰For the whole world was illumined with brilliant
light,
and was engaged in unhindered work,
²¹while over those men alone heavy night was spread,
an image of the darkness that was destined to
receive them;
but still heavier than darkness were they to
themselves.

---

account of the terror, expanding on the story in the Book of Exodus. He further implies that paralyzing darkness was a fitting punishment for Egypt's persistence in moral and spiritual darkness. See note 11:1—19:22.

17:2 the holy nation: Israel (Ex 19:6; Deut 7:6). **long night:** The three days of dense darkness that enveloped Egypt (Ex 10:22).

17:3 their secret sins: Such as those mentioned in 14:23. **scattered:** Separated from one another by the blackness. **specters:** It is unclear whether the apparitions were nightmares (18:17), illusions (17:4), the hauntings of a guilty conscience (17:11), or some combination of these.

17:5 no power of fire: The plague caused a supernatural blackout across Egypt that made kindling flames and seeing the night sky impossible.

17:6 except a dreadful ... fire: Lightning, which would have made the experience all the more terrifying.

📖 **17:7 their magic art:** The occult practices of Pharaoh's magicians, who replicated the initial plagues (Ex 7:11, 22; 8:7) but whose abilities were soon outmatched by the power of God (8:18; 9:11).

17:8 drive off the fears: Magic was a common way to alleviate fear in the ancient world, but in this case, it backfired.

17:11 conscience: A term familiar to Hellenistic moralists but first used here in the Bible. Its negative function as an accuser within, causing the sinner anguish over sins committed, is in view (CCC 1776–89). See word study: *Conscience* at 1 Tim 1:19.

17:14 powerless: Darkness inspires fear but is not itself fearsome. **Hades:** Greek name for the realm of the dead. See note on 16:13. **the same sleep:** Perhaps referring to those who perished in 17:10, here viewed as deceased souls in the netherworld.

17:16 a prison: The darkness in which they were bound (17:17).

17:20 world was illumined: The blockage of sunlight was confined to Egypt.

17:21 image of the darkness: The plague was a foretaste of death and the gloom of Hades.

ʰ Or, with other authorities, *unobserved, they were darkened behind a dark curtain of forgetfulness, terribly.*
ᶦ The Greek text of this line is uncertain and probably corrupt.
ʲ Other ancient authorities read *anticipated.*

18 But for your holy ones there was very great light.

Their enemies[k] heard their voices but did not see their forms,

and counted them happy for not having suffered,

[2]and were thankful that your holy ones,[k] though previously wronged, were doing them no injury;

and they begged their pardon for having been at variance with them.[1]

[3]Therefore you provided a flaming pillar of fire as a guide for your people's[m] unknown journey,

and a harmless sun for their glorious wandering.

[4]For their enemies[n] deserved to be deprived of light and imprisoned in darkness,

those who had kept your sons imprisoned,

through whom the imperishable light of the law was to be given to the world.

[5]When they had resolved to kill the infants of your holy ones,

and one child had been exposed and rescued,

in punishment you took away a multitude of their children;

and you destroyed them all together by a mighty flood.

[6]That night was made known beforehand to our fathers,

so that they might rejoice in sure knowledge of the oaths in which they trusted.

[7]The deliverance of the righteous and the destruction of their enemies

were expected by your people.

[8]For by the same means by which you punished our enemies

you called us to yourself and glorified us.

[9]For in secret the holy children of good men offered sacrifices,

and with one accord agreed to the divine law,

that the saints would share alike the same things,

both blessings and dangers;

and already they were singing the praises of the fathers.[o]

[10]But the discordant cry of their enemies echoed back,

and their piteous lament for their children was spread abroad.

[11]The slave was punished with the same penalty as the master,

and the common man suffered the same loss as the king;

[12]and they all together, by the one form of death, had corpses too many to count.

For the living were not sufficient even to bury them,

since in one instant their most valued children had been destroyed.

[13]For though they had disbelieved everything because of their magic arts,

yet, when their first-born were destroyed, they acknowledged your people to be God's son.

[14]For while gentle silence enveloped all things, and night in its swift course was now half gone,

---

18:1 your holy ones: The Israelites, who were untouched by the darkness (Ex 10:23).

18:2 begged their pardon: Inferred from the interactions in Ex 12:35–36.

18:3 pillar of fire: A manifestation of God's glory that guided Israel on its wilderness journey toward Canaan (Ex 13:21–22). **harmless sun:** Reflects a belief that the divine cloud formed a protective canopy over the pilgrims fleeing Egypt (10:17; Ps 105:39; 1 Cor 10:1).

18:4 light of the law: The Torah is a moral and spiritual lamp that reveals the path of life for God's people (Ps 19:8; 119:105; Rom 2:17–20). **given to the world:** Israel, entrusted with divine revelation, was tasked with enlightening other nations with God's wisdom and truth (Deut 4:5–8; Is 42:6; 49:6). The author deduces from this that Egypt, by keeping the people of Israel captive, was attempting to hold God's plan of salvation for the world in bondage.

18:5–25 The sixth Exodus antithesis: God sent a plague of death on all the first-born of Egypt (Ex 12:29–32) as fitting punishment for Pharaoh's edict to drown all the newborn sons of Israel in the Nile (Ex 1:22), whereas Israel only suffered a brief plague that was stopped short by the intervention of Aaron, the first high priest of Israel (Num 16:41–50).

18:5 one child: Moses, set adrift on the Nile and saved by the Pharaoh's daughter (Ex 2:1–10). **mighty flood:** Refers to the drowning of Egypt's army in the sea (Ex 14:26–28). Jewish tradition outside the Bible also viewed this judgment by water as retribution for the Egyptian mandate to destroy Israel's infant boys in the Nile (*Jubilees* 48, 14).

18:6 That night: Passover night (Ex 12:42). **made known beforehand:** Israel's departure from Egypt was foretold to Abraham (Gen 15:13–14) and Jacob (Gen 46:3–4). **the oaths:** The Lord's covenants with the Patriarchs laid the groundwork for the Exodus deliverance (Ex 6:2–8). See note on 12:21.

18:8 the same means: The miracles of the Exodus, which manifested God's wrath as well as his redemption.

18:9 sacrifices: The lambs offered for the feast of Passover (Ex 12:27) and eaten in Israelite homes (Ex 12:5–8). **singing:** Participants at a Passover meal traditionally sang Ps 113–18, known as the Hallel Psalms (cf. Mt 26:30).

18:10 discordant cry: The wailing that rang out over Egypt at the tenth plague (Ex 12:30).

18:11 common man ... king: The plague of the first-born struck every family in Egypt, even the Pharaoh's (Ex 12:29).

18:13 magic arts: See note on 17:7. **God's son:** An interpretation of Ex 12:31, where the Egyptians finally submit to the Lord's demands, in conjunction with Ex 4:22, where the Lord threatens Pharaoh's first-born with death if he refuses to free Israel, who is God's "first-born son" (CCC 441).

18:14–16 The word of God is personified as a swordsman who administered the tenth plague. The author uses poetical imagery, not to dispute that God inflicted the plague through "the destroyer" (Ex 12:23) or a band of "destroying angels" (Ps 78:49), but to stress the irrevocable

---

[k] Gk *they*.

[1] The meaning of the Greek of this line is uncertain.

[m] Gk *their*.

[n] Gk *those men*.

[o] Other authorities read *dangers, the fathers already leading the songs of praise.*

15your all-powerful word leaped from heaven, from
the royal throne,
into the midst of the land that was doomed,
a stern warrior 16carrying the sharp sword of
your authentic command,
and stood and filled all things with death,
and touched heaven while standing on the
earth.
17Then at once apparitions in dreadful dreams
greatly troubled them,
and unexpected fears assailed them;
18and one here and another there, hurled down half
dead,
made known why they were dying;
19for the dreams which disturbed them forewarned
them of this,
so that they might not perish without knowing
why they suffered.

20The experience of death touched also the
righteous,
and a plague came upon the multitude in the
desert,
but the wrath did not long continue.
21For a blameless man was quick to act as their
champion;
he brought forward the shield of his ministry,
prayer and propitiation by incense;
he withstood the anger and put an end to the
disaster,
showing that he was your servant.

22He conquered the wrath[p] not by strength of body,
and not by force of arms,
but by his word he subdued the punisher,
appealing to the oaths and covenants given to
our fathers.
23For when the dead had already fallen on one
another in heaps,
he intervened and held back the wrath,
and cut off its way to the living.
24For upon his long robe the whole world was
depicted,
and the glories of the fathers were engraved on
the four rows of stones,
and your majesty on the diadem upon his head.
25To these the destroyer yielded, these he[q] feared;
for merely to test the wrath was enough.

God's Continuing Help for His People

19 But the ungodly were assailed to the end by
pitiless anger,
for God[r] knew in advance even their future actions,
2that, though they themselves had permitted[s]
your people to depart
and hastily sent them forth,
they would change their minds and pursue them.
3For while they were still busy at mourning,
and were lamenting at the graves of their dead,
they reached another foolish decision,
and pursued as fugitives those whom they had
begged and compelled to depart.
4For the fate they deserved drew them on to this
end,

---

certainty of the Lord's word concerning the death of the first-born (Ex 11:4–7). • This passage appears to be echoed in Rev 19:11–16, where Christ descends from heaven as "the Word of God" who executes judgment with a "sharp sword" from his mouth. • Catholic tradition has often read 18:15 as anticipating the Incarnation of Christ, the eternal "Word" of the Father who descended into the world and "dwelt among us" as a man (Jn 1:14).

✠ **18:15 all-powerful ... from the royal throne:** The same things are said of wisdom in 7:23 and 9:4, 10. • At midnight God sent down his Word from heaven to bring the judgment of death on the ungodly. What is the Word of the Lord except the Son of God. Elsewhere he is called the arm of the Lord and the right hand of the Lord. This Word now saves us through the waters of Baptism, wherein he also destroys the host of spiritual enemies (Rabanus Maurus, *On Sirach* 3, 15).

18:17–19 Details that dramatize the panic that must have seized the Egyptians but are not found in the Book of Exodus.

18:19 dreams ... forewarned them: Parallels the experience of Pilate's wife in Mt 27:19.

18:20 a plague: Sent against Israel (Num 16:41–50) in the aftermath of Korah's rebellion (Num 16:1–40).

18:21 a blameless man: Aaron, the high priest. **prayer:** Not mentioned in the account of the plague in Numbers but a reasonable supposition in view of the priestly responsibility

in Num 6:22–27. **propitiation by incense:** God's wrath was averted and the plague against Israel halted when Aaron used a censer to make atonement for the people (Num 16:47–48).

18:22 the punisher: Seemingly "the destroyer" of 18:25, i.e., the same angel who unleashed the tenth plague on the first-born in Egypt (Ex 12:23; 1 Cor 10:10). For angels as mediators of divine judgment, see 2 Kings 19:35; 1 Chron 21:15; Rev 16:1–21. **oaths and covenants:** See note on 12:21.

18:24 long robe: A vestment of the high priest (Ex 28:4). Jewish writings outside the Bible also indicate that the robe was ornamented with designs representing various elements of the cosmos (Philo of Alexandria, *Life of Moses* 2, 117–21; Josephus, *Antiquities of the Jews* 3, 180–84). **the glories:** The names of the twelve tribes of Israel, inscribed on gemstones set in the linen breastpiece of the high priest (Ex 28:15–21). **diadem:** A golden headpiece worn by the high priest and engraved with the words: "Holy to the Lord" (Ex 28:36).

18:25 the destroyer: See note on 18:22.

✠ **19:1–22** The seventh and final Exodus antithesis: Because the Israelites were freed by the plagues but not fully saved and the Egyptians were chastised by the plagues but not fully punished, God performed a mighty miracle at the sea, bringing complete deliverance to Israel (Ex 14:21–25) and complete defeat upon Egypt (Ex 14:26–28). See note on 11:1—19:22.

19:1 knew in advance: The divine foreknowledge revealed in Ex 14:3–4 and verified by the Egyptian pursuit of Israel in Ex 14:5–9.

19:2 change their minds: As indicated in Ex 14:5.

19:3 their dead: The first-borns who perished in the tenth plague (Num 33:4).

---

p Cn: Gk *multitude.*
q Other authorities read *they.*
r Gk *he.*
s Other authorities read *had changed their minds to permit.*

and made them forget what had happened,
in order that they might fill up the punishment
which their torments still lacked,
⁵and that your people might experience ᵗ an
incredible journey,
but they themselves might meet a strange
death.

⁶For the whole creation in its nature was
fashioned anew,
complying with your commands,
that your children ᵘ might be kept unharmed.
⁷The cloud was seen overshadowing the camp,
and dry land emerging where water had stood
before,
an unhindered way out of the Red Sea,
and a grassy plain out of the raging waves,
⁸where those protected by your hand passed
through as one nation,
after gazing on marvelous wonders.
⁹For they ranged like horses,
and leaped like lambs,
praising you, O Lord, who delivered them.
¹⁰For they still recalled the events of their sojourn,
how instead of producing animals the earth
brought forth gnats,
and instead of fish the river spewed out vast
numbers of frogs.
¹¹Afterward they saw also a new kind ᵛ of birds,
when desire led them to ask for luxurious food;
¹²for, to give them relief, quails came up from the
sea.

¹³The punishments did not come upon the sinners
without prior signs in the violence of thunder,

for they justly suffered because of their wicked
acts;
for they practiced a more bitter hatred of
strangers.
¹⁴Others had refused to receive strangers when
they came to them,
but these made slaves of guests who were their
benefactors.
¹⁵And not only so, but punishment of some sort
will come upon the former
for their hostile reception of the strangers;
¹⁶but the latter, after receiving them with festal
celebrations,
afflicted with terrible sufferings
those who had already shared the same rights.
¹⁷They were stricken also with loss of sight—
just as were those at the door of the righteous
man—
when, surrounded by yawning darkness,
each tried to find the way through his own
door.

¹⁸For the elements changed ʷ places with one
another,
as on a harp the notes vary the nature of the
rhythm,
while each note remains the same. ˣ
This may be clearly inferred from the sight of
what took place.
¹⁹For land animals were transformed into water
creatures,
and creatures that swim moved over to the
land.
²⁰Fire even in water retained its normal power,
and water forgot its fire-quenching nature.

19:6 the whole creation: The entire natural world is at the service of God to execute his will for the righteous and the wicked alike (also 5:17-23; 16:24-25). **fashioned anew:** The miracle of the sea crossing in Ex 14 parallels the creation of the world in Gen 1. Two points of correspondence are clear: **(1)** the parting of the waters took place as darkness was giving way to morning (Ex 14:20-24), just as creation began with darkness yielding to light (Gen 1:2-3); and **(2)** the waters of the sea were drawn back to reveal dry land (Ex 14:21, 29) and vegetation (grass, 19:7), just as God called back the prevailing waters at creation so that the dry land could appear and put forth vegetation (Gen 1:9-11). **your children:** The Israelites.
19:7 the Red Sea: For possible sites of the sea crossing, see note on Ex 13:18.
19:9 leaped like lambs: Imagery drawn from Ps 114:4. **praising you:** Refers to the Song of the Sea (Ex 15:1-18) and the Song of Miriam (Ex 15:20-21).

19:10 gnats: The third plague (Ex 8:16-19). **frogs:** The second plague (Ex 8:1-15).
19:11 new kind of birds: Migratory quails sent by the Lord to satisfy Israel's craving for meat (Ex 16:11-13; Num 11:31-32).
19:13-17 The inhospitality of the Egyptians is compared to the sin of the Sodomites. • In spite of the sacred duty throughout the Near East to show kindness to strangers, the men of Sodom wished to abuse Lot's guests in a perverted, sexual way (Gen 19:1-7), only to be struck blind for their wickedness (19:17, referring to Gen 19:11). The men of Egypt likewise forced the Israelites, once honored guests in the land (Gen 45:16-20), into slavery (Ex 1:8-14), only to be deprived of sight with the plague of darkness (19:17, referring to Ex 10:21-29).
19:15 the former: The Sodomites.
19:16 the latter: The Egyptians.
19:17 the righteous man: Lot, the nephew of Abraham (10:6; 2 Pet 2:7).
19:18 the elements changed: The Exodus miracles transcended the laws of nature.
19:19 water creatures: Israel's flocks and herds passed through the sea as if they were aquatic animals. **over to the land:** The frogs of the second plague forsook the Nile as if they were land-dwelling mammals.
19:20 Fire: Perhaps the plague of hail and lightning is in view (as in 16:16-17, which is based on Ex 9:22-26).

ᵗ Other authorities read *accomplish*.
ᵘ Or *servants*.
ᵛ Or *production*.
ʷ Gk *changing*.
ˣ The meaning of this verse is uncertain.

[21]Flames, on the contrary, failed to consume
    the flesh of perishable creatures that walked
        among them,
    nor did they melt[y] the crystalline, easily melted
        kind of heavenly food.

[22]For in everything, O Lord, you have exalted and
        glorified your people;
    and you have not neglected to help them at all
        times and in all places.

19:22 O Lord: The final verse is a prayer of divine praise. The author of Wisdom has shown in chaps. 10–19 that throughout salvation history God is ever faithful to his covenant people, delivering them from danger and from those who mistreat them. These lessons from the past are also lessons for the present. Readers can take courage in knowing that wisdom is still at work in the world and that God is still the mighty Savior of those who serve him.

---

[y] Cn: Gk *nor could be melted.*

STUDY QUESTIONS
The Wisdom of Solomon

Chapter 1

For understanding

1. **1:1—5:23.** Through what literary device is immortality, the theme of Wis 1–5, explored? What belief about life is a recurring motif in Scripture?
2. **1:4.** Personified as an indwelling tutor from God, with what is wisdom closely linked? In biblical teaching, what does wisdom do? What does the soul-body language suggest that the author finds about the compatibility between the Greek view of man and Israel's view? What NT view does this body-and-soul anthropology anticipate? What kind of person is enslaved to sin? Who in the NT warns about slavery to sin? According to St. Gregory of Nyssa, why does the soul that is immersed in God not delight in things that deceptively seem good?
3. **1:7.** Where is the Spirit of God diffused, and where does wisdom permeate? What does the biblical teaching on divine omnipresence mean? What similar statement does Paul make about Jesus Christ?
4. **1:12.** As a subject of a theological debate in the book, what do the wicked mistakenly suppose about death and what happens after? What do they do as a consequence? Being ignorant of the Lord's designs, of what are they unaware about bodily death and even an early death? For Wisdom's author, what is physical death far less dreadful than? What does he mean by this? How did spiritual death enter human history, and to whom does it come?
5. **1:15.** With what does the author imply that God rewards the righteous? Why is righteousness the antidote to sinfulness and mortality? If the Book of Wisdom neither affirms nor denies the immortality of the soul on philosophical grounds, on what fundamentally Jewish doctrine does its belief in a blessed immortality depend?

For application

1. **1:2.** How might a person who claims to be seeking the Lord actually be putting him to the test in the process? How can a seeker trust the one he is still seeking?
2. **1:6.** What is blasphemy? Given the definition of blasphemy in the *Catechism* and noting its grave (i.e., mortal) sinfulness (CCC 2148), what would it take to make a person truly guilty of it? Would an expression of mere impatience with God qualify?
3. **1:12–13.** How have you dealt with the death of someone deeply loved? How did it affect your attitude toward God? What have you thought regarding your own death?
4. **1:14.** Since substances toxic to humans do exist in the environment, what do you think the author means by saying that there is no "destructive poison" in created things? How can even poisonous substances be beneficial?

Chapter 2

For understanding

1. **2:1–20.** How are the twisted thoughts and motives of the wicked revealed? By what five ideologies do they live? According to 2:12 and 3:10 who do the wicked appear to be?
2. **2:12–20.** To what does hatred of the righteous, provoked by their opposition to evildoing, lead? With what are these verses commonly read in connection? In particular, what do vv. 18–20, which detail how the righteous man is made to suffer in order to test his claim to be God's son, closely parallel?
3. **2:23.** What is the incorruption that wisdom offers? What is the point being made about spiritual death and separation from God, and what about physical death? How is the original divine intention finally realized? According to St. Ambrose, how can the soul once controlled by unrighteousness receive virtue and grace?
4. **Word Study: Envy (2:24).** How many times does the Greek word *phthonos* appear in the Bible, and where? Since classical times, how has envy been defined? In the Book of Wisdom, to what is envy directly opposed, and as what is it exposed? How was envy also at work in the condemnation of Jesus, the new Adam? How is envy unlike jealousy? How does the moral teaching of the Church categorize envy?

For application

1. **2:2–4.** What do you think is the meaning and value of your life? Do you believe you were born by chance rather than by divine plan? What legacy would you like to leave behind?
2. **2:11.** How is the utilitarian philosophy of this verse reflected in our society? How do the laws of our country favor the strong over the weak? What should be the Christian response to them, and on what grounds?
3. **2:12–16.** Which doctrines of Christianity do its critics most often deplore? How do they justify their criticisms? How do they put their opposition to Christian ways into effect?
4. **2:24.** Read the word study on envy at this verse. Since the devil is superior in nature to human beings, what about us could have made him envious? Why is his malice so relentless?

Chapter 3

For understanding

1. **3:1.** What are the "souls of the righteous"? What doctrine does the Book of Wisdom neither explicitly affirm nor deny? What does it mean to say that the souls of the righteous are in the hands of God? What will the righteous experience in heaven? According to St. Augustine, what lesson should those traveling to such a home learn from the saints?
2. **3:5.** How does Wisdom view the trials and ordeals of life? Consequently, how should one view the suffering of the righteous?

3. **3:12.** In what sense are the wives and children of evildoers considered evil? Of what else may the author be accusing the wicked? What are we to note about the barren woman in v. 13 and the enuch in v. 14? What might this suggest are the primary targets of criticism in v. 12?
4. **3:16.** Why will the children of adulterers not come to maturity? Beyond this, what may the author also have in mind about them? On this reading, what will fail to endure or afford consolation on the Day of Judgment?

For application
1. **3:4.** What hope of immortality do you have? What is the ultimate goal of that hope?
2. **3:5.** Review the note for this verse. If you have or care for children, how do you discipline them, and for what purpose? Upon reflection, what has the Lord's discipline in the spiritual life been like for you, and what have you learned from it?
3. **3:11.** How successful is a person likely to be who undertakes a skilled profession without acquiring the necessary training? How successful is a person likely to be in the spiritual life who believes that spiritual direction is unnecessary? What kind of training can spiritual direction provide?
4. **3:12.** Read the note for this verse. What does virtue do for a person's character? How does one acquire a virtue? What virtue would you most like to acquire?

Chapter 4

For understanding
1. **4:1.** How were both childlessness and having children experienced in biblical times? Here, however, what is more highly esteemed than natural offspring? What is virtue? Which virtues does the author of Wisdom commend?
2. **4:7–19.** What view about an early death does Wisdom contest? How, on the contrary, should a life pleasing to God be measured?
3. **4:10–15.** Why does the author support his claim in 4:7–9 by alluding to Enoch, the patriarch in Genesis? How does he view Enoch's translation into heaven? For what purpose does the author of Wisdom often take this approach of referring to persons and stories of the OT? Why does he do this without citing their names?
4. **4:20—5:23.** At the final Judgment, whom will the faithful departed face, and what will they receive from the Lord? By contrast, what will happen to the wicked?

For application
1. **4:1–2.** Who is the most virtuous person you have known? What about this person's life inspires you? What aspect of his life would you most like to imitate?
2. **4:8–9.** How do you feel about growing old? What do you most anticipate? What do you most fear? How true do you think it is that wisdom and understanding come with old age?
3. **4:11.** What is your opinion about the death of the young, even of infants? How comforting would most people find the sentiment in this verse when a child dies? Comforting or not, how true do you think the statement is?
4. **4:12.** According to St. James (Jas 1:14–15), what leads people into sin? Why do people find wickedness fascinating and virtue boring? What fascinates you?

Chapter 5

For understanding
1. **5:5.** Of whom are the expressions "sons of God" and "saints" sometimes used? According to some scholars, whom does Wisdom envision the righteous dead joining? What does this *not* mean, however?
2. **5:7.** What do the three terms (translated "journeyed", "untrodden", and "wilderness") also describe in Israel's history? What typological connection is implied?
3. **5:16.** What does "a glorious crown" represent, as in the NT? From where does the image of a "crown" or "diadem" in the Lord's "hand" come, and what does it symbolize?
4   **5:17.** On what is the image of God arming himself with his attributes based? In Ephesians, what exhortation does Paul draw from both Isaiah and Wisdom?

For application
1. **5:5.** Can you think of a notorious sinner who converted on his deathbed or received the Sacrament of Confession there? What questions does that raise for you? What does it tell you about the mercy of God?
2. **5:8–12.** At death, what can you take with you? On what will you be judged? According to these verses, if you have lived a successful life but wanted nothing to do with God, what will remain to you? In such a case, what will have been the point of having lived?
3. **5:15–16.** What characteristics of eternal life are mentioned in these verses? For example, of what would care and protection for someone in heaven consist? How does this description of eternal life compare with your understanding of it?

Chapter 6

For understanding
1. **6:1.** How does the Latin Vulgate begin this chapter? What does the biblical idiom "the ends of the earth" mean? What empire do some scholars believe is in view here, and why?
2. **6:4.** What indicates that God's kingship over the world is a prominent theme in the OT? How do political rulers participate in God's government of the world? How is the theme of the "kingdom of God" deepened and expanded in the NT? What law is presumably meant in this verse?

3.   **6:12.** How is wisdom personified here? How is her depiction as a woman based on the biblical terms for "wisdom"? How does the imagery in Wis 6–9 draw from and develop Prov 1–9?
4.   **6:17.** What two virtues does the desire for wisdom presuppose?

For application
1.   **6:3.** Scripture enjoins citizens to respect governing authorities (Rom 13:1–2; 1 Pet 2:13–14; CCC 2238–40). If governing authority is given from the Lord, what allegiance do you owe when authorities misuse it, for example, when they impose restrictions on Christian morality or require you to support immoral behavior?
2.   **6:4.** In what ways are you a servant of God's kingdom? Whether you have much or little authority over others, how have you used the authority you have? Have you ever sought the Lord for help in using authority? If so, in what ways?
3.   **6:16.** Read the note for this verse. Upon reflection, have you ever seen God taking the initiative in your life, even before you were aware of his action? For example, when you felt an impulse to pray, what prompted that impulse? What name do we give this initiative of God?
4.   **6:23.** In addition to envy, what other vices oppose the gaining of wisdom? For example, how might sloth or greed impede growth in wisdom?

Chapter 7

For understanding
1.   **7:7–21.** As recollections based on Solomon's prayer for wisdom in 1 Kings 3:5–14, what do these verses illustrate?
2.   **7:17.** What knowledge did Solomon, taught by divine wisdom, have? What does the author seem to hint about Solomon's understanding of philosophical and scientific matters? What is one implication of this verse regarding divine revelation and human reason?
3.   **7:20.** What did Jewish tradition hold about Solomon? To what might his understanding of the potency of "roots" point? At least by NT times, what power was the Messiah expected to wield?
4.   **7:22—8:1.** What do these verses comprise? How does it build on earlier texts of the OT and make use of terms drawn from Greek philosophy? What is most striking about the figure of wisdom? Of what is this poem the nearest thing to a revelation in the OT? How are characteristics here attributed to wisdom attributed to the Son and the Spirit in the NT?

For application
1.   **7:1–6.** How would you apply these verses to your view of yourself? What good does it do to remind yourself that in certain respects you are just like everyone else? In what ways are you unique? How often do you thank the Lord for what makes you human?
2.   **7:7.** In the normal course of life, how does one naturally acquire wisdom, as distinct from skill? What kind of wisdom can come only through prayer? As one of the gifts of the Holy Spirit, what makes divine wisdom different from natural wisdom?
3.   **7:13.** How does instruction or discipline teach wisdom? Why must one who acquires divine wisdom share it with others?
4.   **7:22–24.** How do these verses describe what God is like? What does each attribute mean to you? For example, why does wisdom require purity?

Chapter 8

For understanding
1.   **8:7.** What are virtues? Which are those that are specified in classical antiquity and here in the Jewish life of wisdom? How are these four cornerstones of human formation defined? What does Catholicism likewise commend them as being?
2.   **8:8.** Why can knowledge of the past and future only be imparted by God? What was one of Solomon's more famous intellectual abilities? For what is the expression "signs and wonders" biblical terminology?
3.   **8:13.** What double meaning does immortality have in the context of this verse?
4.   **8:19–20.** In this brief reflection on the author's natural endowments, what was it apparent that God had already given him in his youth? What do some scholars read these verses to mean with respect to their author's beliefs? For what two reasons is this unlikely?

For application
1.   **8:2.** The note for this verse says that a "loving union with wisdom [8:18] amounts to a loving friendship with God himself." How do you approach God: as a judge, as a distant parent, as someone to be afraid of, or as a friend? Why do the saints compare union with God to marriage? Do you think such a union is possible for yourself? If not, why not?
2.   **8:7.** Of the four cardinal virtues, of which do you think you are most in need? Of which would someone who knows you well (e.g., a spouse) say you are in need?
3.   **8:9–20.** Bearing in mind that the speaker in these verses is Solomon, the king, what is to prevent the reader from attributing these verses to a power-hungry narcissist? How might the list of these attributes actually be considered a humble admission?

Chapter 9

For understanding
1.   **9:1–18.** On what is Solomon's prayer for divine wisdom based? For what does the king seek wisdom? With what does the prayer link God's wisdom? How does the NT reveal the mystery of the Trinity in terms that recall these OT portraits of wisdom?

2. **9:8.** What did the terms of the Davidic covenant specify that David's royal heir should do? What is the name of God's "holy mountain"? Of what were the sanctuaries of Israel supposed to be earthly replicas? To whom was its pattern first shown, and to whom was it later revealed as an inspired blueprint?
3. **9:13.** Why did human ignorance of divine things make a deep impression on the author? What makes the counsel of God accessible to humans?
4. **9:15.** What language did Greek thinkers use to describe the trials of the human condition? While the same is true of the author, how does his Jewish perspective influence his view of the body? What does "this earthly tent" mean?

For application
1. **9:1-3.** Just as every Christian enjoys the "common priesthood of the faithful", so each is privileged to play a kingly role, exercising dominion over certain aspects of creation. What does "dominion" mean to you, and how is it different from domination? Where do you exercise dominion in your environment (e.g., in your family, over your time)?
2. **9:5.** According to 1 Cor 3:18–20, the wisdom of this age is folly with God, and the thoughts of the wise are futile. How would you describe the wisdom of the age in which we live? What about it is futile from God's viewpoint?
3. **9:7.** The note for this verse names Solomon's brothers Amnon, Absalom, and Adonijah. What about their characters might explain the wisdom of God's preference for Solomon? How do you see the wisdom of God at work in placing you where you are in life?
4. **9:13.** How do you try to discern the will of God for your life? What makes discernment difficult for you? According to v. 17, from where does the ability to discern God's will come?

Chapter 10

For understanding
1. **10:1-21.** What activity does chap. 10 review? In addition to examining the leading personalities in Genesis and Exodus, what additional allusions does it also make? Why is salvation history retold this way? How is God's work in the world described?
2. **10:1.** Who is the "first-formed"? How does Genesis portray him? What does the text imply that he did after his first transgression against God, although this is not mentioned in Genesis?
3. **10:6.** Whom does the author call the "righteous man" in this verse? What are the Five Cities, and which four are named in Scripture?
4. **10:10.** Who is the righteous man in this verse, and from what did he flee? How is the kingdom of God understood here? What dream is alluded to in this verse?

For application
1. **10:7-8.** Scripture is full of stories of people whose unwise behavior proved disastrous for subsequent generations. Can you think of any historical person whose failures had such consequences for those who followed them? How can the pursuit of divine wisdom help you avoid decisions that negatively affect people for whom you are responsible?
2. **10:9.** By the same token, how has the pursuit of divine wisdom protected you and yours from trouble? What encouragement can you derive from the lives of the saints?
3. **10:10-12.** These verses call the patriarch Jacob, whom Genesis portrays as a trickster and a shrewd manipulator, a "righteous man" protected by wisdom. According to v. 12, how did Jacob learn that "godliness is more powerful than anything" (hint: see Gen 32:23–29)? Through what struggles is the Lord teaching this lesson to you?
4. **10:21.** Who are the "mute" and the "infants" of this verse? What kind of language is needed for praising God? How does the grace of God help you build a vocabulary of praise?

Chapter 11

For understanding
1. **11:1—19:22.** How do the final chapters of Wisdom continue tracing the events of salvation history? What is emphasized here? In the overall argument of the book, for what do these saving actions of God in the past give hope? What is a *midrash*? How does the author also make use of a Greek rhetorical device known as *synkrisis* or "comparison"? How many antitheses punctuate this part of the book?
2. **11:4-14.** What is the first Exodus antithesis?
3. **11:9-10.** What kind of time was Israel's testing in the wilderness? How was it an exercise of the Father's mercy? Whether preventative or corrective, at what does divine discipline aim?
4. **11:20.** To what does "the breath of your power" refer here? According to what laws is the cosmos ordered? How does this biblical outlook stand in marked contrast to pagan world views? What would the biblical conviction that a divine rationality is inscribed into creation later inspire? According to St. Augustine, how was every creature, without exception, made?

For application
1. **11:4-14.** Read the note for these verses. How many antitheses can you detect in your reading of other parts of Scripture (e.g., what appears as folly to one group is salvation to another, as in 1 Cor 1:18)? How might you view general human experience in terms of antitheses, such as what is a bane for one group proves a boon to another?
2. **11:9-10.** How is God's discipline of his servants different from the wrath of his judgment on his enemies, even when both are undergoing similar difficulties? What is the purpose of God's discipline?
3. **11:16.** What examples can you think of to illustrate the truth of this verse? For example, how might one be punished by sinning with food?
4. **11:20.** Read the note for this verse, paying attention to the comment about divine rationality and the natural sciences. What happens to the natural sciences when scientists reject divine rationality? What happens to the minds of the scientists?

Chapter 12

For understanding

1. **12:3–11.** What point does this aside on the conquest of Canaan illustrate? Why were the Canaanites robbed of life and land? Since the Lord could have annihilated the Canaanites at a stroke for their crimes, why did he parcel out punishments "little by little"?
2. **12:10.** What is the ultimate reason that God tempers his judgment with mercy? Why does this verse not mean that the Canaanites were created evil or predestined for damnation? What idea is being presented?
3. **12:12–18.** Of what do the critics of Israel's conquest of Canaan accuse God? In what three ways does the author challenge these allegations?
4. **12:21.** Who are the fathers? In the biblical world, how were covenants established? When God makes a promise on oath, what is he giving?

For application

1. **12:2.** When it comes to the correction of children, which is more beneficial: to correct misbehavior a little at a time or to store up offenses and then apply correction once for everything? Why?
2. **12:13–14.** To whom is God accountable? When there is a difference of opinion between God and man, whose opinion must change? Why?
3. **12:19.** The note for this verse suggests that kindness toward others is an attribute of divine wisdom, an idea that anticipates Jesus' teaching on love of enemies. What motive does the verse itself give for being kind? How might such a motive affect your relations with people you regard as enemies?
4. **12:26.** What does a parent do to a child who fails to learn from gradual disciplines, or an employer do to an employee who fails to respond to repeated admonitions? How does failure to respond to discipline prepare one for the final Judgment?

Chapter 13

For understanding

1. **13:1—15:17.** Against what does this excursus on the foolishness of Gentile idolatry seek to strengthen Jewish readers? At several points, of what literary approach does the author make use? In what four ways do both Wisdom and Paul in the NT treat the subject of idolatry?
2. **13:1–9.** For what does the author fault idolaters? Instead of coming to know the Creator, at what did they stop short and fail to recognize? What teaching of Scripture does the Catholic Church uphold in this regard?
3. **13:5.** In a remarkably positive assessment of human reason, what does the author contend that the mind can do by applying the philosophical principle of analogy?
4. **3:6.** What mitigates the blame that can be assigned to worshipers of creation? What three categories of blame does the author delineate?

For application

1. **13:2.** While secular scientists claim not to deify nature, how do they think the world operates? Where do they believe such principles of operation originate?
2. **13:7.** How do you determine that something is beautiful? How can beauty become a way of leading people to faith in God? To what kinds of beauty would you refer someone as pointing to God?
3. **13:13–19.** What religious images do you own? Where do you place them in your home, and what veneration do you give them? Since Scripture forbids the making of "graven images", why does the Church allow their use (CCC 2132)?

Chapter 14

For understanding

1. **Word Study: Providence (14:3).** To what does the Greek word *pronoia*, translated "providence" or "provision", refer? Appearing first in the OT in the Book of Wisdom in this verse, what does it designate here? For what is it used in the NT? In ancient Greek writings, what does *pronoia* denote? How did Latin speakers designate this benevolent rule and wise ordering of the cosmos? Although Hebrew had no single word that expressed the idea of God's Providence, what belief did numerous passages express about it? Under what notion is biblical teaching on divine Providence often subsumed? In Catholic teaching, to what does divine Providence lead creation?
2. **14:7.** What "blessed wood" is referred to here, and who made it? To what wood did the Fathers of the Church often apply this verse?
3. **14:12.** How is the abandonment of God for idols the "beginning of fornication"? What makes this more than just a metaphor?
4. **14:15–21.** To which ancient customs is idolatry traced? What two cases are given in the note?

For application

1. **14:3.** Read the word study on Providence, which refers to CCC 302. If, according to CCC 303, God has "absolute sovereignty over the course of events", how is God's Providence and solicitude over creation manifested in natural disasters and man-made terrors?
2. **14:7.** Read the note for this verse. How many hymns and prayers can you think of that celebrate the wood of the Cross? What does the Cross or crucifix mean to you personally?
3. **14:12.** Why were so many idols of ancient society associated with fertility or sexual potency? In modern times, how does our culture idolize sex? How is that idolatry usually represented or portrayed?
4. **14:22–31.** Compare these verses with Rom 1:22–32. In terms of our culture, how accurate do you think this assessment is? How does the assessment affect your own life? What should be the Christian response to it?

Chapter 15

For understanding
1. **15:1.** What were three divine attributes made known to Moses in Ex 34:6? In what senses is the Lord true?
2. **15:8.** What irony does this verse point out? At death, what was believed to happen to the "living spirit" divinely infused in man?
3. **15:17.** In relation to human nature, what is obvious about idols? What did the ancient Jewish philosopher Philo similarly declare it absurd for persons with souls to do?

For application
1. **15:2.** In sacramental terms, how do you know that God accounts you as his? When you sin, how do you make a perfect act or purpose of contrition? According to the *Catechism*, when is going to the Sacrament of Reconciliation necessary (CCC 1446, 1856)?
2. **15:3.** For a human person, what constitutes holiness? This verse says that knowledge of God is "complete righteousness"; in the biblical understanding of knowledge, what sort of knowledge is this?
3. **15:7.** Christian hymns sometimes address the Lord as a divine Potter molding the human spirit. How would you like this Potter to mold yours? What kind of reshaping might he need to do to you so as to answer that request?
4. **15:16–17.** Modern technology is trying to create an artificial intelligence that is virtually human, capable of learning and operating on its own. How might these verses apply to such an effort? In what sense might such a device actually be alive, and in what sense would it be dead? What questions about being human would such a device raise?

Chapter 16

For understanding
1. **16:1–4.** What is the second Exodus antithesis in Wisdom?
2. **16:5–14.** What is the third Exodus antithesis?
3. **16:13.** Since all living things are in the hand of God and subject to his absolute Lordship, what point is Wisdom making here? What was the realm of the dead, known in Greek as Hades and in Hebrew as Sheol, imagined to be? Once a deceased "soul" passed within, what happened to it?
4. **16:15–29.** What is the fourth Exodus antithesis?
5. **16:20.** What was the "food of angels" and the "bread from heaven"? How have Catholic liturgy and hymnody used both expressions? What detail is not mentioned in the biblical accounts of the manna?

For application
1. **16:3.** How is a modicum of suffering good for the soul? Why do the saints often mortify themselves, and why does the Church insist that some mortification is necessary in the pursuit of holiness (CCC 2015)?
2. **16:6.** The note for this verse refers to the bronze serpent made by Moses (Num 21:9), which King Hezekiah later smashed because it had become an object of idolatry (2 Kings 18:4). What kinds of religious articles (e.g., icons, crucifixes, statues, rosaries) do you own? Why do you have them? At what point would these articles cease contributing to genuine devotion and become objects of superstition?
3. **16:12.** In what sense is the word of God "living and active" (Heb 4:12)? How does it provide healing?
4. **16:20.** The Church calls the Eucharist the "source and summit of the Christian life" (CCC 1324). What does that mean in practice? How would you explain Catholic devotion to the Eucharist, both within and outside of Mass, to a non-Christian?

Chapter 17

For understanding
1. **17:1—18:4.** What is the fifth Exodus antithesis? What sort of account of the terror does the author give? What does he further imply?
2. **17:3.** What scattered the "lawless men" (v. 2) from one another? What is unclear about the specters that appalled them?
3. **17:11.** Though familiar to Hellenistic moralists, where is the term *conscience* first used in the Bible? What function of conscience is in view?
4. **17:21.** Of what was the plague of darkness a foretaste?

For application
1. **17:3.** Why is there no such thing as a perfectly private sin? What effects do personal sins that we think are unobserved have on our relationships with others, especially family members and friends?
2. **17:11.** In what sense is wickedness cowardly by nature? How do specific vices, such as lying or stealing, oppose the virtue of fortitude? What does the author mean by saying that wickedness exaggerates difficulties for the conscience?
3. **17:18–21.** Why are people afraid of the dark? If you were alone in a cave with no light, of what would you be most afraid? What does light reveal? Why do Christians refer to God in terms of light?

Chapter 18

For understanding
1. **18:4.** What kind of lamp is the Torah? With what was Israel, entrusted with divine revelation, tasked? What does the author deduce from this about Egypt?
2. **18:5–25.** What is the sixth Exodus antithesis?

3.   **18:5.** Who was the one child who was exposed and rescued? What was the mighty flood referred to here? How did Jewish tradition outside the Bible view this judgment by water?
4.   **18:14–16.** How is the word of God personified here? Why does the author use such poetic imagery? How does this passage appear to be echoed in Rev 19:11–16? What has Catholic tradition often read 18:15 as anticipating?

For application
1.   **18:4.** According to 2 Tim 3:15–16, for what is Scripture useful? What is the ultimate personal goal of reading it?
2.   **18:9.** Where in today's world must Christianity be practiced in secret? What dangers do people in that area face for practicing it? Although you enjoy relative freedom of religion, what (if any) are some of the restrictions that local laws or policies place on practicing your Christian faith?
3.   **18:14–16.** How does the word of God cut so as to be compared to a sword? As Heb 4:12 describes, how has it helped you discern "the thoughts and intentions of [your] heart"?
4.   **18:21.** What is your experience with intercessory prayer? For whom or what do you typically intercede? How confident are you that your prayers are being heard? Have you noticed any results from persistent intercession?

Chapter 19

For understanding
1.   **19:1–22.** What is the seventh and final Exodus antithesis?
2.   **19:6.** For what purpose is the entire natural world at the service of God? In paralleling the miracle of the sea crossing in Ex 14 to the creation of the world in Gen 1, what two points of correspondence are clear?
3.   **19:13–17.** To what is the inhospitality of the Egyptians compared? In spite of the sacred duty throughout the Near East to show kindness to strangers, what did the men of Sodom wish to do, and what happened to them? What likewise happened to the men of Egypt?
4.   **19:22.** What has the author of Wisdom shown in chaps. 10–19? How are these lessons from the past also lessons for the present?

For application
1.   **19:1–3.** When are strong emotions morally good, and when are they evil (CCC 1768)? Why is making a major decision in the heat of anger a bad idea? From a more positive viewpoint, how can the passion of anger work for good?
2.   **19:4.** In the story of the Exodus, what compulsion drove Pharaoh to recapture the Israelites, despite the recent deaths of their first-born? Did God's foreknowledge of events determine Pharaoh's behavior? Why do we view compulsive behavior as a problem?
3.   **19:6.** According to the *Catechism* (CCC 280), what is the end for which God created the universe? What will its realization mean both for the universe itself and for mankind (CCC 1042–47)?
4.   **19:9.** Be it a sporting, a political, or a military victory, how do people tend to celebrate it? How does a rehearsal or review of the events leading up to the victory enhance the celebration? Why is it right to include praise of God in the celebration?

INTRODUCTION TO SIRACH

Author and Date The Book of Sirach holds the distinction of being the only wisdom book in the Bible that can be dated with precision, give or take a decade, and whose author is not subject to any scholarly controversy. We owe this, first, to the author's signature at the end of the book and, second, to the book's prologue, written by his grandson.

The author identifies himself as "Jesus the son of Sirach [Ben Sira], son of Eleazar, of Jerusalem" (50:27). Despite variations of his name in the Hebrew text of 50:27 and 51:30, his grandson also refers to him as "my grandfather Jesus" in the prologue. He was a sage and professional scribe devoted to the Scriptures of Israel and desirous to pass on his wisdom to others through his own writing. Some have suggested that his description of the life of the scribe in 39:1–11 is autobiographical. He appears to have led a school or academy, to which he invited the unlearned to study wisdom (51:23).

The prologue tells us that Ben Sira wrote the book in Hebrew (probably in Jerusalem). An important clue to the book's date comes from the author's description of the priest Simon, son of Onias (50:1–21). This figure is commonly identified with Simeon II, who according to most scholars was high priest from 219 to 196 B.C. Sirach describes Simon's ministry as if he had personally witnessed it, and yet it seems that Simon is deceased at the time of the book's writing (50:1). Additionally, there is no clear evidence in the book of the tensions between Jews and Greeks that increased sharply after the accession of the Seleucid King Antiochus IV Epiphanes to the throne in 175 B.C., or of the persecution of the Jews that he initiated in 169 B.C. (though 36:1–17 is a possible exception). This makes it likely that Ben Sira had published the book before that date, probably somewhere between 196 and 175 B.C., with 180 B.C. being a commonly proposed date.

Ben Sira's grandson, who is never named in the book, translated the book into Greek after coming to Egypt "in the thirty-eighth year of the reign of Euergetes" (prologue). This Euergetes is King Ptolemy VII Physcon (sometimes numbered VIII), who reigned from 170 to 164 and 146 to 117 B.C. The thirty-eighth year from the beginning of his reign is 132 B.C., so Sirach's grandson likely translated the book shortly after that date.

Title The book is known in Greek manuscripts as "The Wisdom of Jesus Son of Sirach" or simply "Wisdom of Sirach". This title is likely based on the Hebrew version of 50:27, which reads: "The Wisdom of Jesus son of Eleazar son of Sira". The Babylonian

Talmud (*Hagigah* 13a, *Niddah* 16b) refers to it as *Sepher Ben Sira* ("The Book of Ben Sira"). In the Vulgate, as in the Latin Christian tradition generally, the book is known as *Ecclesiasticus* ("book of the Church"), but this title is losing ground today, largely because it is easily confused with the book of Ecclesiastes. Nowadays the book is commonly known as *Sirach*, the Greek form of the Hebrew *Sira*—the name of the author's father or grandfather. Scholars typically refer to the book's author by his Hebrew name, *Ben Sira* ("Son of Sirach").

Place in the Canon Although Sirach was originally written in Hebrew, it was not accepted into the Hebrew Bible, possibly due to the relatively late date of its composition. Its inclusion in the Septuagint attests that it was a sacred writing for Greek-speaking Jews. Nevertheless, ancient rabbis excluded it from the Jewish Bible, or Tanakh. Despite its exclusion, the Hebrew text of Sirach is frequently cited in the Talmud (sometimes introduced by the formula "it is written"), indicating that some rabbis held it in extremely high regard. The canonicity of Sirach was also disputed in the early Church. It is quoted as authoritative in early Christian writings such as the *Didache* and *Epistle of Barnabas*, but the Eastern Fathers were divided over its status, e.g., St. Clement of Alexandria, St. Cyril of Jerusalem, and St. John Chrysostom accepted it as canonical, whereas Origen of Alexandria and St. Athanasius provide conflicting evidence, sometimes referring to the book as "Scripture" but sometimes excluding it from the canon. Eusebius saw the book as valuable but disputed. Among the Western Fathers, most viewed Sirach as part of the Bible, including St. Cyprian of Carthage, St. Hilary of Poitiers, and St. Augustine of Hippo. One notable exception was St. Jerome, who considered Sirach distinct from the canonical books of the Hebrew Old Testament.

Early Church synods at Hippo (A.D. 393) and Carthage (397) included Sirach in the canon of Scripture, the latter calling it one of the "five books of Solomon" (with Proverbs, Ecclesiastes, Song of Songs, and Wisdom). This decision was confirmed at the later Synod of Carthage in 419. Thereafter Sirach's canonical status was uncontested until the Protestant Reformation, when Martin Luther and the other Reformers relegated it to the Apocrypha and adopted the shorter Jewish Bible as the Protestant canon of the Old Testament. In response to this, the Council of Trent reaffirmed Sirach as one of the canonical books of Scripture. In Catholic Bibles, the book is placed last among the wisdom books of the Old Testament. Sirach is also accepted as canonical in Eastern Orthodox and Oriental Orthodox churches.

Structure Like Proverbs, Sirach is an anthology of wisdom texts, though it tends to organize its materials in larger thematic units than Proverbs. It is difficult to discern an intentional structure in a book that contains little narrative and is primarily composed of poems, moral exhortations, and pieces of advice for the wise. Not surprisingly, there is no consensus among scholars on the book's internal organization.

That said, Sirach may be divided into three main parts (chaps. 1–23; 24–43; 44–50), framed by a prologue and an epilogue (chap. 51). The Greek text includes headings that mark off this basic division: "The Praise of Wisdom" at 24:1 (many consider this chapter to be the climax of the book), and "Hymn in Honor of our Ancestors" at 44:1. Alternatively, some have suggested that the third part should begin with the hymn on creation at 42:15. Others divide the book into five parts, also framed by the prologue and epilogue, thereby replicating the structure of the Pentateuch. On the fivefold division, each unit begins with a doctrinal section that is followed by practical teachings (1:1—16:23; 16:24—23:27; 24:1—32:13; 32:14—42:14; 42:15—50:29). Still others divide the book into eight parts, each beginning with a poem on wisdom. The present volume outlines the contents of the book by combining the threefold parts (Books One, Two, Three) and the eightfold divisions (Parts I–VIII). See *Outline*.

Literary Background The textual situation of Sirach is complicated, not least because the original Hebrew text was lost from about A.D. 400 to 1900, during which time the book survived mainly in Greek, Syriac, and Latin versions. The Greek version, moreover, has been preserved in two forms: one short form, which is a translation of the original Hebrew text (GI), and one longer form, which includes more than 300 additional lines and translates an expanded form of the Hebrew text (GII). St. Jerome did not produce a new translation of Sirach for the Latin Vulgate; instead, he adopted the text of the Old Latin version, which is based on the expanded GII text (plus some additions not found in GII).

In the late nineteenth century, fragments of the Hebrew version of Sirach were found in a Cairo Synagogue Geniza (a storeroom for discarded manuscripts); this was followed by the discovery of more fragments at Qumran and Masada in the twentieth century. About two-thirds of the Hebrew text is now recovered. These archaeological finds have confirmed the existence of shorter (HI) and longer (HII) editions of the Hebrew text. In many instances, the Hebrew manuscripts agree with the Greek and Syriac; in other instances, they disagree.

The text of the Clementine Vulgate generally follows the longer Greek version, with further additions of its own. Adding to the complexity of the situation, the New Vulgate, upon which the RSV2CE is largely based, sometimes diverges from the Clementine Vulgate in order to follow the Greek text more closely (e.g., 3:10, 24).

Because of this state of affairs, there are variations in the text and verse numbers of modern translations. Whereas earlier modern English translations (KJV, Douay-Rheims) are based on the longer Greek (and/or Latin) text, more recent translations (RSV) rely primarily on the shorter Greek text (resulting in some verses that are either missing or relegated to the footnotes). Other modern translations (NAB, NRSV) also follow the shorter Greek text while making extensive use of the Hebrew and longer Greek texts. The RSV2CE is eclectic: it often favors the Greek text (4:17, 20–21; 7:30; 24:31–33) but sometimes prefers the longer Latin text of the New Vulgate (1:5, 7; 4:18; 24:1–3, 8, 12, 20).

Historical Context The Book of Sirach was shaped by the historical, political, and cultural context of Hellenism. Alexander the Great's rapid conquest of the Persian Empire in 332 B.C. permanently transformed the ancient Near East. After his death in 323, his vast empire was divided among his generals, and thereafter the land of Judea became a battleground between the Ptolemies of Egypt and Seleucids of Syria. In 301 B.C., the Ptolemies gained control of the area and maintained it for the next century. With the growth of commercial opportunities, many Judean Jews migrated to colonies throughout the known world, contributing to what became known as the Diaspora (= the dispersion of the Jewish people to foreign lands). In time Jews learned to speak Greek and adopted Greek customs and ideas. Around 250 B.C. in Alexandria, Egypt, the Hebrew Scriptures began to be translated into Greek, producing the Septuagint.

In 198 B.C., the Seleucid King Antiochus III the Great defeated the Ptolemies and took control of Judea. The Jews initially welcomed the Seleucids, who brought a time of peace and stability under Antiochus III and his son Seleucus IV Philopator (187–175). The decades that preceded the accession to the throne of Antiochus IV Epiphanes likely provide the context in which Ben Sira lived. According to 2 Maccabees, under the pious high priest Onias III, "the holy city was inhabited in unbroken peace and the laws were very well observed" (2 Mac 3:1). Nevertheless, the Ptolemies and Seleucids promoted an aggressive policy of Hellenization (= the imposition of Greek culture) that gave rise to increasing tensions in Jewish society. Many Jews were attracted to the Greek way of life and dabbled in Greek philosophy and religion. Others, such as Ben Sira, saw Hellenization as a threat to Judaism and set out to resist it.

The Book of Sirach is thus an apologetic defense of Judaism against the challenges of Hellenism. Ben Sira attempts to counter the rising influence of Greek thought among Jews by insisting that true wisdom resides in the Torah given to Israel. He does this largely through the integration of sacred history into wisdom: whereas older wisdom books (Job, Proverbs, Ecclesiastes) made few references to Israel's life and history, Sirach connects wisdom with the religious traditions of Israel. The work is thus full of references and allusions to biblical persons and events, e.g., the creation account (39:16), the Garden of Eden (24:25–27), Adam (33:10; 40:1) and Eve (25:24), the fallen angels (16:7), the flood (40:10), Lot, Sodom and Gomorrah (16:8), the Israelites in the wilderness (16:9–10), the Law of Moses (24:23), the Tabernacle (24:10, 15), and Mt. Zion (24:10; 36:13–15). Ben Sira's praise of ancient heroes (chaps. 44–50) provides the most comprehensive summary of salvation history in the Bible. Beginning with Enoch, it celebrates the Patriarchs, the Exodus from Egypt, the conquest and period of the Judges, the united and divided monarchies, the Prophets, and the postexilic restoration up to the days of Simon the high priest.

The irony in Ben Sira's resistance to Hellenism is that he is not entirely immune to its influences. Some have found in the book traces of Stoicism, according to which the universe is ruled by the divine Logos (= word, rationality). Men and women must conform themselves to nature and reason as reflections of the Logos—obeying a type of natural law—if they wish to live well and find harmony between the individual and the whole. Some see hints of this philosophy in Sirach's ideal of human dignity (41:14—42:8), of the unity of the world (43:27), and of the human race (36:1–4). Others see in Sirach traces of Epicureanism, which sought a balanced life ruled by reason, free from bodily pain and inner disquiet (14:11–16; 30:21–25; 31:27–29). Still others detect Hellenistic traits in Sirach's quasi-identification of virtue with knowledge and wickedness with folly, in his endorsement of the Greek culture of banquets and of medical practices, and in his use of philosophical arguments to defend divine justice.

Content and Themes Sirach is a long book. It touches on so many subjects that it is difficult to draw up a succinct list of its teachings. Nevertheless, there are a few key themes that are central to the book's theology.

(1) *Wisdom.* The quest for wisdom lies at the heart of the book. But what—or who—is wisdom? Ben Sira answers this question by means of wisdom poems (opening each of the eight parts of the book—see *Outline* below) that disclose her metaphysical nature and short maxims that teach men how to acquire and exercise wisdom. From these, we learn about the following aspects of wisdom: (a) *Preexistence*: Wisdom is an emanation from God and his eternal word (24:3); although she

was created in some sense, she existed before the world came into being (1:4, 9) and will never cease to exist (1:1; 24:9). (b) *Role in creation and history*: Wisdom created the universe and guided the course of human history—especially Israel's history (16:24—18:14; 24:5–6; 39:12–35; 42:15—50:24). (c) *Nature*: Wisdom is much more than knowledge gained through study; she is personified as wife and mother (4:11–19; 14:20—15:8), and men are invited to enter a loving relationship with her. She grants them facility in distinguishing between good and evil, along with the ability to choose the good so that they may stand in a right relationship with God and lead a blessed life. (d) *Acquisition*: Wisdom is a gift that comes from God, who gives her to those who love him (1:10). Yet men and women must do their part to obtain her: they must have a reverential fear of the Lord—the "crown" and the "root" of wisdom (1:11–30)—and they must pursue her and submit to her discipline, even at great cost (4:17; 6:24–25), including keeping the commandments (1:26). (e) *Rewards*: Even though the quest for wisdom is difficult, she turns out to be worth the effort in the end. To those who find her, she provides fruits and desirable goods, health, knowledge, and glory (1:16–19), abundant life blessed by God's favor and love (4:11–14), rest, protection, glorious garments, and a crown of gladness (6:28–31). Souls remain thirsty when they refuse to draw near to her (51:24).

(2) *Torah.* Wisdom resides in "the book of the covenant of the Most High God, the law which Moses commanded us" (24:23). The prominence given to the Law of Moses in Sirach distinguishes it from Proverbs and the other wisdom books. This does not imply a legalistic view of wisdom, for the Hebrew term *torah* is only imperfectly rendered by the English word "law". More than legal obligation, Torah is "teaching" or "instruction" about how to live a godly life. The identification of the Torah with wisdom that emanates "from the mouth of the Most High" and is the "first-born before all creatures" (24:3, 9) implies the preexistence of the Torah. This is the first occurrence of what would later become a teaching of rabbinic Judaism: although the Torah was *revealed* in the time of Moses, its existence preceded the creation of the world (see, e.g., Midrash *Genesis Rabbah* 8) and would endure forever (Bar 4:1). It is no wonder, then, that for Ben Sira "he who holds to the law will obtain wisdom" (15:1), and "he who devotes himself to the study of the law of the Most High will seek out the wisdom of all the ancients, and will be concerned with prophecies" (39:1).

(3) *Retribution.* Sirach subscribes to the classic Deuteronomistic theology of retribution: seeking and finding wisdom by obeying God's commandments brings blessings, prosperity, and happiness (Deut 28:1–14); despising wisdom by disregarding the commandments leads to curses, disaster, and misery (Deut 28:15–68). The choice is set before each person, who has the ability and the responsibility to choose good over evil (15:11–20). Ben Sira believes that divine retribution takes place in this life. He has no clear concept of judgment after death apart from the idea that the just live on through their good name, memory, and descendants (30:4–5; 37:26; 41:12–13). On the whole, he appears to view death as final and Hades as the destination of all the deceased; thus, man must make the best of the few days he has on earth (14:11–19; 38:16–23; 41:1–4). That said, two prayers for the "revival of bones" (46:12; 49:10) dimly point toward a future resurrection.

(4) *Temple Worship.* Although wisdom is universal and older than creation, she "sought a resting place" where she might lodge in history (24:7). She contracts herself, as it were, to dwell in Israel, in Jerusalem, and ultimately in Israel's sanctuary, where she ministers before God (24:8–12). Wisdom is thus present and active in the liturgy of the Jewish Temple, which is portrayed as a type of Garden of Eden (24:13–17). The use of language similar to that found in chapter 24 also implies the presence of wisdom in the ministry of the high priest Simon (50:1–24). Sirach's reverence for the Temple service is also discernable in his exhortation to honor the sanctuary priests (7:29–31) and the sacrifices they offer (34:18–20). Although he tends toward spiritualizing cultic rituals, so that keeping the Torah, performing deeds of kindness, and acting justly are considered equivalent to offering sacrifices (35:1–3), he never treats the latter as dispensable but continues to require their observance as part of Israel's divinely ordained worship (35:4–11).

(5) *Prayer.* Since wisdom is a gift from God, the quest for her is never a secular enterprise but one grounded in a relationship with the Lord. Teachings on prayer are found throughout the book. Ben Sira recommends petitions for mercy (21:1; 28:2–4; 39:5), wise counsel (37:15), healing (38:9, 13–14), and, of course, for wisdom (51:13). Keeping the commandments is a prerequisite to having one's prayers heard (3:5). He also urges readers to offer praise to the Lord (17:10; 39:14–15; 43:30). The book itself includes three lengthy prayers: one asking God for control of one's thoughts, words, and desires (22:27—23:6), a second asking for the redemption of Zion (36:1–17), and a third a psalm of thanksgiving (51:1–12).

(6) *Life in Society.* Ben Sira's moral teachings cover a wide range of topics. These include counsel on controlling the tongue (19:4–17; 20:5–8; 23:12–15), the family and duty of caring for one's parents (3:1–16), humility (3:17–24; 7:16–17), social justice and almsgiving (3:30–31; 4:2–10; 29:1–20), wealth and poverty (10:30–31; 11:10–20; 13:15—14:10; 31:1–11), and authentic versus false friendship (6:5–17; 9:10–16; 11:29—12:18). His concerns for chastity and his warnings against loose women and prostitutes (9:1–9; 26:9–12; 42:12–14) seem at times to color his view of women in a negative way (22:3; 25:16–26; 42:14); but he also has words of high praise for good wives (26:1–4).

Christian Perspective Sirach is not quoted in the New Testament, but a few passages seem to allude to it. The strongest echo is found in Jesus' invitation to shoulder his easy yoke (Mt 11:28–30), which evokes Wisdom's summons to bear her yoke (6:24–26; 51:26–27). Jesus' promise to the Samaritan woman that "whoever drinks of the water that I shall give him will never thirst" (Jn 4:13–14) reads like a response to Wisdom's assertion that "those who drink me will thirst for more" (24:21). One can see the personification of wisdom in Sirach as a preparation for Jesus as the incarnation of Wisdom (Jn 1:1–18) and her role in creation as a prefiguration of Christ's identity as "the first-born of all creation" through whom all things were made (Col 1:15–20; Heb 1:1–2). Finally, the Letter of James has a number of allusions to Sirach on topics such as double-mindedness (1:28; 2:12; Jas 1:6, 8), temptations (2:1; 15:11–20; Jas 1:2–4, 13–15), being swift to hear (5:11; Jas 1:19), controlling the tongue (28:12–26; Jas 3:1–12), and true wisdom (19:20–25; Jas 3:13–18).

OUTLINE OF SIRACH

Translator's Prologue

1. Book One (chaps. 1–23)

    A. Part I (1:1—4:10)
        1. Introduction: The Origin of Wisdom (1:1–10)
        2. Fear of the Lord Is Wisdom for Mankind (1:11–30)
        3. Trust in God (2:1–18)
        4. The Honor Due Father and Mother (3:1–16)
        5. Humility and Pride (3:17–31)
        6. Almsgiving and Social Conduct (4:1–10)

B. Part II (4:11—6:17)
  1. Wisdom's Rewards and Warnings (4:11–19)
  2. Exhortations about Speech (4:20–31)
  3. Avarice, Presumption, Duplicity, Unruly Passions (5:1—6:4)
  4. True and False Friendship (6:5–17)

C. Part III (6:18—14:19)
  1. Encouragement to Strive for Wisdom (6:18–37)
  2. Conduct toward God and Neighbor (7:1–17)
  3. Maxims for Family Life, Religion, and Charity (7:18–36)
  4. Prudence in Dealing with Others (8:1–19)
  5. Advice concerning Women and the Choice of Friends (9:1–18)
  6. About Rulers and the Sin of Pride (10:1–18)
  7. True Honor and the Deceptiveness of Appearances (10:19—11:9)
  8. Providence and Trust in God (11:10–28)
  9. Care in Choosing Friends; Beware of Enemies (11:29—12:18)
  10. The Rich and the Poor (13:1–26)
  11. The Use of Wealth (14:1–19)

D. Part IV (14:20—23:28)
  1. The Search for Wisdom and Its Blessings (14:20—15:10)
  2. Free Will and Responsibility (15:11—16:23)
  3. Divine Wisdom and Mercy in the Creation of Man (16:24—18:14)
  4. Prudential Warnings (18:15—19:17)
  5. Wisdom and Folly in Word and in Deed (19:18—20:32)
  6. Sin and Folly of Various Kinds (21:1—22:18)
  7. The Preservation of Friendship (22:19–27)
  8. Warning against Destructive Sins (23:1–28)

2. Book Two (chaps. 24–43)

A. Part V (24:1—33:17)
  1. Praise of Wisdom (24:1–34)
  2. Gifts That Bring Happiness (25:1–12)
  3. Wicked and Virtuous Women (25:13—26:27)
  4. Hazards to Integrity and to Friendship (26:28—27:21)
  5. Malice, Anger, Vengeance, and the Evil Tongue (27:22—28:26)
  6. Loans, Alms, and Surety (29:1–20)
  7. Frugality and the Training of Children (29:21—30:13)
  8. Health, Cheerfulness, and Riches (30:14—31:11)
  9. Food, Wine, and Banquets (31:12—32:13)
  10. The Providence of God (32:14—33:17)

B. Part VI (33:18—38:23)
  1. Property and Servants (33:18–31)
  2. Trust in the Lord and Not in Dreams (34:1–17)
  3. True Worship of God and His Response (34:18—36:17)
  4. Choice of Associates (36:18—37:15)
  5. Wisdom and Temperance (37:16–31)
  6. Sickness and Death (38:1–23)

C. Part VII (38:24—43:33)
  1. Vocations of the Skilled Worker and the Scribe (38:24—39:11)
  2. Praise of God the Creator (39:12–35)
  3. Joys and Miseries of Life (40:1—41:13)
  4. True and False Shame; Fathers and Daughters (41:14—42:14)
  5. The Works of God in Creation (42:15—43:33)

3. Book Three (chaps. 44–50)

Part VIII (44:1—50:24)
1. Praise of Israel's Great Ancestors (44:1–15)
2. The Early Patriarchs (44:16–23)
3. Praise of Moses, Aaron, and Phinehas (45:1–26)
4. Joshua, Caleb, the Judges, and Samuel (46:1–20)
5. Nathan, David, and Solomon (47:1–22)
6. The Northern Kingdom: Elijah and Elisha (47:23—48:15)
7. Judah: Hezekiah and Isaiah (48:16–25)
8. Josiah and the Prophets: Heroes Early and Late (49:1–16)
9. Simeon, Son of Jochanan (50:1–24)
10. Judah's Neighbors; Postscript (50:25–29)

Epilogue (chap. 51)
A. Song of Thanksgiving (51:1–12)
B. The Author's Search for Wisdom (51:13–30)

THE BOOK OF

SIRACH

The Prologue

Whereas many great teachings have been given to us through the law and the prophets and the others that followed them, on account of which we should praise Israel for instruction and wisdom; and since it is necessary not only that the readers themselves should acquire understanding but also that those who love learning should be able to help the outsiders by both speaking and writing, my grandfather Jesus, after devoting himself especially to the reading of the law and the prophets and the other books of our fathers, and after acquiring considerable proficiency in them, was himself also led to write something pertaining to instruction and wisdom, in order that, by becoming conversant with this also, those who love learning should make even greater progress in living according to the law.

You are urged therefore to read with good will and attention, and to be indulgent[a] in cases where, despite our diligent labor in translating, we may seem to have rendered some phrases imperfectly. For what was originally expressed in Hebrew does not have exactly the same sense when translated into another language. Not only this work, but even the law itself, the prophecies, and the rest of the books differ not a little as originally expressed.

When I came to Egypt in the thirty-eighth year of the reign of Euer′getes and stayed for some time, I found opportunity for no little instruction.[b] It seemed highly necessary that I should myself devote some pains and labor to the translation of the following book, using in that period of time great watchfulness and skill in order to complete and publish the book for those living abroad who wished to gain learning, being prepared in character to live according to the law.

In Praise of Wisdom

1 All wisdom comes from the Lord
and is with him for ever.
[2] The sand of the sea, the drops of rain,
and the days of eternity—who can count them?
[3] The height of heaven, the breadth of the earth,
the abyss, and wisdom—who can search them out?
[4] Wisdom was created before all things,
and prudent understanding from eternity.[c]
[5] The source of wisdom is God's word in the highest heaven,
and her ways are the eternal commandments.

Prologue: the law ... prophets ... others: The earliest known witness to the three parts of the Hebrew Bible (cf. Lk 24:44). **Jesus:** Yeshua, the son of Sirach, who authored the book (50:27). **considerable proficiency:** The entire book attests to the author's remarkable expertise in the Hebrew Scriptures, no doubt the fruit of many years of study. **living according to the law:** The study of wisdom is a commentary on the Torah and its application. **Hebrew:** The original language of the book. **differ not a little:** Semitic languages such as Hebrew and Aramaic are quite different from languages such as Greek and Latin. **thirty-eighth year:** 132 B.C. **Euergetes:** King Ptolemy VII. **the translation:** Ben Sira's grandson translated the book into Greek for the benefit of Jews in Egypt.

1:1–10 The book opens with a poem on the origin of wisdom: she is found in God, and only God truly knows her. God alone, therefore, can bestow her upon others.

1:1 All wisdom: Wisdom is a feminine noun in both Greek (*sophia*) and Hebrew (*ḥokmah*). Thus, in Sirach, as in Proverbs and the Wisdom of Solomon, wisdom is personified as a female figure (4:11–19; 6:18–31; 14:20—15:10; 24:1–34; Prov 8:1–9:6; Wis 6:12–20).

1:2 sand ... drops ... days: Illustrate the immeasurable vastness of creation and, therefore, of wisdom. **who can count?** A rhetorical question implying the answer: "No one but God."

1:3 heaven ... earth ... abyss: The realm of wisdom encompasses the whole creation. **who can search?** Assumes the same answer as the question in 1:2.

1:4 Wisdom was created: Although present at the beginning of creation, wisdom is created by God, according to Sirach (1:9; Prov 8:22; but compare Wis 7:25).

1:5 word: The Greek is *logos*. Wisdom finds her origin in God's eternal word (Jn 1:1–2). **the eternal commandments:** Although the precepts of the Torah were revealed in the time of Moses, for Ben Sira they existed eternally in the mind of God (24:23).

The Book of Sirach (Ecclesiasticus) belongs to the Wisdom literature and was written by Ben Sira, a "sage of Israel," in the early second century B.C. It was originally composed in Hebrew, as we learn from the Prologue, and translated into Greek some fifty years later by his grandson. During these fifty years there had been a violent persecution of the Jews by the Seleucid kings in order to force them to adopt Greek religion and culture. The beginnings of this were already apparent in the time of Ben Sira, and it was to counteract such influences that his book was written. It is full of traditional Jewish wisdom and morals; indeed, full of worldly wisdom and written by one with wide experience of life. He re-emphasizes the traditional truths, but manages to do this in an interesting way and sometimes even from a new angle, e.g., his words on death (40:2; 41:2).

Sirach was included in the Greek Bible but not in the later Jewish canon. The Hebrew text was known to Jerome but later disappeared and was rediscovered, though not complete, only at the end of the nineteenth century in Cairo. Further fragments have been found recently in Palestine.

The Church accepted the book as canonical, but it was the Greek text she accepted. The name Ecclesiasticus was given to it in its Old Latin version—a name which appears to date from the time of St. Cyprian. St. Jerome did not translate the book or revise the Old Latin, so the text is substantially as he found it. It is a version made from the Greek, but a Greek text notably different from the one we use, chiefly in the quantity of additional material. However, these additions do not add anything substantially new to the book except, perhaps, the spirit in which they are written. The version has been described as "a Pharisaic recension of the original work of Ben Sira."

[a] Or *Please read therefore with good will and attention, and be indulgent.*
[b] Other authorities read *a copy affording no little instruction.*
[c] Other authorities omit verse 5.

⁶The root of wisdom—to whom has it been
  revealed?
  Her clever devices—who knows them?ᵈ
⁷The knowledge of wisdom—to whom was it
  manifested?
  And her abundant experience—who has
  understood it?
⁸There is One who is wise, the Creator of all,
  the King greatly to be feared, sitting upon his
  throne, and ruling as God.
⁹The Lord himself created wisdomᵉ in the holy
  spirit;
  he saw her and apportioned her,
  he poured her out upon all his works.
¹⁰She dwells with all flesh according to his gift,
  and he supplied her to those who love him.

¹¹The fear of the Lord is glory and exultation,
  and gladness and a crown of rejoicing.
¹²The fear of the Lord delights the heart,
  and gives gladness and joy and long
  life.
¹³With him who fears the Lord it will go well at
  the end;
  on the day of his death he will be blessed.

¹⁴To fear the Lord is the beginning of wisdom;
  she is created with the faithful in the womb.
¹⁵She madeᶠ among men an eternal foundation,
  and among their descendants she will be
  trusted.
¹⁶To fear the Lord is wisdom's full measure;
  she satisfiesᵍ men with her fruits;
¹⁷she fills their whole house with desirable goods,
  and their storehouses with her produce.
¹⁸The fear of the Lord is the crown of wisdom,
  making peace and perfect health to flourish.
¹⁹He saw her and apportioned her;
  he rained down knowledge and discerning
  comprehension,
  and he exalted the glory of those who held her
  fast.
²⁰To fear the Lord is the root of wisdom,
  and her branches are long life.ʰ

²²Unrighteous anger cannot be justified,
  for a man's anger tips the scale to his ruin.
²³A patient man will endure until the right moment,
  and then joy will burst forth for him.
²⁴He will hide his words until the right moment,
  and the lips of many will tell of his good sense.

1:6–7 Four rhetorical questions underline how the **root ... devices ... knowledge**, and **experience** of wisdom are inaccessible to the unaided human mind.

1:8 Creator of all, the King: An addition from the Latin Vulgate. God is not only the Cause of the universe but also the One who actively rules it (Is 6:1; Ps 9:7). **ruling as God:** An addition from the Latin Vulgate.

1:9 created wisdom: See note on 1:4. **in the holy spirit:** An addition from the Latin Vulgate. **poured her out:** Ben Sira likens wisdom to a liquid that God pours on all that he has made. Evidence of divine wisdom can thus be found throughout creation (Rom 1:20).

1:10 all flesh: Wisdom dwells among all peoples, Jews as well as Gentiles. **those who love him:** The intimate connection between love and wisdom is developed in multiple places in the book (2:15–16; 4:14; 40:20; Wis 6:12, 17–18).

📖 **1:11–30** Men and women have access to wisdom by a humble fear of the Lord. The relationship between wisdom and fear of the Lord is central to Sirach's thought. It is a key theme in the Old Testament, especially in the wisdom literature (Deut 4:9–10; 8:5–6; 2 Chron 19:7; 26:5; Prov 1:7; 9:10; Job 28:28; Ps 111:10). Both are gifts of the Holy Spirit (Is 11:2; CCC 1831). See note on Prov 1:7.

1:11–13 Fear of the Lord is a source of the best things in life. It obtains **joy and long life** as well as protection and blessings at the time of one's **death**.

1:14–20 Fear of the Lord is the **beginning** (1:14), **measure** (1:16), **crown** (1:18), and **root** (1:20) **of wisdom**.

✝ **1:14 the beginning of wisdom:** I.e., its essential point of departure. • Isaiah presents seven spiritual gifts, beginning with wisdom and ending with the fear of God, as

though he is moving downward to our level. In this way he teaches us to climb back up again. Just as he descended from wisdom to fear, so we ascend from fear to wisdom (St. Augustine, *Sermons* 347, 2).

1:15 She made among men an eternal foundation: Literally, "Among humans she nested a foundation of eternity"—i.e., a foundation that will always remain.

1:16 full measure: The more one grows in wisdom, the more one is filled with the fear of the Lord, which in turn increases wisdom. The fact that she **satisfies** or inebriates **men** by **her fruits** is perhaps an allusion to the tree of life (Prov 3:18; 11:30).

1:17 desirable goods: Wisdom's banquet is both metaphorical (Prov 9:1–6) and real (Prov 8:18), for she brings both spiritual riches and material prosperity to one's household.

1:18 crown of wisdom: Fear of the Lord is both the starting point and culmination of the quest for wisdom. See note on 1:16. **peace:** The Hebrew concept of *shalom* implies safety, prosperity, well-being, wholeness, contentment, and satisfaction. **perfect health:** Perhaps includes health of the body (Prov 3:7–8).

1:19 apportioned her: It takes effort to attain wisdom, yet God gives her to those who seek her. **held her fast:** Cultivating wisdom is a condition for exaltation by the Lord.

1:20 root ... branches: Wisdom is pictured as a life-giving tree, implying an identification of wisdom with the tree of life (Gen 2:9; Prov 3:18). Gaining wisdom is equivalent to eating from the tree of life, in contrast to eating from the tree of knowledge, which deceptively appeared "to make one wise" but only brought death (Gen 2:17; 3:6).

1:22–30 Character flaws that prevent men from acquiring the fear of the Lord, contrasting them to virtuous behaviors that lead to attaining it.

1:22 Unrighteous anger: Losing one's temper for no good reason is incompatible with the fear of the Lord.

1:23 A patient man: Exercises self-control and endures sufferings for a time, until his patience is rewarded. He does not complain or engage in idle chatter but remains silent until the opportune time to speak, when his wisdom will earn him praise.

ᵈOther authorities omit verse 7.
ᵉGk *her.*
ᶠGk *made as nest.*
ᵍGk *intoxicates.*
ʰOther authorities add as verse 21, *The fear of the Lord drives away sins; and where it abides, it will turn away all anger.*

²⁵In the treasuries of wisdom are wise sayings,
  but godliness is an abomination to a sinner.
²⁶If you desire wisdom, keep the commandments,
  and the Lord will supply it for you.
²⁷For the fear of the Lord is wisdom and
    instruction,
  and he delights in fidelity and meekness.
²⁸Do not disobey the fear of the Lord;
  do not approach him with a divided mind.
²⁹Be not a hypocrite in men's sight,ⁱ
  and keep watch over your lips.
³⁰Do not exalt yourself lest you fall,
  and thus bring dishonor upon yourself.
The Lord will reveal your secrets
  and cast you down in the midst of the
    congregation,
because you did not come in the fear of the Lord,
  and your heart was full of deceit.

Duties toward God

2 My son, if you come forward to serve the Lord,
  remain in justice and in fear,
  and prepare yourself for temptation.ʲ
²Set your heart right and be steadfast,
  incline your ear, and receive words of
    understanding,
  and do not be hasty in time of calamity.

³Await God's patience, cling to him and do not
    depart,
  that you may be wise in all your ways.
⁴Accept whatever is brought upon you,
  and endure it in sorrow;
  in changes that humble you be patient.
⁵For gold and silver are tested in the fire,
  and acceptable men in the furnace of humiliation.
⁶Trust in God, and he will help you;
  hope in him, and he will make your ways
    straight.
Stay in fear of him, and grow old in him.

⁷You who fear the Lord, wait for his mercy;
  and turn not aside, lest you fall.
⁸You who fear the Lord, trust in him,
  and your reward will not fail;
⁹you who fear the Lord, hope for good things,
  for everlasting joy and mercy.
You who fear the Lord, love him,
  and your hearts will be made radiant.
¹⁰Consider the ancient generations and see:
  who ever trusted in the Lord and was put to
    shame?
Or who ever persevered in his commandmentsᵏ
  and was forsaken?

1:25 treasuries: Storehouses full of wise and valuable sayings. But while wisdom is well received by righteous men, her call to moral excellence is abominable to those who insist on remaining in their sinful ways.

1:26 If you desire wisdom: Wisdom does not consist in abstract philosophical speculation but is attained by keeping God's commandments.

1:28 Do not disobey: I.e., by neglecting to keep the commandments, doubting their efficacy, or approaching them with a **divided mind**, i.e., lacking singlehearted devotion. • How do we deal with the body when the will, which is joined with the body, is weakened in its desire to do good? This applies to people who follow God but who have escaped the world only in part. Their hearts are not detached from worldly things here, and so they are divided within themselves, sometimes looking forward and sometimes back. The wise man addresses them when he says, "Do not come to the Lord with two hearts" (Isaac of Nineveh, *Ascetical Homilies* 37).

1:29 Be not a hypocrite: By pretending to be what one is not or by speaking in one way and acting in another. One who seeks to be wise should guard his lips, lest he lack integrity of speech and be charged with hypocrisy.

1:30 Do not exalt yourself: Arrogance, pride, and pretentious deceit diminish one's reputation in the eyes of the congregation (Prov 11:2; 16:18; 29:23; Tob 4:13).

2:1–18 Fear of the Lord invites trust in God in all circumstances, especially in times of trial and temptation.

2:1–6 God tests those who are faithful to him (4:17; 6:20–21; Job 7:18; Jas 1:2–4).

2:1 My son: A common way for a teacher of wisdom to address a student (Prov 1:8, 10; 2:1). **temptation:** Either the temptation to do wrong or a trial of faith.

2:2 Set your heart right: An exhortation to patience and faithfulness in times of testing. **incline your ear ... understanding:** An addition from the Latin Vulgate.

2:3 cling to him: Trials in life provide some of the greatest opportunities for spiritual growth (Deut 10:20; 13:4; Josh 22:5).

2:4 endure it in sorrow: On the transformative power of suffering, see Rom 5:3–5. • Christ has given suffering new meaning as something that conforms believers to his image and unites them with his redemptive work on the Cross (CCC 1505).

2:5 gold and silver: On the refining fire of suffering, see Is 48:10; Prov 17:3; Wis 3:6; 1 Pet 1:7. • Even the saints, burdened with only minor faults, have been given over to great afflictions, lest they be found to have any spot or stain on the Day of Judgment (St. John Cassian, *Conferences* 1, 7, 25).

2:6 Trust in God: Relying on God amidst severe tribulations reaps rewards when the storms of life have passed (Ps 37:3; Prov 3:5–6). **your ways straight:** The path of life (Prov 10:17; 12:28). It is our duty to seek God's straight way; but God rewards our trust and hope by making straight the paths before him (39:24; Ps 5:8; Prov 3:6; 11:5; Is 45:13; Tob 4:19). **Stay in fear of him, and grow old in him:** An addition from the Latin Vulgate.

2:7–9 Three verses that address those who fear the Lord, exhorting them to **wait**, **trust**, and **hope**. If the faithful persevere in adversity, they will not only avoid falling but will reap a bountiful **reward** with great **joy and mercy**.

2:9 You who fear ... radiant: An addition from the Latin Vulgate.

2:10 Consider the ancient generations: Readers are invited to reflect on the past and consider: Does the Lord ever forsake the righteous? It is tempting to answer "yes" when suffering presses hard (Ps 22:1; Job), but Ben Sira insists the answer is "no", for the Lord has revealed his compassion throughout Israel's history by granting salvation (Ex 34:6; Ps 103:8; 145:8).

ⁱSyr: Gk *in the mouths of men.*
ʲOr *trials.*
ᵏOr *the fear of the Lord.*

Or who ever called upon him and was
   overlooked?
[11]For the Lord is compassionate and merciful;
   he forgives sins and saves in time of affliction,
   and he is the shield of all who seek him in truth.

[12]Woe to timid hearts and to slack hands,
   and to the sinner who walks along two ways!
[13]Woe to the faint heart, for it has no trust!
   Therefore it will not be sheltered.
[14]Woe to you who have lost your endurance!
   What will you do when the Lord punishes
   you?
[15]Those who fear the Lord will not disobey his
   words,
   and those who love him will keep his ways.
[16]Those who fear the Lord will seek his approval,
   and those who love him will be filled with the
   law.
[17]Those who fear the Lord will prepare their hearts,
   and will humble themselves before him.
[18]Let us fall[1] into the hands of the Lord,
   but not into the hands of men;
for as his majesty is,
   so also is his mercy.

Duties toward Parents and Others

3 Listen to me your father, O children;
   and act accordingly, that you may be kept in
   safety.

[2]For the Lord honored the father above the
   children,
   and he confirmed the right of the mother over
   her sons.
[3]Whoever honors his father atones for sins,
   and preserves himself from them.
   When he prays, he is heard;
[4]   and whoever glorifies his mother is like one
   who lays up treasure.
[5]Whoever honors his father will be gladdened by
   his own children,
   and when he prays he will be heard.
[6]Whoever glorifies his father will have long life,
   and whoever obeys the Lord will refresh his
   mother;
[7]   he will serve his parents as his masters.[m]
[8]Honor your father by word and deed,
   that a blessing from him may come upon you.
[9]For a father's blessing strengthens the houses of
   the children,
   but a mother's curse uproots their foundations.

[10]Do not glorify yourself by dishonoring your
   father,
   for your father's dishonor is no glory to you.
[11]For a man's glory comes from honoring his
   father,
   and it is a disgrace for children not to respect
   their mother.

2:11 and he is the shield ... truth: An addition from the Latin Vulgate.

2:12 Woe: Misfortunes await those who lack the fear of the Lord; also noted in 2:13–14.

2:15–18 The righteous who **fear** and **love** the Lord display courage, obedience, and humility and have confidence of success as well. While God's **majesty** places high expectations on those who follow him, his **mercy** makes up for their failures and shortcomings.

3:1–16 A commentary on the fourth commandment of the Decalogue: "Honor your father and your mother" (Ex 20:12; Deut 5:16). Since parents are the primary teachers of their children, children who aspire to be wise must honor and respect them. This commandment is the lynchpin to relating well with all figures of authority for the right ordering of society (CCC 2199).

3:1 your father: Not necessarily a biological father, but a teacher of wisdom speaking to his disciples, whom he considers spiritual sons. **kept in safety:** Literally, "that you may be saved"—i.e., from threats and dangers. Here the concept of "salvation" does not yet imply eternal life in heaven, but refers, rather, to a safe, prosperous, and happy life on earth.

3:2 the Lord honored the father: Whereas in Catholic tradition, the fourth commandment to honor one's father and mother begins the second tablet of the Decalogue, which pertains to love of neighbor (CCC 2197), in Jewish tradition, it appears as the fifth commandment on the first tablet, which pertains to the love of God. The idea is that honoring one's

parents is directly related to honoring God. Conversely, those who are disrespectful to their earthly parents also disrespect their Heavenly Father (3:16).

3:3 atones for sins: Atonement is normally sought through bloody sacrifices in the Temple but is here attributed to acts of kindness (3:14–15, 30; 28:2). This later became a mainstream teaching in Judaism. On forms of penance as an expression of conversion, see CCC 1434–35. **and preserves ... is heard:** An addition from the Latin Vulgate.

3:5 gladdened by his own: The classic doctrine of retribution. What a man sows by honoring his parents, he will reap in his own children's behavior toward him. **he will be heard:** The Lord "hears the prayer of the righteous" (Prov 15:29).

3:6 long life: As stated in Ex 20:12; Deut 5:16. See also Eph 6:2–3 (CCC 2200). **will refresh:** Or, more loosely, "will give his mother no reason to worry".

3:7 his masters: Honoring parents means that children must obey them as slaves obeyed their masters (Prov 6:20–22; Col 3:20; CCC 2216).

3:8 Honor your father: The author now addresses the reader directly. **a blessing:** A father's blessing in the Bible means much more than good wishes. It was believed to have the power to bring about the good things spoken by the father (Gen 9:26–27; 27:27–29; 48:15–16). This blessing could be gratuitous, but often it had to be deserved.

3:9 father's blessing ... mother's curse: Not a division of labor, as though fathers bless and mothers curse. Children should seek the good favor of both parents if they want their family to be well established.

3:10 dishonoring your father: Ben Sira warns against father-son rivalries, lest a son wish to aggrandize himself at his father's expense.

3:11 honoring his father: Literally, "For a man's glory [is] from his father's honor." A man's glory comes not only from

---

[1]Gk *We shall fall.*
[m]In other authorities this line is preceded by *Whoever fears the Lord will honor his father.*

¹²O son, help your father in his old age,
 and do not grieve him as long as he lives;
¹³even if he is lacking in understanding, show
 forbearance;
 and do not despise him all the days of his life.
¹⁴For kindness to a father will not be forgotten,
 and against your sins it will be credited to you
 —a house raised in justice to you.
¹⁵In the day of your affliction it will be remembered
 in your favor;
 as frost in fair weather, your sins will melt
 away.
¹⁶Whoever forsakes his father is like a blasphemer,
 and whoever angers his mother is cursed by
 the Lord.

¹⁷My son, perform your tasks in meekness;
 then you will be loved more than a giver of
 gifts.
¹⁸The greater you are, the more you must humble
 yourself;
 so you will find favor with God.ⁿ

¹⁹There are many who are noble and renowned,
 but it is to the humble that he reveals his
 mysteries.
²⁰For great is the might of the Lord;
 he is glorified by the humble.
²¹Seek not what is too difficult for you,
 nor investigate what is beyond your power.
²²Reflect upon what has been assigned to you,
 and do not be curious about many of his
 works,
 for you do not need to see with your eyes what
 is hidden.
²³Do not meddle in what is beyond your tasks,
 for matters too great for human understanding
 have been shown you.
²⁴For their hasty judgment has led many astray,
 and wrong opinion has caused their thoughts
 to slip.°

²⁶A stubborn mind will be afflicted at the end,
 and whoever loves danger will perish by
 it.

---

honoring his father, but also from the honor his father receives from others (Prov 17:6). **not to respect their mother:** Cf. Prov 15:20, 23:22, 30:17.

3:12 old age: The text shifts from the attitude of respect for parents to the concrete help that children should extend to them "in old age and in times of illness, loneliness, or distress" (CCC 2218).

3:13 lacking in understanding: When his mind fails due to old age. **all the days of his life:** From the Hebrew and Syriac, followed by the New Vulgate. The Greek reads: "in all your strength".

3:14 against your sins ... credited: See note on 3:3.

3:15 remembered in your favor: In times of distress, the Lord will remember a son's kindness to his father. He will count this against his sins, which will **melt away** like **frost in fear weather.** Sirach does not teach that forgiveness can be earned simply by doing good deeds, apart from grace. The ability to merit spiritual blessings is a gift from God that is granted within the context of the covenant (see CCC 2008). • Grace has gone before us, and now we are given what is due. Our merits are thus gifts of God (St. Augustine, *Sermons* 298, 4–5).

3:16 blasphemer ... cursed: Refusal to honor one's father and mother is ultimately an offense against God, since he established them as his representatives and gave them authority to impart the knowledge of God to their children (CCC 2197). See note on 3:2.

3:17–31 A discourse on humility and pride. The right attitude before God is one of humility, for wisdom lies in being unpretentious, aware that one can always be wrong. Humility is the human dimension and expression of the fear of the Lord. Humility, the fear of the Lord, wisdom, and honor are often linked together in wisdom literature (Prov 11:2; 15:33; 18:12; 22:4).

3:17 more than a giver of gifts: From the Hebrew text. The Greek reads: "you will be loved by the accepted man", i.e., by those whom God accepts.

3:18 humble yourself: The Hebrew reads: "make yourself small." The higher your status is in society, the more you should aspire to humble your heart to please the Lord. This theme of humbling oneself is frequently taken up in the New Testament (Mt 20:26–27; Lk 1:50–52; Phil 2:3; Jas 4:6, 10; 1 Pet 5:5–6). • Priests should observe humility precisely because they have been invested with great dignity. Do not feel as though you are exalted above the assembly. Be among them as one of them. You should be humble, fleeing from pride, the source of all evil (Origen of Alexandria, *Homilies on Ezekiel* 9, 2).

3:19 to the humble ... mysteries: See Ps 25:9 and Zeph 3:12.

3:20 glorified by the humble: Paradoxically, the Lord in his infinite power is not glorified by powerful and mighty men but rather by those who are lowly of heart (Ps 25:14; 33:17–18; 147:10–11; Mt 11:25).

3:21–24 Ben Sira turns to the dangers of intellectual pride. He is likely reacting against the influence of Greek philosophy and science that would have appealed to many. He contends that everything his fellow Jews need to know about God and the world has been revealed in the Torah.

3:21 too difficult for you: See Ps 131:1; Eccles 1:13. **what is beyond your power:** Refers to the theoretical speculations of Greek thinkers.

3:22 what has been assigned to you: God's commandments, not idle speculation. **and do not be curious about many of his works:** An addition from the Latin Vulgate. **to see with your eyes:** An addition from the Latin Vulgate. **what is hidden:** You do not need to know secret things that the Lord has not revealed (cf. Deut 29:29).

3:23 matters too great: The same matters assigned to man in 3:22. The Lord has already revealed in the Torah things more marvelous than what the human mind could hope for. Ben Sira argues that his Jewish readers should focus on those things. • We must hold to what we are commanded and believe that God truly exists and rewards those who seek him. But we must not search into the things that surpass our mind and our knowledge (St. Cyril of Alexandria, *Commentary on John,* 5, 7, 27).

3:24 their thoughts to slip: Vain speculations have impaired the judgment of those who engaged in them.

3:26 stubborn mind: Literally, "hard heart"—the same expression used of Pharaoh in Ex 7:14, i.e., obdurate, unwilling to listen or learn.

ⁿOther authorities omit verse 19.
°Other authorities add as verse 25, *If you have no eyes you will be without light; if you lack knowledge do not profess to have it.*

²⁷A stubborn mind will be burdened by troubles,
   and the sinner will heap sin upon sin.
²⁸The affliction of the proud has no healing,
   for a plant of wickedness has taken root in
      them,
   though it will not be perceived.
²⁹The mind of the wise man will ponder the words
      of the wise,
   and an attentive ear is the wise man's desire.
³⁰Water extinguishes a blazing fire:
   so almsgiving atones for sin.
³¹Whoever repays favors gives thought to the
      future;
   at the moment of his falling he will find
      support.

Precepts for Everyday Life

4 My son, deprive not the poor of his living,
   and do not keep needy eyes waiting.
²Do not grieve the one who is hungry,
   nor anger a man in want.
³Do not add to the troubles of an angry mind,
   nor delay your gift to a beggar.

⁴Do not reject an afflicted suppliant,
   nor turn your face away from the poor.
⁵Do not avert your eye from the needy,
   nor give a man occasion to curse you;
⁶for if in bitterness of soul he calls down a curse
      upon you,
   his Creator will hear his prayer.

⁷Make yourself beloved in the congregation;
   bow your head low to a great man.
⁸Incline your ear to the poor,
   and answer him peaceably and gently.
⁹Deliver him who is wronged from the hand of the
      wrongdoer;
   and do not be fainthearted in judging a case.
¹⁰Be like a father to orphans,
   and instead of a husband to their mother;
   you will then be like a son of the Most High,
   and he will love you more than does your mother.

¹¹Wisdom breathes life into her sons
   and gives help to those who seek her.

3:27 sin upon sin: The hard-hearted are not open to correction. Refusing this wisdom, they will accumulate sins and face the curses that result (see Deut 28:15–68).

3:28 no healing: Because the proud man lacks fear of the Lord, he refuses to repent and be converted (Prov 12:3). **wickedness has taken root:** The proud man is unable to bear good fruit, in contrast to the righteous, who flourish like strong trees (Ps 92:12–14; Mt 7:17–19). **though it will not be perceived:** An addition from the Latin Vulgate.

3:29 mind of the wise: Literally, "a wise heart", in contrast to the stubborn mind or "hard heart" of 3:26–27. **words of the wise:** An addition from the Latin Vulgate. The wise man actively seeks words of good advice and is always ready to learn. **attentive ear:** An appeal to pay close attention to wisdom (Mt 13:9).

3:30–31 The topic of almsgiving, further developed in 4:1–10.

3:30 Water extinguishes ... almsgiving atones: The parallelism underscores the efficacy of giving alms. On the atoning power of good deeds, see notes on 3:3 and 3:14–15.

3:31 gives thought to the future: Giving alms and repaying favors are "stored" in a treasury of merits that God can recall at an opportune time. Ben Sira thus develops the thought of Prov 19:17: "He who is kind to the poor lends to the LORD, and he will repay him for his deed." Kindness is an investment that will bring returns in the future (Tob 4:7–11; 14:10–11).

4:1–10 The responsibility of the wise toward the poor. Five pairs of admonitions on how *not* to treat the poor (4:1–6) are followed by four pairs of exhortations outlining the generosity required of one who seeks to be wise (4:7–10).

4:1 deprive not the poor: Ben Sira considers almsgiving, not as an optional work of mercy left to the discretion of the giver, but as a grave obligation incumbent upon every disciple.

4:2 Do not grieve ... nor anger: By withholding charity from one in need, the stingy person becomes indirectly guilty of the poor man's suffering.

4:3 nor delay: The just person will give promptly (Prov 3:28; 2 Cor 9:7).

4:4 nor turn ... from the poor: In imitation of God himself, who does not turn his face away from the afflicted but takes care of them (Ps 22:24; Tob 4:7; Mt 5:42).

4:6 a curse upon you: One who lacks compassion and refuses to help the needy bears some responsibility if they utter a curse against him (Prov 28:27). **his Creator will hear:** God always hears the prayer of the needy when they cry for justice (Prov 17:5). He can even send punishments on those who refuse to help them (Ex 22:22–23; Prov 14:31).

4:7–10 Counsel on how to act toward others besides the poor. This includes people of importance as well as those who are oppressed, orphans, and widows. God's concern for the latter is repeatedly emphasized throughout the Bible (Deut 24:17–22; Is 1:17; Job 29:11–16; Jas 1:27).

4:7 Make yourself beloved: By acting humbly and mercifully toward the classes of people mentioned in the next three verses. **bow your head low:** To show deference, continuing the theme of humility in 3:17–24.

4:8 peaceably and gently: The Hebrew text reads: "Return him peace." It is not enough to give assistance to the poor; one must also treat them with kindness and respect.

4:9 Deliver him who is wronged: God's people should take an active role in curbing and opposing injustice when it lies within their power to do so (Ps 82:2–4).

4:10 Be like a father to orphans: By taking on the role of spiritual father or mentor, caring for orphans as his own children. **Instead of a husband to their mother:** Not a call to marry widows but to be "like a husband" to them, protecting them and providing for them (Ps 68:5). **like a son of the Most High:** A rare expression in the Old Testament, used to refer to Jesus in the Gospels (Mk 5:7; Lk 1:32; 8:28). **he will love you:** Concludes the thought introduced in 4:7: he who makes himself beloved among men by acts of mercy will also be loved by God. **more than does your mother:** God's love expressed as motherly love is rare in Scripture but not unheard of (see Is 49:15; 66:13). This passage sets the stage for the following depiction of wisdom as a loving mother.

4:11–19 A second poem praising Wisdom. In 1:1–10, she was introduced as the first of God's created works; here she is presented as a caring mother who exercises "tough love" with her children, disciplining them in order to exalt them.

4:11 Wisdom breathes life into her sons: Follows the Latin Vulgate. Wisdom is portrayed as a woman who gives life to her children and exalts them by teaching them the right way to live (cf. Prov 3:16, 18; 8:35; Wis 8:16–17).

12Whoever loves her loves life,
and those who seek her early
will win the Lord's good favor.
13Whoever holds her fast will obtain glory,
and the Lord will bless the place she[p] enters.
14Those who serve her will minister to the Holy One;[q]
the Lord loves those who love her.
15He who obeys her will judge the nations,
and whoever gives heed to her will dwell
secure.
16If he has faith in her he will obtain her;
and his descendants will remain in possession
of her.
17For she will walk with him in disguise,
and at first she will put him to the test;
she will bring fear and cowardice upon him,
and will torment him by her discipline
until he holds her in his thoughts,
and she trusts him.
18Then she will come straight back to him and
strengthen him,
she will gladden him and will reveal her
secrets to him,
and store up for him knowledge
and the discernment of what is right.
19But if he goes astray she will forsake him,
and give him over into the hands of his foe.

20Observe the right time, and beware of evil;[r]
and do not bring shame on yourself.
21For there is a shame which brings sin,
and there is a shame which is glory and
favor.
22Do not show partiality, to your own harm,
or deference, to your downfall.
23Do not refrain from speaking at the crucial time,[s]
and do not hide your wisdom.[t]
24For wisdom is known through speech,
and education through the words of the
tongue.
25Never speak against the truth,
but be mindful of your ignorance.
26Do not be ashamed to confess your sins,
and do not try to stop the current of a river.
27Do not subject yourself to a foolish fellow,
nor show partiality to a ruler.

4:12 Whoever loves her: To find wisdom, it is not enough to acquire intellectual knowledge. One must pursue her as a man courts a woman he loves (Prov 8:17).

4:13 holds her fast: As the beloved one holds on to her lover so as not to lose him (Song 3:4). **obtain glory ... will bless:** The fullness of life found in wisdom includes God's own glory and blessing.

4:14 the Holy One: A common way of referring to God in later Jewish literature. Serving wisdom is depicted as worshiping God. See note on Is 1:4.

4:15–19 In the Hebrew text, personified Wisdom speaks in the first person. In the Greek text (followed by the RSV), the narrator continues to speak of her in the third person.

4:15 judge the nations: The just one who acquires wisdom will have the authority to sit in judgment and rule over others (Wis 3:8; 1 Cor 6:2; Rev 3:21).

4:16 If he has faith in her: Or "if he entrusts himself to her". **his descendants:** Implies that wisdom should be passed on from generation to generation.

4:17 in disguise: Appears in the Latin Vulgate. **put him to the test:** Wisdom's attractiveness is not on display for all to see. At first, she acts harshly, testing the wise with severe trials until they prove themselves worthy of her. Once the wise man passes the test, she strengthens, gladdens, and reveals her secrets to him (4:18). This process describes well the spiritual life, which can alternate between times of desolation, when it seems as if God is distant, and times of consolation, when God's presence is tangibly felt through increased love, joy, devotion, etc.

4:18 store up ... what is right: An addition from the Latin Vulgate.

4:19 But if he goes astray: One who becomes negligent and wanders away from wisdom's path of discipline will not find her, for she will leave him to his own devices. **into the hands of his foe:** The reading of the Latin Vulgate. The Greek text reads: "to his ruin".

4:20–31 Reveals the connections underlying wisdom, speech, sin, and shame. Ben Sira expounds on the principle in Ecclesiastes that there is "a time to keep silence, and a time to speak" (Eccles 3:7); the wise person will know how to tell the difference.

4:20 Observe the right time: Watch for the opportune time to do good. **do not bring shame:** Shame is a consequence of sin that goes back to the fall of Adam and Eve in the garden (Gen 2:25; 3:7).

4:21 shame which brings sin: Appears to reverse the causal relationship between sin and shame (normally it would seem that sin causes shame, and not vice versa). Perhaps the meaning is that sin and shame initiate a vicious circle whereby sin engenders shame, and guilt-laden shame leads to more sin. **shame ... glory and favor:** May refer to being ashamed of one's sins, a posture that leads to repentance and conversion (4:26) or, possibly, to appearing shameful in the eyes of others by speaking the truth and doing what is right. See also 41:14—42:8. • Just as shame is praiseworthy in the face of evil, so it is reproachful in dealing with what is good. To blush because of evil is wise; to blush because of good is foolish (St. Gregory the Great, *Homilies on Ezekiel* 1, 10, 17).

4:22 Do not show partiality: I.e., do not be biased or show preference toward anyone. Impartiality is an attribute of God (Deut 10:17; Sir 35:16) that his people are called to emulate (Lev 19:15; Prov 18:5; Ps 82:2; Sir 42:1).

4:23 Do not refrain from speaking: The wise are called to share their wisdom with others (even when it is not welcome). The wisdom of the wise is of little use unless they speak at the opportune time to instruct, counsel, exhort, or admonish.

4:25 Never speak against the truth: Wisdom is incompatible with falsehood. **be mindful of your ignorance:** Those who are truly wise have the humility to recognize that their knowledge is always limited.

4:26 do not try to stop the current of a river: Perhaps means: "Trying to hide your sins is as futile as trying to stop the current of a river, so it is much wiser to confess them."

4:27 foolish fellow: Legitimate authorities are to be respected, but the wise person should not let a fool dominate him.

---

[p] Or *he*.
[q] Or *at the holy place*.
[r] Or *an evil man*.
[s] Cn: Gk *at a time of salvation*.
[t] So some Gk Mss and Heb Syr Vg: other Gk Mss omit *and do not hide your wisdom*.

[28]Strive even to death for the truth
  and the Lord God will fight for you.

[29]Do not be reckless in your speech,
  or sluggish and remiss in your deeds.
[30]Do not be like a lion in your home,
  nor be a faultfinder with your servants.
[31]Let not your hand be extended to receive,
  but withdrawn when it is time to repay.

5 Do not set your heart on your wealth,
  nor say, "I have enough."
[2]Do not follow your inclination and strength,
  walking according to the desires of your heart.
[3]Do not say, "Who will have power over me?"
  or "Who will bring me down because of my
    deeds?"
  for God will surely punish you.

[4]Do not say, "I sinned, and what happened to me?"
  for the Most High is slow to anger.
[5]Do not be so confident of atonement
  that you add sin to sin.
[6]Do not say, "His mercy is great,
  he will forgive[u] the multitude of my sins,"
for both mercy and wrath are with him,
  and his anger rests on sinners.

[7]Do not delay to turn to the Lord,
  nor postpone it from day to day;
for suddenly the wrath of the Lord will go forth,
  and at the time of punishment you will perish.

[8]Do not depend on dishonest wealth,
  for it will not benefit you in the day of
    calamity.
[9]Do not winnow with every wind,
  nor follow every path:
  the double-tongued sinner does that.
[10]Be steadfast in your understanding,
  and let your speech be consistent.
[11]Be quick to hear,
  and be deliberate in answering.
[12]If you have understanding, answer your
    neighbor;
  but if not, put your hand on your mouth.
[13]Glory and dishonor come from speaking,
  and a man's tongue is his downfall.

[14]Do not be called a slanderer,
  and do not lie in ambush with your tongue;
for shame comes to the thief,
  and severe condemnation to the
    double-tongued.

4:28 Strive even to death: An appeal to fight for the Torah and the Jewish way of life, even to the point of martyrdom. **the Lord God will fight:** Particularly when God's people stand for truth even to the point of death (Ex 14:14; 2 Mac 7).

4:29 reckless in your speech: It is better to be slow to speak and quick to act than the other way around. Actions speak louder than words (Jas 1:19-25).

4:30 a lion in your home: A man should not rule his household tyrannically, roaring at his wife and children.

4:31 your hand be extended: An appeal to be generous to others (Acts 20:35).

5:1—6:4 In a series of eight prohibitions ("Do not ..."), Ben Sira warns the reader against avarice and presumption (5:1-8). He then addresses sincerity, consistency, and self-restraint in speech, warning against duplicity, fickleness, and unruly passions (5:9-6:4).

5:1 your heart on your wealth: For similar warnings, see Ps 52:7; 62:10; Mt 6:24; Lk 12:15; 1 Tim 6:17. **nor say, "I have enough":** Ben Sira is not encouraging greed. On the contrary, he continues his warning against it: "Do not think money is all you need."

5:2 your inclination: Following one's **heart** can lead to disaster unless the Lord's word guides one's path (Prov 3:5-6).

5:3 "Who will have power over me?": An arrogant expression of autonomy from one who vainly thinks that he is accountable to no one—not even to God. **or "Who will bring me down because of my deeds?"** An addition from the Latin Vulgate.

5:4 I sinned, and what happened ...?: The wicked man thinks he can sin with impunity. Although God is **slow to anger** (Ex 34:6; Num 14:18), he will execute judgment on all evildoers (Eccles 8:11-13).

5:5 so confident of atonement: Jews sought forgiveness of sins primarily through blood sacrifice (Ex 30:10). Jewish oral law warns against the presumption that one will always have a chance to repent of sin (e.g., Mishnah *Yoma* 8, 9).

5:6 mercy and wrath: God extends the former to those who repent and the latter to those who do not (16:11; Rom 2:4-5; CCC 2092).

5:7 Do not delay: It is a mark of wisdom to repent quickly, for no one knows the day of the Lord's judgment and the moment of one's death (2 Cor 6:2). • Let us repent quickly, since the more we put off repentance, the greater our chance that death will bring us damnation rather than salvation (St. Fulgentius, *On the Forgiveness of Sins* 2, 5).

5:8 dishonest wealth: Will be useless on the day of God's judgment (Prov 10:2; 11:4; Ezek 7:19; Mt 6:19-21).

5:9 Do not winnow: Farmers winnow grain by tossing it in the air, allowing the wind to separate the grain from the husks. If continued when the winds change, the chaff would blow back into the grain, undoing what was done. Similarly, when **the double-tongued sinner** speaks dishonestly in order to accommodate everyone, he scatters his words with neither purpose nor direction.

5:10 let your speech be consistent: Literally, "let your word be one", so that people may always rely on what you say.

5:11 Be quick to hear: Be diligent in listening to others. **be deliberate in answering:** Literally, "in patience utter an answer" (Prov 18:13; Jas 1:19).

5:12 If ... understanding: Only answer when you know what you are talking about. **hand on your mouth:** As a sign of respect for the speaker (Prov 30:32; Mic 7:16).

5:13 Glory and dishonor: Words can build or destroy one's reputation—either that of the speaker or that of the person spoken about (Prov 12:18; 18:21; Mt 12:37; Jas 3:2-10).

5:14 a slanderer: Or a gossiper, someone who speaks evil of others. **do not ... ambush:** Do not wait for opportunities to attack others with your words. **the thief:** Perhaps one who has robbed another of his good reputation through slander. **the double-tongued:** The duplicitous, or one who says one thing with his mouth and another with his heart.

---

[u] Heb: Gk *he* (or *it*) *will atone for.*

¹⁵In great or small matters do not act amiss,
and do not become an enemy instead of a
friend;

6 for a bad name incurs shame and reproach:
so fares the double-tongued sinner.

²Do not exalt yourself through your soul's counsel,
lest your soul be torn in pieces like a bull.ᵛ
³You will devour your leaves and destroy your
fruit,
and will be left like a withered tree.
⁴An evil soul will destroy him who has it,
and make him the laughingstock of his enemies.

⁵A pleasant voice multiplies friends and softens
enemies,
and a gracious tongue multiplies courtesies.
⁶Let those that are at peace with you be many,
but let your advisers be one in a thousand.
⁷When you gain a friend, gain him through
testing,
and do not trust him hastily.
⁸For there is a friend who is such at his own
convenience,
but will not stand by you in your day of trouble.
⁹And there is a friend who changes into an enemy,
and will disclose a quarrel to your disgrace.

¹⁰And there is a friend who is a table companion,
but will not stand by you in your day of
trouble.
¹¹In prosperity he will make himself your equal,
and be bold with your servants;
¹²but if you are brought low he will turn against
you,
and will hide himself from your presence.
¹³Keep yourself far from your enemies,
and be on guard toward your friends.
¹⁴A faithful friend is a sturdy shelter:
he that has found one has found a treasure.
¹⁵There is nothing so precious as a faithful friend,
and no scales can measure his excellence.
¹⁶A faithful friend is an elixir of life;
and those who fear the Lord will find him.
¹⁷Whoever fears the Lord directs his friendship
aright,
for as he is, so is his neighbor also.

¹⁸My son, from your youth up choose instruction,
and until you are old you will keep finding
wisdom.
¹⁹Come to her like one who plows and sows,
and wait for her good harvest.
For in her service you will toil a little while,
and soon you will eat of her produce.

5:15 do not act amiss: Literally, "do not be ignorant." The Hebrew has: "Do not act corruptly."

6:1 a bad name: Duplicity in speech results in antagonistic relations with others and creates a bad reputation, which in turn brings **shame and reproach**.

6:2 Do not exalt yourself through your soul's counsel: The Hebrew text reads: "Do not fall into the hand of your soul," i.e., into the grip of your passions. **torn in pieces:** An uncontrolled temper will wreak havoc in a person's life.

6:3 You will devour: Uncontrolled passions will leave one like a tree that is fruitless and **withered**, in contrast to the wise person, who prospers in all that he does (Ps 1:3).

6:4 An evil soul: Evil passion will be the downfall of the one who lacks self-mastery.

6:5-17 A discourse on friendship, the first of several in the book (9:10-16; 19:13-17; 22:19-26; 27:16-21; 37:1-6).

6:5 pleasant voice: Kind and gentle speech. **multiplies friends:** In contrast to those who fail to rule their passions and multiply enemies. **softens enemies:** An addition from the Latin Vulgate. **gracious tongue:** Speaks well of others.

6:6 Let ... be many: Have many friendly acquaintances, but choose **advisers** and those who will influence you carefully.

6:7 through testing: By passing through difficulties and overcoming trials, a friend will prove his loyalty to you. **do not trust him hastily:** Do not be too quick to trust him until you know whether he is loyal (19:4). Lady Wisdom likewise tests the faithfulness of her followers (4:17).

6:8-13 Warnings against false friends who seek to take advantage of their companions.

6:8 friend ... at his own convenience: The fair-weather friend offers companionship only when it serves him; he disappears when he has nothing more to gain from the friendship.

6:9 changes into an enemy: Even worse than letting you down, some may turn hostile by resorting to gossip or slander.

6:10 a table companion: A friend who gladly accepts your hospitality but disappears in your time of need.

6:11 bold with your servants: A fair-weather friend might seek to wield authority in your household, "making himself at home", so to speak.

6:12 if you are brought low: If you are humbled, lose your wealth, or, according to the Hebrew text, "if evil overtakes you", your former companion will not be interested in sharing your adversity.

6:13 enemies ... friends: The wise person should not only avoid enemies; he should also be able to distinguish false friends from genuine ones.

6:14-17 Following his warning against false friends (6:8-13), Ben Sira praises the value of a true friend.

6:14 a sturdy shelter: A true friend protects his companions from threats and dangers. **a treasure:** Such a friend is rare and, therefore, of great worth—like wisdom (Prov 8:18).

6:16 elixir of life: Or life-saving medicine. The Hebrew reads: "a bundle of life", implying that a good friendship is a place where the soul is secure (1 Sam 25:29). **those who fear the Lord will find him:** A faithful friend is a gift from the Lord to those who fear him.

6:17 directs ... aright: One who fears the Lord will pursue wisdom and virtue in his friendships. **as he is, so is his neighbor:** His neighbor is as dear to him as himself (Lev 19:18; Mt 19:19).

6:18-37 A return to the theme of seeking wisdom, following 1:1-20 and 4:11-19. Ben Sira develops the idea that although this quest requires discipline at first, she proves to be well worth the effort in the end.

6:18 My son: The fatherly exhortation begins a new unit. **instruction:** Or "discipline" (Gk., *paideia*). **until you are old:** The search for wisdom is a life-long quest.

6:19 like one who plows and sows: Like a farmer, who labors and waits for growth, one who toils for wisdom must persevere in study, but then he can look forward to enjoying the benefits she produces.

ᵛThe meaning of the Greek of this verse is obscure.

20She seems very harsh to the uninstructed;
  a weakling will not remain with her.
21She will weigh him down like a heavy testing
    stone,
  and he will not be slow to cast her off.
22For wisdom is like her name,
  and is not manifest to many.

23Listen, my son, and accept my judgment;
  do not reject my counsel.
24Put your feet into her chains,
  and your neck into her collar.
25Put your shoulder under her and carry her,
  and do not fret under her bonds.
26Come to her with all your soul,
  and keep her ways with all your might.
27Search out and seek, and she will become known
    to you;
  and when you get hold of her, do not let her go.
28For at last you will find the rest she gives,
  and she will be changed into joy for you.
29Then her chains will become for you a strong
    protection,
  and her collar a glorious robe.
30Her yoke*w* is a golden ornament,
  and her bonds are a cord of blue.

31You will wear her like a glorious robe,
  and put her on like a crown of gladness.

32If you are willing, my son, you will be taught,
  and if you apply yourself you will become
    clever.
33If you love to listen you will gain knowledge,
  and if you incline your ear you will become
    wise.
34Stand in the assembly of the elders.
  Who is wise? Cling to him.
35Be ready to listen to every*x* narrative,
  and do not let wise proverbs escape you.
36If you see an intelligent man, visit him early;
  let your foot wear out his doorstep.
37Reflect on the statutes of the Lord,
  and meditate at all times on his
    commandments.
It is he who will give insight to*y* your mind,
  and your desire for wisdom will be granted.

Advice for Right Conduct

7 Do no evil, and evil will never befall you.
2Stay away from wrong, and it will turn away
    from you.
3My son, do not sow the furrows of injustice,
  and you will not reap a sevenfold crop.

6:20 seems very harsh: I.e., to those who are undisciplined. **a weakling:** One who lacks the courage and determination to remain with wisdom.

6:24 her chains ... her collar: One who seeks wisdom must be willing to submit to her, ready to follow where she leads.

6:25 carry her: Wisdom is compared to a yoke (51:26; Mt 11:29–30). Paradoxically, the one who bears her load will find rest, joy, and protection (6:28–29). According to Jewish tradition, one who accepts the yoke of the Torah will be relieved of the yoke of worldly concerns (e.g., *Pirqe Avot* 3, 5). **do not fret:** Do not resent her commands.

6:26 all your soul ... might: An appeal to follow wisdom's ways wholeheartedly (Deut 6:5).

6:27 Search out: Like a hunter tracks down an animal. **she will become known:** Wisdom will reward the seeker by revealing herself to him. **do not let her go:** Do not take wisdom for granted, for you may still lose her if you do not hold on to her (Prov 4:13).

6:28 the rest she gives: One who labors to find wisdom will eventually find rest, and her apparent harsh demeanor will then become **joy** (Mt 11:29).

6:29–31 Images of slavery and bondage are transformed into metaphors of power, beauty, and royalty—the final inheritance of those who find wisdom.

6:29 strong protection: Or "sturdy shelter", like that of the faithful friend (6:14). **glorious robe:** Like the vestment of the high priest (6:31; 50:11).

6:30 cord of blue: The expression used in Num 15:38–39 for the tassels worn by the people of Israel to remind them of God's commandments. Wisdom's "bonds" thus serve as a reminder to observe the Torah.

6:31 like a glorious robe: The image of "wearing wisdom" anticipates the NT idea of "putting on Christ" (Rom 13:14; Gal 3:27). **crown of gladness:** Points to the splendor of royalty (1:11; 15:6).

6:32–37 The rewards of those who diligently seek wisdom. The freedom of each person to invest in this pursuit is emphasized by the use of conditional clauses (**If ... if ... If ... if ...**).

6:32 will be taught: If you desire it, you will acquire wisdom through discipline and education. **if you apply yourself:** Literally, "if you set your heart on it".

6:34 elders: Wiser people, older people with more life experience, or authorities such as synagogue elders. **Cling to him:** One should adhere to the wise and their teachings as a man clings to his wife. The same Greek verb is used in Gen 2:24.

6:35 every narrative: The Greek specifies every "godly narrative". **do not ... escape you:** Pay attention to the wisdom caught in everyday conversations with the wise.

6:36 wear out his doorstep: A rhetorical exaggeration that exhorts readers to seek frequently the company of the wise.

6:37 his commandments: The ultimate source of wisdom is the Torah (Ps 1:2). **wisdom will be granted:** Wisdom is the end and goal of every wise man's pursuit.

7:1–17 Miscellaneous advice for right conduct toward God and neighbor, mostly in the form of negative admonitions ("Do not ... ").

7:1 evil will never befall you: There is a correlation between sowing and reaping evil (Hos 10:12; Job 4:8; Prov 22:8; Gal 6:8). Evil does not strike randomly but is closely related to the behavior of each person.

7:2 Stay away: Avoiding wrongdoing is the best protection against evil. Although the righteous man can still suffer evil from others (Eccles 8:14; Job), he is always able to guard himself from moral evil.

7:3 the furrows of injustice: The metaphor slightly shifts so it is now the field (not the seed) that represents injustice. **you will not reap:** I.e., a crop of injustice in your own life.

---

*w*Heb: Gk *Upon her.*
*x*Heb: Greek adds *divine.*
*y*Heb: Gk *will confirm.*

⁴Do not seek from the Lord the highest office,
   nor the seat of honor from the king.
⁵Do not assert your righteousness before the Lord,
   nor display your wisdom before the king.
⁶Do not seek to become a judge,
   lest you be unable to remove iniquity,
  lest you be partial to a powerful man,
   and thus put a blot on your integrity.
⁷Do not offend against the public,
   and do not disgrace yourself among the people.

⁸Do not commit a sin twice;
   even for one you will not go unpunished.
⁹Do not say, "He will consider the multitude of my
    gifts,
   and when I make an offering to the Most High
    God he will accept it."
¹⁰Do not be fainthearted in your prayer,
   nor neglect to give alms.

¹¹Do not ridicule a man who is bitter in soul,
   for there is One who abases and exalts.
¹²Do not devise ᶻ a lie against your brother,
   nor do the like to a friend.

¹³Refuse to utter any lie,
   for the habit of lying serves no good.
¹⁴Do not prattle in the assembly of the elders,
   nor repeat yourself in your prayer.

¹⁵Do not hate toilsome labor,
   or farm work, which were created by the Most
    High.
¹⁶Do not count yourself among the crowd of
    sinners;
   remember that wrath does not delay.
¹⁷Humble yourself greatly,
   for the punishment of the ungodly is fire and
    worms. ᵃ

¹⁸Do not exchange a friend for money,
   or a real brother for the gold of Ophir.
¹⁹Do not deprive yourself of a wise and good wife,
   for her charm is worth more than gold.
²⁰Do not abuse a servant who performs his work
    faithfully,
   or a hired laborer who devotes himself to you.
²¹Let your soul love ᵇ an intelligent servant;
   do not withhold from him his freedom.

7:4–7 Appeals to avoid presumption and pursue humility (Jas 4:6; 1 Pet 5:5).

7:4 highest office ... seat of honor: Do not seek a position of political power or prestige, either from God or from ruling authorities (cf. Mt 20:21–28).

7:5 Do not assert your righteousness: Do not justify yourself by trying to convince God of your own goodness (Eccles 7:16; Lk 18:11). **the Lord ... the king:** The same parallel structure as 7:4.

7:6 Do not seek ... judge: One should not set his heart on becoming a judge unless he has a strong sense of justice and integrity of character, so that he is able to resist the lure of bribes and the temptation to favor men of power and influence—both of which are harmful to the common good of society.

7:8 Do not commit a sin twice: A warning against presumption, i.e., thinking one can commit the same sins over and over so long as sacrifices are made to God (Is 1:10–16; Amos 5:21–24).

7:10 Do not be fainthearted: Do not grow weary in prayer. On the contrary, pray with perseverance and faith—in the present context, presumably a prayer of confession and repentance for sin (Jas 1:6; Mt 21:21–22; Mk 11:24). **give alms:** Since almsgiving has atoning power (3:30—4:10).

7:11 Do not ridicule ... bitter in soul: Do not mock someone humiliated by poverty or adverse circumstances. **One who abases and exalts:** The Lord, who bestows adversity or prosperity upon each person and can reverse any situation (2 Sam 22:28; Job 5:11; Ps 147:6; Lk 1:51–53).

7:12 Do not devise a lie: Literally, "do not plow a lie." **your brother ... a friend:** One should be truthful to all people, particularly to those closest to us.

7:13 lying serves no good: Nothing profitable endures if obtained by telling lies.

7:14 Do not prattle: I.e., engage in idle chatter. **in the assembly:** Possibly in the synagogue (6:34). **nor repeat ... your prayer:** On vain repetitions in prayer, see Mt 6:7.

7:15 Do not hate toilsome labor: Manual work is held in high esteem in rabbinic writings. According to one Jewish tradition, the father who fails to teach his son to work teaches him to rob (e.g., Babylonian Talmud, *Qiddushin* 99a). **created by the Most High:** Perhaps an allusion to Gen 2:15, where God tasks Adam with tilling the ground, or to Gen 3:17–19, where farm work becomes a heavy burden to man after the Fall.

7:16 Do not count yourself ... sinners: I.e., do not join the company of sinners. **wrath does not delay:** Divine judgment will not be postponed indefinitely.

📖 **7:17 Humble yourself:** Do not think too highly of yourself. **fire and worms:** A likely allusion to Is 66:24, where the corpses of the wicked are consigned to a fate of worms and fire. It would become an image of eternal damnation (Jud 16:17; Mk 9:47–48).

7:18–36 Counsel on household management, i.e., on a wise man's duties to his friends, family, and servants as well as to priests and the poor.

7:18 friend for money: Since a true friend is "precious" (6:15), one should be careful not to sacrifice friendship for the sake of material gain. **Ophir:** Famous in biblical times for its fine gold (Ps 45:9; Is 13:12). See note on 1 Kings 9:28.

7:19 a wise and good wife: Not to be lightly dismissed because finding such a woman is a great blessing from God, equivalent to finding wisdom (Prov 18:22; 31:10). **her charm is worth more than gold:** Her charm is due not so much to her external beauty as to her graceful inner disposition. The Hebrew text has instead: "and a well-favored wife is above pearls."

7:20 Do not abuse: Echoes the teaching of the Mosaic Law (Deut 15:12–18; 23:16).

7:21 love an intelligent servant: Goes beyond the injunction of the previous verse: treat intelligent and diligent servants with deep affection. According to the Hebrew text: "A wise servant love as your soul [as yourself]." **his freedom:** Refers to the commandment to release Hebrew servants after six years (Ex 21:2; Deut 15:12–15).

ᶻ Heb: Gk *plow*.
ᵃ The Hebrew text reads *for the expectation of man is worms*.
ᵇ The Hebrew text reads *Love like yourself*.

²²Do you have cattle? Look after them;
   if they are profitable to you, keep them.
²³Do you have children? Discipline them,
   and make them obedient^c from their youth.
²⁴Do you have daughters? Be concerned for their
      chastity,^d
   and do not show yourself too indulgent with
      them.
²⁵Give a daughter in marriage; you will have
      finished a great task.
   But give her to a man of understanding.

²⁶If you have a wife who pleases you,^e do not cast
      her out;
   but do not trust yourself to one whom you detest.
²⁷With all your heart honor your father,
   and do not forget the birth pangs of your mother.
²⁸Remember that through your parents^f you were
      born;
   and what can you give back to them that equals
      their gift to you?

²⁹With all your soul fear the Lord,
   and honor his priests.

³⁰With all your might love your Maker,
   and do not forsake his ministers.
³¹Fear the Lord and honor the priest,
   and give him his portion, as is commanded
      you:
   the first fruits, the guilt offering, the gift of the
      shoulders,
   the sacrifice of sanctification, and the first
      fruits of the holy things.

³²Stretch forth your hand to the poor,
   so that your blessing may be complete.
³³Give graciously to all the living,
   and withhold not kindness from the
      dead.
³⁴Do not fail those who weep,
   but mourn with those who mourn.
³⁵Do not shrink from visiting a sick man,
   because for such deeds you will be loved.
³⁶In all you do, remember the end of your life,
   and then you will never sin.

Prudence

8 Do not contend with a powerful man,
   lest you fall into his hands.

7:22–26 Counsel on managing the domestic economy.

7:23 Discipline them: On the duty of fathers to discipline their children, see 30:1–3, 12–13; Prov 23:13.

7:24 their chastity: Fathers must protect their daughters, making sure they remain virgins until marriage. **do not show yourself too indulgent:** While this expression sounds harsh, perhaps the wayward daughters in 26:10–12 and 42:9–14 are in mind.

7:25 finished a great task: The Hebrew text reads: "Marry your daughter, and sorrow will depart." **give her to a man of understanding:** Jewish fathers typically arranged marriages for their daughters. Finding a wise husband was a great responsibility, and succeeding in that task would have brought a father great relief.

7:26 a wife who pleases you: Literally, "a wife according to your soul". **do not cast her out:** Possibly means: "do not divorce her." **one whom you detest:** Or "a hated wife" (cf. Deut 21:15–17, which protects the rights of a "hated wife" and her children). Ben Sira does not favor divorce, but he cautions against trusting a wife who has proven untrustworthy.

7:27–30 all your heart ... soul ... might: Echoes the *Shema* prayer of Deut 6:4–5. Applying language for loving of God to others such as parents, priests, and ministers implies that these figures act as God's representatives.

7:27 honor your father: Literally, "give glory to your father." **do not forget the birth pangs:** Remember how much your mother suffered when you came into the world.

7:28 what can you give back: Children owe a debt of gratitude to their parents, not only for giving them life, but also for providing for them throughout their childhood.

7:29–31 Responsibilities toward the Lord's priests and ministers are outlined.

7:29 honor his priests: Or "marvel at his priests". The Hebrew and Latin read "sanctify" his priests. Priests were the descendants of Aaron, who ministered in the Jerusalem Temple.

7:30 love your Maker: Parallels 7:29 with the same structure and thought, indicating that priests and ministers act as God's representatives in the community of Israel. **do not forsake:** Israelites are to fulfill their obligations toward priests and Levites as mandated by the Law (Num 18:8–19; Deut 12:19; 18:1–5). **his ministers:** A synonym either for the Aaronic priests or perhaps for their assistants, the Levites.

7:31 first fruits: From the first harvest of grain and fruit (Num 18:13; Deut 18:4). **guilt offering:** Made in atonement for sins (Lev 5:6; Num 18:9). **gift of the shoulders:** Given to the priests for their service (Deut 18:3). **sacrifice of sanctification:** Possibly the grain offering (Lev 2:1–16). **first fruits of the holy things:** Perhaps referring to Num 18:8–11.

7:32 Stretch forth your hand: With the intent to give generously. **the poor:** Managing one's household wisely includes duties to the poor (Sir 3:30—4:10). **that your blessing may be complete:** On the duty to donate part of one's crop to the poor, and on how God blesses those who give generously, see Deut 14:28–29.

7:33 Give graciously to all: The Greek is difficult, perhaps saying "a gift has grace before all living." **withhold not kindness:** Do not refuse the deceased a dignified burial or fail to comfort those who mourn their passing. See note on Tob 1:17.

7:34 Do not fail ... weep: Do not withdraw from those in need of support during times of loss. **mourn with those who mourn:** Mourning the dead normally lasted seven days (Sir 22:12; cf. Rom 12:15).

7:35 Do not shrink: Or "do not delay." Visiting the sick is an essential duty, a way of fulfilling the commandment to "love your neighbor as yourself" (Lev 19:18), so that one is also loved in return (Job 2:11–13; Mt 25:39, 44).

7:36 the end of your life: Literally, "your last days". To avoid sin, Jewish tradition advises people to remember where they came from, where they are going, and to Whom they must give an account of their lives (e.g., *Pirqe Avot* 3, 1).

8:1–19 Advice on dealing with the rich and powerful, sinners and penitents, the aged and the deceased, and the wise and the foolish. Life provides only limited time and resources to do good. It is important to "choose our battles" by avoiding futile conflicts that cannot be won and by investing time and

---

^c Gk *bend their necks.*
^d Gk *body.*
^e Heb Syr omit *who pleases you.*
^f Gk *them.*

²Do not quarrel with a rich man,
  lest his resources outweigh yours;
for gold has ruined many,
  and has perverted the minds of kings.
³Do not argue with a chatterer,
  nor heap wood on his fire.

⁴Do not jest with an ill-bred person,
  lest your ancestors be disgraced.
⁵Do not reproach a man who is turning away from
    sin;
  remember that we all deserve punishment.
⁶Do not disdain a man when he is old,
  for some of us are growing old.
⁷Do not rejoice over any one's death;
  remember that we all must die.
⁸Do not slight the discourse of the sages,
  but busy yourself with their maxims;
because from them you will gain instruction
  and learn how to serve great men.
⁹Do not disregard the discourse of the aged,
  for they themselves learned from their fathers;
because from them you will gain understanding
  and learn how to give an answer in time of
    need.

¹⁰Do not kindle the coals of a sinner,
  lest you be burned in his flaming fire.
¹¹Do not get up and leave an insolent fellow,
  lest he lie in ambush against your words.
¹²Do not lend to a man who is stronger than you;
  but if you do lend anything, be as one who has
    lost it.
¹³Do not give surety beyond your means,
  but if you give surety, be concerned as one
    who must pay.

¹⁴Do not go to law against a judge,
  for the decision will favor him because of his
    standing.
¹⁵Do not travel on the road with a foolhardy fellow,
  lest he be burdensome to you;
for he will act as he pleases,
  and through his folly you will perish with him.
¹⁶Do not fight with a wrathful man,
  and do not cross the wilderness with him;
because blood is as nothing in his sight,
  and where no help is at hand, he will strike
    you down.
¹⁷Do not consult with a fool,
  for he will not be able to keep a secret.

---

energy into healthy relationships. All injunctions in this section are expressed as prohibitions ("Do not ... "). The first part also warns readers against spiritual and intellectual pride (8:1–9).

8:1 a powerful man: It is normally pointless to oppose a powerful or influential man because, humanly speaking, you have little chance of winning, and he can inflict great harm.

8:2 a rich man: It is best to avoid conflict with the wealthy, for they can use their money against you, even to the point of perverting justice by bribery.

8:3 a chatterer: It is futile to argue with someone who constantly talks and never listens to anyone else. **heap wood on his fire:** In modern idiom, this is adding fuel to the fire of the babbler, giving him a pretext to keep on talking (28:8–12; Prov 15:1; 26:20–2; Jas 3:5–6).

8:4 an ill-bred person: An uneducated person with bad manners. **lest your ancestors be disgraced:** I.e., either by mocking an uneducated man or by such a one cursing them.

8:5 we all deserve punishment: Everyone is a sinner, so we should not condemn repentant sinners (1 Kings 8:46; Eccles 7:20; Jn 8:7).

8:6 when he is old: On the honor due to the elderly, see 3:12; 25:4–6; Lev 19:32; Wis 4:8–9. **some of us are growing old:** Understated for rhetorical effect—*all* of us are growing old, not just some of us. The elderly should be honored as we would like to be honored.

8:7 Do not rejoice over ... death: Even if the deceased is an enemy or you have something to gain, such as an inheritance.

8:8 Do not slight: I.e., do not neglect or disregard the words of the wise. **their maxims:** Proverbs or short sayings. Even today, it is typical of people in the Middle East to sprinkle their speech with proverbs or wisdom sayings. **gain instruction:** Or learn discipline, including social skills. **to serve great men:** The Hebrew reads: "to stand before princes".

8:9 discourse of the aged: This verse follows the same parallel structure as 8:8, while continuing the thought initiated in 8:6 on the wisdom of the elderly. **learned from their fathers:** Wisdom is passed down from generation to generation (Deut 4:9; 11:18–19; Job 8:8–10). **you will gain understanding:** Otherwise, every new generation would have to "reinvent the

wheel". Why learn from the painful trial and error of your own mistakes when the wise advice and lessons of the more experienced are freely offered to you? (Job 12:12). **in time of need:** By learning from your elders, you will be able to help others.

8:10–19 Returns to the topic in 8:1–3, counseling that one should avoid provoking those who can inflict harm because they are either powerful or evil.

8:10 Do not kindle the coals: Do not encourage a sinner to continue sinning or tacitly approve of his deeds. **lest you be burned:** I.e., lest you suffer the consequences of his sin or be drawn into sinning yourself.

8:11 lest he lie in ambush: The insolent man may try to provoke you into saying something that he can use against you.

8:12 be as one who has lost it: If you lend money to someone more powerful or influential than you, how will you enforce repayment of the debt? You are free to make such a loan, but there is no guarantee that you will see your money again.

8:13 give surety: This occurs when a lender demands that someone else guarantee to repay the loan if the borrower fails to do so (29:14–20; Prov 6:1–5; 11:15; 17:18; 22:26–27). The person who guarantees another's loan must do so prudently and be prepared to pay it off if need be.

8:14 against a judge: Litigating against a judge is like entering a race against a professional racer. **the decision will favor him:** I.e., you have no chance of winning.

8:15 Do not travel ... with a foolhardy fellow: I.e., choose your travel companion wisely. Traveling was a perilous business in the ancient Near East. **you will perish with him:** If your travel companion takes life-threatening risks, he will endanger you as well.

8:16 a wrathful man: A man with a hot temper. **do not cross the wilderness with him:** Do not find yourself alone with him, where there are no witnesses. **blood is as nothing in his sight:** He does not hesitate to resort to violence when no one is looking.

8:17–19 The last three verses of the chapter deal with discretion in sensitive or secret matters.

8:17 a fool: A person who lacks wisdom and prudence is the most unreliable person to whom to entrust a secret.

[18]In the presence of a stranger do nothing that is to
  be kept secret,
  for you do not know what he will divulge.[g]
[19]Do not reveal your thoughts to every one,
  lest you drive away your good luck.[h]

On Conduct toward Others

9 Do not be jealous of the wife of your bosom,
  and do not teach her an evil lesson to your
  own hurt.
[2]Do not give yourself to a woman
  so that she gains mastery over your
  strength.
[3]Do not go to meet a loose woman,
  lest you fall into her snares.
[4]Do not associate with a woman singer,
  lest you be caught in her intrigues.
[5]Do not look intently at a virgin,
  lest you stumble and incur penalties for her.
[6]Do not give yourself to harlots
  lest you lose your inheritance.
[7]Do not look around in the streets of a city,
  nor wander about in its deserted sections.

[8]Turn away your eyes from a shapely woman,
  and do not look intently at beauty belonging to
  another;
  many have been misled by a woman's beauty,
  and by it passion is kindled like a fire.
[9]Never dine with another man's wife,
  nor revel with her at wine;
  lest your heart turn aside to her,
  and in blood[i] you be plunged into
  destruction.

[10]Forsake not an old friend,
  for a new one does not compare with him.
  A new friend is like new wine;
  when it has aged you will drink it with
  pleasure.

[11]Do not envy the honors of a sinner,
  for you do not know what his end will be.
[12]Do not delight in what pleases the ungodly;
  remember that they will not be held guiltless
  as long as they live.

8:18 a stranger: Avoid disclosing your business in the presence of someone whom you do not know, for he may go and repeat what he has heard to others.

8:19 your thoughts: Literally, "your heart". **to every one:** Ben Sira now extends the need for prudence and discretion to thoughts in general. It is not a good idea to "think aloud" unless surrounded with close, trustworthy friends, for you do not know who may use your words against you. **your good luck:** Your happiness.

9:1-18 Advice about relationships with women (in a series of negative exhortations, 9:1-9) and choosing friends and companions (9:10-18).

9:1 the wife of your bosom: A Hebrew idiom for "the wife you love" (Deut 13:6; 28:54). **to your own hurt:** Being jealous toward one's wife may cause her to become jealous, resulting in a breakdown of trust between spouses.

9:2 so that she gains mastery: I.e., with the result that your will to do good is overpowered. Ben Sira may have in mind especially the women of questionable morals mentioned in 9:3-4.

9:3 a loose woman: Or "strange woman", meaning a prostitute or adulteress with whom one is tempted to be intimate (Prov 2:16; 5:3; 7:5). **lest you fall into her snares:** Lest you become trapped by her deceptive charms (Prov 7:22-23; Eccles 7:26). Contrast the chains, bonds, or yoke of wisdom (Sir 6:24-25, 29-30).

9:4 a woman singer: Perhaps a poetic designation for a prostitute. In ancient Israel, women who sang publicly were considered morally suspect (Is 23:16).

9:5 a virgin: A young, unmarried woman. **lest you stumble:** Lest you fall into some sexual sin with her. **and incur penalties:** According to the Torah, a man who had relations with an unmarried woman had to pay a fine to her father and marry her (Ex 22:16-17; Deut 22:28-29).

9:6 harlots: The injunction to avoid prostitutes is common in wisdom literature (Prov 5:3-14; 6:26; 23:27). **lest**

you lose your inheritance: Not necessarily being disowned or cut out of a will, but losing your present possessions in paying the prostitutes or perhaps through divine punishment (Prov 29:3).

9:7 streets of a city: Avoid places where prostitutes may be found (Prov 7:7-12). In other words, do your utmost to avoid "the near occasion of sin".

9:8 a shapely woman: The Hebrew reads: "a graceful woman". **beauty belonging to another:** The beauty of another man's wife (Mt 5:28). **misled by a woman's beauty:** The problem is not the woman's beauty, but the lustful inclination in men lacking self-control. **passion is kindled like a fire:** For fire as a metaphor for sexual passion, see Job 31:9, 12.
• Beauty is a work of God's wisdom, and God's work cannot be a cause of wickedness. Looking on it with evil intentions is the result of a corrupted will. A wise man therefore exhorted: "Do not gaze on another's beauty" (St. John Chrysostom, *Homilies on Hosea* 3, 4).

9:9 Never dine: A warning against placing oneself in an imprudent situation that could lead to temptation and sin. **lest your heart turn aside to her:** With the desire to commit adultery. **in blood you be plunged into destruction:** Putting oneself in compromising circumstances that lead to sin can end up wreaking havoc in one's life. According to the Torah, the penalty for adultery was death (Lev 20:10; Deut 22:22; Jn 8:4-5). Or, perhaps the "destruction" refers to the husband's vengeance (Prov 6:32-34).

9:10-18 Practical exhortations concerning friends and companions. For the author, this applies to friendships between men, but in a modern context, his counsel can be extended to friendships between women or between both sexes.

9:10 an old friend: Points to a long-lasting friendship. **when it has aged:** Like a good wine, friendships get better as they grow older. On friendship, see 6:5-17; 37:1-6.

9:11 Do not envy: Do not be jealous of a sinner who appears to be successful (Prov 3:31-32; 24:1; Ps 73:2-16). **what his end will be:** His prosperity is only temporary, and punishment for his misdeeds is sure to come (18:12; Ps 37:1-2, 13-15, 38; 73:18-19).

9:12 what pleases the ungodly: The passing pleasures of the world. **as long as they live:** They will not escape judgment indefinitely.

---

[g]Or *it will bring forth.*
[h]Heb: Gk *let him not return a favor to you.*
[i]Heb: Gk *by your spirit.*

¹³Keep far from a man who has the power to kill,
 and you will not be worried by the fear of death.
But if you approach him, make no misstep,
 lest he rob you of your life.
Know that you are walking in the midst of snares,
 and that you are going about on the city
 battlements.

¹⁴As much as you can, aim to know your neighbors,
 and consult with the wise.
¹⁵Let your conversation be with men of
 understanding,
 and let all your discussion be about the law of
 the Most High.
¹⁶Let righteous men be your dinner companions,
 and let your glorying be in the fear of the Lord.
¹⁷A work will be praised for the skill of the
 craftsmen;
 so a people's leader is proved wise by his
 words.
¹⁸A babbler is feared in his city,
 and the man who is reckless in speech will be
 hated.

10 A wise magistrate will educate his people,
 and the rule of an understanding man will
 be well ordered.

²Like the magistrate of the people, so are his
 officials;
 and like the ruler of the city, so are all its
 inhabitants.
³An undisciplined king will ruin his people,
 but a city will grow through the understanding
 of its rulers.
⁴The government of the earth is in the hands of
 the Lord,
 and over it he will raise up the right man for
 the time.
⁵The success of a man is in the hands of the Lord,
 and he confers his honor upon the person of
 the scribe. ʲ

⁶Do not be angry with your neighbor for any
 injury,
 and do not attempt anything by acts of
 insolence.
⁷Arrogance is hateful before the Lord and before
 men,
 and injustice is outrageous to both.
⁸Sovereignty passes from nation to nation
 on account of injustice and insolence and
 wealth.
⁹How can he who is dust and ashes be proud?
 for even in life his bowels decay. ᵏ

9:13 the power to kill: Possessed by tyrants (Prov 20:2). **make no misstep:** If you must do business with an unjust ruler, be very careful. **lest he rob you of your life:** Lest he kill you or cause you some other harm. **going about on the city battlements:** Walking on top of the city walls in full view of the enemy makes one vulnerable. The Hebrew reads: "You are walking on nets."
 9:14 know your neighbors: Discern which are wise, pious, or righteous. **consult with the wise:** And not with fools (8:17; 11:9). On seeking the company of the wise, see 6:34; 8:8; Prov 13:14, 20.
 9:15 the law of the Most High: For Ben Sira, wisdom dwells among men in the Torah revealed through Moses (19:17). The wise thus constantly meditate on the Law of the Lord (24:23; Ps 1:2; Bar 4:1).
 9:16 your dinner companions: Table fellowship provides significant opportunities for social interaction, and so the wise should choose carefully who sits at their table. **let your glorying be in ... the Lord:** I.e., take delight in serving God.
 9:17-18 Contrasts one who is wise in act and speech with one who speaks vainly and accomplishes nothing.
 9:17 wise by his words: Just as the quality of a work of art reveals the skill of the artist, so wise speech demonstrates the leader's competence over his people.
 9:18 babbler: One who speaks thoughtlessly accomplishes little and earns the respect of no one.
 10:1-18 Figures of authority such as judges and kings have a responsibility to acquire wisdom and exercise it for the good of their subjects (10:1-5). Because they are subject to God's rule, they must be vigilant to avoid pride, a fault to which men in authority are especially prone (10:6-18).
 10:1 a wise magistrate: Refers to any king, governor, or ruler who exercises leadership over others. The key to good leadership is wisdom (Prov 8:15-16). **educate his people:** A

good leader will form his people not only in knowledge but especially in moral discipline. **understanding man:** The wise magistrate of the preceding line.
 10:2 magistrate ... officials ... ruler ... inhabitants: This verse underlines the hierarchical nature of wisdom. The two halves of the verse are in parallel, with the magistrate being the same person as the ruler. The quality of a leader (or lack thereof) is often reflected in his officials and subjects.
 10:3 undisciplined king: In contrast to the wise magistrate of 10:1. On bad rulers, see Prov 28:15-16; 29:2; 31:3-5.
 10:4-5 The focus shifts from human rulers to the divine Ruler. God is in control of the earth's **government**, over which he raises up leaders, as well as man's **success** (Heb., "government"), probably referring to the rule of the same leaders. If he governs justly and wisely, the Lord **confers his honor** upon **the scribe**, or "lawgiver".
 10:6 Do not be angry: Do not return evil for evil. **for any injury:** No one is perfect, and everyone makes mistakes. A wise person should overlook and forgive the little faults of others (28:2; Lev 19:17; Mt 18:21). **do not attempt anything by acts of insolence:** The Hebrew reads: "Walk not in the way of pride."
 10:7 before the Lord and before men: Most people have an instinctive aversion to arrogance; how much more does this displease the Lord. **injustice:** Implies that a haughty attitude often leads to more unrighteous acts.
 10:8 from nation to nation: Ben Sira views political regime changes, not as accidents of history, but as a consequence of human pride at a national level. If "pride goes before destruction, and a haughty spirit before a fall" (Prov 16:18), how precarious is the situation of rich and powerful states that arrogantly dominate other nations. Perhaps Ben Sira has in mind the recent takeover of the Holy Land by the Seleucids over the Ptolemies (198 B.C.).
 10:9-11 Reflecting on one's mortality is proposed as an antidote to temptation.
 10:9 dust and ashes: Man was created out of dust and will return to dust (17:32; 40:3; Gen 2:7; 3:19; 18:27).

ʲ Or *the official.*
ᵏ Heb: Greek is obscure.

[10]A long illness baffles the physician;[1]
    the king of today will die tomorrow.
[11]For when a man is dead,
    he will inherit creeping things, and wild
      beasts, and worms.
[12]The beginning of man's pride is to depart from
    the Lord;
    his heart has forsaken his Maker.
[13]For the beginning of pride is sin,
    and the man who clings to it pours out
      abominations.
Therefore the Lord brought upon them
    extraordinary afflictions,
    and destroyed them utterly.
[14]The Lord has cast down the thrones of rulers,
    and has seated the lowly in their place.
[15]The Lord has plucked up the roots of the
    nations,[m]
    and has planted the humble in their place.
[16]The Lord has overthrown the lands of the
    nations,
    and has destroyed them to the foundations of
      the earth.
[17]He has removed some of them and destroyed
    them,
    and has extinguished the memory of them
      from the earth.
[18]Pride was not created for men,
    nor fierce anger for those born of women.

[19]What race is worthy of honor? The human race.
    What race is worthy of honor? Those who fear
      the Lord.
    What race is unworthy of honor? The human
      race.
    What race is unworthy of honor? Those who
      transgress the commandments.
[20]Among brothers their leader is worthy of honor,
    and those who fear the Lord are worthy of
      honor in his eyes.[n]
[22]The rich, and the eminent, and the poor—
    their glory is the fear of the Lord.
[23]It is not right to despise an intelligent poor man,
    nor is it proper to honor a sinful man.
[24]The nobleman, and the judge, and the ruler will
    be honored,
    but none of them is greater than the man who
      fears the Lord.
[25]Free men will be at the service of a wise servant,
    and a man of understanding will not
      grumble.
[26]Do not make a display of your wisdom when you
    do your work,
    nor glorify yourself at a time when you are in
      want.
[27]Better is a man who works and has an abundance
    of everything,
    than one who goes about boasting, but lacks
      bread.

10:10 A long illness: The text is difficult in both the Hebrew and Greek, but the point is that physicians are powerless in the face of prolonged, fatal illnesses. **die tomorrow:** Even the most powerful monarch will eventually die.

10:11 beasts ... worms: Reminders that the body of every human being is destined to decompose and be eaten by predators or worms.

10:12 The beginning of man's pride: Ben Sira shifts from the consequences of pride to examining its origins. In contrast to wisdom, which originates in the fear of the Lord (1:14), pride begins when a person strays from the Lord, **his Maker**.

10:13 the beginning of pride is sin: Seems to say that sin is the source of pride; but the Vulgate reverses this: "for pride is the beginning of all sin." The idea of a vicious circle where sin engenders pride, which in turn causes more sin, is plausible and compatible with the rest of the verse, e.g., **the man who clings to it** (pride, sin, or both) **pours out** a flood of **abominations** detestable to God. The Hebrew reads: "For sin is a reservoir of insolence, and its source overflows with vice." **Therefore:** Ben Sira returns to the topic of rulers and governments (10:1–5). Since all pride originates in a sinful departure from God, this explains why God's judgment on prideful rulers and nations is so harsh (10:8).

10:14 cast down the thrones ... seated the lowly: God's humiliation of the powerful and proud and his exaltation of the weak and humble are common themes in the Bible (1 Sam 2:7–8; Ps 113:7–8; 147:6; Lk 1:52).

10:15 plucked up ... planted: Parallels the thought of 10:14.

10:16 overthrown ... destroyed: Emphasizes the severity of divine judgment on prideful nations. Examples abound in biblical history, from the judgment of Egypt by plagues (Ex 7–12), to the fall of Assyria (612 B.C.), of Babylon (539 B.C.), of Persia (331 B.C.), etc.

10:19—11:9 A section on true honor and the deceptiveness of appearances. Prideful people seek honor but are unworthy of it; only those who fear the Lord, the wise, and the humble are worthy (10:19–11:1). Judging according to appearances or hearsay is discouraged (11:2–9).

10:19 worthy ... unworthy: The human race is honorable when it fears the Lord and dishonorable when it disobeys the Lord's commandments.

10:22 rich ... eminent ... poor: The Hebrew reads: "sojourner and stranger, alien and poor". The point is that all people, whatever their situation in life, have equal access to the **glory** that comes with fearing the Lord.

10:23 intelligent poor man: Because people often judge by external appearances, they may be tempted to withhold honor from a poor man, who may be wise. Conversely, it is inappropriate to **honor** a sinner based on looks, wealth, or social standing.

10:24 nobleman ... judge ... ruler: People of influence who are honored by virtue of their position.

10:25 Free men: Wisdom is so worthy of honor that even free citizens would place themselves under a wise servant without complaining (Prov 17:2).

10:26 your wisdom: Can also include technical skills beyond knowledge and virtue. **when you are in want:** Suggests that one should not call undue attention to his troubles.

10:27 abundance: The person who diligently goes about his business will prosper, in contrast to the braggard who goes hungry because of his idleness (Prov 12:9).

---

[1] Heb Vg: Greek is uncertain.
[m] Some authorities read *proud nations*.
[n] Other authorities add as verse 21, *The fear of the Lord is the beginning of acceptance; obduracy and pride are the beginning of rejection*.

²⁸My son, glorify yourself with humility,
  and ascribe to yourself honor according to
    your worth.
²⁹Who will justify the man that sins against himself?
  And who will honor the man that dishonors
    his own life?
³⁰A poor man is honored for his knowledge,
  while a rich man is honored for his wealth.
³¹A man honored in poverty, how much more in
    wealth!
  And a man dishonored in wealth, how much
    more in poverty!

11 The wisdom of a humble man will lift up his
    head,
  and will seat him among the great.

²Do not praise a man for his good looks,
  nor loathe a man because of his appearance.
³The bee is small among flying creatures,
  but her product is the best of sweet things.
⁴Do not boast about wearing fine clothes,
  nor exalt yourself in the day that you are
    honored;
  for the works of the Lord are wonderful,
    and his works are concealed from men.
⁵Many kings have had to sit on the ground,
  but one who was never thought of has worn
    a crown.

⁶Many rulers have been greatly disgraced,
  and illustrious men have been handed over to
    others.

⁷Do not find fault before you investigate;
  first consider, and then reprove.
⁸Do not answer before you have heard,
  nor interrupt a speaker in the midst of his words.
⁹Do not argue about a matter which does not
    concern you,
  nor sit with sinners when they judge a case.

¹⁰My son, do not busy yourself with many matters;
  if you multiply activities you will not go
    unpunished,
  and if you pursue you will not overtake,
    and by fleeing you will not escape.
¹¹There is a man who works, and toils, and presses on,
  but is so much the more in want.
¹²There is another who is slow and needs help,
  who lacks strength and abounds in poverty;
  but the eyes of the Lord look upon him for his good;
    he lifts him out of his low estate
¹³and raises up his head,
  so that many are amazed at him.

¹⁴Good things and bad, life and death,
  poverty and wealth, come from the Lord.°

10:28 glorify yourself with humility: According to this paradox, there is nothing wrong with a modest self-esteem or with recognizing when we rightly deserve credit proportionate to our accomplishments.

10:29 dishonors his own life: This verse continues the thought of 10:28, warning against counterfeits of true humility such as low self-esteem and self-depreciation.

10:30 poor man ... rich man: Not a claim that all poor men have knowledge, that all rich men deserve to be honored, or that a rich man cannot get knowledge. The point is that even a poor man can be honored if he acquires knowledge, a form of wealth that cannot be lost or stolen.

10:31 how much more: The two parts of the verse are parallel: Wealth increases the honor of the wise, and poverty the dishonor of the foolish.

11:2–9 A warning against hasty judgments regarding things that are seen (11:2–6) and heard (11:7–9).

11:2 his appearance: A person's true worth is not visible to the naked eye, and so the wise person should not be misled by external appearances (1 Sam 16:7).

11:3 The bee: An example supporting the previous verse. Although the bee looks like an insignificant insect, it plays a vital role in pollinating plants and in producing sweet honey.

11:4 fine clothes: Not the true quality or measure of a person. **nor exalt yourself:** Because honor, like clothing, can be easily stripped away. The Hebrew text expresses the first half of this verse differently: "Do not mock him who is clothed in rags, and do not despise those whose days are bitter."

11:5 sit on the ground: Powerful kings have been toppled from their thrones. **one who was never thought of:** Unknown

people have risen from obscurity to kingship. Perhaps Ben Sira is thinking of David (1 Sam 16:1–13).

11:6 handed over: Beyond losing power, some rulers lost their freedom when they were toppled, perhaps by being sold into slavery.

11:7 before you investigate: Advises caution before passing a judgment on things heard, lest one jump to conclusions without having first carefully considered the matter.

11:8 before you have heard: Letting others speak without interrupting them is not only a common courtesy but a trait of the wise (5:11–12; Prov 18:13).

11:9 nor sit with sinners when they judge: Means either "do not participate in a judgment when the members of the council are sinners" or, perhaps, "do not get involved in disputes between sinners" (Ps 1:1).

11:10–28 On Providence and trust in God.

11:10 My son: The beginning of a new unit. **many matters:** A caution against excessive multitasking in business matters. It is difficult to perform well too many activities at the same time. **you will not go unpunished:** Implies that too much business can lead to a dilapidation of soul that puts one at risk for sin (26:29—27:3; 31:5–11; Prov 28:20). **and if you pursue:** Possibly wealth. **and by fleeing:** The responsibilities of your many activities.

11:11 works, and toils, and presses on: A warning against workaholism, which is ultimately unproductive and does not satisfy man.

11:12 lacks strength and abounds in poverty: The weak and poor, if they work with a humble disposition, draw the kindness of the Lord, who is able to raise them up to a position of honor and make them prosperous, to the astonishment of many. Success in life thus does not always arise out of one's own efforts (Ps 31:16; 127:1; Eccles 5:18–19).

11:14 Good ... bad ... poverty ... wealth: Represent all aspects of human life, which ultimately come from the Lord. The one exception is moral evil, which originates, not in the

---

°Other authorities add as verses 15 and 16, ¹⁵*Wisdom, understanding, and knowledge of the law come from the Lord; affection and the ways of good works come from him.* ¹⁶*Error and darkness were created with sinners; evil will grow old with those who take pride in malice.*

¹⁷The gift of the Lord endures for those who are
   godly,
   and what he approves will have lasting
      success.
¹⁸There is a man who is rich through his diligence
   and self-denial,
   and this is the reward allotted to him:
¹⁹when he says, "I have found rest,
   and now I shall enjoy ᵖ my goods!"
he does not know how much time will pass
   until he leaves them to others and dies.
²⁰Stand by your covenant ᑫ and attend to it,
   and grow old in your work.

²¹Do not wonder at the works of a sinner,
   but trust in the Lord and keep at your toil;
for it is easy in the sight of the Lord
   to enrich a poor man quickly and suddenly.
²²The blessing of the Lord is ʳ the reward of the
   godly,
   and quickly God causes his blessing to flourish.
²³Do not say, "What do I need,
   and what prosperity could be mine in the
      future?"

²⁴Do not say, "I have enough,
   and what calamity could happen to me in the
      future?"
²⁵In the day of prosperity, adversity is forgotten,
   and in the day of adversity, prosperity is not
      remembered.
²⁶For it is easy in the sight of the Lord
   to reward a man on the day of death according
      to his conduct.
²⁷The misery of an hour makes one forget luxury,
   and at the close of a man's life his deeds will
      be revealed.
²⁸Call no one happy before his death;
   a man will be known through his children.

²⁹Do not bring every man into your home,
   for many are the wiles of the crafty.
³⁰Like a decoy partridge in a cage, so is the mind of
   a proud man,
   and like a spy he observes your weakness; ˢ
³¹for he lies in wait, turning good into evil,
   and to worthy actions he will attach blame.
³²From a spark of fire come many burning coals,
   and a sinner lies in wait to shed blood.

Creator, but in the free choice of creatures (Gen 3:16–19). God permits rather than perpetrates evil, and only because he can bring good out of it (Gen 50:20; CCC 312).

11:18 diligence and self-denial: Normally praised as virtues but here describe the vices of the avaricious person who hoards wealth by denying himself everything and never spends. It is wise to prepare for one's financial future (Prov 6:6–8), but life must also be lived well now, and wealth must be used to bless others.

11:19 until he leaves them … dies: Since no one knows the day of his death, the miser who hoards riches does not know if he will ever live to enjoy them (14:3–10; Eccles 2:21; 6:1–3; Ps 49:10; Lk 12:16–21).

11:20 Stand by your covenant: Fulfill your covenant obligations to God, or following the Hebrew: "Be steadfast in your task."

11:21 quickly and suddenly: Since poverty and wealth come from the Lord (11:14), he can reverse anyone's fortune at any time.

11:22 blessing of the Lord: The context suggests wealth or material benefits are in view, though spiritual benefits can be indicated as well (Prov 10:22).

11:23 What do I need: The attitude of the greedy person, never satisfied with what he has and always seeking to increase his wealth and possessions.

11:24 I have enough: Although the opposite attitude of that found in the previous verse, Ben Sira also looks upon it with disapproval. **what calamity could happen to me:** A presumptuous and false sense of security. As quickly as God is able to impart his blessing (11:22), so he is able to withdraw it.

11:25 prosperity … adversity: When things go well, people quickly forget about hard times; when hard times come, they forget just as quickly the blessings of the past.

11:26–28 Ben Sira insists that a person's true worth is revealed at death. These verses resolve the tension expressed in 11:21–25 concerning the fleeting prosperity of sinners.

11:26 the day of death: Past fortunes or misfortunes are not reliable indicators of divine favor or wrath. The Lord may allow temporary chastisements upon the righteous or prosperity upon the wicked, for it is ultimately at man's last hour that the Lord will reward him **according to his conduct** (35:19; Prov 24:12; Mt 16:27; Rom 2:6; Rev 20:12). Perhaps Ben Sira has in mind the circumstances of death, e.g., the just will die content and at peace, but the wicked will die in anguish and distress.

11:27 his deeds will be revealed: The dying person will become aware of the worthiness or unworthiness of his deeds on earth and whether he will leave behind a legacy for good or evil. Others will recognize this legacy as well, perhaps according to the manner of the person's death (Lk 12:2).

🕊 **11:28 happy:** Or "blessed" (Gk., *makarios*; Mt 5:2–11).
before his death: Although everyone experiences pleasurable moments during his lifetime, such moments, liable to be taken away at any instant, are a poor indicator of a man's ultimate happiness. • As long as one continues the struggle of this life, he cannot be without fear or the suspicion of an uncertain end. One can acquire no virtue that cannot be lost (St. John Cassian, *Conferences* 1, 6, 16). **known through his children:** People will know a deceased man's true worth by knowing his children, or, possibly, they will share in his rewards or punishments (see Ex 20:5–6).

11:29–12:18 A discussion on prudence when inviting people into one's home (11:29–34), discerning to whom to extend generosity (12:1–7), how to tell a true friend from a false one (12:8–12), and the consequences of mistaking an enemy for a friend (12:13–18).

11:29 Do not bring every man: Advocates caution when inviting someone into one's home, since the home is a sanctuary for the family. **the wiles of the crafty:** Some people are dishonest and may take advantage of your hospitality.

11:30 a proud man: The wicked person who seeks to trap you.

11:31 turning good into evil: The proud man waits in ambush, ready to take advantage of even good deeds or interpreting them as selfishly motivated.

11:32 burning coals: Just as a single spark can light a damaging fire, so can a sinner inflict much harm on others.

ᵖ Gk *eat of.*
ᑫ Heb *task.*
ʳ Gk *is in.*
ˢ Heb: Gk *downfall.*

³³Beware of a scoundrel, for he devises evil,
  lest he give you a lasting blemish.
³⁴Receive a stranger into your home and he will
    upset you with commotion,
  and will estrange you from your family.

Friends and Enemies

12 If you do a kindness, know to whom you do
  it,
  and you will be thanked for your good deeds.
²Do good to a godly man, and you will be repaid—
  if not by him, certainly by the Most High.
³No good will come to the man who persists in evil
  or to him who does not give alms.
⁴Give to the godly man, but do not help the sinner.
⁵ Do good to the humble, but do not give to the
    ungodly;
  hold back his bread, and do not give it to him,
    lest by means of it he subdue you;
  for you will receive twice as much evil
    for all the good which you do to him.
⁶For the Most High also hates sinners
  and will inflict punishment on the ungodly.ᵗ
⁷Give to the good man, but do not help the sinner.

⁸A friend will not be knownᵘ in prosperity,
  nor will an enemy be hidden in adversity.
⁹A man's enemies are grieved when he prospers,
  and in his adversity even his friend will
    separate from him.

¹⁰Never trust your enemy,
  for like the rusting of copper, so is his
    wickedness.
¹¹Even if he humbles himself and goes about
    cringing,
  watch yourself, and be on your guard against
    him;
  and you will be to him like one who has polished
    a mirror,
  and you will know that it was not hopelessly
    tarnished.
¹²Do not put him next to you,
  lest he overthrow you and take your place;
  do not have him sit at your right,
  lest he try to take your seat of honor,
  and at last you will realize the truth of my words,
  and be stung by what I have said.
¹³Who will pity a snake charmer bitten by a
    serpent,
  or any who go near wild beasts?
¹⁴So no one will pity a man who associates with a
    sinner
  and becomes involved in his sins.
¹⁵He will stay with you for a time,
  but if you falter, he will not stand by you.

¹⁶An enemy will speak sweetly with his lips,
  but in his mind he will plan to throw you into
    a pit;

11:34 a stranger ... will upset you: An appeal for careful discernment in the exercise of hospitality, lest a dangerous scoundrel be invited into one's home (see 11:30–33). This verse concludes the discussion begun in 11:29.

12:1 know to whom you do it: I.e., make sure that the character of the beneficiary is worthy of your generosity. **you will be thanked:** Literally, "there will be favor for your good deeds"—not necessarily that the giver will gain from his own generosity, but that there will be benefits to the receiver and, perhaps, to society in general.

12:2 you will be repaid: By the Lord, who gives to all as their works deserve (11:26).

12:3 No good will come ... persists in evil: The Hebrew text is quite different: "No good comes to him who relieves an evil man, and no act of mercy has he done" (i.e., by helping an evil man). The meaning of the Hebrew is elaborated in 12:4–7.

12:4 the sinner: The person who persists in evil without repentance (12:3). For different perspectives on acts of kindness, see Prov 25:21–22; Rom 12:20; Mt 5:43–47; Lk 6:27–28.

12:5 his bread: His food. **lest ... he subdue you:** Although Ben Sira's adamant stance not to help the wicked seems harsh, his rationale is that the wicked will continue to do evil even after they have benefited from acts of kindness. Feeding the wicked may even give them further strength to return evil for good. **twice as much evil:** An ancient Jewish saying claims that doing good to an evil person is an act of evil (*Qoheleth Rabbah* 5.1). The NT offers a different perspective, insisting that we should love our enemies and do good to them (Mt 5:43–47; Rom 12:20).

12:6 sinners: See note on 12:4.

12:8 A friend will not be known: When all is well, it is difficult to tell who your true friends are (6:8–13). **nor will an enemy be hidden:** When troubles come, it becomes easier to tell real friends from those who are self-serving.

12:9 enemies are grieved when he prospers: The Hebrew text conveys a different idea, which better fits the context: "One's enemy is friendly when one prospers" (Prov 19:4). **his friend will separate:** Not true friends, but self-serving, false friends.

12:10 copper: Refers to the mirror of 12:11. Mirrors made of bronze had to be polished frequently to maintain a distinct reflection. Likewise, one must be constantly on guard against the ever-shifting wickedness of an enemy.

12:11 humbles himself: An enemy may put on a show of modesty and innocence. **be on your guard:** Despite the enemy's trickery, the wise person remains vigilant.

12:12 next to you: Putting your enemy next to you implies letting down your guard and treating him as a friend—a position of which he can take advantage.

12:13 snake charmer: A person who takes unnecessary risks (Eccles 10:11). He should not expect any sympathy for bearing the consequences of his own actions. One who cavorts with a sinner likewise endangers himself.

12:15 he will not stand by you: A sinner may be a friend of convenience, but when adversity comes, he will flee when he has nothing more to gain from the friendship (12:9).

12:16 his lips ... his mind: An enemy cannot be trusted because what he says is very different from what he thinks. **throw you into a pit:** Despite his smooth talk, the enemy really plans to trap you and take advantage of you. **weep with his eyes:** External appearances are deceptive. The enemy may pretend to share your sorrows, but he is really planning your downfall. **his thirst for blood:** He will not hesitate to harm you.

ᵗ Other authorities add *and he is keeping them for the mighty day of their punishment.*

ᵘ Other authorities read *punished.*

an enemy will weep with his eyes,
 but if he finds an opportunity his thirst for
  blood will be insatiable.
¹⁷If calamity befalls you, you will find him there
  ahead of you;
 and while pretending to help you, he will trip
  you by the heel;
¹⁸he will shake his head, and clap his hands,
 and whisper much, and change his
  expression.

Responsible Use of Riches

13 Whoever touches pitch will be defiled,
 and whoever associates with a proud man
  will become like him.
²Do not lift a weight beyond your strength,
 nor associate with a man mightier and richer
  than you.
How can the clay pot associate with the iron
  kettle?
 The pot will strike against it, and will itself be
  broken.
³A rich man does wrong, and he even adds
  reproaches;
 a poor man suffers wrong, and he must add
  apologies.
⁴A rich manᵛ will exploit you if you can be of use
  to him,
 but if you are in need he will forsake you.
⁵If you own something, he will live with you;
 he will drain your resources and he will not
  care.

⁶When he needs you he will deceive you,
 he will smile at you and give you hope.
He will speak to you kindly and say, "What do
  you need?"
⁷He will shame you with his foods,
 until he has drained you two or three times;
 and finally he will deride you.
Should he see you afterwards, he will forsake you,
 and shake his head at you.

⁸Take care not to be led astray,
 and not to be humiliated in your feasting.ʷ
⁹When a powerful man invites you, be reserved;
 and he will invite you the more often.
¹⁰Do not push forward, lest you be repulsed;
 and do not remain at a distance, lest you be
  forgotten.
¹¹Do not try to treat him as an equal,
 nor trust his abundance of words;
 for he will test you through much talk,
 and while he smiles he will be examining you.
¹²Cruel is he who does not keep words to himself;
 he will not hesitate to injure or to imprison.
¹³Keep words to yourself and be very watchful,
 for you are walking about with your own
  downfall.ˣ

¹⁵Every creature loves its like,
 and every person his neighbor;
¹⁶all living beings associate by species,
 and a man clings to one like himself.

12:18 shake . . . clap . . . whisper: Expressions of contempt and mockery (Ps 22:7; Lam 2:15; Ps 41:7). **change his expression:** The enemy will no longer feign friendship but will then show his true face.

13:1–26 Counsel on how to relate to the rich (13:2–8) and powerful (13:9–13), followed by a discussion of the differences between the rich and the poor (13:15–26).

13:1 pitch: A black, thick, and sticky substance derived from petroleum. **associates with a proud man:** Just as pitch defiles and is difficult to clean off, so pride contaminates those with whom it comes into contact (1 Cor 15:33).

13:2 beyond your strength: As lifting a heavy weight can cause injury, so keeping company with the rich and powerful can be harmful. **clay pot . . . iron kettle:** Just as the pot will break if hit by the kettle, so you may be harmed by too close a contact with the rich and powerful.

13:3 rich man . . . adds reproaches: The wealthy sometimes boast about wronging others because they are unafraid of retribution. **poor man . . . must add apologies:** The poor man is helpless in the face of injustice and must even apologize to the person hurting him.

13:4 exploit you: The Hebrew reads: "enslave you". **he will forsake you:** Leaving you helpless.

13:5 he will live with you: In order to gain control of your belongings.

13:6 smile at you: He will feign to be your friend and to care for you.

13:7 shame you with his foods: By extending hospitality to you, the rich man will oblige you to return his invitations, leading you to overspend and come to financial ruin. **deride you:** The reaction of a malicious rich person. **shake his head:** See note on 12:18.

13:9–13 Ben Sira now turns his attention to the powerful.

13:9 invites you: Or "summons you". **be reserved:** I.e., do not rush in responding.

13:10 push forward . . . remain at a distance: Two extremes to be avoided, i.e., one's response should not be overeager or excessively shy.

13:11 as an equal: Even if a powerful person speaks in a friendly way toward you, you should not be overly casual but still approach him with deference. **examining you:** His friendly demeanor may be masking an ulterior motive; he may be trying to put you at ease to catch you off guard and obtain information that he will later use against you.

13:12 Cruel is he: Presumably the powerful man mentioned in 13:9–11. **words to himself:** He will use the words you have spoken to harm you.

13:13 walking about . . . downfall: By keeping company with the rich and powerful, you are walking on precarious grounds. The Hebrew has instead: "do not walk with violent men."

13:15–24 Illustrations of the principle that like associates with like.

13:15 Every creature loves its like: The Hebrew reads: "All flesh loves its kind." Animals keep company with animals of the same species. **his neighbor:** Not in the sense of loving one's neighbor here, but in the sense that every person is drawn to others like himself.

ᵛGk *He.*
ʷOther authorities read *folly.*
ˣOther authorities add *When you hear these things in your sleep, wake up!* ¹⁴*During all your life love the Lord, and call on him for your salvation.*

17What fellowship has a wolf with a lamb?
> No more has a sinner with a godly man.
18What peace is there between a hyena and a
> dog?
> And what peace between a rich man and
> a poor man?
19Wild donkeys in the wilderness are the prey of
> lions;
> likewise the poor are pastures for the rich.
20Humility is an abomination to a proud man;
> likewise a poor man is an abomination to a
> rich one.

21When a rich man totters, he is steadied by
> friends,
> but when a humble man falls, he is even
> pushed away by friends.
22If a rich man slips, his helpers are many;
> he speaks unseemly words, and they justify
> him.
> If a humble man slips, they even reproach him;
> he speaks sensibly, and receives no attention.
23When the rich man speaks all are silent,
> and they extol to the clouds what he says.
> When the poor man speaks they say, "Who is this
> fellow?"
> And should he stumble, they even push him
> down.

24Riches are good if they are free from sin,
> and poverty is evil in the opinion of the
> ungodly.
25A man's heart changes his countenance,
> either for good or for evil.ʸ
26The mark of a happy heart is a cheerful face,
> but to devise proverbs requires painful
> thinking.

14 Blessed is the man who does not blunder with
his lips
> and need not suffer grief for sin.
2Blessed is he whose heart does not condemn him,
> and who has not given up his hope.

3Riches are not seemly for a stingy man;
> and of what use is property to an envious
> man?
4Whoever accumulates by depriving himself,
> accumulates for others;
> and others will live in luxury on his goods.
5If a man is mean to himself, to whom will he be
> generous?
> He will not enjoy his own riches.
6No one is meaner than the man who is grudging
> to himself,
> and this is the retribution for his baseness;
7even if he does good, he does it unintentionally,
> and betrays his baseness in the end.

13:17 a sinner with a godly man: Lambs avoid wolves, not only because they are different, but because they are a threat. Likewise, godly men should avoid sinners, not only because they have nothing in common, but because sinners are spiritually dangerous to the righteous (Mt 7:15; 10:16).

13:18 a hyena and a dog: In ancient Israel, dogs guarded the flocks from hyenas, so that the two were notorious enemies. Ben Sira compares the rich man's greed with the hyena's predatory instinct.

13:19 pastures: The poor are compared to feeding grounds for the rich, who are likened to voracious lions (Ps 34:10; 35:17).

13:20 Humility: Typically associated with the poor man as distinct from the rich man, who is often characterized as proud.

13:21 a humble man: The Hebrew and some Greek manuscripts have instead: "a poor man". While the rich man's wealth draws the support of many, the humble or poor man often finds himself alone, without help, because he is unable to repay favors done to him.

13:22 If a rich man slips: He is still defended and helped by many, regardless of what he says. The humble (or poor) man, by contrast, is rarely given the benefit of the doubt or aided in such ways.

13:23 extol to the clouds: All listen attentively to the rich and praise extravagantly what he says. This implies that his credibility derives from his wealth, and not from the intelligence of his words. **Who is this fellow:** Few listen to the poor man of no repute (Eccles 9:16).

13:24 Riches are good: Wealth is not intrinsically evil, at least if gained honestly (Prov 28:20; Mt 19:23–24). **poverty is evil in the opinion of the ungodly:** Poverty is undesirable but not always the result of sins such as laziness (Prov 6:6–11), worthless pursuits (Prov 28:19), idle talk (Prov 14:23), or pleasure seeking (Prov 21:17).

13:25 A man's heart: The seat of the emotions or "the depths of one's being" (CCC 368). **for good or for evil:** One's inner disposition is reflected in one's face (Prov 15:13; Eccles 8:1).

14:1–19 A discussion on how to use wealth responsibly.

14:1 Blessed: Or "happy" (11:28). **does not blunder:** In contrast to the person who speaks carelessly (13:22), the one who speaks prudently and innocently lives with a clear conscience and can be counted as blessed or happy.

14:2 heart: Or "soul". **does not condemn him:** The just person finds peace in a clear conscience (1 Jn 3:19–22); his serenity of mind also gives him **hope** for the future.

14:3 stingy man: The Hebrew reads: "small heart", i.e., a small-minded miser, one who never spends money, even on himself. **envious man:** A covetous person who desires the riches of others.

14:4 accumulates for others: The hoarder who refuses to spend money is laying it up for others who will inherit it after he dies (11:19; 14:15; Eccles 6:2).

14:5 mean to himself: I.e., refuses to spend money on himself. Such a person will be even less generous with others.

14:6 No one is meaner: A miser is, in a sense, even worse than a selfish person who does not give to others for the sake of self-indulgence. At least the self-indulgent person enjoys the good things of life, which brings him some joy (Eccles 2:24), whereas the miser deprives even himself of joy. **retribution:** Stinginess is its own punishment.

14:7 unintentionally: Not even occasional acts of kindness are praiseworthy for the miser, since he does those almost by accident. **betrays his baseness:** Eventually his true nature is revealed.

ʸ Other authorities add *and a glad heart makes a cheerful countenance.*

⁸Evil is the man with a grudging eye;
    he averts his face and disregards people.
⁹A greedy man's eye is not satisfied with a portion,
    and mean injustice withers the soul.
¹⁰A stingy man's eye begrudges bread,
    and it is lacking at his table.

¹¹My son, treat yourself well, according to your
    means,
    and present worthy offerings to the Lord.
¹²Remember that death will not delay,
    and the decree ᶻ of Hades has not been shown
    to you.
¹³Do good to a friend before you die,
    and reach out and give to him as much as you
    can.
¹⁴Do not deprive yourself of a happy day;
    let not your share of desired good pass by you.
¹⁵Will you not leave the fruit of your labors to
    another,
    and what you acquired by toil to be divided
    by lot?
¹⁶Give, and take, and beguile yourself,
    because in Hades one cannot look for luxury.

¹⁷All living beings become old like a garment,
    for the decree ª from of old is, "You must
    surely die!"
¹⁸Like flourishing leaves on a spreading tree
    which sheds some and puts forth others,
    so are the generations of flesh and blood:
    one dies and another is born.
¹⁹Every product decays and ceases to exist,
    and the man who made it will pass away with it.

²⁰Blessed is the man who meditates on ᵇ wisdom
    and who reasons intelligently.
²¹He who reflects in his mind on her ways
    will also ponder her secrets.
²²Pursue wisdom ᶜ like a hunter,
    and lie in wait on her paths.
²³He who peers through her windows
    will also listen at her doors;
²⁴he who encamps near her house
    will also fasten his tent peg to her walls;
²⁵he will pitch his tent near her,
    and will lodge in an excellent lodging place;
²⁶he will place his children under her shelter,
    and will camp under her boughs;

14:8 the man with a grudging eye: A selfish person. **he averts his face:** To avoid seeing and helping people in need, he turns his back on them (contrast 4:4–5; Tob 4:7–11).

14:9 withers the soul: Avarice dries up a person's soul and his vitality of life.

14:11 My son: Ben Sira addresses readers in a fatherly way to explain how to make good use of wealth. **treat yourself well:** I.e., be good to yourself. The commandment "you shall love your neighbor as yourself" (Lev 19:18) presupposes that one must first love oneself and avoid excessively harsh forms of asceticism.

14:12 the decree of Hades: Or "the covenant of Hades", i.e., the moment of your death. Hades is the underworld and abode of the dead (Heb., *Sheol*) (17:27; 21:10). There was not yet a clear understanding of heaven and hell in the Old Testament (Is 28:15, 18; Ps 16:10) prior to the Book of Wisdom (Wis 3:1–5).

14:13 Do good: Since the moment of each person's death is unknown, no one knows how much time he has to do good. **give to him:** Be as generous as possible to your friends while you are able to do so (Prov 3:27–28).

14:14 do not deprive yourself: I.e., enjoy good things while they last, lest one miss an opportunity to make the best of life (Eccles 7:14; 9:7–10).

14:15 the fruit . . . to another: If you die without having made the best use of your resources and wealth (11:19; 14:4; Ps 49:10). **divided by lot:** Your possessions will be given to your heirs.

14:16 Give, and take: See 14:13–14. **beguile yourself:** Seems to mean "enjoy yourself". **in Hades:** Generally, in the Old Testament, it was believed that rewards and punishments were meted out in this life, not in the next (Eccles 5:17; 9:9–10).

📖 **14:17 All living beings:** Literally, "all flesh". **like a garment:** All creatures with bodies will wear out like old

clothes (Is 50:9; Ps 102:26). **the decree:** Literally, "the covenant" (Gk., *hē diathēkē*). **"You must surely die!":** Death is the curse of the primordial covenant that God made with Adam. Ben Sira refers specifically to the penalty attached to the tree of the knowledge of good and evil in Gen 2:17.

14:18 flesh and blood: The mortal human body (17:31; Mt 16:17; 1 Cor 15:50). Human lives are precarious; they are as passing as the leaves that fall from the trees in autumn (Is 34:4; 40:6–8).

14:19 Every product: Literally, "every work" will rot and pass away, along with its human producers.

14:20—15:10 A fourth poem in the book encouraging the pursuit of wisdom (1:1–20; 4:11–19; 6:18–37). The first part emphasizes the determination needed to find her (14:20–27). The second part describes the benefits she grants to those who find her and remain with her (15:1–10).

14:20 meditates on wisdom: See 6:37; Ps 1:1–2; 119:15, 23, 148.

14:21 her ways: Keeping the "ways" of wisdom is equivalent to keeping God's commandments (2:15; cf. Prov 3:17; 8:32). Only after learning obedience is one able to **ponder her secrets:** I.e., to learn the deeper, more advanced lessons accessible to those who have followed her for some time (4:18; 39:3, 7).

14:22 like a hunter: The Hebrew reads: "like a spy". The point is that the seeker of wisdom must employ intelligence to find her.

14:23 peers through her windows: Either this continues the spy metaphor, or it evokes courtship with an allusion to Song 2:9. **listen at her doors:** Wisdom is portrayed dwelling in a house (Prov 8:34).

14:24 encamps near her house: The pursuer of wisdom becomes her neighbor, so to speak. He lives next to her so that he may better learn her secrets. To learn the deeper teachings of wisdom, it is not enough to pay her an occasional visit. One must learn to dwell with her permanently.

14:25 lodge in an excellent lodging place: The Hebrew reads: "dwells/tabernacles in a good dwelling/tabernacle".

14:26 under her boughs: The metaphor shifts to wisdom as a sheltering tree, protecting her followers and their children under her branches.

ᶻGk *covenant.*
ªGk *covenant.*
ᵇOther authorities read *dies in.*
ᶜGk *her.*

²⁷he will be sheltered by her from the heat,
  and will dwell in the midst of her glory.

Freedom of Choice and Its Consequences

15 The man who fears the Lord will do this,
  and he who holds to the law will obtain
  wisdom.ᵈ

²She will come to meet him like a mother,
  and like the wife of his youth she will welcome
  him.

³She will feed him with the bread of understanding,
  and give him the water of wisdom to drink.

⁴He will lean on her and will not fall,
  and he will rely on her and will not be put to
  shame.

⁵She will exalt him above his neighbors,
  and will open his mouth in the midst of the
  assembly;
she will fill him with a spirit of wisdom and
  understanding,
  and clothe him with a robe of glory.

⁶He will find gladness and a crown of rejoicing,
  and will acquire an everlasting name.

⁷Foolish men will not obtain her,
  and sinful men will not see her.

⁸She is far from men of pride,
  and liars will never think of her.

⁹A hymn of praise is not fitting on the lips of a
  sinner,
  for it has not been sent from the Lord.

¹⁰For a hymn of praise should be uttered in
  wisdom,
  and the Lord will prosper it.

¹¹Do not say, "Because of the Lord I left the right
  way";
  for heᵉ will not do what he hates.

¹²Do not say, "It was he who led me astray";
  for he has no need of a sinful man.

¹³The Lord hates all abominations,
  and they are not loved by those who fear
  him.

¹⁴It was he who created man in the beginning,
  and he left him in the power of his own
  inclination.

¹⁵If you will, you can keep the commandments,
  they will save you;
  if you trust in God, you too shall live.

14:27 from the heat: Wisdom will shelter her followers from the "heat" of life's trials.

15:1 will do this: Ben Sira identifies the person determined to pursue wisdom as the one who fears the Lord—a familiar theme (1:9–18, 27–30; 2:7–10, 15–17; 19:20; 21:11). **holds to the law:** One who fears the Lord will strive to keep the commandments of the Torah (1:26; 2:16; 6:37; 9:15; 24:23).

15:2 mother ... wife of his youth: Wisdom is personified as a woman through a double metaphor. She is like a mother welcoming her son and like a young bride eagerly waiting for her husband. On motherly imagery, see Is 49:15; 66:13; Wis 7:12. On bridal imagery, see Prov 4:6–9; Wis 8:2.

15:3 bread ... water: Wisdom metaphorically nourishes her seekers and quenches their thirst (Prov 9:1–5; Is 55:1–2; cf. Jn 4:10–15; 6:35).

15:4 lean on her: Wisdom is the support of one who fears the Lord. The wise person who fears the Lord does not sin and, thus, is not **put to shame** (24:22; Gen 2:25; 3:7).

15:5 exalt him: Wisdom raises the wise to a position of honor. **in the midst of the assembly:** Wisdom will give a position of prominence to the wise man in the public forum. A similar expression is used of wisdom herself in 24:1–2. **she will fill him ... a robe of glory:** This second half of the verse comes from the Latin Vulgate. **spirit of wisdom and understanding:** See Is 11:2. **robe of glory:** See 6:29, 31; 45:10; 50:11.

15:6 crown of rejoicing: One who finds wisdom finds great joy (1:11). **everlasting name:** The wise will be remembered forever (Is 56:5).

15:7 Foolish ... sinful: While those who fear the Lord and keep his commandments are sure to find wisdom, she remains hidden to the wicked.

15:8 men of pride: Heb., "mockers".

15:9 A hymn of praise: Songs of praise to God are the natural response of the righteous, for they recognize God for who he is. Praise is a form of prayer that lauds God for who he is and not merely for what he does (CCC 2639). It is unfitting on **the lips of a sinner**, because sinners violate God's will and their praise is insincere.

15:10 uttered in wisdom: Praise is the outer manifestation of the wisdom of the just.

15:11–20 Ben Sira addresses sin, free will, human responsibility, and the origin of evil. He refutes the claim that some people sin because God leads them to do so. People must take responsibility for their own sins.

15:11 "Because of the Lord I left the right way": The Hebrew reads: "From God is my transgression." **what he hates:** Since God hates evil, sin can never have its origin in God (Amos 5:15; Jas 1:13).

15:12 he who led me astray: Implies that God is responsible for human sin. The idea may derive from a misinterpretation of some OT passages, e.g., Ex 11:10; 2 Sam 24:1; Is 45:7. Or, it may allude to the rabbinic idea of the *yeṣer ha-ra*, the "evil inclination" (see note on 15:14). **no need of a sinful man:** Those who sin are of no use to God.

15:13 not loved: The wise love what the Lord loves and hate what he hates. They will diligently avoid, therefore, whatever he declares to be evil.

15:14 created man in the beginning: The Hebrew adds an extra clause in the middle of the verse: "and delivered him into the hand of him that spoils him"—possibly a reference to Satan. **inclination:** Heb., *yeṣer*; Lat., *concupiscentia*. This verse refutes the idea that God created the evil inclination (Heb., *yeṣer ha-ra*). God created man good, but sin came into the world because man abused his free will by straying from God's will. Thus, evil originates in man, not in God (Rom 5:12). • According to the Church, God is never the cause of moral evil, either directly or indirectly. He permits it, but only because he can derive good from it (CCC 311).

15:15 you can keep the commandments: A strong affirmation of human free will, which can obey or disobey God's law. **they will save you:** Not apart from faith, but together with it (Mt 19:17–21; Gal 5:6; Jas 2:14–26). The Hebrew text adds here: "And it is understanding to do his good pleasure." **if you trust in God, you too shall live:** Follows the Hebrew text; the Greek of this line is cryptic.

ᵈGk *her*.
ᵉHeb: Gk *you*.

¹⁶He has placed before you fire and water:
  stretch out your hand for whichever you wish.
¹⁷Before a man ᶠ are life and death, good and evil,
  and whichever he chooses will be given to him.
¹⁸For great is the wisdom of the Lord;
  he is mighty in power and sees everything.
¹⁹The eyes of the Lord are on those who fear him,
  and he knows every deed of man.
²⁰He has not commanded any one to be ungodly,
  and he has not given any one permission to
  sin.

16 Do not desire a multitude of useless children,
  nor rejoice in ungodly sons.
²If they multiply, do not rejoice in them,
  unless the fear of the Lord is in them.
³Do not trust in their survival,
  and do not rely on their multitude;
  for one is better than a thousand,ᵍ
  and to die childless is better than to have
  ungodly children.
⁴For through one man of understanding a city will
  be filled with people,
  but through a tribe of lawless men it will be
  made desolate.

⁵Many such things my eye has seen,
  and my ear has heard things more striking
  than these.
⁶In an assembly of sinners a fire will be kindled,
  and in a disobedient nation wrath was kindled.
⁷He was not propitiated for the ancient giants
  who revolted in their might.
⁸He did not spare the neighbors of Lot,
  whom he loathed on account of their insolence.
⁹He showed no pity for a nation devoted to
  destruction,
  for those destroyed in their sins;
¹⁰nor for the six hundred thousand men on foot,
  who rebelliously assembled in their
  stubbornness.
¹¹Even if there is only one stiffnecked person,
  it will be a wonder if he remains unpunished.
  For mercy and wrath are with the Lord;ʰ
  he is mighty to forgive, and he pours out wrath.
¹²As great as his mercy, so great is also his reproof;
  he judges a man according to his deeds.
¹³The sinner will not escape with his plunder,
  and the patience of the godly will not be
  frustrated.

15:16 fire and water: Correspond to "life and death" in the following verse. **whichever you wish:** Ben Sira insists that a person has the power to choose his destiny and act to pursue it. The NT balances this statement by emphasizing the need for divine grace to help man make the right choices and stay on the straight path (Eph 2:8–10).

15:17 life and death, good and evil: The choice set before each human person is at the heart of the biblical message and of God's covenant with man (Deut 11:26–28; 30:15–20).

15:18 great is the wisdom of the Lord: The Hebrew reads: "Sufficient is the wisdom of the Lord" (i.e., to make the right decision and choose life and good over death and evil). **sees everything:** Including the choices man makes for good and evil.

15:20 not commanded any one to be ungodly: Rebuts the allegations in 15:11–12. One can never excuse sin by saying "God made me do it." The Hebrew adds: "And he has no mercy on him who commits falsehood, nor on him who reveals secrets."

16:1–23 Treats of God's punishment of sinners. Rebellious children are no exception (16:1–5). God punished sin in the past (16:6–10), and he will do so in the future (16:11–16), because no deed escapes his notice (16:17–23).

16:1 ungodly sons: Although Scripture sees children as a blessing (Gen 15:5, Ps 127:3–5; 128:3–4), Ben Sira recognizes that children are hardly a source of joy if they are children of the wicked (40:15–16; 41:5–6).

16:3 their survival: Literally, "their life"—because the wicked will come to an untimely end (Deut 28:15–19; Ps 55:23; Job 24:24; Wis 14:15). The next clause is unclear in Hebrew and Greek; the Latin Vulgate clarifies it with a gloss: **for one** (who fears God) **is better than a thousand** (wicked sons). **to die childless:** It is more profitable to be fruitful in godliness and virtue than in ungodly offspring (Wis 3:10—4:6).

16:4 through one man of understanding: The Hebrew text reads: "through one childless man who fears the Lord"—a probable allusion to Abraham, who became the father of a great multitude even though his wife Sarah was initially barren (Gen 15:2–5). **tribe of lawless men:** Possibly an allusion to the Sodomites, who were destroyed for their grave sin (Gen 18:16–32).

16:5 my eye has seen, and my ear has heard: An appeal to personal experience.

16:6 assembly of sinners: Possibly a reference to Korah, Dathan, Abiram, and their followers, who were consumed by heavenly fire because of their rebellion against Moses and Aaron in the desert (45:18–19; Num 16:1–35; Ps 106:18).

16:7 ancient giants: Or "princes of old", according to the Hebrew text. A reference to the "mighty men" or giants whose wickedness unleashed the flood (Gen 6:1–4; Wis 14:6).

16:8 neighbors of Lot: The evil inhabitants of Sodom, who perished when God destroyed their city (Gen 19:1–25). **their insolence:** Attributes their wickedness to pride, though other sources identify it with sexual immorality (Jude 7).

16:9 devoted to destruction: The Canaanites, infamous for their immoral practices (Ex 23:33; 34:11–16; Deut 7:1–2; Num 33:51–56; Wis 12:3–7).

16:10 six hundred thousand: The generation of Israelites who rebelled against God and Moses in the wilderness (46:7–8; Ex 12:37; Num 11:21; 14:1–24).

16:11 stiffnecked person: An expression usually associated with the generation of the Exodus (Ex 32:9; 33:3, 5) but employed here to refer to anyone who stubbornly resists God's will. If the wilderness generation did not escape punishment, neither will those who repeat their mistake. **mercy and wrath:** Two facets of God's character (see note on 5:6).

16:12 his mercy ... his reproof: God's punishment is as severe as his mercy is great. **according to his deeds:** As also noted at 12:2.

16:13 The sinner ... the godly: God will render to each one according to what he deserves; the just should patiently wait for their reward.

ᶠ Gk *men.*
ᵍ The text of this line is uncertain.
ʰ Gk *him.*

¹⁴He will make room for every act of mercy;
      every one will receive in accordance with his
            deeds.ⁱ

¹⁷Do not say, "I shall be hidden from the Lord,
      and who from on high will remember me?
   Among so many people I shall not be known,
      for what is my soul in the boundless
            creation?
¹⁸Behold, heaven and the highest heaven,
      the abyss and the earth, will tremble at his
            visitation.
¹⁹The mountains also and the foundations of the
            earth
      shake with trembling when he looks upon
            them.
²⁰And no mind will reflect on this.
      Who will ponder his ways?
²¹Like a tempest which no man can see,
      so most of his works are concealed.
²²Who will announce his acts of justice?
      Or who will await them? For the covenant is
            far off."

²³This is what one devoid of understanding thinks;
      a senseless and misguided man thinks
            foolishly.

²⁴Listen to me, my son, and acquire knowledge,
      and pay close attention to my words.
²⁵I will impart instruction by weight,
      and declare knowledge accurately.

²⁶The works of the Lord have existed from the
            beginning by his creation,ʲ
      and when he made them, he determined their
            divisions.
²⁷He arranged his works in an eternal order,
      and their dominionᵏ for allˡ generations;
   they neither hunger nor grow weary,
      and they do not cease from their labors.
²⁸They do not crowd one another aside,
      and they will never disobey his word.
²⁹After this the Lord looked upon the earth,
      and filled it with his good things;
³⁰with all kinds of living beings he covered its surface,
      and to it they return.

16:14 every act of mercy: God will not overlook a single act of kindness, but mercy will be rewarded with mercy.

16:15 hardened Pharaoh: Recalls the Exodus from Egypt, when God made the king of Egypt too stubborn to acknowledge him (Ex 7:3; 9:12; 10:27; 11:10). See note on Ex 4:21. **that his works might be known:** The hardening of Pharaoh led to Israel's deliverance from slavery—a great testimony of God's power.

16:16 His mercy is manifest: The Exodus was a demonstration not only of divine power but of God's mercy toward Israel.

16:17–22 The speech of one who hopes his deeds will go unnoticed by the Lord, which Ben Sira dismisses as foolish in 16:23. Verse 18 is a parenthesis on the supreme power of God over all creation.

16:17 so many people: The speaker foolishly supposes that God will not notice him amidst the enormous population of the world. **the boundless creation:** The speaker downplays his personal worth, as if he were not important to God.

16:18 the highest heaven: Literally, "the heaven of heavens" (Deut 10:14; 1 Kings 8:27). **the abyss:** Or "the deep" (Heb., *tehom*)—the subterranean abyss of waters (Gen 7:11). **tremble at his visitation:** The commotion that will seize creation when God comes to judge the earth (Ps 18:7–8; 97:4–5; Is 29:6; Joel 2:10).

16:20 And no mind will reflect on this. Who will ponder his ways?: The Hebrew text has instead: "Also, he sets not his heart upon me, and who observes my ways?"—continuing the thought of 16:17: The universe is so vast that God cannot give attention to one's actions.

16:21 Like a tempest: The Hebrew reads: "If I sin no eye will see me, or if I deal untruly in all secrecy, who will know it?"

16:22 who will await: The speaker wonders when—or if—God's justice will be manifest. **the covenant is far off:** For the speaker, God's retribution seems far and distant.

16:23 devoid of understanding: Ben Sira's negative assessment of the speaker in 16:17–22.

16:24—17:14 Reaffirms the Lord's wisdom in creation. Following an introduction (16:24–25), Ben Sira depicts God's wisdom in creating the universe (16:26–30); he treats of God's wisdom in creating mankind (17:1–10); and he turns to God's wisdom in giving the Torah to Israel (17:11–14).

16:24 my son: The fatherly address and exhortation to listen marks the beginning of a new section (2:1; Prov 1:8). **pay close attention:** Literally, "set your heart".

16:25 instruction: The Hebrew text reads: "my spirit" (Prov 1:23).

16:26 from the beginning: Recalls Gen 1:1. **determined their divisions:** When God created the world, he assigned to each of his creatures their specific realms, boundaries, and functions. Ben Sira summarizes in 16:26–28 the first four days of creation (Gen 1:1–19), minus the creation of plant life on the third day (Gen 1:11–13).

16:27 He arranged his works: Specifically, the heavenly bodies—the sun, moon, and stars. **their dominion:** Refers to their rule over day and night (Gen 1:16; Ps 136:8–9), which endures as long as the present order of the universe lasts. **neither hunger nor grow weary:** A statement about the stability of the created order. Its laws show no sign of weakening with the passing of time (Is 40:26; Jer 31:35–36).

16:28 They do not crowd: The heavenly bodies—the planetary and galactic systems—keep their course with astonishing regularity, being all part of a finely tuned, well-ordered system. **never disobey his word:** In contrast to humans, whose free will allows them to stray from God's purposes, the inanimate heavenly bodies always "obey" God's order of creation (Ps 104:19; 148:5–6).

16:29 the earth: This verse transitions from heaven to earth. **filled it with his good things:** The sea creatures and birds created on the fifth day of creation (Gen 1:20–23).

16:30 living beings: The land animals created on the sixth day (Gen 1:24–25). **to it they return:** All animals die and return to the earth (40:11; Ps 104:24–30; Eccles 3:20).

ⁱ Other authorities add ¹⁵*The Lord hardened Pharaoh so that he did not know him; in order that his works might be known under heaven.* ¹⁶*His mercy is manifest to the whole of creation, and he divided his light and darkness with a plumb line.*
ʲ Heb: Gk *judgment.*
ᵏ Or *elements.*
ˡ Gk *their.*

Wisdom concerning God's Gifts to Men

17 The Lord created man out of earth,
  and made him into his own image;
[2]he turned him back into earth again,
  but clothed him in strength like his own.°
[3]He gave to men[m] few days, a limited time,
  but granted them authority over the things
  upon the earth.[n]
[4]He placed the fear of them[p] in all flesh,
  and granted them dominion over beasts and
  birds.[q]
[6]He made for them[r] discretion, with a tongue and
  eyes and ears;
  he gave them a mind for thinking,
  and filled them with the discipline of
  discernment.
[7]He created in them the knowledge of the spirit;
  he filled their hearts with understanding,
  and showed them good and evil.
[8]He placed the fear of him into their hearts,
  showing them the majesty of his works.[s]
[9]He made them glory in his wondrous deeds,

[10] that they might praise his holy name,
  to proclaim the grandeur of his works.
[11]He bestowed knowledge upon them,
  and allotted to them the law of life.
[12]He established with them an eternal covenant,
  and showed them his justice and his
  judgments.
[13]Their eyes saw his glorious majesty,
  and their ears heard the glory of his voice.
[14]And he said to them, "Beware of all
  unrighteousness."[t]
  And he gave commandment to each of them
  concerning his neighbor.

[15]Their ways are always before him,
  they will not be hidden from his eyes.[u]
[17]He appointed a ruler for every nation,
  but Israel is the Lord's own portion.[v]
[19]All their works are as the sun before him,
  and his eyes are continually upon their ways.
[20]Their iniquities are not hidden from him,
  and all their sins are before the Lord.[w]

17:1–14 Extols God's wisdom in creating mankind and granting gifts to humanity (17:1-10) as well as Israel (17:11-14). No Hebrew text is extant for this section, and there is considerable confusion between the ancient versions, resulting in different verse numbers between modern English translations for the first ten verses of the chapter. The RSV2CE text generally follows the New Vulgate.

17:1 out of earth: See Gen 2:7. **his own image:** See Gen 1:26-27. This clause follows the Latin Vulgate; it appears in 17:3 in the Greek and in other English translations. The "earth" made into God's image indicates that man is a union of matter and spirit, body and soul. • According to the Church, man is both corporeal and spiritual and is the only one of God's visible creatures who is willed for its own sake and is called to share in the divine life (CCC 362, 356).

17:2 back into earth: After the Fall, man became mortal (Gen 3:19; Ps 146:4; CCC 400). This clause follows the Vulgate; it appears in 17:1 in the Greek LXX and some English translations. **clothed him in strength like his own:** Or "clothed him with appropriate strength". This clause appears in 17:3 in the Greek LXX and some English translations.

17:3 few days: Since the Fall, the length of man's days on earth is limited (18:9-10; Gen 6:3; Ps 90:10; Job 14:1-2). **authority:** God granted man the authority to rule over all other creatures (Gen 1:28; 9:2; Ps 8:6-9; Wis 9:2-3). This

verse appears in 17:2 in the Greek LXX and some English translations.

17:4 fear ... in all flesh: Points to man's dominion over all animals (Gen 1:28; 9:2).

17:6 discretion: The same Greek word that is translated as "inclination" in 15:14, possibly meaning "free will" and the ability to discern and make rational decisions. **a mind for thinking:** Or "an understanding mind" (1 Kings 3:9). **and filled them ... discernment:** From the Latin Vulgate.

17:7 He created in them the knowledge of the spirit: From the Latin Vulgate. The Greek text reads: "He filled them with knowledge and understanding." **good and evil:** Adam and Eve obtained knowledge of these as a result of their sin (Gen 2:17; 3:5, 22).

17:8 fear ... into their hearts: From the New Vulgate.

17:10 praise his holy name: God bestows gifts so that men and women might recognize his goodness and respond to him in praise.

17:11 bestowed knowledge: The special kind of knowledge that God gave to Israel in the Torah, which is a source of life (24:23-29; 45:5; Bar 4:1).

17:12 eternal covenant: The covenant God made with Israel at Mt. Sinai (Ex 19:5; Deut 5:1-5).

17:13 his glorious majesty ... his voice: The manifestations of God's power and presence at Mt. Sinai (45:5; Ex 19:16-19; 24:15-17).

17:14 unrighteousness: The sins prohibited by the Torah, such as idolatry and violating the Sabbath. **concerning his neighbor:** Especially the precepts of the Decalogue that prohibit murder, adultery, theft, bearing false witness, and coveting.

17:15–24 Ben Sira counters those who doubt or deny that God will act as Judge and repay every human action with rewards and punishments.

17:15 always before him: The Lord is always aware of what people do.

17:17 a ruler for every nation: Either a civil ruler or perhaps an angelic ruler (Deut 32:8-9; Dan 10:13-21). **the Lord's own portion:** Unlike the other nations, Israel is God's treasured possession (Ex 19:5; Deut 7:6; Ps 135:4).

17:19 as the sun: The Lord sees all human actions as in daylight (17:15; 23:19).

17:20 iniquities ... sins: The Lord is aware of all evil things in the world.

---

[m]Gk *them.*
[n]Gk *it.*
°Cn: Gk *proper to them.*
[p]Syr: Gk *him.*
[q]Other authorities add [5]*They obtained the use of the five operations of the Lord; as sixth he distributed to them the gift of mind, and as seventh reason, the interpreter of his operations.*
[r]Syr: Gk *Inclination and.*
[s]Other authorities add [9]*and he gave them to boast of his marvels for ever.*
[t]Or *every unrighteous man.*
[u]Other authorities add [16]*Their ways from youth tend toward evil, and they are unable to make for themselves hearts of flesh in place of their stony hearts.* [17]*For in the division of the nations of the whole earth.*
[v]Other authorities add [18]*whom, being his first-born, he brings up with discipline, and allotting to him the light of his love, he does not neglect him.*
[w]Other authorities add [21]*But the Lord, who is gracious and knows his creatures, has neither left nor abandoned them, but spared them.*

²²A man's almsgiving is like a signet with the Lord,ˣ

and he will keep a person's kindness like the apple of his eye.

²³Afterward he will arise and repay them,

and he will bring their recompense on their heads.

²⁴Yet to those who repent he grants a return,

and he encourages those whose endurance is failing,

and he has appointed to them the lot of truth.

²⁵Turn to the Lord and forsake your sins;

pray in his presence and lessen your offenses.

²⁶Return to the Most High and turn away from iniquity,ʸ

and hate abominations intensely.

Know the justice and the judgments of God,

and stand firm in the lot that is set before you,

in prayer to God, the Almighty.

²⁷Who will sing praises to the Most High in Hades,

as do those who are alive and give thanks?

Tarry not in the waywardness of the ungodly,

and give thanks before death.

²⁸From the dead, as from one who does not exist,

thanksgiving has ceased;

he who is alive and well sings the Lord's praises.

²⁹How great is the mercy of the Lord,

and his forgiveness for those who turn to him!

³⁰For all things cannot be in men,ᶻ

since a son of man is not immortal.

³¹What is brighter than the sun? Yet its light fails.ᵃ

So flesh and blood devise evil.

³²He marshals the host of the height of heaven;

but all men are dust and ashes.

God and Man

18 He who lives for ever created the whole universe;

2 the Lord alone will be declared righteous.ᵇ

⁴To none has he given power to proclaim his works;

and who can search out his mighty deeds?

⁵Who can measure his majestic power?

And who can fully recount his mercies?

⁶It is not possible to diminish or increase them,

nor is it possible to trace the wonders of the Lord.

⁷When a man has finished, he is just beginning,

and when he stops, he will be at a loss.

⁸What is man, and of what use is he?

What is his good and what is his evil?

17:22 a signet: A ring that carried an engraved mark of identification, like a signature (49:11). A person's almsgiving is a similarly valuable mark of identification of the righteous before God. **like the apple of his eye:** Indicates how precious a person's good deeds are before the Lord (Deut 32:10; Ps 17:8; Zech 2:8).

17:23 Afterward: In the end. **he will arise:** On the Day of Judgment. **repay them:** In response to the skeptics who think that God does not act (16:22), Ben Sira insists the Lord will render to each according to his works. **on their heads:** A metaphor for judgment (Ps 7:16; Jer 23:19; Ezek 22:31).

17:24 grants a return: The Lord welcomes those who repent back to himself and to a good life (Ezek 33:11). **and he has appointed ... truth:** From the Latin Vulgate.

17:25–32 Because God will judge all sin, Ben Sira issues a call to forsake sin, repent, praise God, and serve him.

17:25 Turn to the Lord: See word study: *Return* at Jer 3:1. **pray in his presence:** Perhaps "pray in the Temple" or "pray in earnest". **lessen your offenses:** Either the manifestation or fruit of earnest prayer.

17:26 hate abominations: As the Lord does (15:13). **Know the justice ... the Almighty:** From the Latin Vulgate.

17:27 Who will sing praises: Praising God is a privilege and joy of this life. **Hades:** The gloomy abode of the dead in OT times, known in Hebrew as *she'ol*, where it was believed that no one could praise God (14:16; 41:4; Ps 30:9; 115:17–18; Is 38:18–19; Bar 2:17). **Tarry not ... before death:** From the Latin Vulgate.

17:28 as ... does not exist: Not that the dead of the OT do not exist, but that their state is *as if* they no longer exist, since it barely qualifies as living. This perspective changes in the New Testament with the revelation of eternal life in heaven.

17:29 How great is the mercy: Stress on God's forgiveness is part of an appeal for repentance (Ps 86:5, 15; 103:8; 111:4; 145:7–9).

17:30 all things cannot be in men: Perhaps referring to the divine mercy and forgiveness of 17:29. **a son of man:** A human being. **not immortal:** Because humans are mortal, they cannot grasp the extent of God's mercy.

17:31 its light fails: After sundown or because of an eclipse. **flesh and blood devise evil:** If the sun can be eclipsed, how much more does evil darken human thoughts (Job 25:4–6).

17:32 host ... of heaven: If God rules over the heavenly powers, such as the sun, moon, and stars (Is 24:21), how much more over man, who is but **dust and ashes** (Gen 18:27).

18:1–14 God's majesty and his role as benevolent judge are emphasized. The chapter begins with God (18:1–7), then turns to man (18:8–10), then considers God's attitude toward man (18:11–14).

18:1 He who lives for ever: The eternal God.

18:2 declared righteous: Means the Lord alone (and no man) will be proven right and true and wise in all things.

18:4 power to proclaim: No man can describe or comprehend the grandeur of God's magnificent works (1:3; 42:17; Ps 145:3; Job 9:10).

18:5 Who can measure ... recount? Implies that no man can gauge God's infinite strength or recall the manifold times when he revealed his mercy.

18:7 When a man has finished: When anyone thinks he is done recounting the Lord's merciful actions and wonders (Ps 77:12–13), he is really only beginning. **he will be at a loss:** He will recognize his inability to contemplate God's works.

18:8 What is man: Ben Sira shifts attention from God to man. Man is truly insignificant compared to his Maker (Ps 8:4; 144:3). **what use is he?:** What is the purpose of man? What is he good for? **What is his good ... his evil?:** Not a denial

---

ˣGk *him*.

ʸOther authorities add *for he will lead you out of darkness to the light of health*.

ᶻThe Greek text of this line is uncertain.

ᵃOr *suffers eclipse*.

ᵇOther authorities add *and there is no other beside him;* ³*he steers the world with the span of his hand, and all things obey his will; for he is king of all things, by his power separating among them the holy things from the profane*.

⁹The number of a man's days is great if he reaches
   a hundred years.
¹⁰Like a drop of water from the sea and a grainᶜ of
   sand
   so are a few years in the day of eternity.
¹¹Therefore the Lord is patient with them
   and pours out his mercy upon them.
¹²He sees and recognizes that their end will be evil;
   therefore he grants them forgiveness in
   abundance.
¹³The compassion of man is for his neighbor,
   but the compassion of the Lord is for all living
   beings.
 He rebukes and trains and teaches them,
   and turns them back, as a shepherd his flock.
¹⁴He has compassion on those who accept his
   discipline
   and who are eager for his judgments.

¹⁵My son, do not mix reproach with your good
   deeds,
   nor cause grief by your words when you
   present a gift.
¹⁶Does not the dew assuage the scorching heat?
   So a word is better than a gift.

¹⁷Indeed, does not a word surpass a good gift?
   Both are to be found in a gracious man.
¹⁸A fool is ungracious and abusive,
   and the gift of a grudging man makes the eyes
   dim.

¹⁹Before you speak, learn,
   and before you fall ill, take care of your health.
²⁰Before judgment, examine yourself,
   and in the hour of visitation you will find
   forgiveness.
²¹Before falling ill, humble yourself,
   and when you are on the point of sinning, turn
   back.
²²Let nothing hinder you from paying a vow
   promptly,
   and do not wait until death to be released from
   it.
²³Before making a vow,ᵈ prepare yourself;
   and do not be like a man who tempts the Lord.
²⁴Think of his wrath on the day of death,
   and of the moment of vengeance when he
   turns away his face.
²⁵In the time of plenty think of the time of hunger;
   in the days of wealth think of poverty and need.

---

of the morality of human actions, which are strongly affirmed (17:20–26). Perhaps this refers to the circumstances of man's life and the events that befall him: "How does man know what is truly good and truly evil for him?"

18:9 a hundred years: Even this is brief in God's eyes (Ps 90:10).

18:10 Like a drop of water: Compared to eternity, the length of human life on earth is barely more than a moment (1:2; Ps 90:3–6).

18:11 the Lord is patient: Precisely because man is so fragile and short-lived.

18:12 their end will be evil: The reason why the Lord is so merciful to man.

18:13 compassion of the Lord: Extends to all living creatures. **rebukes ... teaches:** God's mercy is often expressed as "tough love" (Wis 12:19–22; 2 Mac 6:12–16). **shepherd:** The image of God as good shepherd guiding his flock is common in Scripture (Is 40:11; Ezek 34:11–16; Ps 23; Jn 10:11–18; 1 Pet 2:25).

18:14 those who accept his discipline: Recipients of the Lord's special favors, over and above what all receive.

18:15–29 Exhorts the reader to imitate the Lord by giving graciously (18:15–18) and to be prepared for all situations (18:19–29).

18:15 My son: The fatherly address opens a new section. **do not mix:** Do not spoil your good works by tainting them with a wrong intention or attitude. **grief by your words:** The value of giving a gift may be diminished by harsh or uncharitable words.

18:16 assuage the scorching heat: Just as dew gives relief from extreme heat (43:22), so a kind or cheerful word spoken while giving a gift can be greater than the gift itself.

18:18 A fool is ungracious: Unlike the wise man, who gives cheerfully and gracefully (2 Cor 9:7), as God himself does (Jas 1:5). It is the mark of fools to give grudgingly or

with reproach (20:14–15). **makes the eyes dim:** Perhaps with tears, when the recipient realizes that the gift was not given in a good spirit.

18:19 Before you speak, learn: Know what you are talking about before speaking. This advice opens a series of injunctions on preparedness, all beginning with "before ... ". **take care of your health:** Either to prevent illness or to strengthen the body in advance of it.

18:20 examine yourself: Even more important than preparation for speaking or falling ill, one should make ready for God's judgment by examining one's conscience. **the hour of visitation:** The Lord's coming in judgment, either when sickness strikes or at death (16:18). **forgiveness:** Self-examination reveals faults, inviting one to seek mercy.

18:21 Before falling ill: For Ben Sira, illness is sometimes a form of divine punishment and sometimes a prelude to death. **humble yourself:** By humbling oneself, it is possible to avert God's punishment (2:17; 7:16–17). **on the point of sinning:** Literally, "at the time of sins". **turn back:** It is better to avoid sin than to repent after sinning. See note on 17:24.

18:22 paying a vow: Fulfilling a solemn promise made to God. **promptly:** Or, better, "at the appropriate time" (Eccles 5:4–5). **do not wait until death:** It is unwise to postpone indefinitely, thinking that death will release you from your vows and promises to God.

18:23 prepare yourself: I.e., give thought to your vow and make sure you have the means to fulfill it. It is unwise to make a rash vow that you are unlikely to keep. This would be the equivalent of tempting the Lord or testing his patience (Deut 6:16; Prov 20:25; Mt 4:7).

18:24 wrath ... day of death: God will hold one accountable for unfulfilled vows at the moment of death (18:22). **turns away his face:** One who fails to keep vows has turned his back on God; God, in turn, will "hide his face" or turn his back on him (Deut 31:17–18; Ps 30:7).

18:25 hunger ... poverty: Possibly an appeal to store up provisions in preparation for times of scarcity (Prov 6:6–11). More likely, since hunger and poverty are often viewed as punishments for sin, this is a reminder not to take God's blessings

---

ᶜGk *pebble.*
ᵈOr *offering a prayer.*

26From morning to evening conditions change,
  and all things move swiftly before the Lord.

27A wise man is cautious in everything,
  and in days of sin he guards against
    wrongdoing.
28Every intelligent man knows wisdom,
  and he praises the one who finds her.
29Those who understand sayings become skilled
    themselves,
  and pour forth apt proverbs.

30Do not follow your base desires,
  but restrain your appetites.
31If you allow your soul to take pleasure in base
    desire,
  it will make you the laughingstock of your
    enemies.
32Do not revel in great luxury,
  lest you become impoverished by its expense.
33Do not become a beggar by feasting with
    borrowed money,
  when you have nothing in your purse.

True Wisdom Contrasted to Cleverness and Evil

19 A workman who is a drunkard will not
  become rich;

he who despises small things will fail little by
    little.
2Wine and women lead intelligent men astray,
  and the man who consorts with harlots is very
    reckless.
3Decay and worms will inherit him,
  and the reckless soul will be snatched away.

4One who trusts others too quickly is lightminded,
  and one who sins does wrong to himself.
5One who rejoices in wickedness **e** will be
    condemned, **f**
6and for one who hates gossip evil is lessened.
7Never repeat a conversation,
  and you will lose nothing at all.
8With friend or foe do not report it,
  and unless it would be a sin for you, do not
    disclose it;
9for some one has heard you and watched you,
  and when the time comes he will hate you.
10Have you heard a word? Let it die with you.
  Be brave! It will not make you burst!
11With such a word a fool will suffer pangs
  like a woman in labor with a child.
12Like an arrow stuck in the flesh of the thigh,
  so is a word inside a fool.

---

for granted and to remain faithful to him in days of abundance (Deut 8:10–20; 28:33).

18:26 morning to evening: The span of a single day. **conditions change:** One's life can be altered radically (Job 4:19–21). **all things move swiftly:** The Lord can suddenly turn one's fortune from prosperity to want.

18:27 cautious in everything: Prudence is a mark of the wise person. **days of sin:** Days when sin is prevalent or perhaps when the wise person is tempted to sin. **guards against wrongdoing:** The wise are particularly vigilant to resist temptation.

18:28 knows wisdom: The wise can recognize wisdom in other people. **praises the one who finds her:** The wise person also encourages others to pursue her.

18:29 apt proverbs: The wise become sources of wisdom for others.

18:30 your appetites: Not only sinful desires, but even legitimate appetites must be restrained lest they dominate a person's life (Rom 1:27; 2 Tim 2:22; Jas 1:14).

18:31 laughingstock: Lack of self-control leads to embarrassment and shame (6:4; 42:11).

18:32 impoverished: Living lavishly has a great cost—it can lead to financial ruin.

18:33 feasting with borrowed money: Self-indulgence is particularly destructive when it entails living beyond one's means.

19:1–17 Continues the theme of prudence and self-control in the areas of passions and appetites (19:1–3), of speaking wisely and avoiding gossip (19:4–17), and of discerning true wisdom from counterfeit wisdom (19:18–30).

19:1 a drunkard: On the correlation between drunkenness and poverty, see Prov 21:17; 23:21. The Hebrew reads: "He that does this", referring to the previous verse, i.e., he who becomes a beggar by feasting with borrowed money will not

become rich. **despises small things:** Neglect of small matters leads to the neglect of greater matters, until this leads to ruin (Mt 25:21, 23).

19:2 Wine and women: Represent drunkenness and sexual temptations (31:25–30; Hos 4:11; Prov 31:3–7). Not only fools but **intelligent men** are vulnerable to these temptations.

19:3 Decay and worms: A metaphor for death as the ultimate consequence of sin (Prov 5:5; 7:26–27; 9:18; Rom 6:23; Gal 6:8). **reckless soul:** One who indulges in pleasure.

19:4 trusts others too quickly: Trusting others or believing what they say too quickly or uncritically encourages gossip.

19:5 rejoices in wickedness: By taking delight in malicious gossip. **will be condemned:** Either by God or other people.

19:6 hates gossip: Either by not speaking it or not listening to it.

19:7 Never repeat a conversation: Literally, "a word" (Prov 25:9). **you will lose nothing:** One has nothing to lose by refraining from gossip; by gossiping, on the other hand, one risks losing friends and reputation (Prov 17:9; 25:9–10).

19:8 unless ... a sin: One should not disclose a confidential matter or speak ill of anyone unless by silence one becomes complicit in another's sin or puts another in danger.

19:9 heard ... watched: As a person engaged in gossip. **he will hate you:** Those who gossip are eventually despised, because "whoever gossips to you will gossip about you."

19:10 a word: A rumor about someone. **Let it die with you:** Do not repeat it; let it go no farther. **Be brave! It will not make you burst:** A sarcastic remark, implying that fools are hardly able to restrain themselves from gossiping, thinking that they will explode if they do not repeat rumors they have heard (Job 32:18–19).

19:11 a fool will suffer pangs: Fools are so unable to control their speech that gossip must come out of them as inevitably as a newborn from his mother's womb. Restraining themselves hurts them as much as a woman's labor pains.

19:12 Like an arrow: As an arrow in the leg causes great pain until removed, so a fool suffers agony until he lets words out of his mouth.

---

e Other authorities read *heart*.
f Other authorities add *but he who withstands pleasures crowns his life.*
6*He who controls his tongue will live without strife.*

¹³Question a friend, perhaps he did not do it;
>   but if he did anything, so that he may do it no
>   more.
¹⁴Question a neighbor, perhaps he did not say it;
>   but if he said it, so that he may not say it
>   again.
¹⁵Question a friend, for often it is slander;
>   so do not believe everything you hear.
¹⁶A person may make a slip without intending it.
>   Who has never sinned with his tongue?
¹⁷Question your neighbor before you threaten
>   him;
>   and let the law of the Most High take its
>   course. ᵍ

²⁰All wisdom is the fear of the Lord,
>   and in all wisdom there is the fulfilment of the
>   law. ʰ
²²But the knowledge of wickedness is not wisdom,
>   nor is there prudence where sinners take
>   counsel.
²³There is a cleverness which is abominable,
>   but there is a fool who merely lacks wisdom.
²⁴Better is the God-fearing man who lacks
>   intelligence,
>   than the highly prudent man who transgresses
>   the law.

²⁵There is a cleverness which is scrupulous but
>   unjust,
>   and there are people who distort kindness to
>   gain a verdict.
²⁶There is a rascal bowed down in mourning, ¹
>   but inwardly he is full of deceit.
²⁷He hides his face and pretends not to hear;
>   but where no one notices, he will forestall you.
²⁸And if by lack of strength he is prevented from
>   sinning,
>   he will do evil when he finds an opportunity.
²⁹A man is known by his appearance,
>   and a sensible man is known by his face, when
>   you meet him.
³⁰A man's attire and open-mouthed laughter,
>   and a man's manner of walking, show what
>   he is.

On Silence and Speech

20 There is a reproof which is not timely;
>   and there is a man who keeps silent but
>   is wise.
²How much better it is to reprove than to stay
>   angry!
>   And the one who confesses his fault will be
>   kept from loss. ʲ
⁴Like a eunuch's desire to violate a maiden
>   is a man who executes judgments by violence.

19:13 Question a friend: To find out if a damaging rumor is true or false. **perhaps he did not:** The rumor may be false. **if he did anything:** If the rumor is true, then frankly discussing it with the friend is better than talking behind his back.
19:14 Question a neighbor: To find out the source of the rumor. **perhaps he did not say it:** The rumor may have been a misunderstanding. **if he said it:** Gently admonishing the neighbor may prevent future gossip coming from his lips.
19:15 Question a friend, for often it is slander: Perhaps false rumors were spread maliciously about the friend. **do not believe everything:** Confirms 19:4.
19:16 without intending it: Some things are said carelessly without any malicious intent.
19:17 Question your neighbor before you threaten him: False rumors can stir up anger, so one should verify the facts before taking steps to reprove someone. **let the law ... take its course:** Probably refers to Lev 19:17–18.
19:18—20:32 Miscellaneous advice on exercising wisdom and avoiding folly.
19:20 wisdom is the fear of the Lord: Reiterates the essence of authentic wisdom, set out many times throughout the book (1:9–30; 2:7–17; 10:19–20; 21:6). **fulfilment of the law:** Fearing the Lord is expressed by keeping the law (9:15; 15:1; 21:11; 24:23; Bar 4:1).

19:22 knowledge of wickedness: Whether this refers to knowing about wickedness or to the knowledge possessed by wicked people—neither of these is wisdom (Wis 1:4). **where sinners take counsel:** The advice of sinners is never a good one to follow (Ps 1:1).
19:23 cleverness ... abominable: Intelligence used for evil is not only unwise; it is detestable—far worse than mere foolishness.
19:24 God-fearing man: The devout man is better than a shrewd transgressor of the Law.
19:25 scrupulous but unjust: One can be meticulous and precise, yet dishonest. **distort kindness:** As when one shows kindness deceptively, for the sake of an ulterior motive or to gain a personal favor.
19:26 a rascal bowed down: A duplicitous man who puts on a show of false humility.
19:27 he will forestall you: After putting you off guard, he will seek an opportunity to take advantage of you when you least expect it.
19:29 known by his appearance: Even though deceivers mask their true intentions, the wise are able to "read" people and recognize one who is sensible.
19:30 attire ... laughter ... manner of walking: Ben Sira sees these things as indicators of a man's true character.
20:1–8 Counsel on the proper time for speech, i.e., on knowing that there is "a time to keep silence, and a time to speak" (Eccles 3:7).
20:1 reproof ... not timely: It is appropriate to rebuke someone who has done wrong (Mt 18:15–17), but doing so at the wrong time can have adverse effects. **keeps silent but is wise:** Sometimes silence is wiser than speaking.
20:2 better it is to reprove: Conflicts are better resolved by addressing problems than by keeping anger bottled up. **kept from loss:** Candidly admitting one's faults can protect one from greater failure or embarrassment.
20:4 a eunuch's desire ... maiden: Not only evil but utterly futile, since eunuchs were typically castrated. No less futile is a man's desire to control others by force.

ᵍ Other authorities add *and do not be angry. ¹⁸The fear of the Lord is the beginning of acceptance, and wisdom obtains his love. ¹⁹The knowledge of the Lord's commandments is life-giving discipline; and those who do what is pleasing to him enjoy the fruit of the tree of immortality.*
ʰ Other authorities add *and the knowledge of his omnipotence. ²¹When a servant says to his master, "I will not act as you wish," even if later he does it, he angers the one who supports him.*
¹ Gk *blackness.*
ʲ Other authorities add ³*How good it is to show repentance when you are reproved, for so you will escape deliberate sin!*

⁵There is one who by keeping silent is found
    wise,
       while another is detested for being too
       talkative.
⁶There is one who keeps silent because he has no
    answer,
       while another keeps silent because he knows
       when to speak.
⁷A wise man will be silent until the right moment,
    but a braggart and fool goes beyond the right
    moment.
⁸Whoever uses too many words will be loathed,
    and whoever usurps the right to speak will be
    hated.

⁹There may be good fortune for a man in
    adversity,
       and a windfall may result in a loss.
¹⁰There is a gift that profits you nothing,
    and there is a gift that brings a double return.
¹¹There are losses because of glory,
    and there are men who have raised their heads
    from humble circumstances.
¹²There is a man who buys much for a little,
    but pays for it seven times over.

¹³The wise man makes himself beloved through his
    words,
       but the courtesies of fools are wasted.
¹⁴A fool's gift will profit you nothing,
    for he has many eyes instead of one.

¹⁵He gives little and upbraids much,
    he opens his mouth like a herald;
       today he lends and tomorrow he asks it back;
       such a one is a hateful man.
¹⁶A fool will say, "I have no friend,
    and there is no gratitude for my good deeds;
       those who eat my bread speak unkindly."
¹⁷How many will ridicule him, and how often!

¹⁸A slip on the pavement is better than a slip of the
    tongue;
       so the downfall of the wicked will occur
       speedily.
¹⁹An ungracious man is like a story told at the
    wrong time,
       which is continually on the lips of the ignorant.
²⁰A proverb from a fool's lips will be rejected,
    for he does not tell it at its proper time.

²¹A man may be prevented from sinning by his
    poverty,
       so when he rests he feels no remorse.
²²A man may lose his life through shame,
    or lose it because of his foolish look.
²³A man may for shame make promises to a friend,
    and needlessly make him an enemy.

²⁴A lie is an ugly blot on a man;
    it is continually on the lips of the ignorant.
²⁵A thief is preferable to a habitual liar,
    but the lot of both is ruin.

20:5 keeping silent: On the wisdom of remaining silent, see Prov 17:28.
20:6 he has no answer: "Silence is golden"—either when one has nothing to say or when one waits for the opportune time to speak (Prov 15:23).
20:7 a braggart and fool: A babbler who does not know when to stop talking (20:5).
20:8 whoever usurps the right to speak: One who talks so much that others have no chance to speak is disliked by everyone (Prov 10:19).
20:9-17 A discussion on gain and loss, where things are not always as they seem.
20:9 good fortune ... adversity: Times of trouble may bring unforeseen prosperity. **a windfall:** Conversely, some unexpected good fortune may result in misfortune.
20:10 gift that profits you nothing: Either you receive a gift of little value or you give a gift that brings you nothing in return. **a double return:** Either you receive a gift that makes you doubly indebted to the giver or you receive back twice as much as you gave.
20:11 losses because of glory: May mean that one will have to suffer loss for the sake of seeking glory or that those who attained glory may lose it suddenly. **raised their heads:** A reminder that people of lowly origins have risen to places of high honor (1 Sam 2:4-9; Ps 113:7-9; Lk 1:51-53).
20:12 much for a little: What seems like a bargain may cost you more than expected.
20:13 beloved through his words: The speech of a wise person has a power of attraction. **courtesies of fools:** By contrast, people will see through the flatteries of fools.
20:14 profit you nothing: A fool's gift is of little use to anyone. **many eyes instead of one:** A difficult expression. It

may mean: "The fool thinks his gift is worth much more than it is, and he expects too much in return."
20:15 upbraids much: May mean the fool has little to offer other than criticism. Or, he upbraids by asking to be paid back for his second-rate gifts. **like a herald:** The fool is compared to a public announcer shouting news with a loud voice.
20:16 my good deeds: The fool imagines he has done many good deeds, but those around him know otherwise.
20:18-26 Guidelines on appropriate and inappropriate speech. These deal with the consequences of saying the wrong thing (20:18-20), with being reluctant to speak when one should (20:21-23), and with lying (20:24-26).
20:20 A proverb: Usually commands attention and respect because it communicates wisdom, but not when spoken in an untimely manner by a fool (Prov 26:7-9).
20:21 prevented ... by his poverty: Not that a poor person cannot sin, but that his lack of resources does not afford him the opportunity to commit certain sins. **no remorse:** He is not accused by his conscience for sins he cannot commit.
20:22 lose his life through shame: The meaning of this verse is unclear. Perhaps it says that a man can ruin himself through timidity, i.e., failing to speak at the right time.
20:23 for shame: As when one makes promises to a friend that he cannot keep, leading the friend to confront him on his failure to follow through.
20:24 an ugly blot: A lie is a defect in a person's character (7:13; 25:2; Prov 6:16-19). **the ignorant:** The uneducated fools who continually speak falsehoods.
20:25 preferable to a habitual liar: Not that theft is morally acceptable, but that lying, which is a form of "stealing the truth" from others, can be even worse when it is done constantly.

²⁶The disposition of a liar brings disgrace,
and his shame is ever with him.

²⁷He who speaks wisely will advance himself,
and a sensible man will please great men.
²⁸Whoever cultivates the soil will heap up his
harvest,
and whoever pleases great men will atone for
injustice.
²⁹Presents and gifts blind the eyes of the wise;
like a muzzle on the mouth they avert reproofs.
³⁰Hidden wisdom and unseen treasure,
what advantage is there in either of them?
³¹Better is the man who hides his folly
than the man who hides his wisdom. ᵏ

Various Sins and Foolishness

21 Have you sinned, my son? Do so no more,
but pray about your former sins.
²Flee from sin as from a snake;
for if you approach sin, it will bite you.
Its teeth are lion's teeth,
and destroy the souls of men.
³All lawlessness is like a two-edged sword;
there is no healing for its wound.

⁴Terror and violence will lay waste riches;
thus the house of the proud will be laid waste.

⁵The prayer of a poor man goes from his lips to
the ears of God, ¹
and his judgment comes speedily.
⁶Whoever hates reproof walks in the steps of the
sinner,
but he that fears the Lord will repent in his
heart.
⁷He who is mighty in speech is known from afar;
but the sensible man, when he slips, is aware
of it.

⁸A man who builds his house with other people's
money
is like one who gathers stones for his burial
mound.ᵐ
⁹An assembly of the wicked is like tow gathered
together,
and their end is a flame of fire.
¹⁰The way of sinners is smoothly paved with stones,
but at its end is the pit of Hades.

¹¹Whoever keeps the law controls his thoughts,
and wisdom is the fulfilment of the fear of the
Lord.
¹²He who is not clever cannot be taught,
but there is a cleverness which increases
bitterness.

20:26 brings disgrace: A habitual liar ruins his own credibility and reputation.
20:27–31 If fools should remain quiet, the wise should assert themselves and speak.
20:27 advance himself: I.e., will be successful.
20:28 atone for injustice: Just as cultivating the soil leads to a good harvest, so pleasing influential men wins their goodwill, makes amends for errors, and earns their favor at a later time.
20:29 Presents and gifts: Bribes. These are forbidden because they subvert justice and affect the judgment even of wise people (Ex 23:8; Deut 16:19; Prov 15:27; 17:8, 23). **like a muzzle:** Bribes inhibit authorities from giving reproof and correction to others, much as a muzzle prevents a dog from barking or biting.
20:30 Hidden wisdom: As useless as a hidden treasure. To be beneficial, wisdom must be shared with others.
20:31 Better is the man: Essentially means: "It is good for a fool to hide his folly, but it is not good for the wise to hide his wisdom." These two verses recur in 41:14–15. • Persons who can preach the gospel but shrink back out of excessive humility should be admonished. If they hide money from neighbors in need, they facilitate their ruin. So too, if they withhold preaching from sinners, they are guilty of hiding the remedies of life from dying souls. If people are perishing from famine, and others kept food hidden, they are authors of death. So too, they are liable to punishment who do not supply the bread of grace when souls are perishing from a famine of the word of God (St. Gregory the Great, *Pastoral Rule* 3, 25).
21:1 about your former sins: Pray to obtain forgiveness from God along with the moral strength to avoid these mistakes in the future.

21:2 as from a snake: Brings to mind the serpent who tempted Eve in the Garden of Eden (Gen 3:1–5). **it will bite you:** Sin is personified as a snake that attacks if approached (cf. Prov 23:32). One should avoid sin as much as a snake, for both are deadly. **lion's teeth:** A personification of sin as a predator (27:10; Gen 4:7; 1 Pet 5:8) that kills souls (Mt 10:28).
21:3 a two-edged sword: A sword filed sharp on both edges is particularly deadly (Judg 3:16; Ps 149:6). **no healing:** Emphasizes the deadliness of sin (Prov 5:4).
21:5 to the ears of God: God hears and responds quickly to the prayers of the poor (Ps 18:6; 34:15; 86:1).
21:6 Whoever hates reproof: Whoever resents being corrected for his wrongdoing (32:17). **repent in his heart:** The fear of the Lord, as the mark of true wisdom, is seen in a person who acknowledges his sins, repents of them, and strives to avoid them in the future.
21:7 mighty in speech: Possibly an ironic reference to a boastful person, famous for his eloquence.
21:8 A man who builds: One who increases his wealth at the expense of others. **gathers stones for his burial:** By using other people's wealth to build his own fortune, he is erecting his own tomb, i.e., inviting a premature death.
21:9 tow gathered together: Tow consists of fibers from the flax plant used for spinning into thread. It is highly flammable. **a flame of fire:** Not necessarily a form of punishment in the afterlife (the doctrine of hell was not fully developed at the time of Sirach), but a quick and decisive end of the wicked in this life.
21:10 smoothly paved: On the idea of an apparently secure way that ultimately leads to death, see Prov 14:12; 16:25; Mt 7:13. **Hades:** The abode of the dead (14:16; 17:27).
21:11–28 The wise and the foolish are contrasted in their words and actions.
21:11 his thoughts: Or "his impulses".
21:12 cleverness ... bitterness: While cleverness is a good to be sought (34:10), it can also be used to deceive or hurt others, making them resentful (19:23).

ᵏOther authorities add ³²*Unwearied patience in seeking the Lord is better than a masterless charioteer of one's own life.*
¹Gk *his ears.*
ᵐOther authorities read *for the winter.*

¹³The knowledge of a wise man will increase like a
flood,
and his counsel like a flowing spring.
¹⁴The mind of a fool is like a broken jar;
it will hold no knowledge.

¹⁵When a man of understanding hears a wise
saying,
he will praise it and add to it;
when a reveler hears it, he dislikes it
and casts it behind his back.
¹⁶A fool's narration is like a burden on a journey,
but delight will be found in the speech of the
intelligent.
¹⁷The utterance of a sensible man will be sought in
the assembly,
and they will ponder his words in their minds.

¹⁸Like a house that has vanished, so is wisdom to
a fool;
and the knowledge of the ignorant is
unexamined talk.
¹⁹To a senseless man education is chains on his feet,
and like manacles on his right hand.
²⁰A fool raises his voice when he laughs,
but a clever man smiles quietly.
²¹To a sensible man education is like a golden
ornament,
and like a bracelet on the right arm.

²²The foot of a fool rushes into a house,
but a man of experience stands respectfully
before it.
²³A boor peers into the house from the door,
but a cultivated man remains outside.
²⁴It is ill-mannered for a man to listen at a door,
and a discreet man is grieved by the
disgrace.
²⁵The lips of strangers will speak of these things,[n]
but the words of the prudent will be weighed
in the balance.
²⁶The mind of fools is in their mouth,
but the mouth of wise men is in[o] their mind.
²⁷When an ungodly man curses his adversary,[p]
he curses his own soul.
²⁸A whisperer defiles his own soul
and is hated in his neighborhood.

On Wisdom, Folly, and Self-Control

22 The indolent may be compared to a filthy
stone,
and every one hisses at his disgrace.
²The indolent may be compared to the filth of
dunghills;
any one that picks it up will shake it off his
hand.

³It is a disgrace to be the father of an undisciplined
son,
and the birth of a daughter is a loss.

21:13 like a flood: Abundant knowledge is akin to a source of life-giving water. **a flowing spring:** Literally, "a fountain of life" (Ps 36:9; Prov 10:11; 18:4).

21:14 a broken jar: Cannot contain anything (cf. Jer 2:13). In contrast to the "flood" and "flowing spring" of the wise man, the fool cannot remember anything worthwhile.

21:15 add to it: An intelligent man welcomes words of wisdom and adds his own wise insights to the conversation. **a reveler:** A shallow person who is fond of luxury and the easy life swiftly dismisses any spoken wisdom and changes the subject.

21:16 like a burden: The discourse of fools is tiresome and tedious. **the speech of the intelligent:** Pleasant and refreshing (Prov 22:11; Eccles 10:12).

21:18 Like a house ... vanished: Fools are unable to see the "house of wisdom" (Prov 9:1). **unexamined talk:** The Greek is unclear. It may mean: "To the ignorant, knowledge is incomprehensible speech."

21:19 chains ... manacles: The fool considers discipline a hamper on his freedom, whereas the reality is the opposite (6:23–31; 21:21).

21:21 golden ornament ... bracelet: In contrast to the fool's view of education (21:19), submitting to the education of wisdom is a source of rest, joy, and protection. Wisdom is thus likened to precious jewelry.

21:22–24 The bad social manners of fools are contrasted with the good manners of the wise: the former is **ill-mannered** and rude; the latter is patient, **discreet**, and considerate of others.

21:25 speak of these things: One manuscript has instead: "Babblers speak things that are not their own." **weighed in the balance:** In contrast to babblers, wise people weigh their words before they speak (16:25; 28:25).

21:26 their mouth ... their mind: Fools speak before they think, but the wise think before they speak. • If the heart of a fool is in his mouth, it is because he does not speak after thinking but only thinks after speaking. The tongue of the wise, by contrast, comes from meditation on wisdom and, like the pen of a scribe, does nothing that is wrongly ordered or uncertain. Instead, it subjects itself to what has been considered and read according to reason's judgment (St. Hilary of Poitiers, *Homilies on the Psalms* 51, 7).

21:27 curses his adversary: Or "curses Satan". This may refer to a wicked person who curses Satan as the one responsible for his sins.

21:28 A whisperer: A gossip who hurts his own reputation more than that of the person about whom he is gossiping (5:14; 19:4–17; 28:13).

22:1–18 More contrasts between fools and the wise. Fools are lazy (22:1–2); they raise undisciplined children (22:3–6); they are unteachable (22:7–12); and they are best avoided (22:13–15). The stability and strength of the wise should be sought instead (22:16–18).

22:1–2 The indolent: Sluggards, whom Ben Sira views as filthy and disgusting as excrement (Prov 6:9–11; 10:4–5; 15:19; 20:4; 24:30–34; 26:13–16).

22:3 undisciplined: An unruly child is an embarrassment to a father. **a daughter is a loss:** Reflects the fact that women in the ancient world were financially dependent upon males, normally fathers or husbands.

---

[n] The Greek text of this line is uncertain.
[o] Other authorities omit *in*.
[p] Or *curses Satan*.

[4]A sensible daughter obtains her husband,
but one who acts shamefully brings grief to her father.
[5]An impudent daughter disgraces father and husband,
and will be despised by both.
[6]Like music in mourning is a tale told at the wrong time,
but chastising and discipline are wisdom at all times.

[7]He who teaches a fool is like one who glues potsherds together,
or who rouses a sleeper from deep slumber.
[8]He who tells a story to a fool tells it to a drowsy man;
and at the end he will say, "What is it?"[q]
[11]Weep for the dead, for he lacks the light;
and weep for the fool, for he lacks intelligence;
weep less bitterly for the dead, for he has attained rest;
but the life of the fool is worse than death.
[12]Mourning for the dead lasts seven days,
but for a fool or an ungodly man it lasts all his life.

[13]Do not talk much with a foolish man,
and do not visit an unintelligent man;
guard yourself from him to escape trouble,
and you will not be soiled when he shakes himself off;
avoid him and you will find rest,
and you will never be wearied by his madness.
[14]What is heavier than lead?
And what is its name except "Fool"?
[15]Sand, salt, and a piece of iron
are easier to bear than a stupid man.

[16]A wooden beam firmly bonded into a building
will not be torn loose by an earthquake;
so the mind firmly fixed on a reasonable counsel
will not be afraid in a crisis.
[17]A mind settled on an intelligent thought
is like the stucco decoration on the wall of a colonnade.[r]
[18]Fences set on a high place
will not stand firm against the wind;
so a timid heart with a fool's purpose
will not stand firm against any fear.

[19]A man who pricks an eye will make tears fall,
and one who pricks the heart makes it show feeling.
[20]One who throws a stone at birds scares them away,
and one who reviles a friend will break off the friendship.
[21]Even if you have drawn your sword against a friend,
do not despair, for a renewal of friendship is possible.

22:4 obtains her husband: The Latin reads: "is an inheritance to her husband". The sense is that she is "a treasure to her husband". A well-raised daughter will attract a good husband who will cherish her.

22:5 impudent daughter: Brings grief and shame not only to her father, but to her husband as well.

22:6 told at the wrong time: Lecturing children to correct misbehavior is ill-advised when ill-timed. **chastising:** Refers to corporal punishment.

22:7–8 These two verses follow the order of the Vulgate. They are numbered 22:9–10 in the Greek text and in other English translations.

22:7 glues potsherds: A broken pot, even if repaired, will not hold its contents reliably. It is just as futile to try to teach a fool (Prov 1:22; 23:9; 24:7).

22:8 a drowsy man: It is useless to explain something to someone who is barely awake. So too, the fool—who is mentally and spiritually drowsy—will not retain what he is taught.

22:11 weep for the fool: While one naturally mourns the dead, one should mourn the fool even more, because, lacking sense—which is essential to a fully human life—it is as if he was never alive in the first place.

22:12 seven days: The customary mourning period in biblical times (Gen 50:10; Job 2:13; Jud 16:24). Jews continue this tradition today.

22:13 do not visit an unintelligent man: The Syriac version reads: "Consort not with a pig." **you will not be soiled:** The fool is likened to a pig that shakes itself off after wallowing in the mud, soiling everything around him.

22:14 heavier than lead: Being in the company of fools is like carrying a burdensome load.

22:15 Sand, salt ... iron: Items that are difficult to carry (Job 6:3; Prov 27:3)—yet not as burdensome as a fool.

22:16 fixed on a reasonable counsel: As a well-constructed building can withstand an earthquake, a well-formed mind can withstand the crises of life.

22:17 like the stucco decoration: Perhaps means that a well-reasoned mind is as elegant as a wall that is beautifully and expertly covered with plaster.

22:18 Fences: Or, as some manuscripts read, "pebbles", which were placed on the top of garden walls to alert owners of animals climbing over. **a timid heart:** Just as small rocks easily fall off the wall, so a cowardly, unresolved person with foolish thoughts will not be able to stand firm in difficult situations.

22:19–27 Counsel on preserving and repairing friendships (see also 6:5–17; 12:8–18).

22:19 eye ... heart: Two of the most sensitive parts of the human body—the eye, physically, and the heart, metaphorically as the seat of human emotions and affections. Both are easily wounded but not so easily healed.

22:20 birds: Easily scattered by throwing a stone at them but not easily regathered. This illustrates how friendships are easily broken but not easily mended.

22:21–22 Friendships can still be healed after violent arguments, but if a friend is insulted or his trust betrayed, reconciliation will be much more difficult (cf. Prov 20:19; 25:9).

---

[q]Other authorities add [9]*Children who are brought up in a good life, conceal the lowly birth of their parents.* [10]*Children who are disdainfully and boorishly haughty stain the nobility of their kindred.*

[r]Or *on a smooth wall.*

22If you have opened your mouth against your
      friend,
   do not worry, for reconciliation is possible;
but as for reviling, arrogance, disclosure of
      secrets, or a treacherous blow—
   in these cases any friend will flee.

23Gain the trust of your neighbor in his poverty,
   that you may rejoice with him in his prosperity;
stand by him in time of affliction,
   that you may share with him in his inheritance.ˢ
24The vapor and smoke of the furnace precede the
      fire;
   so insults precede bloodshed.
25I will not be ashamed to protect a friend,
   and I will not hide from him;
26but if some harm should happen to me because
      of him,
   whoever hears of it will beware of him.

27O that a guard were set over my mouth,
   and a seal of prudence upon my lips,
that it may keep me from falling,
   so that my tongue may not destroy me!ᵗ

23 O Lord, Father and Ruler of my life,
      do not abandon me to their counsel,
   and let me not fall because of them!
2O that whips were set over my thoughts,
   and the discipline of wisdom over my mind!ᵘ
That they may not spare me in my errors,
   and that it may not pass by myᵛ sins;

3in order that my mistakes may not be multiplied,
   and my sins may not abound;
then I will not fall before my adversaries,
   and my enemy will not rejoice over me.
4O Lord, Father and God of my life,
   do not give me haughty eyes,
5   and remove from me evil desire.
6Let neither gluttony nor lust overcome me,
   and do not surrender me to a shameless soul.

7Listen, my children, to instruction concerning
      speech;
   the one who observes it will never be caught.
8The sinner is overtaken through his lips,
   the reviler and the arrogant are tripped by them.
9Do not accustom your mouth to oaths,
   and do not habitually utter the name of the
      Holy One;
10for as a servant who is continually examined
      under torture
   will not lack bruises,
so also the man who always swears and utters
      the Name
   will not be cleansed from sin.
11A man who swears many oaths will be filled with
      iniquity,
   and the scourge will not leave his house;
if he offends, his sin remains on him,
   and if he disregards it, he sins doubly;
if he has sworn needlessly, he will not be justified,
   for his house will be filled with calamities.

22:23 poverty ... prosperity: By gaining the confidence of your neighbor in his time of need, you will also benefit from his friendship in time of blessings.

22:24 insults precede bloodshed: Just as, when starting a fire, the tinder smolders and smokes before it bursts into flame, so insults create tensions that burst into violence.

22:25 protect a friend: Switching to the first person (I, me, my), the author asserts his own loyalty in friendship.

22:26 will beware of him: If a friend is disloyal and causes harm, his own reputation will be at stake. He will hurt himself more than the one he betrays.

22:27 guard ... over my mouth: Aware that imprudent words easily harm friendships and lead to personal ruin (13:3; 20:7-8, 18-20; 22:22; 28:24-26; Prov 6:2; Ps 141:3), Ben Sira expresses the desire to exert better control over what he says.

23:1-6 A prayer for self-control over one's thoughts (23:1-3), which rule speech and desires (23:4-6). These are treated in the rest of the chapter in instructions concerning speech (23:7-15) and sex (23:16-28).

23:1 O Lord, Father and Ruler: Three titles for God expressing his loving care and divine authority. **their counsel:** The counsel of the mouth, lips, and tongue mentioned in 22:27.

23:2 discipline of wisdom: Alludes to God's fatherly discipline as an expression of his love (Prov 3:11-12). Wisdom's discipline over the mind is really self-discipline. **That they may not spare me:** I.e., that the whips of chastisement might correct one's sins.

23:3 my mistakes ... my sins: Uncontrolled thoughts lead to a multitude of errors and transgressions that can lead to one's downfall and to the triumph of one's enemies.

23:4 O Lord, Father and God: Almost identical to 23:1. **haughty eyes:** Either an arrogant attitude or, more probably, a brazen, lustful look (26:9; Gen 39:7; Mt 5:28).

23:5 evil desire: Or "lust".

23:6 gluttony nor lust: The two most carnal of the seven capital sins (CCC 1866). **do not surrender me to a shameless soul:** Or "do not hand me over to shameless passion."

23:7 Listen, my children: Ben Sira addresses readers as a father would. **will never be caught:** The wise man will not be ensnared by his words (20:18; Prov 6:2).

23:9 oaths: Oaths are solemn pledges made by invoking God's name. Oaths should be sworn only in the gravest of circumstances (Mt 5:34-37; Jas 5:12). **the Holy One:** God (4:14; 43:10; 47:8).

23:10 always swears ... the Name: One who takes the name of the Lord in swearing rash oaths violates the commandments of the Torah (Ex 20:7; Lev 19:12).

23:11 swears many oaths: On careless swearing, see 27:14. **the scourge:** Signifies God's punishment. **his house:** The family of a sinner, which can suffer the consequences of his transgressions. **if he offends:** By rashly swearing an oath or not fulfilling it. **if he disregards it:** If he dismisses or ignores his oath, he is doubly guilty.

ˢ Other authorities add *For one should not always despise restricted circumstances, nor admire a rich man who is stupid.*
ᵗ Or *Who will set a guard...destroy me?*
ᵘ Or *Who will set whips...my mind?*
ᵛ Gk *their.*

¹²There is an utterance which is comparable to
    death;ʷ
    may it never be found in the inheritance of
        Jacob!
    For all these errors will be far from the godly,
        and they will not wallow in sins.
¹³Do not accustom your mouth to lewd vulgarity,
        for it involves sinful speech.
¹⁴Remember your father and mother
        whenˣ you sit among great men;
    lest you be forgetful in their presence,
        and be deemed a fool on account of your
            habits;
    then you will wish that you had never been born,
        and you will curse the day of your birth.
¹⁵A man accustomed to using insulting words
        will never become disciplined all his days.

¹⁶Two sorts of men multiply sins,
        and a third incurs wrath.
    The soul heated like a burning fire
        will not be quenched until it is consumed;
    a man who commits fornication with his near of
        kinʸ
    will never cease until the fire burns him up.
¹⁷To a fornicator all bread tastes sweet;
        he will never cease until he dies.
¹⁸A man who breaks his marriage vows
        says to himself, "Who sees me?

Darkness surrounds me, and the walls hide me,
        and no one sees me. Why should I fear?
    The Most High will not take notice of my sins."
¹⁹His fear is confined to the eyes of men,
        and he does not realize that the eyes of the
            Lord
        are ten thousand times brighter than the sun;
    they look upon all the ways of men,
        and perceive even the hidden places.
²⁰Before the universe was created, it was known to
        him;
    so it was also after it was finished.
²¹This man will be punished in the streets of the city,
        and where he least suspects it, he will be seized.
²²So it is with a woman who leaves her husband
        and provides an heir by a stranger.
²³For first of all, she has disobeyed the law of the
        Most High;
    second, she has committed an offense against
        her husband;
    and third, she has committed adultery through
        harlotry
    and brought forth children by another man.
²⁴She herself will be brought before the assembly,
        and punishment will fall on her children.
²⁵Her children will not take root,
        and her branches will not bear fruit.
²⁶She will leave her memory for a curse,
        and her disgrace will not be blotted out.

23:12 comparable to death: Some sins of speech, such as blasphemy, are very serious; they are punishable by death in the Old Testament (Lev 19:12; 22:2–3, 32; 24:15–16). **the inheritance of Jacob:** The people of Israel.

23:13 lewd vulgarity: A warning to avoid foul and impure talk (Eph 5:4; Col 3:8; Jas 1:21).

23:14 father and mother: The commandment to "honor your father and your mother" (Ex 20:12) includes honoring them in speech, even in their absence. **among great men; lest you be forgetful:** It may be tempting to speak coarsely among men of social importance, forgetting the formation given by one's parents and disgracing them and yourself in the process. **curse the day of your birth:** An allusion to Job 3:3; Jer 20:14.

23:15 will never become disciplined: Contrast with the prayer in 23:1–3.

23:16–28 Warnings against sexual sins.

23:16 Two sorts of sins . . . and a third: A numerical proverb (25:1–2, 7–11; 26:5–6; Prov 6:16–19), referring to the three types of sexual sins that follow. **like a burning fire:** A person consumed by sexual passion. **fornication with his near of kin:** Literally, "a fornicator in the body of his flesh", which may refer to incest (Lev 18:6–18) or to someone who is sexually licentious generally.

23:17 all bread tastes sweet: A euphemism for addiction to sexual pleasure (Prov 9:17).

✠ **23:18 Who sees me? . . . Why should I fear?:** The adulterer wrongly thinks that his sin is hidden and that

it will even escape the notice of God (16:17–23; Job 24:15). This type of rationalization is typical of sinners (Is 29:15; Ezek 8:12). • Let us take care of our body as our own, since we must give an account to the Lord for everything done in the body. Do not tell yourself: No one sees me. Do not think there are no witness to what you have done, for the One who made us sees it. Just as a scar remains after a wound in the body has healed, so sin, after wounding us, leaves its mark on us (St. Cyril of Jerusalem, *Catechesis* 18, 20).

23:19 His fear is confined: The adulterer's only concern is to escape the punishment and public disgrace he would suffer (23:21). He fails to realize that the Lord sees even our most hidden thoughts and actions (17:19–20; Prov 15:3, 11; Ps 33:13–15).

23:20 known to him: A reference to God's omniscience (42:18; Ps 139:1–16).

23:21 punished in the streets: According to the Law, punishment for adultery was death by stoning (Lev 20:10; Deut 22:22–24; Jn 8:4–5).

23:22 leaves her husband: Means that the adulteress betrays her husband, not that she abandons or divorces him. **an heir by a stranger:** A child conceived by another man.

23:23 she . . . she . . . she: The adulteress has sinned against God, sinned against her husband, and become the mother of illegitimate children.

23:24 the assembly: A public trial is envisioned. **children:** Will be declared illegitimate.

23:25 will not take root: Illegitimate Jewish children were not considered part of the congregation of Israel and thus were unable to find a respectable place in society or marry into the Jewish community (Deut 23:2; Wis 3:16–19; 4:3–6).

23:26 memory . . . curse: The consequences of adultery are bitter and long-lasting.

ʷOther authorities read *clothed about with death.*
ˣGk *for.*
ʸGk *in the body of his flesh.*

27Those who survive her will recognize
  that nothing is better than the fear of the
    Lord,
and nothing sweeter than to heed the
  commandments of the Lord. ᶻ

The Praise of Wisdom

24 Wisdom will praise herself and is honored in
  God,
  and will glory in the midst of her people. ᵃ
2In the assembly of the Most High she will open
  her mouth,
  and in the presence of his host she will glory.
In the midst of her people she is exalted;
  in holy fulness she is admired.
In the multitude of the chosen she finds praise,
  and among the blessed she is blessed, saying:
3"I came forth from the mouth of the Most High,
  the first-born before all creatures.
I ordained that an unfailing light
  should arise in the heavens,
  and I covered the earth like a mist.
4I dwelt in high places,
  and my throne was in a pillar of cloud.

5Alone I have made the circuit of the vault of
  heaven
  and have walked in the depths of the abyss.
6In the waves of the sea, in the whole earth,
  and in every people and nation I have gotten a
    possession.
7Among all these I sought a resting place;
  I sought in whose territory I might lodge.

8"Then the Creator of all things gave me a
    commandment,
  and the one who created me assigned a place
    for my tent.
And he said, 'Make your dwelling in Jacob,
  and in Israel receive your inheritance,
  and among my chosen put down your roots.'
9From eternity, in the beginning, he created me,
  and for eternity I shall not cease to exist.
10In the holy tabernacle I ministered before him,
  and so I was established in Zion.
11In the beloved city likewise he gave me a resting
    place,
  and in Jerusalem was my dominion.

23:27 nothing is better than the fear of the Lord: A fitting summary and conclusion to the first part of the book. **nothing sweeter:** Keeping the commandments is the best expression of the fear of the Lord that leads to the attainment of wisdom.

24:1–34 This chapter on the praise of wisdom is the central and most important passage of the book. In contrast to most other English translations, the RSV2CE largely follows the text of the New Vulgate throughout this chapter.

24:1–7 A reflection on Lady Wisdom's divine origin and omnipresence in creation.

24:1 praise herself: Personified Lady Wisdom is about to utter a long discourse praising her own excellence (24:3–22). **honored in God:** A Latin addition, not in the Greek text. **her people:** The people of Israel, with whom she primarily dwells.

24:2 assembly of the Most High: The angelic hosts in heaven (Ps 82:1). **open her mouth:** Metaphorically, in order to speak the word of God (Prov 8:6–8). **she is blessed, saying:** The rest of the verse, further describing the praise wisdom receives from her "audience," is an addition from the Latin Vulgate.

24:3 I came forth: Lady Wisdom speaks in the first person (Prov 8:4–36). **from the mouth:** Wisdom's origin suggests that she is closely associated with God's word spoken at creation (Is 45:23; 48:3; 55:11; Prov 2:6; Wis 7:25). **the first-born ... in the heavens:** From the Latin Vulgate. **first-born before all creatures:** For Ben Sira, Wisdom existed before the founding of the world; nevertheless, she is still described as (in some sense) a created being (24:8, 10). **I ordained ... unfailing light:** Underlines wisdom's role in the creation of light. **covered the earth like a mist:** Highlights wisdom's role on the first day of creation (Gen 2:6; Prov 8:27), perhaps indicating an association with the Spirit of God who "hovered" over the waters at creation (Gen 1:2). Wisdom is associated with the Spirit also in Wis 1:6–7; 9:17.

24:4 I dwelt in high places: In heaven. **a pillar of cloud:** Wisdom is identified with God's presence leading the Israelites out of Egypt and through the desert (Ex 13:21–22; 14:19; Wis 10:17).

24:5 the vault of heaven: The firmament, by which God separated the heavens from the earth on the second day of creation (Gen 1:6–8). Wisdom has circled the heavenly realms above (43:12; Job 22:14) as well as the watery **abyss** below (called "the deep" Gen 1:3). She is present in every realm of creation—heaven, earth, and below the earth (Prov 8:27–28).

24:6 the sea ... earth: Recalls the separation of the waters from the dry land on the third day of creation (Gen 1:9–10). **every people:** Wisdom is present among all nations. The human race is traced back to the sixth day of creation (Gen 1:26–31).

24:7 I sought a resting place: Although Lady Wisdom was present with God before creation, she longs to dwell in the midst of a historical people. The following verses thus describe how she leaves her heavenly abode to make her home in Israel. See note on Prov 8:22–31.

24:8 gave me a commandment: Lady Wisdom always acts in perfect conformity with God's will. Although she is God's Wisdom, the hymn portrays her as distinct from God. **created me:** See also 1:4. **my tent:** Or "tabernacle" (24:10). **Make your dwelling:** Or "Pitch your tabernacle" (Jn 1:14). **in Israel:** Wisdom will dwell among the people of Israel. **among my chosen ... roots:** From the Latin Vulgate. It reinforces Israel's status as God's chosen people.

24:9 From eternity: I.e., since before the foundation of the world. **he created me:** Wisdom proceeds from God, the Origin of all things. **I shall not cease to exist:** Wisdom will have no end.

24:10 the holy tabernacle: Wisdom dwelt in the Tabernacle that accompanied Israel on its journey through the wilderness. This was the place where God met with his people (Ex 25:8–9; 33:9–10; 40:34). **I ministered before him:** Wisdom performed a liturgical ministry before the Lord. The Tabernacle was an earthly representation of the heavenly sanctuary (Ex 25:8–9; Wis 9:8). **in Zion:** In Jerusalem (2 Sam 5:7), where Solomon built a Temple as the new seat of God's presence that replaced the Tabernacle (1 Kings 8:1–11). Wisdom was thus present with Israel at the time of the Exodus and in the days of the kings.

24:11 beloved city: Jerusalem (Ps 87:2; 132:14). **my dominion:** My power or authority.

ᶻ Other authorities add ²⁸*It is a great honor to follow God, and to be received by him is long life.*
ᵃ Or *will glorify herself in the midst of the people.*

¹²So I took root in an honored people,
  in the portion of the Lord, who is their inheritance,
  and my abode was in the full assembly of the
    saints.

¹³"I grew tall like a cedar in Lebanon,
  and like a cypress on the heights of Hermon.

¹⁴I grew tall like a palm tree in En-ge′di,ᵇ
  and like rose plants in Jericho;
  like a beautiful olive tree in the field,
    and like a plane tree I grew tall.
¹⁵Like cassia and camel's thorn I gave forth the
    aroma of spices,
  and like choice myrrh I spread a pleasant odor,

24:12 So I took root: Anticipates the analogy of trees and plants beginning in the next verse. **an honored people:** Israel. **portion of the Lord:** Another expression for Israel (17:17; Deut 32:9). **and my abode ... saints:** From the Latin Vulgate.

24:13-18 Describes Lady Wisdom growing out of her "root" in Israel, using imagery of lush vegetation and spices that evoke the Song of Solomon, the Garden of Eden, the Temple liturgy, and prophetic promises of future blessings upon the land of Israel. Wisdom invites Israel to a nuptial encounter with her, restoring her people to the lost paradise by means of the Temple liturgy, which also anticipates the idyllic messianic age.

24:13 cedar in Lebanon: A majestic tree that provides strong, durable wood and grows predominantly in Lebanon, north of Israel (Ps 92:12). **cypress:** A large evergreen tree, also known as pine or fir tree. • Cedars and cypresses are often mentioned in the Song of Solomon, as are Lebanon and Hermon (Song 1:17; 3:9; 4:8, 11; 5:15). Ezekiel associates both trees with the Garden of Eden (Ezek 31:8). Both types of wood were used in the construction of the Temple (1 Kings 5:6-10; 6:15-36), and both are characteristic of the messianic age described by the Prophets (Is 14:8; 41:19; 60:13; Hos 14:5-7). **Hermon:** A tall mountain northeast of Israel.

24:14 palm tree: A symbol of peace and prosperity. In the Song of Solomon, the stature of the beloved is like a palm tree (Song 7:8-9). Palm trees decorate the doors of Solomon's Temple (1 Kings 6:29-35) as well as Ezekiel's eschatological temple (Ezek 40:16-37; 41:18-20). **in En-gedi:** An oasis on the western shore of the Dead Sea, also featured in the Song of Songs (Song 1:14). **rose plants:** Flowers (roses or lilies) are prevalent in the Song of Songs (Song 2:1-2, 12, 16; 4:5; 5:13; 6:2-3), in the Tabernacle and Temple furnishings (Ex 25:31-34; 1 Kings 7:19, 22, 26), and in the future messianic age (Is 61:11; Hos 14:5). **Jericho:** In the southern Jordan valley west of the Jordan River. **olive tree:** Widely grown in Israel. Olive oil was used for the lamp in the sanctuary (Ex 27:20) and for the anointing oil (Ex 30:24); it was also offered with sacrifices (Ex 29:2, 40; Lev 2:1-7). The cherubim and doors of the sanctuary were made of olive wood (1 Kings 6:23, 31-33). Olive trees will also be present in the messianic age (Is 41:19; Hos 14:6). According to Ezekiel, **plane trees** were found in the Garden of Eden (Ezek 31:8).

24:15 cassia: Or cinnamon. **camel's thorn:** Or calamus. Both were used to make the anointing oil of the tabernacle, together with **spices** and **myrrh** (Ex 30:23, 34), which are also predominant in nuptial contexts (Ps 45:8; Prov 7:17; Song 1:3, 13; 3:6; 4:6, 13-14; 5:1, 5, 13; 6:2; 8:14). **galbanum, onycha, and stacte** are the ingredients used to make incense for the Tabernacle (Ex 30:34), together with **frankincense**—also featured in the Song of Solomon (Song 3:6; 4:6, 14). Wisdom thus plays a liturgical and priestly role by means of her presence in the Tabernacle worship.

ᵇOther authorities read *on the beaches.*

Nuptial Union with Lady Wisdom through Salvation History

The Bible often portrays the pursuit of wisdom as a romantic courtship and nuptial mystery. Wisdom is personified as a woman who invites men to pursue her (Prov 8:32-36), embrace and love her (Prov 4:6, 8; 8:17; Wis 7:10), dine with her (Prov 9:1-6), and even marry her (Wis 8:2, 9). Ben Sira likewise depicts Lady Wisdom as a welcoming wife and mother. Wise men should love her (Sir 4:11-14), pursue her (Sir 14:22-23), and encamp near her house (Sir 14:24-27). Communion with her is described in terms of sharing a meal with her (Sir 15:1-3; 24:19-21). The heart of Sirach's nuptial symbolism is found in Lady Wisdom's hymn of praise in chapter 24, where she invites the wise to be joined to her. The nuptial nature of this union is underscored by a rich imagery borrowed from the Song of Songs, including trees, plants, and flowers (Sir 24:13-14; Song 1:17; 2:1-2; 5:15; 6:2-3; 7:8-9), spices and frankincense (Sir 24:15; Song 1:13; 3:6; 4:6, 13-14; 5:1), feasting on honey and honeycomb (Sir 24:20; Song 5:1), and streams of water (Sir 24:25-27, 30-31; Song 4:12, 15). At the same time, the imagery of Sirach 24 evokes specific moments in salvation history, implying that Lady Wisdom ceaselessly courts men throughout history.

First, Ben Sira situates wisdom at the origin of creation (Sir 24:3-6; Gen 1) and in the Garden of Eden. The same imagery that evokes the Song of Songs also alludes to Eden and its lush vegetation, rivers (Gen 2:8-14; Ezek 31:8), and even spices and fragrances according to some Second Temple Jewish texts (*Jubilees* 3, 27-28; *Apocalypse of Moses* 29, 3-6). This means that Eden was Wisdom's primordial sanctuary and dwelling, and she was originally given to be "married" to all mankind through Adam and Eve. But she was lost when they ate from the forbidden tree, which promised them a counterfeit wisdom regarding good and evil (Gen 3:5-6, 22) but ultimately brought death (Gen 3:19).

Second, Sirach identifies wisdom with the Torah, the Law that God gave to Israel (19:20; 24:23; Ex 19-24; Bar 4:1). This identification makes sense, because observing the commandments of the Torah and living according to wisdom are both described as remedies to the Fall, sources of life, and the way back to Eden (Deut 4:1; 5:33; 30:19-20; Prov 3:1-2, 16-18, 22; 8:35; Sir 1:18; 4:12). For Ben Sira, the wisdom that was present at creation and lost when Adam sinned was restored when God gave the Torah to Israel. It is significant that Jewish tradition views the Sinai revelation, which was sealed with covenantal feasting (Ex 24:9-11), as God's betrothal to Israel and the Torah as the marriage covenant between the two parties:

like galbanum, onycha, and stacte,
and like the fragrance of frankincense in the
tabernacle.

¹⁶Like a terebinth I spread out my branches,
and my branches are glorious and graceful.

¹⁷Like a vine I caused loveliness to bud,
and my blossoms became glorious and
abundant fruit.ᶜ

¹⁹"Come to me, you who desire me,
and eat your fill of my produce.

²⁰For my teaching is sweeter than honey,
and my inheritance sweeter than the
honeycomb,
and my remembrance lasts throughout all
generations.

²¹Those who eat me will hunger for more,
and those who drink me will thirst for
more.

²²Whoever obeys me will not be put to shame,
and those who work with my help will not
sin."

24:16 terebinth: A large tree related to the oak (Josh 24:26; Judg 6:11). **glorious and graceful:** Such is wisdom, who invites men to return to the Garden of Eden by means of nuptial communion with her in the context of worship.

24:17 Like a vine: The fruit of the vine is often mentioned in nuptial settings (Song 1:6, 14; 6:11; 7:8, 12; 8:11–12). Wine was offered with sacrifices in Israel (Ex 29:40) and will be present in the messianic age (Hos 14:7). **blossoms:** On flower imagery, see 24:14. **glorious and abundant fruit:** On wisdom's fruit, see Prov 8:19. Contrast with the fruit of the tree of knowledge, which was deceptively "a delight to the eyes, and ... the tree was to be desired to make one wise" (Gen 3:6).

24:19–22 Lady Wisdom invites her followers to her nuptial banquet.

 24:19 Come to me: Wisdom invites disciples to be joined to her and to dine with her (Prov 9:1–5; Mt

11:28–30). **you who desire me:** On desiring wisdom, see 1:26; Wis 6:13. **my produce:** Her "fruits" of life, riches, and honors (6:19; Prov 3:16; 8:18–19), as well as the attributes named in 24:18. Eating the fruit of wisdom may be an allusion to partaking of the fruit of the tree of life, in contrast to the fruit of the tree of knowledge, which brought death (Gen 2:9; 16–17).

24:20 sweeter than the honeycomb: God's words or commandments are often described as "sweeter than honey" (Ps 19:10; 119:103; Prov 16:24; 24:13–14). Honey is sometimes mentioned in a nuptial context (Song 4:11; 5:1; Prov 5:3). **and my remembrance ... all generations:** From the Latin Vulgate.

24:21 hunger ... thirst for more: Although Wisdom satiates, "eating" and "drinking" her increases the desire for her even more. Compare Jn 4:14; 6:35.

24:22 shame ... sin: Themes of life, obedience, and work, together with the absence of shame and sin, contrast with eating the fruit of knowledge in Eden, where disobedience and seeking wisdom in the wrong way brought sin, shame, and death into the world (15:4; 51:18, 29; Gen 2:15, 25; 3:6–7; Prov 8:35–36).

ᶜOther authorities add ¹⁸*I am the mother of beautiful love, of fear, of knowledge, and of holy hope; being eternal, I therefore am given to all my children, to those who are named by him.*

"The Lord came from Sinai to receive Israel as a bridegroom comes forth to meet the bride" (*Mekhilta de-Rabbi Ishmael*, Tractate Baḥodesh 3).

Third, Ben Sira situates Wisdom in Israel's sanctuary. Although God restored Wisdom to Israel by giving it the Torah, Lady Wisdom still needed a "place" to dwell after the people departed from Sinai. This dwelling was the Tabernacle and its successor, the Jerusalem Temple. That the sanctuary is the privileged "home" of Wisdom where she "ministered" is evident not only from the explicit statement in Sir 24:10, but also from the imagery of cedars, cypress, palm trees, and flowers—all prominent in the Temple (1 Kings 5–7)—and the spices and fragrances that were used for the anointing oil and incense in the Tabernacle's liturgical ministry (Ex 30:23, 34). Thus, the Temple—like Sinai, a place of covenantal feasting (Lev 7:11–17)—is the place of Wisdom's indwelling where the Sinai revelation is recalled, commemorated, and made present to successive generations in Israel's history. Rabbinic literature also views the Temple as the bridal chamber where God enters into nuptial communion with Israel. According to one tradition, the cherubim in the Holy of Holies embraced each other as a figurative representation of the love between God and Israel (Babylonian Talmud, *Yoma* 54a).

Finally, the imagery in Sir 24 evokes the eschatological vision of the messianic age as depicted by the prophets. Cedars, cypress, palm trees, vines, and flowers irrigated by abundant streams of water are all signs of the idyllic day when the Lord will turn the wilderness into a new Eden (Is 14:8; 35:1–2, 6–7; 41:18–19; 51:3; 55:13; 60:13; Ezek 41:18–20, 25–26; Hos 14:5–9). The rivers and lush vegetation of Sir 24 also recall the life-giving water that will flow out of the eschatological Temple (Ezek 47:1–12; Joel 3:18; Zech 14:8–9). Moreover, the messianic age will be a time of covenantal feasting (Is 25:6; 55:1–3; Jer 31:12), and, according to the Book of Revelation, it will be the consummation of the great marriage between God and his people (Rev 19:7–9; 21:2–3) and the return of humanity to the tree of life (Rev 21:1–2).

In short, the rich imagery in Sir 24 tells the story of Lady Wisdom's romance with Israel and the world throughout salvation history: It describes her initial presence at creation and in the Garden of Eden, her restoration in the Torah, and her indwelling in the Temple's liturgy, which makes the Sinai revelation present for every generation and anticipates her final revelation to the world at the end of times.

²³All this is the book of the covenant of the Most
    High God,
    the law which Moses commanded us
    as an inheritance for the congregations of
    Jacob.ᵈ
²⁵It fills men with wisdom, like the Pi'shon,
    and like the Tigris at the time of the first
    fruits.
²⁶It makes them full of understanding, like the
    Euphrates,
    and like the Jordan at harvest time.
²⁷It makes instruction shine forth like light,
    like the Gi'hon at the time of vintage.
²⁸Just as the first man did not know her perfectly,
    the last one has not fathomed her;
²⁹for her thought is more abundant than the sea,
    and her counsel deeper than the great abyss.

³⁰I went forth like a canal from a river
    and like a water channel into a garden.
³¹I said, "I will water my orchard
    and drench my garden plot";
    and behold, my canal became a river,
    and my river became a sea.

³²I will again make instruction shine forth like the
    dawn,
    and I will make it shine afar;
³³I will again pour out teaching like prophecy,
    and leave it to all future generations.
³⁴Observe that I have not labored for myself
    alone,
    but for all who seek instruction. ᵉ

The Good and the Evil in Daily Life

25 My soul takes pleasure in three things,
    and they are beautiful in the sight of the
    Lord and of men:ᶠ
agreement between brothers, friendship between
    neighbors,
    and a wife and husband who live in harmony.
²My soul hates three kinds of men,
    and I am greatly offended at their life:
a beggar who is proud, a rich man who is a liar,
    and an adulterous old man who lacks good
    sense.

³You have gathered nothing in your youth;
    how then can you find anything in your old
    age?

24:23–29 The Torah is a privileged repository of divine wisdom. This wisdom is a gift from God and a source of life for Israel.

24:23 All this: All that wisdom has described in 24:3–22. What follows is spoken by Ben Sira rather than Lady Wisdom. **the book of the covenant:** Explicitly identifies wisdom with the Torah that God revealed to Moses (9:15; 17:11; 19:20; Ex 24:7–8; Bar 4:1). Since wisdom predates the world (1:4), and wisdom made her home in Israel in the Torah, rabbinic Judaism inferred that the Torah existed before creation (e.g., *Genesis Rabbah* 8). **for ... Jacob:** The Law is Israel's divinely given heritage (Deut 33:4).

24:25–27 The wisdom of the Torah is a source of life comparable to the waters of the Jordan and even to the four rivers that flowed from the Garden of Eden: the Pishon, Tigris, Euphrates, and Gihon (Gen 2:10–14). This may imply that wisdom was present in Eden long before making her abode in Israel. Wisdom is elsewhere compared to a fountain or stream (Prov 16:22; 18:4; Bar 3:12).

24:25 the Tigris: Flows the length of modern Iraq into the Persian Gulf.

24:26 the Euphrates: Rises in Turkey, flows across Syria and Iraq, until it joins with the Tigris. **the Jordan:** Flows through the Jordan Valley in the east of Israel.

24:27 makes instruction shine forth like light: Or "pours forth instruction like the Nile". For the image of the Torah as light, see note on 24:32.

24:28 the first man: Despite the presence of wisdom in Eden, symbolized by the four rivers, Adam did not fully know her. **the last one:** This hypothetical "last man" serves to indicate that no human being will ever be able to fathom her.

24:30–34 Ben Sira describes his vocation to be a teacher of wisdom.

24:30 a canal: Ben Sira channels a small quantity of water from the mighty river of God's wisdom. **into a garden:** By transmitting wisdom, he becomes a source of life and fruitfulness to others.

24:31 canal ... river ... sea: The ever-widening current alludes to the waters that flow out of Ezekiel's eschatological temple, becoming a source of life in the wilderness and producing trees that will bear miraculous fruit (Ezek 47:1–12; Joel 3:18).

24:32 shine forth like the dawn: On the Torah as a shining light to Israel and the nations, see Ps 119:105; Is 2:5; Wis 18:4.

24:33 like prophecy: Ben Sira considers his own mission a prophetic one.

25:1–12 Those who deserve praise or blame are identified. The section includes numerical proverbs: three beautiful things (25:1), contrasted with three detestable things (25:2), and Ben Sira's "ten beatitudes" (25:7–11).

25:1 My soul: A poetic way of saying "I". **brothers ... neighbors ... wife and husband:** One fruit of wisdom is concord and peace in the basic relational units of society (Ps 133).

25:2 three kinds of men: In contrast to the three good things of 25:1. **beggar ... proud:** Pride is always bad (10:7–18), but especially among those who have nothing to boast about. **rich man ... liar:** Lying is always sinful (20:24–26), but especially among those with few material needs and no reason to be dishonest. **adulterous old man:** Adultery is always evil (Ex 20:14), but especially among those who are expected to know better and to be models of wisdom and virtue (25:4–6).

25:3 You have gathered nothing: Refers, not to material goods, but to wisdom, which should be acquired while one is still young. **old age:** If a man neglects to pursue wisdom throughout his life, it will be too late to do so when he is old. • Just as the young are not all fully formed in knowledge and good behavior, so the elderly are not all perfect or exemplary in the same degree. The wealth of the old should be measured, not by gray hair, but by their diligence in youth and the rewards they enjoy from past labors (St. John Cassian, *Conferences* 1, 2, 13).

ᵈOther authorities add ²⁴*"Do not cease to be strong in the Lord, cleave to him so that he may strengthen you; the Lord Almighty alone is God, and besides him there is no savior."*
ᵉGk *it.*
ᶠSyr Vg: Gk *In three things I was beautified and I stood in beauty before the Lord and men.*

⁴What an attractive thing is judgment in gray-
haired men,
and for the aged to possess good counsel!
⁵How attractive is wisdom in the aged,
and understanding and counsel in honorable
men!
⁶Rich experience is the crown of the aged,
and their boast is the fear of the Lord.
⁷With nine thoughts I have gladdened my heart,
and a tenth I shall tell with my tongue:
a man rejoicing in his children;
a man who lives to see the downfall of his foes;
⁸happy is he who lives with an intelligent wife,
and he who has not made a slip with his
tongue,
and he who has not served a man inferior to
himself;
⁹happy is he who has gained good sense,
and he who speaks to attentive listeners.
¹⁰How great is he who has gained wisdom!
But there is no one superior to him who fears
the Lord.
¹¹The fear of the Lord surpasses everything;
to whom shall be likened the one who holds it
fast?ᵍ

¹³Any wound, but not a wound of the heart!
Any wickedness, but not the wickedness of a
wife!

¹⁴Any attack, but not an attack from those who hate!
And any vengeance, but not the vengeance of
enemies!
¹⁵There is no venomʰ worse than a snake's
venom,ʰ
and no wrath worse than an enemy's wrath.
¹⁶I would rather dwell with a lion and a dragon
than dwell with an evil wife.
¹⁷The wickedness of a wife changes her appearance,
and darkens her face like that of a bear.
¹⁸Her husband takes his meals among the
neighbors,
and he cannot help sighingⁱ bitterly.
¹⁹Any iniquity is insignificant compared to a wife's
iniquity;
may a sinner's lot befall her!
²⁰A sandy ascent for the feet of the aged—
such is a garrulous wife for a quiet husband.
²¹Do not be ensnared by a woman's beauty,
and do not desire a woman for her
possessions.ʲ
²²There is wrath and impudence and great disgrace
when a wife supports her husband.
²³A dejected mind, a gloomy face,
and a wounded heart are caused by an evil
wife.
Drooping hands and weak knees
are caused by the wife who does not make her
husband happy.

25:4–6 Qualities that the aged who have lived well and sought wisdom throughout their lives should possess (Wis 4:9; Is 11:2).

25:7 nine thoughts: The beginning of a numerical proverb that extends to 25:11. **gladdened my heart:** These reasons for the wise man to rejoice have been referred to as "Ben Sira's ten beatitudes" (cf. Mt 5:3–11). **a man rejoicing in his children:** He rejoices because they have lived to adulthood and turned out well. **the downfall of his foes:** A common sentiment in the Old Testament (Ps 54:7; 92:11).

25:8 intelligent wife: Finding a good wife is closely related to finding wisdom (Prov 18:22; 31:10–31). The topic is developed in 26:1–4. The Hebrew and Syriac add here: "and the one who does not plow with ox and ass together"— referring to a well-matched husband and wife. **a slip with his tongue:** See 14:1; 20:18; Jas 3:2. **served a man inferior to himself:** Probably refers to serving a man from a lower social class—an embarrassment in the ancient world.

25:9 good sense: The Vulgate and New Vulgate have instead: "a true friend". **who speaks to attentive listeners:** One who commands respect so that others listen to him closely.

25:10 he who has gained wisdom: The next-to-last item of the numerical proverb appears to be the goal of every seeker of wisdom, and yet it is surpassed by the last. **him who fears the Lord:** Fear of the Lord is the prerequisite for acquiring wisdom (1:14) as well as wisdom's crown and full measure (1:16, 18). Hence, one who fears the Lord is considered superior to one who has wisdom—even if the two qualities are inseparable.

25:11 to whom ...?: Implies the answer: "No one is greater than one who fears the Lord."

25:13—26:27 Ben Sira's counsel on women. If this controversial section can appear misogynistic to modern readers, the author's harsh critique of "bad wives" (25:13–26; 26:5–12) must be considered **(1)** as a product of ancient patriarchal society and **(2)** in light of the words of praise he extends to "good wives" (26:1–4, 13–18).

25:13 wound of the heart: A painful, emotional wound. **wickedness of a wife:** Ben Sira is not calling every wife (or woman) wicked (see 26:1–4) but saying that bad things done by a woman to harm a man (or, worse, by a wife to her husband) are particularly injurious.

25:14 enemies: Perhaps rival wives feuding against each other. Polygamy may still have been practiced in Ben Sira's day (26:6; 37:11).

25:16 lion ... dragon: Advises avoiding a hateful woman at all costs (Prov 21:19; 25:24).

25:17 bear: Known for its ferocity (47:3; 1 Sam 17:34–37; 2 Sam 17:8).

25:19 a wife's iniquity: Conjugal injuries can be the most painful of all.

25:20 A sandy ascent: As difficult as it is for an elderly man to climb up a sandy hill, so is it difficult for a quiet husband to endure an excessively talkative or gossipy wife.

25:21 for her possessions: A man should pursue a woman, not for her appearance or wealth, but for her strength of character and godliness (Prov 31:30).

25:22 a wife supports her husband: Financially, as when a man marries a woman for her possessions and lives off her wealth.

25:23 dejected ... gloomy ... Drooping ... weak: The physical signs of discouragement and depression that affect the husband of an evil wife.

ᵍ Other authorities add ¹²*The fear of the Lord is the beginning of love for him, and faith is the beginning of clinging to him.*
ʰ Cn: Gk *head.*
ⁱ Other authorities read *and listening he sighs.*
ʲ Heb Syr: Some Greek authorities read *for her beauty.*

²⁴From a woman sin had its beginning,
  and because of her we all die.
²⁵Allow no outlet to water,
  and no boldness of speech in an evil wife.
²⁶If she does not go as you direct,
  separate her from yourself.

26

Happy is the husband of a good wife;
  the number of his days will be doubled.
²A loyal wife rejoices her husband,
  and he will complete his years in peace.
³A good wife is a great blessing;
  she will be granted among the blessings of the
    man who fears the Lord.
⁴Whether rich or poor, his heart is glad,
  and at all times his face is cheerful.

⁵Of three things my heart is afraid,
  and of a fourth I am frightened:ᵏ
  The slander of a city, the gathering of a mob,
    and false accusation—all these are worse than
    death.
⁶There is grief of heart and sorrow when a wife
    is envious of a rival,
  and a tongue-lashing makes it known to
    all.

⁷An evil wife is an ox yoke which chafes;
  taking hold of her is like grasping a scorpion.
⁸There is great anger when a wife is drunken;
  she will not hide her shame.
⁹A wife's harlotry shows in her lustful eyes,
  and she is known by her eyelids.
¹⁰Keep strict watch over a headstrong daughter,
  lest, when she finds liberty, she use it to her hurt.
¹¹Be on guard against her impudent eye,
  and do not wonder if she sins against you.
¹²As a thirsty wayfarer opens his mouth
    and drinks from any water near him,
  so will she sit in front of every post
    and open her quiver to the arrow.

¹³A wife's charm delights her husband,
  and her skill puts fat on his bones.
¹⁴A sensible and silent wife is a gift of the Lord,
  and there is nothing so precious as a
    disciplined soul.
¹⁵A modest wife adds charm to charm,
  and no balance can weigh the value of a chaste
    soul.
¹⁶Like the sun rising in the heights of the Lord,
  so is the beauty of a good wife in her well-
    ordered home.

25:24 sin had its beginning: A reference to Eve's fall in the Garden of Eden, which led to the fall of Adam as well (Gen 3:6; 2 Cor 11:3; 1 Tim 2:14). **because of her we all die:** Eve is declared responsible for death's entrance into human history, although other texts of Scripture underscore Adam's culpability (Rom 5:12; 1 Cor 15:22).

25:25 no boldness of speech: As a water jar or cistern should not leak, so a man should not allow an evil wife to say anything she wants.

25:26 separate her from yourself: Literally, "cut her away from your flesh." This is probably a reference to divorce, which was permitted under the Mosaic covenant (Deut 24:1–4) but no longer under the New Covenant (Mk 10:2–12), which reverts to the high standard of lifelong monogamy established at creation (Gen 2:24).

26:1 a good wife: A faithful and godly wife (Prov 12:4; 31:10–12). **his days will be doubled:** A hyperbole saying that happily married men tend to live longer—a fact confirmed by modern studies.

26:2 A loyal wife: The same expression (in Hebrew) is used in Prov 31:10 to describe the "virtuous" or "excellent" wife. **his years in peace:** Describes a long, successful, and well-lived life (Prov 3:2, 16–17; Ps 128:1–6).

26:3 man who fears the Lord: Since a good wife is a blessing from God, the key to finding one is to fear the Lord (26:23; Prov 18:22; 19:14).

26:4 glad ... cheerful: Wealth is far less important than a happy marriage. Contrast with the countenance of the miserable man who pursued an evil woman for her wealth (25:21–23).

26:5 three things ... fourth: A numerical proverb. Ben Sira resumes here his critique of the wicked wife. **slander ... false accusation:** The spreading of malicious rumors leading to false charges and corrupt judicial proceedings. These are a prelude to the fourth situation.

26:6 wife: Or "woman". **envious of a rival:** Possibly a reference to polygamy or to a more general jealousy between two women. See note on 25:14. **tongue-lashing:** Slander.

26:7 yoke which chafes: A constant irritation. **grasping a scorpion:** Trying to control an evil wife can be as deadly as a scorpion's sting.

26:8 anger when ... drunken: Because a drunken woman is more prone to shameless behavior.

26:9 lustful eyes: A woman's immorality is seen in her haughty eyes. **eyelids:** Possibly painted (Prov 6:25; Jer 4:30; Ezek 23:40).

26:10 a headstrong daughter: A daughter who is stubborn and wants to have her own way. On daughters, see 7:24–25; 42:9–11.

26:11 if she sins against you: Sexual immorality brings shame upon her family.

26:12 open her quiver to the arrow: A euphemism for a promiscuous daughter who is as eager for sexual intimacy with any man as a thirsty traveler is to drink from any fountain.

26:13 A wife's charm: Ben Sira returns to praising the gracious wife (26:1–4). **puts fat on his bones:** In the ancient world, being fat was a sign of health and prosperity (Deut 31:20; Neh 9:25). A good wife makes her husband healthy and content.

26:14 sensible and silent wife: One who speaks discreetly and not too much, in contrast to the garrulous wife (25:20). **a disciplined soul:** Implies that the wife is self-disciplined. On wisdom's discipline, see 6:18–22.

26:15 A modest wife: The Vulgate and New Vulgate read: "a holy and modest wife". **a chaste soul:** Self-controlled or disciplined.

26:16 the sun rising: The sun at its zenith, i.e., at noon (43:3). **her well-ordered home:** The word for "ordered" in Greek is *kosmos*, which means "world", "universe". The verse could thus be rendered: "A good wife in the cosmos of her home is as beautiful as the noonday sun in the Lord's heaven." Ben Sira likens the good wife's home to a beautiful, well-ordered microcosm. Compare the ministry of the high priest in 50:6–7.

ᵏ The Greek of this line is uncertain.

17Like the shining lamp on the holy lampstand,
  so is a beautiful face on a stately figure.
18Like pillars of gold on a base of silver,
  so are beautiful feet with a steadfast heart. **1**
28At two things my heart is grieved,
  and because of a third anger comes over me:
  a warrior in want through poverty,
  and intelligent men who are treated
    contemptuously;
  a man who turns back from righteousness to
    sin—
  the Lord will prepare him for the sword!

29A merchant can hardly keep from wrongdoing,
  and a tradesman will not be declared innocent
    of sin.

27 Many have committed sin for a trifle,**m**
  and whoever seeks to get rich will avert his
    eyes.
2As a stake is driven firmly into a fissure between
    stones,
  so sin is wedged in between selling and
    buying.

3If a man is not steadfast and zealous in the fear of
    the Lord,
  his house will be quickly overthrown.

4When a sieve is shaken, the refuse remains;
  so a man's filth remains in his thoughts.
5The kiln tests the potter's vessels;
  so the test of just men is in tribulation.
6The fruit discloses the cultivation of a tree;
  so the expression of a thought discloses the
    cultivation of a man's mind.
7Do not praise a man before you hear him speak,
  for this is the test of men.

8If you pursue justice, you will attain it
  and wear it as a glorious robe.
9Birds flock with their kind;
  so truth returns to those who practice it.
10A lion lies in wait for prey;
  so does sin for the workers of iniquity.

11The talk of the godly man is always wise,
  but the fool changes like the moon.

26:17 holy lampstand: The seven-branched menorah in the Temple (Ex 25:31–39; 1 Mac 4:49–50). **a beautiful face on a stately figure:** Ben Sira continues the liturgical analogy by comparing the beauty of the good wife with the splendor of the divine light shining in the sanctuary.

26:18 pillars of gold: Probably the pillars or posts in the Tabernacle and Temple (Song 3:10; 5:15; 1 Mac 1:22–23). **beautiful feet with a steadfast heart:** Or "steadfast heels". The sensible wife plays a role in "holding the world together". Jewish tradition also holds that the world is supported by the Torah, the services of the Temple, and acts of kindness (*Pirqe Avot* 1, 2).

26:28—27:21 Warnings against hazards that threaten personal integrity and friendships.

26:28 two things ... a third: A numerical proverb describing three situation reversals. **the sword:** A violent death awaits the righteous man who turns back to sinful ways.

26:29 wrongdoing: The very nature of commercial activities—where merchants and tradesmen are constantly seeking new opportunities to make a profit—renders them particularly vulnerable to temptations of dishonesty.

27:1 for a trifle: Or "for gain". **avert his eyes:** To avoid witnessing shady transactions (Prov 28:27).

27:2 selling and buying: Ben Sira sees sin as almost inevitable in business transactions.

27:3 steadfast and zealous: While conducting business. **his house will be quickly overthrown:** Wealth gained or used dishonestly will eventually be lost (Prov 12:7; 14:11).

27:4–7 A man's reasoning and conversation reflect his true worth.

27:4 sieve: Used to sift grain or corn. The meal passes through the mesh, while the straw and the dung of the oxen that threshed the grain are filtered out. **a man's filth:** The faults of a bad man cannot be "sieved out"; they become evident when he speaks.

27:5 kiln: As the quality of a potter's vessel is revealed when baked in a furnace (if improperly made, it will crack in the intense heat), so the quality of **just men** is manifest in the furnace of **tribulation**. This text follows the Latin Vulgate. The Greek text reads: "in his reasoning" or "in his conversation".

27:6 cultivation: As the fruit of a tree discloses how well it has been cultivated, so one's utterances reveal how one's **mind** (literally, "heart") has been formed (Mt 7:16–19).

27:8–10 The rewards and retribution for pursuing justice and iniquity.

27:8 pursue justice: Or "follow after righteousness" (Prov 15:9; 21:21; Zeph 2:3; Mt 6:33; Rom 9:30–32). **glorious robe:** An image of wearing wisdom like a majestic garment (6:31; Job 29:14; Is 59:17). Cf. the glorious robe of the high priest in 45:7–13 (Wis 18:24).

27:9 with their kind: Truth is likened to birds flocking with other birds of their own species. Those who seek truth or fidelity will find it.

27:10 lion: The negative counterpart of the birds. Those who insist on sinning will find sin hunting them down (21:2; Gen 4:7; 1 Pet 5:8).

27:11–15 Continues the theme of speech revealing a person's true nature.

27:11 changes like the moon: As the moon changes its appearance from night to night, so the talk of fools is inconsistent and unreliable.

---

1 Other authorities add verses 19–27:

  19*My son, keep sound the bloom of your youth,*
    and do not give your strength to strangers.
  20*Seek a fertile field within the whole plain,*
    and sow it with your own seed, trusting in your fine stock.
  21*So your offspring will survive*
    and, having confidence in their good descent, will grow great.
  22*A harlot is regarded as spittle,*
    and a married woman as a tower of death to her lovers.
  23*A godless wife is given as a portion to a lawless man,*
    but a pious wife is given to the man who fears the Lord.
  24*A shameless woman constantly acts disgracefully,*
    but a modest daughter will even be embarrassed before her husband.
  25*A headstrong wife is regarded as a dog,*
    but one who has a sense of shame will fear the Lord.
  26*A wife honoring her husband will seem wise to all,*
    but if she dishonors him in her pride she will be known to all as
      ungodly.
  Happy is the husband of a good wife;
    for the number of his years will be doubled.
  27*A loud-voiced and garrulous wife is regarded as a war trumpet for*
      putting the enemy to flight,
    and every person like this lives in the anarchy of war.
m One ancient authority reads *gain*.

¹²Among stupid people watch for a chance to leave,
  but among thoughtful people stay on.
¹³The talk of fools is offensive,
  and their laughter is wantonly sinful.
¹⁴The talk of men given to swearing makes one's
  hair stand on end,
  and their quarrels make a man stop his ears.
¹⁵The strife of the proud leads to bloodshed,
  and their abuse is grievous to hear.

¹⁶Whoever betrays secrets destroys confidence,
  and he will never find a congenial friend.
¹⁷Love your friend and keep faith with him;
  but if you betray his secrets, do not run after
  him.
¹⁸For as a man destroys his enemy,
  so you have destroyed the friendship of your
  neighbor.
¹⁹And as you allow a bird to escape from your hand,
  so you have let your neighbor go, and will not
  catch him again.
²⁰Do not go after him, for he is too far off,
  and has escaped like a gazelle from a snare.
²¹For a wound may be bandaged,
  and there is reconciliation after abuse,
  but whoever has betrayed secrets is without hope.

²²Whoever winks his eye plans evil deeds,
  and no one can keep him from them.

²³In your presence his mouth is all sweetness,
  and he admires your words;
  but later he will twist his speech
  and with your own words he will give offense.
²⁴I have hated many things, but none to be
  compared to him;
  even the Lord will hate him.
²⁵Whoever throws a stone straight up throws it on
  his own head;
  and a treacherous blow opens up wounds.
²⁶He who digs a pit will fall into it,
  and he who sets a snare will be caught in it.
²⁷If a man does evil, it will roll back upon him,
  and he will not know where it came from.
²⁸Mockery and abuse issue from the proud man,ⁿ
  but vengeance lies in wait for him like a lion.
²⁹Those who rejoice in the fall of the godly will be
  caught in a snare,
  and pain will consume them before their
  death.

³⁰Anger and wrath, these also are abominations,
  and the sinful man will possess them.

28 He that takes vengeance will suffer vengeance
  from the Lord,
  and he will firmly establish° his sins.
²Forgive your neighbor the wrong he has done,
  and then your sins will be pardoned when you
  pray.

27:12 a chance to leave: Escaping the company of fools is advised. **among thoughtful people stay on:** Time is not wasted in the company of the wise (6:36).

27:13 their laughter is wantonly sinful: Literally, "their laughter is an extravagance of sin" (cf. Prov 10:23).

27:14 given to swearing: Inevitably leads to unbearable strife that no sensible person should want to hear or see (23:11).

27:16–21 Warnings against betraying confidence, a topic Ben Sira touched upon in 22:22.

27:16 destroys confidence: Betraying secrets is a breach of trust that is very difficult to repair.

27:17 keep faith with him: Be loyal to him. **do not run after him:** To try to repair the broken friendship. Perhaps Ben Sira overstates the impossibility of reconciliation as a way of underlining his warning against personal betrayal.

27:19 will not catch him again: Expresses the irreversible effect of betraying a friend's secrets.

27:20 like a gazelle from a snare: Another metaphor expressing how the betrayed friend is irretrievably lost (Prov 6:5).

27:21 reconciliation: A friendship can be healed even after a quarrel when abusive words have been exchanged. **without hope:** Of seeing a betrayed friendship fully restored (22:19–22).

27:22–29 On insincerity and malice. Those who deceive and mislead others will reap the fruit of their own actions.

27:22 winks his eye: As a sign of duplicity (Prov 6:13; 10:10; 16:30; Ps 35:19). **no one can keep him from them:** I.e., from the evil deeds.

27:23 his mouth is all sweetness: The deceptive man appears friendly and speaks kind words to you (12:16).

admires your words: He *pretends* to agree with you. **twist his speech:** When you are no longer present, he will speak very differently. **he will give offense:** He will use your words against you.

27:24 none to be compared: Nothing is as hateful as a man who engages in duplicity and hypocrisy (Prov 6:16–17; 8:13).

27:25 a treacherous blow opens up wounds: The meaning of the Greek is unclear. The Latin reads: "A deceitful blow will wound the deceitful."

27:26 a pit ... a snare: The image of the wicked falling into the pit he has dug or the snare he has set is common in the OT (Ps 7:15; 9:15–16; Prov 26:27; Eccles 10:8).

27:27 it will roll back: See Prov 26:27.

27:28 Mockery and abuse issue from the proud man: Literally, "Mockery and abuse, of the proud", which could also mean "mockery and abuse are the lot of the proud" in the sense that they both issue from and return to them.

27:29 caught in a snare: A famous example of one whose evil deeds turned back on him is that of Haman in the Book of Esther (Esther 5:14; 7:9–10; 9:24–25).

27:30—28:7 On anger, vengeance, and forgiveness.

27:30 Anger and wrath: Rarely guided by sound reason. **the sinful man will possess them:** The Greek is stronger: the sinner "will hold on" or "will cling" to them.

28:1 vengeance: Does not belong to men but to God; he alone is able to enact perfect justice (Deut 32:35; Rom 12:19; Heb 10:30). **he will firmly establish his sins:** Other manuscripts have "he will keep a strict account" of his sins.

28:2 Forgive ... will be pardoned: Ben Sira anticipates a cornerstone of the gospel and Christian prayer (Mt 6:12, 14–15; 18:23–35; Mk 11:25; Jas 2:13). Jewish tradition makes the same point, that God forgives those who forgive others (e.g., Babylonian Talmud, *Rosh Hashanah* 17a).

ⁿOther authorities read *proud men.*
°Other authorities read *closely observe.*

³Does a man harbor anger against another,
 and yet seek for healing from the Lord?
⁴Does he have no mercy toward a man like himself,
 and yet pray for his own sins?
⁵If he himself, being flesh, maintains wrath,
 will he then seek forgiveness from God?
 Who will make expiation for his sins?
⁶Remember the end of your life, and cease from
   enmity,
 remember destruction and death, and be true
   to the commandments.
⁷Remember the commandments, and do not be
   angry with your neighbor;
 remember the covenant of the Most High, and
   overlook ignorance.

⁸Refrain from strife, and you will lessen sins;
 for a man given to anger will kindle strife,
⁹and a sinful man will disturb friends
 and inject enmity among those who are at
   peace.
¹⁰In proportion to the fuel for the fire, so will be the
   burning,
 and in proportion to the obstinacy of strife will
   be the burning;ᵖ
 in proportion to the strength of the man will be
   his anger,

and in proportion to his wealth he will
   heighten his wrath.
¹¹A hasty quarrel kindles fire,
 and urgent strife sheds blood.
¹²If you blow on a spark, it will glow;
 if you spit on it, it will be put out;
 and both come out of your mouth.

¹³Curse the whisperer and deceiver,
 for he has destroyed many who were at peace.
¹⁴Slanderᑫ has shaken many,
 and scattered them from nation to nation,
 and destroyed strong cities,
 and overturned the houses of great men.
¹⁵Slanderᑫ has driven away courageous women,
 and deprived them of the fruit of their toil.
¹⁶Whoever pays heed to slanderʳ will not find rest,
 nor will he settle down in peace.
¹⁷The blow of a whip raises a welt,
 but a blow of the tongue crushes the bones.
¹⁸Many have fallen by the edge of the sword,
 but not so many as have fallen because of the
   tongue.
¹⁹Happy is the man who is protected from it,
 who has not been exposed to its anger,
 who has not borne its yoke,
 and has not been bound with its chains;

28:3 harbor anger: Or "hold a grudge". **seek for healing:** Of injured feelings, as well as mercy and forgiveness.
28:4 no mercy toward a man: On extending mercy to others as a condition for obtaining mercy, see Mt 5:7. **pray for his own sins:** To obtain forgiveness.
28:5 being flesh: I.e., being a mortal human prone to evil (17:31; 1 Cor 15:50; Gal 5:19). **make expiation:** Or "make atonement", a common expression in the OT used to describe the forgiving effect of Levitical sacrifices (Lev 16:16-18, 32-34).
28:6 the end of your life: Literally, "your last things", i.e., your judgment and death, as a reminder that the Lord will render to each one according to his works (7:36; 11:26-28; 38:20).
28:7 commandments: Keeping them is the only thing of lasting value (Eccles 12:13; Mt 19:17). **the covenant:** The covenant that God formed with Israel at Mt. Sinai (11:20; 17:12; 24:23; 39:8; 42:2; Ex 24:7-8). **ignorance:** Here refers to the faults that others commit involuntarily or through lack of knowledge.
28:8-12 Warnings against quarreling.
28:8 Refrain from strife: Engaging in verbal disputes increases the occasions of sin. It is best to avoid them altogether. **a man given to anger:** A hot-tempered man (Prov 15:18; 26:21; 29:22).
28:9 disturb friends: I.e., disrupts peaceful relationships and causes strife. • The contentious are wicked because they sow discord among people who live in peace. Heretics and schismatics are chief among them; they defend their malicious sects and have no qualms about instigating arguments and scandals (Rabanus Maurus, *On Ecclesiasticus* 6, 8).

28:10 in proportion: Just as adding fuel increases the intensity of a fire, so more obstinacy increases the intensity of a quarrel (Prov 26:20; Jas 3:5). **strength ... wealth:** The more powerful and rich a man is, the more he will find reasons to get angry.
28:11 fire ... blood: A verbal argument that flares up suddenly can lead to violence.
28:12 blow on ... spit on: Words have the power to escalate a conflict as well as to extinguish it (Prov 15:1; Jas 3:9-10).
28:13-26 On the evils of slander and vicious talk (cf. Jas 3:1-12).
28:13 whisperer and deceiver: Or "gossiper and double-tongued" (5:9, 14; 19:4-17).
28:14 Slander: Literally, "a third tongue". This may refer to the tongue of the slanderer or, perhaps, to a meddler who interferes in the affairs of others. **destroyed strong cities:** Poetic exaggeration that illustrates how slander has destroyed the lives of many people, whether individuals, societies, or nations.
28:15 courageous women: Seems to indicate faithful women who were divorced by their husbands because of lies told about them (7:26).
28:16 Whoever pays heed: Listening to slander is not a morally neutral activity. It is a choice to give attention to one engaged in sinful speech and therefore involves a measure of participation in the sin.
28:17 a welt: A mark left on the body after whipping. **crushes the bones:** Malicious words can cause deeper wounds than a welt on the skin (Prov 15:4; 25:15).
28:19 the man who is protected: One whom God has shielded from the consequences of slander or from engaging in vicious talk. **its yoke ... its chains:** Slander enslaves the slanderer, the slandered, and those who believe the slander. Contrast this with the liberating "yoke" and "chains" of Wisdom (6:24-25, 29-30; 21:19).

ᵖOther authorities place this line at the end of the verse, or omit it.
ᑫGk a *third tongue.*
ʳGk *it.*

²⁰for its yoke is a yoke of iron,
  and its chains are chains of bronze;
²¹its death is an evil death,
  and Hades is preferable to it.
²²It will not be master over the godly,
  and they will not be burned in its flame.
²³Those who forsake the Lord will fall into its power;
  it will burn among them and will not be put
    out.
  It will be sent out against them like a lion;
    like a leopard it will mangle them.
²⁴See that you fence in your property with thorns,
  lock up your silver and gold,
²⁵make balances and scales for your words,
  and make a door and a bolt for your mouth.
²⁶Beware lest you err with your tongue,ˢ
  lest you fall before him who lies in wait.

On Lending and Borrowing, Home, and Hospitality

29 He that shows mercy will lend to his neighbor,
  and he that strengthens him with his hand
    keeps the commandments.
²Lend to your neighbor in the time of his need;
  and in turn, repay your neighbor promptly.
³Confirm your word and keep faith with him,
  and on every occasion you will find what you
    need.
⁴Many persons regard a loan as a windfall,
  and cause trouble to those who help them.

⁵A man will kiss another's hands until he gets a loan,
  and will lower his voice in speaking of his
    neighbor's money;
  but at the time for repayment he will delay,
    and will pay in words of unconcern,
    and will find fault with the time.
⁶If the lenderᵗ exerts pressure, he will hardly get
    back half,
  and will regard that as a windfall.
  If he does not, the borrowerᵘ has robbed him of
    his money,
    and he has needlessly made him his enemy;
  he will repay him with curses and reproaches,
    and instead of glory will repay him with
    dishonor.
⁷Because of such wickedness, therefore,ᵛ many
    have refused to lend;
  they have been afraid of being defrauded
    needlessly.

⁸Nevertheless, be patient with a man in humble
    circumstances,
  and do not make him wait for your alms.
⁹Help a poor man for the commandment's sake,
  and because of his need do not send him away
    empty.
¹⁰Lose your silver for the sake of a brother or a
    friend,
  and do not let it rust under a stone and be lost.

28:21 an evil death: Calumny causes not only the "death" of one's reputation but suffering, shame, and social stigma. **Hades:** The realm of the dead (14:16).

28:22 It will not be master over the godly: A surprising statement, for Ben Sira says in 28:13–15 that nearly everyone is eventually the target of slander. He means either that the godly are protected from the evil consequences of slander or that they will not engage in it. The exhortation in 28:24–26 seems to support the latter interpretation.

28:23 fall into its power: Those who slander will either suffer the consequences of it or they will destroy themselves and others by engaging in it. **burn among them:** Illustrates the uncontrollable nature of the lies spread by gossip and slander. **like a lion ... leopard:** Underlines the ferocity of words of slander running loose.

28:26 Beware lest you err: A final summary statement on the dangers of slipping with the tongue (14:1; 21:7; 25:8; Jas 3:2–5).

29:1–20 Counsel on assisting those in need by means of loans, alms, and surety.

29:1 shows mercy: Or "does kindness". **his neighbor:** His Jewish neighbor (Lev 19:18, contrast Lk 10:29–37). **he that strengthens him:** He that supports him, lends him a hand. **keeps the commandments:** The Torah requires Israelites to lend money without interest to fellow Israelites (Ex 22:25; Lev 25:35–37; Deut 15:7–11; Prov 19:16–17).

29:2 promptly: Literally, "on time", i.e., when the loan falls due (4:31; Ps 37:21).

29:3 Confirm your word: By keeping your promise to pay the loan back on time. **keep faith:** I.e., be honest (27:17). **find what you need:** If you repay your loans faithfully, you will obtain other loans in the future when needed.

29:4 windfall: Something that is theirs to keep. **cause trouble:** By not paying back the loan.

29:5 kiss another's hands: Feigning humble subjection to the lender. **words of unconcern:** Worthless excuses or empty promises. **fault with the time:** The borrower complains that the date for repayment is too soon.

29:6 windfall: The lender will count himself lucky if he gets even half of the loan back. **If he does not:** If the lender does not insist on getting repaid. **robbed him:** The lender will not get anything back. **enemy:** The lender has turned the borrower against him. **curses ... reproaches ... dishonor:** Perhaps suppressing a sense of shame and guilt, the borrower now shows hostility against the lender instead of returning the **glory** or gratitude due to him.

29:7 Because of such wickedness: Because of bad experiences with borrowers, many are reluctant to lend their money for fear of losing it altogether.

29:8 Nevertheless: Despite the dishonesty of unreliable borrowers, there are other ways of being generous with one's money. **your alms:** It is a religious obligation for God's people to help the needy (3:30–4:6; Prov 14:21, 31; 19:17; 21:13; 22:9).

29:9 the commandment's sake: Giving alms or lending to those in need is one of the precepts of the Torah (Deut 15:7–11).

29:10 Lose your silver: Give your money to someone in need. **do not let it rust:** Actually, "tarnish" in the case of silver (Mt 6:19; 25:18; Jas 5:3). **and be lost:** Or "wasted". It is more profitable to be generous with one's money than to hoard it.

ˢ Gk *with it.*
ᵗ Gk *he.*
ᵘ Gk *he.*
ᵛ Other authorities read *It is not because of wickedness that.*

¹¹Lay up your treasure according to the
　　commandments of the Most High,
　　　and it will profit you more than gold.
¹²Store up almsgiving in your treasury,
　　and it will rescue you from all affliction;
¹³more than a mighty shield and more than a heavy
　　　spear,
　　　it will fight on your behalf against your
　　　　enemy.

¹⁴A good man will be surety for his neighbor,
　　but a man who has lost his sense of shame will
　　　fail him.
¹⁵Do not forget all the kindness of your surety,
　　for he has given his life for you.
¹⁶A sinner will overthrow the prosperity of his
　　　surety,
¹⁷　and one who does not feel grateful will
　　　abandon his rescuer.
¹⁸Being surety has ruined many men who were
　　　prosperous,
　　and has shaken them like a wave of the sea;
　　it has driven men of power into exile,
　　and they have wandered among foreign
　　　nations.
¹⁹The sinner who has fallen into suretyship
　　and pursues gain will fall into lawsuits.

²⁰Assist your neighbor according to your ability,
　　but take heed to yourself lest you fall.

²¹The essentials for life are water and bread
　　and clothing and a house to cover one's
　　　nakedness.
²²Better is the life of a poor man under the shelter
　　　of his roof
　　　than sumptuous food in another man's
　　　　house.
²³Be content with little or much.ʷ
²⁴It is a miserable life to go from house to house,
　　and where you are a stranger you may not
　　　open your mouth;
²⁵you will play the host and provide drink without
　　　being thanked,
　　and besides this you will hear bitter words:
²⁶"Come here, stranger, prepare the table,
　　and if you have anything at hand, let me have
　　　it to eat."
²⁷"Give place, stranger, to an honored person;
　　my brother has come to stay with me; I need
　　　my house."
²⁸These things are hard to bear for a man who has
　　　feeling:
　　scolding about lodgingˣ and the reproach of
　　　the moneylender.

29:12 Store up almsgiving: Giving alms is likened to an "investment" in the "bank" of God's mercy (Prov 19:17; Mt 6:20; 19:21). **it will rescue you:** God will deliver a generous man from future distress; his almsgiving secures him divine favor (3:14–15, 30–31; 7:32; 12:2; Tob 1:3; 4:7–11; 14:9–11). • Many passages indicate the importance of showing mercy in order to cancel our sins. The Lord says, "Enter the kingdom because I was hungry and you gave me food." These will be saved, not because they remained sinless, but because they atoned for their sins with good works (St. Augustine, *Sermons* 389, 5).

29:13 it will fight: I.e., almsgiving will do battle for the generous giver.

29:14–20 The practice of "giving surety" consists of a third party guaranteeing to repay the loan of a borrower if he defaults on his obligation (29:4–6). Proverbs is wary of this practice; Ben Sira is more lenient toward it. See note on Prov 6:1.

29:14 lost his sense of shame: Either one who refuses to give surety to a borrower or a borrower who takes advantage of one giving surety.

29:15 your surety: Not the surety or collateral itself, but the person who provides it. **given his life:** Or "his soul"—an exaggeration to emphasize the financial risk being taken.

29:18 shaken them: Wealthy and powerful men whose surety was abused have suffered financial ruin, losing their homes and even being forced to look for work in foreign lands.

29:19 The sinner ... suretyship: The case of those who become surety for the evil purpose of taking advantage of borrowers by extorting money from them. **and pursues gain:** Perhaps dishonest guarantors became surety to exact interest from borrowers or take their clothes as collateral—two practices explicitly prohibited by the Torah (Ex 22:25; Deut 24:12–13).

29:20 Assist your neighbor: Despite the risks in the practice of surety, Ben Sira does not wholly condemn it. **take heed:** He urges all involved in the practice—lenders, borrowers, guarantors—to be cautious lest they suffer loss.

29:21–28 Counsel on living independently with dignity. In the ancient world, one could seek a better life by living in the household of a richer man, eating better food, and enjoying a more comfortable home, but at the cost of one's independence. Ben Sira prefers a more frugal life in one's own home rather than being dependent on others.

29:21 essentials: Life's basic necessities for survival. **to cover one's nakedness:** To provide privacy.

29:23 Be content: Be satisfied with what you have (Phil 4:11; 1 Tim 6:8; Heb 13:5).

29:24 not open your mouth: One dares not speak freely or openly while living as a sojourner in another's house.

29:25 you will play the host: I.e., you will act as a servant of the housemaster, welcoming guests and pouring drinks, yet without receiving any recognition for your service. **bitter words:** The humiliating words spoken in 29:26–27.

29:26 Come here, stranger: The condescending words spoken by guests to the sojourner. **prepare the table:** The sojourner is evidently treated as a servant.

29:27 Give place, stranger: The host speaks just as condescendingly to the sojourner. **I need my house:** The sojourner is only welcome until a more important guest arrives.

29:28 scolding about lodging and the reproach of the moneylender: A summary of the two topics treated in 29:1–27. A respectable person will find it difficult to be seen as one who defaults on his debts or lives at the expense of others.

ʷOther authorities add *and you will not hear reproach for your sojourning.*

ˣOr *from the household,* or (Syr) *from the host.*

Discipline of Children, Right Attitudes

30 He who loves his son will whip him often,
in order that he may rejoice at the way he
turns out.
[2]He who disciplines his son will profit by him,
and will boast of him among acquaintances.
[3]He who teaches his son will make his enemies
envious,
and will glory in him in the presence of friends.
[4]The[y] father may die, and yet he is not dead,
for he has left behind him one like himself;
[5]while alive he saw and rejoiced,
and when he died he was not grieved;
[6]he has left behind him an avenger against his
enemies,
and one to repay the kindness of his friends.

[7]He who spoils his son will bind up his wounds,
and his feelings will be troubled at every cry.
[8]A horse that is untamed turns out to be stubborn,
and a son unrestrained turns out to be wilful.
[9]Pamper a child, and he will frighten you;
play with him, and he will give you grief.
[10]Do not laugh with him, lest you have sorrow with
him,
and in the end you will gnash your teeth.

[11]Give him no authority in his youth,
and do not ignore his errors.
[12]Bow down his neck in his youth,[z]
and beat his sides while he is young,
lest he become stubborn and disobey you,
and you have sorrow of soul from him.[a]
[13]Discipline your son and take pains with him,
that you may not be offended by his
shamelessness.

[14]Better off is a poor man who is well and strong in
constitution
than a rich man who is severely afflicted in body.
[15]Health and soundness are better than all gold,
and a robust body than countless riches.
[16]There is no wealth better than health of body,
and there is no gladness above joy of heart.
[17]Death is better than a miserable life,
and eternal rest[b] than chronic sickness.

[18]Good things poured out upon a mouth that is
closed
are like offerings of food placed upon a grave.
[19]Of what use to an idol is an offering of fruit?
For it can neither eat nor smell.
So is he who is afflicted by the Lord;

30:1–13 Counsel on the education and training of children. It is assumed that a father should be a firm disciplinarian and that corporal punishment is a normal part of a child's education. Not all of these guidelines should be observed literally in a modern context.

30:1 whip him often: A good father will correct a child's misbehavior with a suitable form of corporal punishment (Prov 13:24; 23:13–14; 29:15). **that he may rejoice:** When the child becomes a respectable and responsible adult.

30:2–3 He who disciplines: By various forms of education and training (Prov 22:6; 29:17). **profit ... boast ... glory:** A father who trains his son well will benefit from him and be proud of him before his friends.

30:4 he is not dead: Or "it is as though he were not dead". **one like himself:** The father lives on in his son—thus the importance of raising him well.

30:6 against his enemies: Protecting the security and honor of one's family was a moral obligation for every male in ancient Israel (Ps 127:4–5).

30:7 He who spoils: The father who does not discipline his son will run into difficulties. **his wounds:** Possibly incurred through reckless play. **troubled:** A father should be strong enough not to be upset every time his son cries.

30:8 untamed ... unrestrained: As a horse remains wild until it is "broken", so a son remains rash and reckless until he is well disciplined.

30:9 he will frighten you: Meaning he will "surprise" you (in a bad way) or "alarm" you. **play with him:** Ben Sira is concerned that a father may lose his child's respect by excessive familiarity.

30:10 Do not laugh: By sharing in the child's frivolity. **lest you have sorrow:** Ben Sira advocates a measure of emotional

detachment between father and son. **gnash your teeth:** In a state of mental anxiety or turmoil (Mt 8:12; 13:42).

30:11 Give him no authority: Do not grant unrestrained freedom to a child.

30:12 Bow down his neck: In the sense of "make him obedient" (7:23). **beat his sides:** Using the analogy of a rider whipping his horse. **lest he become stubborn:** The Torah prescribed the death penalty for a stubborn and rebellious son (Deut 21:18–21)—although there is no record of this sentence ever being carried out.

30:13 take pains with him: The Hebrew reads: "make his yoke heavy"—by giving him lots of work to do.

30:15 a robust body than countless riches: The Hebrew reads: "a good spirit than pearls". The Hebrew version conveys the idea that not only bodily health but also a good attitude of mind is essential for happiness.

30:17 Death is better than a miserable life: Although even the righteous sometimes express a desire to die, they always entrust their life to God's will (Job 3:11; Eccles 4:1–2; Tob 3:6, 10, 13). They recognize, in other words, that God is the sovereign Lord of life and that men and women are stewards rather than owners of the life entrusted to them (CCC 2280). **eternal rest:** Death, which offers rest from the burdens of life. **chronic sickness:** The idea is developed in the following verses. • The Church calls for a special respect to be given to sick or handicapped persons (CCC 2276) and deems euthanasia morally unacceptable (CCC 2277). On the value of redemptive suffering, see note on 2:4.

30:18–20 Ben Sira compares the sick person to three things that cannot enjoy life: a grave, an idol, and a eunuch.

30:18 Good things: Good food. **a mouth that is closed:** Due to illness. **offerings of food placed upon a grave:** A person too sick to eat cannot enjoy good food any more than the dead can.

30:19 an offering of fruit: Offering food and drink to idols was common in Near Eastern religions but ridiculed in Israel (Deut 4:28; Ps 115:4–7; Is 57:6; Dan 14:1–22). **afflicted by the Lord:** Physical suffering is allowed within the scope of

---

[y] Gk *His.*
[z] Other authorities omit this line and the preceding line.
[a] Other authorities omit this line.
[b] Some authorities omit *eternal rest.*

²⁰he sees with his eyes and groans,
　like a eunuch who embraces a maiden and
　　groans.

²¹Do not give yourself over to sorrow,
　and do not afflict yourself deliberately.
²²Gladness of heart is the life of man,
　and the rejoicing of a man is length of days.
²³Delight your soul and comfort your heart,
　and remove sorrow far from you,
for sorrow has destroyed many,
　and there is no profit in it.
²⁴Jealousy and anger shorten life,
　and anxiety brings on old age too soon.
²⁵A man of cheerful and good heart
　will give heed to the food he eats.

Right Conduct

31 Wakefulness over wealth wastes away one's
　flesh,
　and anxiety about it removes sleep.
²Wakeful anxiety prevents slumber,
　and a severe illness carries off sleep.ᶜ
³The rich man toils as his wealth accumulates,
　and when he rests he fills himself with his
　　dainties.
⁴The poor man toils as his livelihood diminishes,
　and when he rests he becomes needy.

⁵He who loves gold will not be justified,
　and he who pursues money will be led astrayᵈ
　　by it.

⁶Many have come to ruin because of gold,
　and their destruction has met them face to
　　face.
⁷It is a stumbling block to those who are devoted
　to it,
　and every fool will be taken captive by it.

⁸Blessed is the rich man who is found
　blameless,
　and who does not go after gold.
⁹Who is he? And we will call him blessed,
　for he has done wonderful things among his
　　people.
¹⁰Who has been tested by it and been found
　perfect?
　Let it be for him a ground for boasting.
Who has had the power to transgress and did
　not transgress,
　and to do evil and did not do it?
¹¹His prosperity will be established,
　and the assembly will relate his acts of
　　charity.

¹²Are you seated at the table of a great man?ᵉ
　Do not be greedyᶠ at it,
　and do not say, "There is certainly much upon
　　it!"
¹³Remember that a greedyᵍ eye is a bad thing.
　What has been created more greedyᵍ than the
　　eye?
　Therefore it sheds tears from every face.

---

divine Providence, sometimes but not always as a punishment for sin.

30:20 a eunuch ... a maiden: A sick man unable to enjoy food is as frustrated as a castrated man unable to enjoy sexual intimacy.

30:21 over to sorrow: Ben Sira holds that chronic unhappiness is not an uncontrolled emotion but the result of a choice.

30:22 Gladness of heart: On the health benefits of cheerfulness, see Prov 17:22.

30:23 Delight your soul: Literally, "deceive your soul" (14:16). Just as one can choose to resist negative emotions, one can "trick oneself" and choose to embrace joy and happiness. **no profit in it:** Cf. Mt 6:34. Jewish tradition makes a similar point that tomorrow's sorrow is not worth worrying about, since one may not live to see tomorrow (Babylonian Talmud, *Yebamot* 63b).

30:24 Jealousy and anger shorten life: Confirmed by modern medicine and psychology.

30:25 give heed to the food: As long as health allows one to do so (Prov 15:15).

31:1-11 Although wealth is a blessing, it can also be hazardous to one's health.

31:1 Wakefulness over wealth: Insomnia due to anxiety or a bad conscience (40:5-8; Eccles 5:12). **wastes away one's flesh:** Causes wariness and harms one's health.

31:3-4 A typical situation of social inequality where the rich become richer and the poor become poorer.

31:5 will not be justified: A person driven by greed will not be able to avoid sinning (Prov 28:20; Eccles 5:10).

31:7 a stumbling block: Wealth easily becomes an idol. Those who pursue it are bound to trip over it and fall. **taken captive:** Enslaved by their own greed (Mt 6:24; Lk 16:9-13).

31:8 Blessed is the rich man: Because wealth can be perilous, Ben Sira praises those who have become rich without losing their integrity or succumbing to greed. **after gold:** The Hebrew reads: "after mammon".

31:9 Who is he?: Implies that a righteous rich man is hard to find (Mt 19:23-24; Mk 10:23-25). **wonderful things:** He has acquired wealth without committing sin.

31:10 Who ... found perfect?: The implied answer: "very few people".

31:11 His prosperity will be established: Ultimately, wealth is a blessing from God (Deut 30:5, 9). It is not money that is evil, but the "love of money" (1 Tim 6:10). The person who has acquired wealth honestly deserves to benefit from it. **acts of charity:** Assumes that the righteous rich man is also generous.

31:12—32:13 Guidelines on etiquette at banquets. Ben Sira advocates moderation in eating (31:12-24), drinking (31:25-31), and conversation (32:1-13).

31:12 at the table: For some banquet or festive occasion. **Do not be greedy:** Literally, "do not open your throat." It seems to encompass impatience at table as well as gluttony.

31:13 a greedy eye: Signifies gluttony in this context. **more greedy than the eye:** The eye covets many things and is thus a major cause of sin (14:9; 1 Jn 2:16). **it sheds tears:** Because it cannot have everything it wants.

ᶜ Other authorities read *sleep carries off a severe illness.*
ᵈ Heb Syr: Gk *will be filled.*
ᵉ Heb Syr: Gk *at a great table.*
ᶠ Gk *open your throat.*
ᵍ Gk *evil.*

¹⁴Do not reach out your hand for everything you
see,
and do not crowd your neighbor[h] at the dish.
¹⁵Judge your neighbor's feelings by your own,
and in every matter be thoughtful.
¹⁶Eat like a human being what is set before you,
and do not chew greedily, lest you be hated.
¹⁷Be the first to stop eating, for the sake of good
manners,
and do not be insatiable, lest you give offense.
¹⁸If you are seated among many persons,
do not reach out your hand before they do.

¹⁹How ample a little is for a well-disciplined man!
He does not breathe heavily upon his bed.
²⁰Healthy sleep depends on moderate eating;
he rises early, and feels fit.[i]
The distress of sleeplessness and of nausea
and colic are with the glutton.
²¹If you are overstuffed with food,
get up in the middle of the meal, and you will
have relief.
²²Listen to me, my son, and do not disregard me,
and in the end you will appreciate my words.
In all your work be industrious,
and no sickness will overtake you.

²³Men will praise the one who is liberal with food,
and their testimony to his excellence is
trustworthy.
²⁴The city will complain of the one who is miserly
with food,
and their testimony to his miserliness is accurate.

²⁵Do not aim to be valiant over wine,
for wine has destroyed many.

²⁶Fire and water prove[j] the temper of steel,
so wine tests hearts in the strife of the proud.
²⁷Wine is like life to men,
if you drink it in moderation.
What is life to a man who is without wine?
It has been created to make men glad.
²⁸Wine drunk in season and temperately
is rejoicing of heart and gladness of soul.
²⁹Wine drunk to excess is bitterness of soul,
with provocation and stumbling.
³⁰Drunkenness increases the anger of a fool to his
injury,
reducing his strength and adding wounds.

³¹Do not reprove your neighbor at a banquet of
wine,
and do not despise him in his merrymaking;
speak no word of reproach to him,
and do not afflict him by making demands of
him.

32 If they make you master of the feast, do not
exalt yourself;
be among them as one of them;
take good care of them and then be seated;
² when you have fulfilled your duties, take your
place,
that you may be merry on their account
and receive a wreath for your excellent
leadership.

³Speak, you who are older, for it is fitting that you
should,
but with accurate knowledge, and do not
interrupt the music.
⁴Where there is entertainment, do not pour out talk;
do not display your cleverness out of season.

31:14 Do not reach out your hand: Making a show of
greediness at the dinner table. **crowd your neighbor:** To reach
the dish and obtain the best portions.

31:15 be thoughtful: Of others and not just of yourself
(Mt 7:12).

31:16 Eat like a human being: I.e., not like an animal.

31:17-18 A well-mannered person should not be the first
one to start eating; he should also display moderation and be
the first one to stop.

31:19-20 A moderate person is satisfied with a small
quantity of food; he sleeps better and feels better than the
glutton (37:29-31; Prov 13:25).

31:21 get up in the middle of the meal: To vomit—not following the Roman custom to go vomit so that one could eat
more, but as an emergency action to find relief from overeating.

31:22 be industrious: The Hebrew reads: "be modest."

31:23-24 Commends generosity and condemns stinginess
regarding food.

31:24 their testimony: Those who are generous or miserly
in hosting others will inevitably create for themselves a reputation that will precede them (Prov 23:6-8).

31:25 valiant over wine: Do not try to prove your man-
hood by heavy drinking (Is 5:22). **wine has destroyed many:**
Scripture has many warnings against excessive drinking (Prov
20:1; 23:29-35; 31:4-5; Amos 6:6; Hos 7:5; Is 5:11-12;
28:1; Jud 13:2).

31:26 wine tests hearts: Alcohol brings out the true character of prideful people when they quarrel.

31:27 Wine is like life: Wine is a blessing to the temper-
ate. **created to make men glad:** Also indicated in Ps 104:15.

31:28-30 A contrast between the good of drinking
responsibly and the evil of drinking irresponsibly. • God
gave wine knowing that moderation brings health but that
gulping without restraint brings vice. To human freedom he
gave the choice between sobriety and drunkenness. But the
Lord also made wine a means of salvation, with the forgiveness
of sins deriving from it (St. Ambrose, *Hexameron* 5, 17, 72).

31:31 Do not reprove: Because this will spoil a joyful occasion. A banquet is not the proper time to preach morality and
make unreasonable demands of other guests.

32:1 master of the feast: A banquet manager who pre-
sides over the feast (2 Mac 2:27; Jn 2:8). **be among them:**
He should not act more important than his guests but should
modestly mix with them.

32:2 a wreath: A garland of flowers worn on the head of
honored guests (Wis 2:8; cf. Is 28:1).

---

[h] Gk *him.*
[i] Gk *his soul is with him.*
[j] Gk *The furnace by dipping proves.*

⁵A ruby seal in a setting of gold
  is a concert of music at a banquet of wine.
⁶A seal of emerald in a rich setting of gold
  is the melody of music with good wine.

⁷Speak, young man, if there is need of you,
  but no more than twice, and only if asked.
⁸Speak concisely, say much in few words;
  be as one who knows and yet holds his tongue.
⁹Among the great do not act as their equal;
  and when another is speaking, do not babble.

¹⁰Lightning speeds before the thunder,
  and approval precedes a modest man.
¹¹Leave in good time and do not be the last;
  go home quickly and do not linger.
¹²Amuse yourself there, and do what you have in
    mind,
  but do not sin through proud speech.
¹³And for these things bless him who made you
  and satisfies you with his good gifts.

¹⁴He who fears the Lord will accept his discipline,
  and those who rise early to seek him[k] will find
    favor.
¹⁵He who seeks the law will be filled with it,
  but the hypocrite will stumble at it.

¹⁶Those who fear the Lord will form true judgments,
  and like a light they will kindle righteous deeds.
¹⁷A sinful man will shun reproof,
  and will find a decision according to his liking.

¹⁸A man of judgment will not overlook an idea,
  and an insolent[l] and proud man will not
    cower in fear.[m]
¹⁹Do nothing without deliberation;
  and when you have acted, do not regret it.
²⁰Do not go on a path full of hazards,
  and do not stumble over stony ground.
²¹Do not be overconfident on a smooth[n] way,
²² and give good heed to your paths.[o]
²³Guard[p] yourself in every act,
  for this is the keeping of the commandments.

²⁴He who believes the law gives heed to the
    commandments,
  and he who trusts the Lord will not suffer loss.

Practical Advice

33 No evil will befall the man who fears the Lord,
  but in trial he will deliver him again and
    again.
²A wise man will not hate the law,
  but he who is hypocritical about it is like a
    boat in a storm.

32:5–6 Parallel verses compare the value of music and wine at a banquet with precious jewels (Is 5:12; 24:7–9; Eccles 2:8).

32:10 approval precedes a modest man: As lightning precedes thunder, so a modest man's reputation will precede him and he will be welcome wherever he goes.

32:11 Leave in good time: It is bad manners to overstay one's welcome.

32:12 Amuse yourself there: Presumably at home, after the banquet. **sin through proud speech:** The pleasant atmosphere at banquets makes people prone to speak carelessly. Ben Sira reminds them to keep some restraint on their speech.

32:13 bless him who made you: Give thanks to God, your Creator. **satisfies you:** Literally, "intoxicates", "makes drunk". Though Ben Sira cares deeply about good manners, he is not overly austere or ascetic. He believes one should be grateful to God for the enjoyment of good food, good music, and good conversation.

32:14—33:17 Life is best lived by honoring God and keeping his commandments.

32:14 fears the Lord: There is a close connection between fearing the Lord and accepting his discipline (Heb., *musar*; Gk., *paideia*)—his training, correction, or chastening (4:17; 18:14; 21:19; 22:6; Prov 3:11–12; 6:23; 12:1; Heb 12:5). **rise early:** See 4:12; 6:36; 39:5.

32:15 seeks the law: By searching out its meaning (Ezra 7:10). **will be filled with it:** Includes putting it into practice (2:16; 6:37). **hypocrite:** To one who studies the Torah but has

no intention of observing it, it becomes a trap (Mt 23:23–28; Jas 1:23–24).

32:16 kindle righteous deeds: The Hebrew reads: "And out of darkness he will draw forth a course of action." On the Torah as light, see Prov 6:23; Ps 119:105.

32:17 shun reproof: The sinful man rejects criticism and correction. **find a decision according to his liking:** The Hebrew reads: "forces the Law to suit his purpose". Instead of following the Torah, he reinterprets it according to his liking.

32:18 an idea: Another man's thoughtful suggestion, understanding, or direction. **will not cower in fear:** The insolent man is reckless and does not consider the consequences of his actions (Prov 12:15).

32:19 Do nothing without deliberation: Think carefully about your actions beforehand (37:16).

32:20 a path full of hazards: Do not take a course of action that is dangerous. **do not stumble over stony ground:** The Hebrew reads: "Do not stumble over an obstacle twice", meaning "do not make the same mistake twice."

32:21 a smooth way: Perhaps the meaning is: "Be cautious on an apparently safe but unfamiliar road, for it may hide unexpected pitfalls."

32:23 Guard yourself: Be prudent and cautious in all that you do. **the commandments:** A reference to Deut 4:9 (Prov 16:17; 19:16).

32:24 He who believes ... commandments: The Hebrew reads: "He who observes the Torah guards his soul." **will not suffer loss:** Trusting the Lord, believing the Torah, and observing its commandments is a path to flourishing (2:16; 15:1; 19:20).

33:1 No evil: Although the righteous man is not always shielded from hardships, God will keep him safe through them. He will also protect him from moral evil (Job 5:19; Prov 12:21). **in trial:** Or "in temptation".

33:2 like a boat in a storm: Those who are hypocritical about the law, perhaps by giving it lip service but not observing it, are tossed around by life and unstable in all that they do.

---

[k] Other authorities omit *to seek him*.
[l] Heb: Gk *alien*.
[m] The meaning of this line is uncertain. Other authorities add the phrases *and after acting, with him, without deliberation*.
[n] Or an *unexplored*.
[o] Syr Vg: Gk *and beware of your children*.
[p] Heb Syr: Gk *Trust*.

³A man of understanding will trust in the law;
    for him the law is as dependable as an inquiry
      by means of Urim.

⁴Prepare what to say, and thus you will be heard;
    bind together your instruction, and make your
      answer.
⁵The heart of a fool is like a cart wheel,
    and his thoughts like a turning axle.
⁶A stallion is like a mocking friend;
    he neighs under every one who sits on him.

⁷Why is any day better than another,
    when all the daylight in the year is from the
      sun?
⁸By the Lord's decision they were distinguished,
    and he appointed the different seasons and
      feasts;
⁹some of them he exalted and hallowed,
    and some of them he made ordinary days.
¹⁰All men are from the ground,
    and Adam was created of the dust.
¹¹In the fulness of his knowledge the Lord
    distinguished them
    and appointed their different ways;
¹²some of them he blessed and exalted,
    and some of them he made holy and brought
      near to himself;
    but some of them he cursed and brought low,
    and he turned them out of their place.
¹³As clay in the hand of the potter—
    for all his ways are as he pleases—

so men are in the hand of him who made them,
    to give them as he decides.

¹⁴Good is the opposite of evil,
    and life the opposite of death;
    so the sinner is the opposite of the godly.
¹⁵Look upon all the works of the Most High;
    they likewise are in pairs, one the opposite of
      the other.
¹⁶I was the last on watch;
    I was like one who gleans after the
      grape-gatherers;
    by the blessing of the Lord I excelled,
    and like a grape-gatherer I filled my wine press.
¹⁷Consider that I have not labored for myself alone,
    but for all who seek instruction.
¹⁸Hear me, you who are great among the people,
    and you leaders of the congregation, listen.

¹⁹To son or wife, to brother or friend,
    do not give power over yourself, as long as
      you live;
    and do not give your property to another,
    lest you change your mind and must ask for it.
²⁰While you are still alive and have breath in you,
    do not let any one take your place.
²¹For it is better that your children should ask from
      you
    than that you should look to the hand of your
      sons.
²²Excel in all that you do;
    bring no stain upon your honor.

33:3 inquiry by means of Urim: The Urim and the Thummim were sacred objects worn on the high priest's breastplate and used to determine God's will (45:10; Ex 28:30; Lev 8:8; 1 Sam 14:41; 28:6).

33:5 cart wheel ... turning axle: The thoughts of a fool go round and round, meaning he lacks firm convictions and constantly changes his mind.

33:6 a mocking friend: One who lavishes affections on everyone but has no real loyalty to anyone.

33:7-15 A reflection on why people are so different. It underlines the divine responsibility for these differences.

33:7 better than another: "Better" is meant in the sense of "holier", referring to the Jewish religious holidays.

33:8 the Lord's decision: The Hebrew reads: "the Lord's wisdom". **seasons and feasts:** God ordained and set apart the religious festivals to reveal through them his purposes to Israel and the world (Gen 2:3; Ex 34:21–23; Lev 23; Deut 16:1–17).

33:10 created of the dust: All humans, like Adam, are made from the dust of the earth (Gen 2:7; 3:19; Job 4:19; 10:9; Ps 103:14; Eccles 3:20).

33:11 the Lord distinguished: God made undeniable distinctions and appointed different roles, functions, and destinies to various people.

33:12 some ... he blessed: Especially the people of Israel (Gen 12:2; Ex 32:13). **brought near to himself:** The Aaronic priests (Ex 28:1). **some ... he cursed:** Probably a reference to the Canaanites, who were ousted from the Promised Land because of their wickedness (cf. Gen 9:25; Lev 18:24–30; Deut 18:9–12).

33:13 As clay: People and their destinies are in the hand of God, to be molded as he sees fit (Is 29:16; 45:9; 64:8; Jer 18:4; Rom 9:21; Wis 15:7–8).

33:14 Good ... evil ... life ... death ... the sinner ... the godly: These three pairs of opposites are not metaphysical necessities in the world—since God created man "very good" (Gen 1:31; cf. CCC 339)—but the result of man's ethical choices.

33:16 the last on watch: Ben Sira considers himself the last in a succession of Israel's wisdom teachers. **one who gleans:** One who gathers what harvesters have left behind. Ben Sira has gleaned from the vineyard of wisdom harvested by his predecessors. **I filled my wine press:** By gathering the "wine" of wisdom (Prov 9:2, 5) from the study of Scripture and Israel's tradition.

33:17 not labored for myself alone: Ben Sira has gathered wisdom not only for his own self-edification but also for the benefit of others who seek it (24:34).

33:18-23 Counsel on property and personal independence.

33:18 leaders of the congregation: Perhaps the religious or secular leaders of the Jewish community.

33:19 power over yourself: The result of prematurely giving away your possessions to those close to you. **your property:** Any belongings, not just real estate. Ben Sira is advising, not against generosity, but against bequeathing assets that may still be needed.

33:20 take your place: Advice against letting others acquire your possessions and thereby control your life.

33:21 look to the hand: Being financially dependent on your children is discouraged.

²³At the time when you end the days of your life,
   in the hour of death, distribute your
      inheritance.

²⁴Fodder and a stick and burdens for a donkey;
   bread and discipline and work for a servant.
²⁵Set your slave to work, and you will find rest;
   leave his hands idle, and he will seek
      liberty.
²⁶Yoke and thong will bow the neck,
   and for a wicked servant there are racks and
      tortures.
²⁷Put him to work, that he may not be idle,
   for idleness teaches much evil.
²⁸Set him to work, as is fitting for him,
   and if he does not obey, make his chains
      heavy.
²⁹Do not act immoderately toward anybody,
   and do nothing without discretion.

³⁰If you have a servant, let him be as yourself,
   because you have bought him with blood.
³¹If you have a servant, treat him as a brother,
   for as your own soul you will need him.
   If you ill-treat him, and he leaves and runs
      away,
      which way will you go to seek him?

Fear of the Lord, Sacrifices, Justice, and Prayer

34 A man of no understanding has vain and
   false hopes,
   and dreams give wings to fools.
²As one who catches at a shadow and pursues the
      wind,
   so is he who gives heed to dreams.
³The vision of dreams is this against that,
   the likeness of a face confronting a face.
⁴From an unclean thing what will be made clean?
   And from something false what will be true?
⁵Divinations and omens and dreams are folly,
   and like a woman with labor pains the mind
      has fancies.
⁶Unless they are sent from the Most High as a
      visitation,
   do not give your mind to them.
⁷For dreams have deceived many,
   and those who put their hope in them have
      failed.
⁸Without such deceptions the law will be fulfilled,
   and wisdom is made perfect in truthful lips.

⁹An educated[q] man knows many things,
   and one with much experience will speak with
      understanding.

33:23 distribute your inheritance: I.e., at the end of your life. It appears that written wills were not common in Israel in the days of Ben Sira.

33:24–31 Instructions on the treatment of domestic servants. Ben Sira advocates severity for the lazy or wicked slave (33:24–28) but kindness toward the good slave (33:29–31). His counsel reflects the harshness of a time when slavery was common.

33:24 a donkey ... a servant: Shows the demeaning nature of human slavery.

33:25 Set your slave to work: Lest he be idle.

33:26 Yoke and thong: The slave is compared to a beast of burden that must be harnessed to be kept under control. **racks and tortures:** Or "stocks and chastisements", instruments to discipline disobedient servants (Lk 12:46). Israelite law limited punishment on servants and protected their rights (Ex 21:1–11, 20–21, 26–27; 23:12; Deut 15:12–18). • Catholic teaching, on the basis of the seventh commandment, denounces the enslavement of human beings as a sin against their dignity and fundamental rights (CCC 2414).

33:29 Do not act immoderately: A counterbalance to Ben Sira's advice on the harsh treatment of lazy slaves.

33:30 bought him with blood: I.e., you have bought him with your own livelihood.

33:31 as your own soul: The kind treatment of a servant helps to ensure his faithful service to you (7:20–21). **runs away:** The Torah prohibits the people of Israel to return runaway slaves to their masters or to oppress them (Deut 23:15–16; Philem 10–18).

34:1–8 Warnings against seeking hidden information through dreams and occult practices.

34:1 give wings to fools: Dreams can sometimes excite delusive hopes that have no chance of coming to pass.

34:2 pursues the wind: Equivalent to chasing vain fantasies (Eccles 1:14; 2:17).

34:3 a face confronting a face: Like a reflection in a mirror, a dream can be the reflection of the dreamer's own wishful thinking (Prov 27:19).

34:4 from something false: Just as something clean cannot come from something unclean, so reality cannot emerge from the illusion of a dream.

34:5 Divinations and omens: Occult practices by which one attempts to know the future are strictly forbidden by the Torah (Lev 19:26; Deut 18:10–14; Jer 29:8). • The Church continues to forbid divination, conjuring the dead, service to demons, horoscopes, astrology, palm reading, etc., in search of knowledge about the future, as these things contradict the fear and love we owe to God alone (CCC 2116).

34:6 Unless they are sent: An acknowledgment that God sometimes speaks through dreams, as seen throughout the Bible (see Gen 28:10–17; 31:10–13; 37:5–10; 40:8–19; 41:1–32; Dan 2:1–19, 27–45; Mt 1:20–21; 2:12–13, 19, 22). The author recognizes this without providing any guidelines for discerning whether a dream comes from God.

34:7 dreams have deceived many: See Jer 23:25–27; 29:8–9. • One should not be inclined to have faith in dreams. The saints can distinguish illusions from revelations and discover the meaning of their words and images. However, if a soul is not prudent in the matter of dreams, it can be misled into a forest of vanity by the deceiving spirit, who can sometimes predict things accurately and thereby imprison a soul by a single lie (St. Gregory the Great, *Dialogue* 4, 50, 6).

34:8 the law will be fulfilled: The Torah is a sufficient guide for living a good life and attaining wisdom without the need for dreams.

34:9–12 Ben Sira recommends gaining experience and wisdom through travel.

34:9 An educated man: In contrast to the dreamer, the intelligent person derives a broad knowledge from his education, travel, and life experience.

---

[q]Other authorities read *A traveled.*

¹⁰He that is inexperienced knows few things,
　　but he that has traveled acquires much
　　　cleverness.
¹¹I have seen many things in my travels,
　　and I understand more than I can express.
¹²I have often been in danger of death,
　　but have escaped because of these experiences.

¹³The spirit of those who fear the Lord will live,
　　for their hope is in him who saves them.
¹⁴He who fears the Lord will not be timid,
　　nor play the coward, for he is his hope.
¹⁵Blessed is the soul of the man who fears the
　　Lord!
　　To whom does he look? And who is his
　　　support?
¹⁶The eyes of the Lord are upon those who love
　　him,
　　a mighty protection and strong support,
　　a shelter from the hot wind and a shade from
　　　noonday sun,
　　a guard against stumbling and a defense
　　　against falling.
¹⁷He lifts up the soul and gives light to the eyes;
　　he grants healing, life, and blessing.

¹⁸If one sacrifices from what has been wrongfully
　　obtained, the offering is blemished;ʳ
　　the giftsˢ of the lawless are not acceptable.

¹⁹The Most High is not pleased with the offerings
　　of the ungodly;
　　and he is not propitiated for sins by a
　　　multitude of sacrifices.
²⁰Like one who kills a son before his father's eyes
　　is the man who offers a sacrifice from the
　　　property of the poor.
²¹The bread of the needy is the life of the poor;
　　whoever deprives them of it is a man of blood.
²²To take away a neighbor's living is to murder
　　him;
　　to deprive an employee of his wages is to shed
　　　blood.

²³When one builds and another tears down,
　　what do they gain but toil?
²⁴When one prays and another curses,
　　to whose voice will the Lord listen?
²⁵If a man washes after touching a dead body, and
　　touches it again,
　　what has he gained by his washing?
²⁶So if a man fasts for his sins,
　　and goes again and does the same things,
　　who will listen to his prayer?
　　And what has he gained by humbling himself?

The Law and Sacrifice—Divine Justice

35 He who keeps the law makes many offerings;
　　he who heeds the commandments sacrifices
　　　a peace offering.

34:10 inexperienced: Untried or untested. **much cleverness:** The one who travels grows in skill and resourcefulness,
having had unique opportunities to put wisdom into practice.

34:11 I have seen: A brief autobiographical note about
the experience and understanding Ben Sira gained through his
own travels and how these helped him escape various dangers
(51:13).

34:13 The spirit: Or "the soul". **will live:** In the face of
the dangers mentioned in 34:12. **their hope is in him:** Their
hope is well established in God rather than in elusive dreams
(34:1).

34:14 will not be timid: Those who fear the Lord find
great courage in him, so that they need not fear life's perils.
See note on 2:15–18.

34:15 Blessed is the soul: The fear of the Lord is not a
servile fear but a reverence for God that draws forth his blessings (Ps 112:1–9).

34:16 The eyes of the Lord: See 15:19; Ps 33:18; 34:15. **a
mighty protection:** God's role as a protective shield (Gen 15:1;
Deut 33:29; Ps 3:3; 18:2–3; 61:3–4; Is 4:6; 25:4–5; Prov
30:5) and **support** of Israel (Ps 91:11–12; 121:3) is repeated
throughout Scripture.

34:17 lifts up the soul ... light to the eyes: Two metaphors illustrate the happiness that God grants to those who
love and fear him. **healing, life, and blessing:** Gifts from God
(Ps 21:4; 30:2; 36:9; 133:3).

34:18–26 Ben Sira, like many before him, criticizes those
who sacrifice in the Temple with the wrong disposition or with
disregard for social justice. These offerings are empty rituals

that the Lord does not accept (cf. 1 Sam 15:22; Is 1:11–13;
Hos 6:6; Amos 5:21–24).

34:18 wrongfully obtained: God considers an animal that
was stolen or gotten unjustly as unacceptable for sacrifice (Lev
22:18–25; Deut 15:21; Mal 1:8). **gifts of the lawless:** God
rejects the gifts of those who do not observe his Law (Prov
15:8; 21:27).

34:19 not propitiated for sins: God does not forgive sins
based on how many sacrifices people offer so long as they
refuse to repent (5:6; 7:9; Ps 50:8–15).

34:20 one who kills a son before his father's eyes: The
shocking comparison (alluding to 2 Kings 25:6–7) illustrates
how offensive to the Lord is a sacrifice that was stolen from
the poor, because it robs them of their livelihood. God, after
all, is the father of the poor and needy (Ps 68:5).

34:21 bread of the needy: Not a luxury, but essential to
survival. Whoever steals it is called **a man of blood**, i.e., a mur-
derer. The same goes for withholding **wages** (34:22) from an
employee (4:1–6; Deut 24:14–15; Tob 4:14; Jas 5:4).

34:23–26 Ben Sira contends that a pious act is cancelled
out by its opposite.

34:26 if a man fasts: Fasting is worthless without repentance. God will not listen to the prayers of a man who appears
to humble himself but does not turn away from his sin (Is
58:3–7; Jer 14:12).

35:1–11 Describes worship that is acceptable to God.

35:1 makes many offerings: This can be interpreted in
two ways: **(1)** the man who keeps the Law will offer the
sacrifices that the Law prescribes (Lev 1–7), or **(2)** keeping
the ethical precepts of the Law is the spiritual equivalent
of the bringing of sacrificial offerings. The following two
verses seem to favor the second interpretation, while 35:4–
11 appears to support the first. **peace offering:** A sacrifice of
fellowship with God. See note on Lev 3:1–17.

ʳ Other authorities read *is made in mockery.*
ˢ Other authorities read *mockeries.*

²He who returns a kindness offers fine flour,
  and he who gives alms sacrifices a thank
    offering.
³To keep from wickedness is pleasing to the
    Lord,
  and to forsake unrighteousness is atonement.
⁴Do not appear before the Lord empty-handed,
5   for all these things are to be done because of
    the commandment.
⁶The offering of a righteous man anoints the
    altar,
  and its pleasing odor rises before the Most
    High.
⁷The sacrifice of a righteous man is acceptable,
  and the memory of it will not be forgotten.
⁸Glorify the Lord generously,
  and do not stint the first fruits of your
    hands.
⁹With every gift show a cheerful face,
  and dedicate your tithe with gladness.
¹⁰Give to the Most High as he has given,
  and as generously as your hand has found.
¹¹For the Lord is the one who repays,
  and he will repay you sevenfold.

¹²Do not offer him a bribe, for he will not accept it;
  and do not trust to an unrighteous sacrifice;
 for the Lord is the judge,
  and with him is no partiality.

¹³He will not show partiality in the case of a poor
    man;
  and he will listen to the prayer of one who is
    wronged.
¹⁴He will not ignore the supplication of the
    fatherless,
  nor the widow when she pours out her story.
¹⁵Do not the tears of the widow run down her cheek
  as she cries out against him who has caused
    them to fall?
¹⁶He whose service is pleasing to the Lord will be
    accepted,
  and his prayer will reach to the clouds.
¹⁷The prayer of the humble pierces the clouds,
  and he will not be consoled until it reaches the
    Lord;ᵗ
 he will not desist until the Most High visits him,
  and the just judge executes judgment.
¹⁸And the Lord will not delay,
  neither will he be patient with them,
 till he crushes the loins of the unmerciful
  and repays vengeance on the nations;
 till he takes away the multitude of the insolent,
  and breaks the scepters of the unrighteous;
¹⁹till he repays man according to his deeds,
  and the works of men according to their
    devices;
 till he judges the case of his people
  and makes them rejoice in his mercy.

35:2 fine flour: A cereal or grain offering. See note on Lev 2:1–16. **thank offering:** A type of peace offering offered in thanksgiving to God. The point is that acts of kindness and giving alms are the equivalent of making freewill offerings in the Temple. See note on Lev 7:12.

35:3 pleasing: As the odor of sacrifices is pleasing to the Lord (Lev 1:13). **to forsake unrighteousness is atonement:** Not committing sins in the first place is better than presenting sin offerings to atone for them and obtain forgiveness later (5:5; 17:29).

35:4 empty-handed: I.e., without any sacrifice to offer at God's sanctuary (7:29–31; Ex 23:15; 34:20; Deut 16:16). Ben Sira underscores the spiritual significance of the Temple sacrifices; at the same time, he does not lessen the obligation of his fellow Jews to perform the rites of worship prescribed in the Torah.

35:5 the commandment: Not one commandment in particular, but the whole body of legislation pertaining to sacrifices in Lev 1–7, etc.

35:6 anoints the altar: I.e., with the fat that drips from the animals burning on the altar hearth. **its pleasing odor:** A common expression to describe sacrifices acceptable to the Lord (Lev 1:9, 13).

35:7 the memory of it: Refers to the memorial portion of the cereal offering that was mixed with oil and frankincense and burned on the altar (Lev 2:1–2).

35:8 Glorify the Lord: With your sacrifices. **generously:** Literally, "with a good eye" (Prov 22:9).

35:9 a cheerful face: See 2 Cor 9:7. **your tithe:** Ten percent of one's harvest or income (Deut 12:6; 14:23; Tob 1:6–7).

35:10 as he has given: One should strive to give back to God as generously as he bestows his gifts upon man. **as your hand has found:** According to what the Lord has given you.

35:11 repay you sevenfold: According to the generosity of your gift (Ps 79:12).

35:12–20 The Lord answers the prayers of his people and brings judgment upon wicked nations.

35:12 a bribe: God cannot be "bought off" with sacrifices as a corrupt judge is swayed by gifts. **no partiality:** God is perfectly just, meaning he does not show favoritism when rendering judgment (Deut 10:17; 2 Chron 19:7; Acts 10:34; Rom 2:11).

35:13 partiality ... poor man: Prejudice either *against* the poor or *for* the poor (Lev 19:15).

35:14–15 fatherless ... widow: The Torah grants special protection to these vulnerable social groups (Ex 22:22–23; Deut 10:17–18; 24:17; 27:19; Ps 68:5). **tears of the widow:** An allusion to Lam 1:1–2, where Jerusalem is described as a bereaved widow (also Bar 4:12, 16).

35:16 whose service is pleasing: Includes the people of Israel, oppressed by their enemies (35:18–19). Their prayer is found in 36:1–17.

✠ **35:17 pierces the clouds:** A figurative way of saying that Israel's persevering and humble prayer reaches God in heaven (contrast with Lam 3:44). **until the Most High visits him:** Israel persists in prayer until the Lord answers and punishes the oppressors—perhaps the Seleucids in the early second century B.C. • Victory over the adversary is won only when we fight with tears and prayers in constant humility of heart (St. Fulgentius, *Letters* 4, 9, 5).

35:18 will not delay: The Lord will soon judge the nations that oppress Israel (Lk 1:71–75; 18:7–8; 2 Pet 3:9). **the unmerciful ... unrighteous:** Israel's enemies.

35:19 till he repays man: The judgment of the heathen nations. **the case of his people:** God judges *in favor* of his people against their oppressors. **rejoice in his mercy:** The Hebrew reads: "in his salvation" (Is 25:9).

ᵗ Or *until the Lord draws near.*

20Mercy is as welcome when he afflicts them
    as clouds of rain in the time of drought.

A Prayer for God's People; Wise Sayings

36 Have mercy upon us, O Lord, the God of all,
    and look upon us,
    and show us the light of your mercy;
2   send fear of you upon the nations.
3Lift up your hand against foreign nations
    and let them see your might.
4As in us you have been sanctified before them,
    so in them may you be magnified before us;
5and let them know you, as we have known
    that there is no God but you, O Lord.
6Show signs anew, and work further wonders;
    make your hand and your right arm glorious.
7Rouse your anger and pour out your wrath;
    destroy the adversary and wipe out the enemy.
8Hasten the day, and remember the appointed time,u
    and let people recount your mighty deeds.
9Let him who survives be consumed in the fiery
    wrath,
    and may those who harm your people meet
    destruction.
10Crush the heads of the rulers of the enemy,
    who say, "There is no one but ourselves."
11Gather all the tribes of Jacob,
    and givev them their inheritance, as at the
    beginning.

12Have mercy, O Lord, upon the people called by
    your name,
    upon Israel, whom you have likened to aw first-
    born son.
13Have pity on the city of your sanctuary,x
    Jerusalem, the place of your rest.
14Fill Zion with the celebration of your wondrous
    deeds,
    and your templey with your glory.
15Bear witness to those whom you created in the
    beginning,
    and fulfil the prophecies spoken in your
    name.
16Reward those who wait for you,
    and let your prophets be found trustworthy.
17Listen, O Lord, to the prayer of your servants,
    according to the blessing of Aaron for your
    people,
    and direct us in the way of righteousness,
  and all who are on the earth will know
    that you are the Lord, the God of the ages.

18The stomach will take any food,
    yet one food is better than another.
19As the palate tastes the kinds of game,
    so an intelligent mind detects false words.
20A perverse mind will cause grief,
    but a man of experience will pay him back.

35:20 rain in the time of drought: A most welcome arrival (Ps 72:6; Prov 16:15; Is 45:8; Zech 10:1).

36:1 Have mercy upon us: In speaking in the first-person plural (we, us, our), Ben Sira is praying as the representative of Israel. **the God of all:** The prayer addresses God as the Lord of all creation.

36:3 Lift up your hand: To execute judgment. **foreign nations:** Especially the Greek Seleucids, who occupied the land of Israel at this time.

36:4 in us ... sanctified: God revealed his holiness to the nations by punishing Israel for its sins, allowing his people to become subject to foreign domination (Ezek 20:41; 28:25; 39:27). **be magnified:** Israel asks God to reveal his glory and power by judging the foreign nations (Ezek 38:21-23).

36:5 no God but you: See also Ex 6:7; 1 Kings 8:60; 1 Chron 17:20; Is 45:14.

36:6 signs ... wonders: An allusion to God's great deeds when he delivered Israel from Egypt (Ex 7:3). **make your hand ... glorious:** A way of saying "show your power" (Ex 15:6; Is 62:8; 63:12; Ps 98:1).

36:7 wipe out the enemy: Overt hostility against the enemy points to tense relations between the Jews and the reigning Seleucids.

36:8-9 Hasten the day: A petition that God would quickly execute his judgment on Israel's enemies (Is 2:12-17; 14:21). The Hebrew reads: "Hasten the end", i.e., of the present age.

36:10 Crush the heads: Possibly an allusion to Num 24:17. **no one but ourselves:** The arrogant words of the foreign rulers (Is 47:8, 10).

36:11 Gather all the tribes of Jacob: Even though many Jews had returned to Judea from exile in Babylon, many more Israelites remained scattered in foreign lands. Ben Sira prays that the whole people of Israel may recover their homeland as it was in **the beginning**, referring to the conquest of the land that began under Joshua and was completed under David (2 Sam 7:1). God's promise to gather the 12 tribes of Israel back to their land is the most frequently attested prophecy in the Bible (Is 11:11-12; 27:13; Jer 3:18; 30:3; 31:8, 10; Ezek 36:8-11; 39:25-27; Amos 9:14).

36:12 by your name: God renamed the patriarch Jacob "Israel" (Gen 32:28; 35:10; Is 63:19; Jer 14:9). **first-born son:** The nation of Israel (Ex 4:22; Jer 31:9; Hos 11:1; Wis 18:13).

36:13 city of your sanctuary: Or "your holy city", where the Temple stands. **the place of your rest:** The Temple is the place of God's dwelling on earth (Ex 15:17; Deut 12:10-11; 1 Kings 8:13; Ps 132:8).

36:14 your glory: The Lord filled the Temple with his glory at the major moments of encounter with his people (Ex 40:34-35; 1 Kings 8:11; Hag 2:7).

36:15 created in the beginning: Ben Sira asks God to acknowledge Israel, his first-born, and the great redemptive deeds that he accomplished for it at the beginning of its history. **fulfil the prophecies:** I.e., of God's victory over Israel's enemies.

36:17 Listen, O Lord: The final appeal of Ben Sira's prayer. **your servants:** The people of Israel (1 Kings 8:30; Dan 9:17). **the blessing of Aaron:** See Num 6:22-27. The Hebrew reads: "according to your goodwill toward your people". **God of the ages:** Or "eternal God" (Is 40:28).

36:18—37:15 Brief counsel on discernment (36:18-20) that is applied to choosing a wife (36:21-26), friends (37:1-6), and advisers (37:7-15).

36:19 detects false words: Ben Sira draws a parallel between discernment of the senses and discernment of the intellect. As a well-trained palate can discern good food from

---

u Other authorities read *remember your oath.*
v Other authorities read *I gave.*
w Other authorities read *have named your.*
x Or *on your holy city.*
y Heb Syr: Gk Vg *people.*

²¹A woman will accept any man,
    but one daughter is better than another.
²²A woman's beauty gladdens the countenance,
    and surpasses every human desire.
²³If kindness and humility mark her speech,
    her husband is not like other men.
²⁴He who acquires a wife gets his best possession,ᶻ
    a helper fit for him and a pillar of support.ᵃ
²⁵Where there is no fence, the property will be
        plundered;
    and where there is no wife, a man will wander
        about and sigh.
²⁶For who will trust a nimble robber
    that skips from city to city?
So who will trust a man that has no home,
    and lodges wherever night finds him?

Concerning Good Counsel, Reason, and Moderation

37 Every friend will say, "I too am a friend";
    but some friends are friends only in
        name.
²Is it not a grief to the death
    when a companion and friend turns to enmity?
³O evil imagination, why were you formed
    to cover the land with deceit?
⁴Some companions rejoice in the happiness of a
        friend,
    but in time of trouble are against him.
⁵Some companions help a friend for their stomachs'
        sake,
    and in the face of battle take up the shield.

⁶Do not forget a friend in your heart,
    and be not unmindful of him in your wealth.

⁷Every counselor praises counsel,
    but some give counsel in their own interest.
⁸Be wary of a counselor,
    and learn first what is his interest—
    for he will take thought for himself—
  lest he cast the lot against you
⁹   and tell you, "Your way is good,"
    and then stand aloof to see what will happen
        to you.
¹⁰Do not consult with one who looks at you
        suspiciously;
    hide your counsel from those who are jealous
        of you.
¹¹Do not consult with a woman about her rival
    or with a coward about war,
  with a merchant about barter
    or with a buyer about selling,
  with a grudging man about gratitude
    or with a merciless man about kindness,
  with an idler about any work
    or with a man hired for a year about
        completing his work,
  with a lazy servant about a big task—
    pay no attention to these in any matter of
        counsel.
¹²But stay constantly with a godly man
    whom you know to be a keeper of the
        commandments,

---

bad, so an intelligent man is able to tell truth from falsehood and to turn the tables on the deceptions and troubles caused by a perverse mind.

36:21–26 Ben Sira returns to the topic of women (25:13—26:18), focusing on the blessing of a good wife.

36:21 accept any man: Women in Ben Sira's day had little or no say in choosing a spouse. Husbands were typically chosen for them. **one daughter is better:** Men, by contrast, could choose a wife. A wise selection was to his advantage.

36:22 surpasses every human desire: Men typically seek women of great beauty (26:16), but they do better to choose a woman of kind and humble speech (Prov 15:4).

36:24 helper fit for him: Echoes the language used for the creation of Eve (Gen 2:18, 20).

36:25 property will be plundered: The Hebrew reads: "The vineyard is laid waste" (Is 5:5; Prov 24:30–31). **will wander about and sigh:** The Hebrew reads: "is a fugitive and a wanderer", echoing Cain's pathetic statement after he murdered Abel (Gen 4:12, 14). Ben Sira, speaking in an OT context, implies that the unmarried man lives in a type of exile and is as vulnerable as an unfenced vineyard. In a NT context, celibacy is elevated by Jesus to become a radiant sign of the kingdom of God (Mt 19:12; 1 Cor 7:1, 8; CCC 1579).

36:26 no home: An unmarried man without a fixed residence is as restless and untrustworthy as an armed man who wanders from city to city (Prov 27:8).

37:1–6 On discerning true friends from false friends (cf. 6:5–17; 12:8–18; 22:19–26).

37:1 friends only in name: Not all those who claim to be friends are really friends (Prov 20:6). It is particularly painful when those who we thought were friends turn into enemies (22:19–26; 27:16–21).

37:3 O evil imagination: A cry of distress at the deception that taints so many friendships (Ps 41:9; 55:12–14).

37:4 against him: Refers to the fair-weather friend who is eager to share in good times—especially by enjoying hospitality—but disappears during bad times (6:8–12).

37:5 for their stomachs' sake: The Hebrew text is quite different and fits better with the second half of the verse: "A good friend fights against (one's) enemy." **the shield:** A real friend does not hesitate to defend his companion (Ps 35:2).

37:7–15 Counsel on avoiding bad advisors (37:7–11) and choosing good ones (37:12–15).

37:7 in their own interest: Some advisors are really looking for their own advantage. This verse parallels 37:1 on discerning between true and false friends.

37:8 what is his interest: Before listening to a counselor, be aware first of what he has to gain from his own advice.

37:11 Do not consult: Nine types of people are listed from whom one should not seek counsel, either because they have a vested interest in their own advice or because they are of dubious moral character. **a woman about her rival:** Perhaps in a polygamous marriage or in some other form of romantic rivalry (26:6).

37:12 godly man: One should turn to a God-fearing, pious man for reliable advice (10:19–20; 18:27). If he is faithful to God's Law, he will likely be faithful to you as well. **in accord with your soul:** One who understands the person seeking counsel and wants to see him succeed in life.

ᶻHeb: Gk *enters upon a possession.*
ᵃHeb: Gk *rest.*

whose soul is in accord with your soul,
and who will sorrow with you if you fail.
¹³And establish the counsel of your own heart,
for no one is more faithful to you than it is.
¹⁴For a man's soul sometimes keeps him better
informed
than seven watchmen sitting high on a
watchtower.
¹⁵And besides all this pray to the Most High
that he may direct your way in truth.

¹⁶Reason is the beginning of every work,
and counsel precedes every undertaking.
¹⁷As a clue to changes of heart
¹⁸   four turns of fortune appear,
good and evil, life and death;
and it is the tongue that continually rules
them.
¹⁹A man may be shrewd and the teacher of many,
and yet be unprofitable to himself.
²⁰A man skilled in words may be hated;
he will be destitute of all food,
²¹for grace was not given him by the Lord,
since he is lacking in all wisdom.
²²A man may be wise to his own advantage,
and the fruits of his understanding may be
trustworthy on his lips.
²³A wise man will instruct his own people,
and the fruits of his understanding will be
trustworthy.
²⁴A wise man will have praise heaped upon him,
and all who see him will call him happy.

²⁵The life of a man is numbered by days,
but the days of Israel are without number.
²⁶He who is wise among his people will inherit
confidence,ᵇ
and his name will live for ever.

²⁷My son, test your soul while you live;
see what is bad for it and do not give it that.
²⁸For not everything is good for every one,
and not every person enjoys everything.
²⁹Do not have an insatiable appetite for any luxury,
and do not give yourself up to food;
³⁰for overeating brings sickness,
and gluttony leads to nausea.
³¹Many have died of gluttony,
but he who is careful to avoid it prolongs his life.

Concerning Physicians, Tradesmen, and Craftsmen

38 Honor the physician with the honor due him,ᶜ
according to your need of him,
for the Lord created him;
²for healing comes from the Most High,
and he will receive a gift from the king.
³The skill of the physician lifts up his head,
and in the presence of great men he is admired.
⁴The Lord created medicines from the earth,
and a sensible man will not despise them.
⁵Was not water made sweet with a tree
in order that hisᵈ power might be known?
⁶And he gave skill to men
that heᵉ might be glorified in his marvelous
works.

37:13–14 establish the counsel of your own heart: Or "heed your own heart's counsel." If you fear the Lord, your own deliberations may constitute the best advice, because no one looks after your interests more than you do (1:11–30; 6:32–37). **a man's soul:** A person's conscience can be more reliable than several counselors who may not have your best interest in mind.

37:15 pray: Prayer for divine guidance is essential to wise living (Prov 16:9).

37:16–31 On true and false wisdom (37:16–26) and the virtue of temperance (37:27–31).

37:16–18 Wise living depends on thoughtful deliberation and seeking counsel (37:7–15).

37:18 four turns of fortune: The Hebrew reads: "It sprouts four branches." The idea is that our choices lead us to good and life or evil and death (33:14; Deut 30:19).

37:19 unprofitable to himself: A person may appear to be wise in teaching others and yet be unable to manage his own affairs wisely.

37:20–21 hated: Eloquence without wisdom can offend people and lead to hardships. **grace:** Here means the gifts of tact, prudence, and sensitivity given by the Lord.

37:22 his own advantage: A wise person should benefit from his wisdom (Prov 12:14). **trustworthy on his lips:** Some manuscripts read "praiseworthy". The text may mean that people will praise the wisdom of a man who knows how to manage his own affairs.

37:24 happy: Or "blessed", "fortunate".

37:25 days ... without number: The people of Israel are promised a long-lasting history (Jer 31:35–37).

37:26 his name will live for ever: The wise of Israel will be remembered forever (39:9; 41:13; 44:13–14).

37:27 test your soul while you live: I.e., learn from your own experience. **what is bad:** The context suggests this refers to eating unhealthy foods or overeating (31:12–24).

37:28 not everything is good: See 1 Cor 6:12; 10:23.

37:31 died of gluttony: Suggests a connection between overeating (or lack of discipline in general) and an early death (Prov 5:23). **prolongs his life:** A benefit of eating with moderation, which confirms that practical wisdom is life-giving (1:10, 18; Prov 3:1–2, 16–17, 22; 4:10, 22; 9:11).

38:1–23 A discussion on physicians and sickness (38:1–15) and mourning the dead (38:16–23).

38:1 Honor the physician: Ben Sira's respect for doctors is progressive for his time. The OT usually sees illness as punishment for sin, suggesting to many that one should turn to God and not to doctors to find healing (2 Chron 16:12). Ben Sira's positive view of physicians is consonant with the practical wisdom he exhibits throughout the book, holding that God often works for the good of man through human agency. Indeed, the skill of the physician comes from God.

38:2–3 gift from the king: A doctor's ability to heal makes him admired even by ruling powers (Prov 22:29).

38:4 The Lord created medicines: The healing properties of herbs and plants are part of God's wise design of creation.

38:5 water made sweet: Refers to the incident when Moses sweetened bitter waters by throwing a tree branch into them, revealing God's power to Israel (Ex 15:23–25).

ᵇOther authorities read *honor.*
ᶜOther authorities omit *with the honor due him.*
ᵈOr *its.*
ᵉOr *they.*

⁷By them he heals and takes away pain;
8   the pharmacist makes of them a compound.
 His works will never be finished;
   and from him health ᶠ is upon the face of the
   earth.

⁹My son, when you are sick do not be negligent,
   but pray to the Lord, and he will heal you.
¹⁰Give up your faults and direct your hands aright,
   and cleanse your heart from all sin.
¹¹Offer a sweet-smelling sacrifice, and a memorial
   portion of fine flour,
   and pour oil on your offering, as much as you
   can afford. ᵍ
¹²And give the physician his place, for the Lord
   created him;
   let him not leave you, for there is need of him.
¹³There is a time when success lies in the hands of
   physicians, ʰ
14   for they too will pray to the Lord
   that he should grant them success in diagnosis ⁱ
   and in healing, for the sake of preserving life.
¹⁵He who sins before his Maker,
   may he fall into the care ʲ of a physician.

¹⁶My son, let your tears fall for the dead,
   and as one who is suffering grievously begin
   the lament.
 Lay out his body with the honor due him,
   and do not neglect his burial.

¹⁷Let your weeping be bitter and your wailing
   fervent;
   observe the mourning according to his merit,
 for one day, or two, to avoid criticism;
   then be comforted for your sorrow.
¹⁸For sorrow results in death,
   and sorrow of heart saps one's strength.
¹⁹In calamity sorrow continues,
   and the life of the poor man weighs down his
   heart.
²⁰Do not give your heart to sorrow;
   drive it away, remembering the end of life.
²¹Do not forget, there is no coming back;
   you do the dead ᵏ no good, and you injure
   yourself.
²²"Remember my doom, for yours is like it:
   yesterday it was mine, and today it is yours."
²³When the dead is at rest, let his remembrance
   cease,
   and be comforted for him when his spirit has
   departed.

²⁴The wisdom of the scribe depends on the
   opportunity of leisure;
   and he who has little business may become
   wise.
²⁵How can he become wise who handles the plow,
   and who glories in the shaft of a goad,
 who drives oxen and is occupied with their work,
   and whose talk is about ˡ bulls?

38:9 pray to the Lord: Since healing comes from God (38:2; Ex 15:26), it is important to rely on prayer no less than physicians when seeking healing (2 Chron 16:12; Hos 6:1).

38:10 cleanse your heart: Implies a correlation between physical and spiritual health. Sickness can be a punishment that God inflicts for violations of the law (Deut 29:21–29). Turning away from sin can thus be an important step toward recovering health (Ps 24:4; Prov 3:7–8; Job 17:9).

38:11 a sweet-smelling sacrifice: The cereal or grain offering described in Lev 2:1–3, which included flour offered with oil and frankincense and signified communion with God (35:2). The passage implies that prayer, repentance, and fulfilling religious obligations all have an impact on one's health.

38:14 they too will pray: Assumes doctors know they have received their skills from God (38:2).

38:15 may he fall: Not an insult against doctors, but a wish of bad luck to sinners, saying in effect: "May they fall ill and need the care of a physician, because God will not help them."

38:16 let your tears fall: It is proper to mourn the deceased. **the lament:** The Hebrew has *qinah*, which refers to a traditional lamentation for the dead (2 Sam 1:17; Jer 7:29; Ezek 19:1; Amos 5:1). **burial:** Burying the dead is a sacred duty in both Judaism and Christianity. See note on Tob 1:17.

38:17 Let your weeping be bitter: In Middle Eastern cultures, people do not suppress their grief at the death of a loved one; it is appropriate to express it freely and loudly (Is 22:4; Jer

16:7; Zech 12:10). **according to his merit:** Every person who dies deserves some amount of mourning. **one day, or two:** Of weeping and wailing. Anything less would bring charges of insensitivity against the mourner. The formal period of mourning in Judaism lasts seven days (22:12). **then be comforted:** The mourner should regain his composure after the initial days of mourning.

38:18 results in death: Excessive sorrow can afflict the soul so much that it can lead to the mourner's death (Gen 42:4, 38; 44:29). Jewish tradition likewise states that excessive grief for the dead will create weeping for another death, i.e., that of the mourner (Babylonian Talmud *Moed Qatan* 27b).

38:19 sorrow continues: The Greek of this verse is unclear.

38:20 the end of life: Life is short, and so excessively prolonged mourning is unwise.

38:21 no coming back: Mourning will not bring the dead back to life (Wis 2:1). It is of no use to the dead and potentially harmful to one's self.

38:22 Remember my doom ... today it is yours: The first person (I, me, my) is used to portray the dead person reminding the mourner that they share a common fate (41:2–3). The Hebrew text is in the third person, continuing the thought of the narrator ("Remember his doom ... ").

38:24—39:11 Ben Sira compares skilled workers (38:24–34) with the scribe (39:1–11).

38:24 scribe: A professional religious scholar who specialized in studying and teaching the Torah and other sacred traditions. **leisure:** The Greek term is *scholē*, from which we get the English words *school* and *scholar*. The etymology confirms Ben Sira's point in this section, namely, that the scribe or scholar must have sufficient leisure time, unencumbered by manual labor, to engage in intellectual pursuits and grow in wisdom.

38:25 who handles the plow: The farmer, whose work is necessary and profitable but whose labor affords him little time to study. **a goad:** A sharp stick used to lead cattle.

ᶠ Or *peace*.
ᵍ Heb: Vulgate omits *as much as you can afford*; Greek is obscure.
ʰ Gk *in their hands*.
ⁱ Heb: Gk *rest*.
ʲ Gk *hands*.
ᵏ Gk *him*.
ˡ Or *among*.

26He sets his heart on plowing furrows,
   and he is careful about fodder for the heifers.
27So too is every craftsman and master workman
      who labors by night as well as by day;
   those who cut the signets of seals,
      each is diligent in making a great variety;
   he sets his heart on painting a lifelike image,
      and he is careful to finish his work.
28So too is the smith sitting by the anvil,
      intent upon his handiwork in iron;
   the breath of the fire melts his flesh,
      and he wastes away in[m] the heat of the
         furnace;
   he inclines his ear to the sound of the hammer,[n]
      and his eyes are on the pattern of the object.
   He sets his heart on finishing his handiwork,
      and he is careful to complete its decoration.
29So too is the potter sitting at his work
      and turning the wheel with his feet;
   he is always deeply concerned over his work,
      and all his output is by number.
30He moulds the clay with his arm
      and makes it pliable with his feet;
   he sets his heart to finish the glazing,
      and he is careful to clean the furnace.

31All these rely upon their hands,
      and each is skilful in his own work.
32Without them a city cannot be established,
      and men can neither sojourn nor live there.
33Yet they are not sought out for the council of the
         people,
   nor do they attain eminence in the public
      assembly.

They do not sit in the judge's seat,
   nor do they understand the sentence of
      judgment;
they cannot expound discipline or judgment,
   and they are not found using proverbs.
34But they keep stable the fabric of the world,
   and their prayer is in the practice of their
      trade.

The Student of the Law; and Praise of God

39 On the other hand he who devotes himself
   to the study of the law of the Most High
will seek out the wisdom of all the ancients,
   and will be concerned with prophecies;
2he will preserve the discourse of notable men
   and penetrate the subtleties of parables;
3he will seek out the hidden meanings of proverbs
   and be at home with the obscurities of
      parables.
4He will serve among great men
   and appear before rulers;
he will travel through the lands of foreign nations,
   for he tests the good and the evil among men.
5He will set his heart to rise early
   to seek the Lord who made him,
   and will make supplication before the Most
      High;
he will open his mouth in prayer
   and make supplication for his sins.

6If the great Lord is willing,
   he will be filled with the spirit of
      understanding;
he will pour forth words[o] of wisdom
   and give thanks to the Lord in prayer.

38:27 who cut the signets of seals: Artisans who engrave seals in jewelry and precious stones, to be pressed into soft wax as the owner's unique signature. His work is useful (45:11; Ex 28:11), but it prevents him from dedicating himself to the pursuit of wisdom.

38:28 the smith: The metalworker, whose demanding occupation leaves him little time or energy left for the study of wisdom.

38:29 the potter: Too busy with his trade to dedicate himself to the pursuit of wisdom.

38:32 a city cannot be established: Manual laborers make human civilization possible.

38:33 the council of the people: Lack of extensive schooling means that manual laborers are rarely suited for judicial offices and other positions of civil leadership.

38:34 the fabric of the world: Far from being dispensable, manual laborers provide the sure foundation for every human society. **their prayer ... their trade:** Manual labor is not without spiritual value; indeed, it can be a form of prayer that substitutes for a life of study and spiritual reflection.

39:1–11 In Ben Sira's view, the profession of the scribe surpasses all occupations, since he alone can devote himself to the quest for wisdom.

39:1 law ... wisdom ... prophecies: The scribe's object of study is the Hebrew Scriptures in its three traditional divisions (cf. prologue). The Torah, the Law of Moses, is the foundation of all wisdom and the focus of the scribe's attention. It provides the foundation for the two other categories of sacred texts, the Prophets and Wisdom Books.

39:2–3 The scribe is an expert in Israel's oral traditions as well as in the Scriptures. He memorizes, interprets, and expounds a wealth of wisdom sayings passed down in various forms (Prov 1:2, 6; Wis 8:8).

39:4 appear before rulers: Because of his wisdom, the scholar is influential among leaders of society, often occupying government positions such as that of ambassador. **foreign nations:** The sage is ideally a well-traveled man who has gained much experience about the world and different cultures (34:9–12).

39:5 set his heart: The same expression is used in 38:26, 27, 28, 30. Ben Sira thus likens the scholar's activities to those of the farmer, craftsman, smith, and potter. **to rise early:** The sage is not only a learned man but also a humble one who begins the day with prayer. **supplication for his sins:** The sage asks for forgiveness daily, because sin is a major obstacle to attaining wisdom (Ps 51:6–7; Wis 1:4–6).

39:6 If the great Lord is willing: Even given the sage's efforts, wisdom remains a gift from God. **spirit of understanding:** See Is 11:2. **words of wisdom:** Or "words of wisdom of his own"—not just repeating sayings he has learned, but also developing his own works of wisdom.

---

[m] Cn Compare Syr: Gk *contends with*.
[n] Cn: Gk *the sound of the hammer renews his ear*.
[o] Other authorities read *his words*.

7He will direct his counsel and knowledge
rightly,
and meditate on his secrets.
8He will reveal instruction in his teaching,
and will glory in the law of the Lord's
covenant.
9Many will praise his understanding,
and it will never be blotted out;
his memory will not disappear,
and his name will live through all generations.
10Nations will declare his wisdom,
and the congregation will proclaim his praise;
11if he lives long, he will leave a name greater than
a thousand,
and if he goes to rest, it is enough[p] for him.

12I have yet more to say, which I have thought
upon,
and I am filled, like the moon at the full.
13Listen to me, O you holy sons,
and bud like a rose growing by a stream of
water;
14send forth fragrance like frankincense,
and put forth blossoms like a lily.
Scatter the fragrance, and sing a hymn of praise;
bless the Lord for all his works;
15ascribe majesty to his name
and give thanks to him with praise,
with songs on your lips, and with lyres;
and this you shall say in thanksgiving:
16"All things are the works of the Lord, for they are
very good,
and whatever he commands will be done in his
time."

17No one can say, "What is this?" "Why is that?"
for in God's[q] time all things will be sought
after.
At his word the waters stood in a heap,
and the reservoirs of water at the word of his
mouth.
18At his command whatever pleases him is done,
and none can limit his saving power.
19The works of all flesh are before him,
and nothing can be hid from his eyes.
20From everlasting to everlasting he beholds
them,
and nothing is marvelous to him.
21No one can say, "What is this?" "Why is that?"
for everything has been created for its use.

22His blessing covers the dry land like a river,
and drenches it like a flood.
23The nations will incur his wrath,
just as he turns fresh water into salt.
24To the holy his ways are straight,
just as they are obstacles to the wicked.
25From the beginning good things were created for
good people,
just as evil things for sinners.
26Basic to all the needs of man's life
are water and fire and iron and salt
and wheat flour and milk and honey,
the blood of the grape, and oil and clothing.

39:7 meditate on his secrets: God will give the sage insight into divine mysteries (1:2–4, 6, 8–10).

39:8 his teaching: The sage will pass on the wisdom he has acquired to others. **the law:** The Torah that God gave to Israel through Moses (17:12; 24:23; 28:7; 42:2).

39:9 Many will praise: The sage will acquire a glowing reputation. **will not disappear:** On account of his wisdom, the sage will be remembered long after his death, like the great men of Israel (37:26; 41:11–13; 44:14; 45:1; Prov 10:7).

39:10 Nations will declare: The sage will be notorious not only in Israel but also among other nations. The verse is repeated in 44:15. **the congregation:** The Jewish community.

39:11 enough for him: The text is unclear. Perhaps the sense is: "If he dies young, he still will have left a sufficient inheritance of wisdom to his people."

39:12–35 A hymn of praise for creation. It is also a theodicy, attempting to explain the presence of evil in the world. The section begins with an invitation to praise God (39:12–15), followed by the hymn itself (39:16–35).

39:12 I have yet more to say: A transition verse. **like the moon:** See 50:6.

39:13–15 Ben Sira, speaking in a fatherly tone, invites readers to worship using terms evocative of the Song of Solomon used elsewhere to describe wisdom (chap. 24) and the ministry of the high priest (chap. 50). These parallels imply that when the wise praise and thank the Lord, they are imitating wisdom, performing a liturgical service, and entering a nuptial relationship with her.

39:13 like a rose: See 24:14; 50:8. **by a stream of water:** See 24:30–31; 50:8; Song 4:15.

39:14 like frankincense: See 24:15; 50:9; Song 4:6, 14. **like a lily:** See 24:17; Song 2:1–2.

39:16 very good: The theme of the hymn is the goodness of God's works of creation (39:33; Gen 1:31). **whatever he commands:** God's creative words brought the universe into existence; he continues his work in the history of the world, blessing the righteous and punishing sinners through the elements of creation (39:22–31; Eccles 3:11).

39:17 all things will be sought: All questions will be answered in God's own time. **waters stood in a heap:** Refers to the gathering of the seas at creation (Gen 1:6–10; Ps 33:7; 104:5–9) or to the parting of the sea during the Exodus (Ex 15:8; Ps 78:13) or both.

39:18 At his command: All creation obeys the word of God and accomplishes his purposes (39:31). **his saving power:** Implies a close correlation between God's creative and salvific power.

39:19 nothing can be hid: God is aware of all human deeds—past, present, and future (15:19; 17:15, 19; 42:18–25).

39:22 a river: The Hebrew reads: "the Nile". **a flood:** The Hebrew reads: "the Euphrates".

39:23 fresh water into salt: An allusion to God's judgment on Sodom and Gomorrah (Gen 13:10; 19:24–28; Deut 29:22–23; Ps 107:34).

39:25 good things ... evil things: God uses creation to enact his justice, giving to the righteous and the wicked as their deeds deserve (40:1).

39:26 water ... clothing: Ten things essential for human life (29:21).

---

[p]Cn: the meaning of Greek is uncertain.
[q]Gk *his*.

²⁷All these are for good to the godly,
　　just as they turn into evils for sinners.

²⁸There are winds that have been created for
　　vengeance,
　　and in their anger they scourge heavily;
　in the time of consummation they will pour out
　　their strength
　　and calm the anger of their Maker.
²⁹Fire and hail and famine and pestilence,
　　all these have been created for vengeance;
³⁰the teeth of wild beasts, and scorpions and vipers,
　　and the sword that punishes the ungodly with
　　destruction;
³¹they will rejoice in his commands,
　　and be made ready on earth for their service,
　　and when their times come they will not
　　transgress his word.

³²Therefore from the beginning I have been
　　convinced,
　　and have thought this out and left it in
　　writing:
³³The works of the Lord are all good,
　　and he will supply every need in its hour.
³⁴And no one can say, "This is worse than that,"
　　for all things will prove good in their season.
³⁵So now sing praise with all your heart and voice,
　　and bless the name of the Lord.

Human Wretchedness and
Joys of Life

40 Much labor was created for every man,
　　and a heavy yoke is upon the sons of Adam,
　from the day they come forth from their mother's
　　womb
　　till the day they return to^r the mother of all.

²Their perplexities and fear of heart—
　　their anxious thought is the day of death,
³from the man who sits on a splendid throne
　　to the one who is humbled in dust and ashes,
⁴from the man who wears purple and a crown
　　to the one who is clothed in burlap;
⁵there is anger and envy and trouble and unrest,
　　and fear of death, and fury and strife.
　And when one rests upon his bed,
　　his sleep at night confuses his mind.
⁶He gets little or no rest,
　　and afterward in his sleep, as though he were
　　on watch,
　he is troubled by the visions of his mind
　　like one who has escaped from the battle-
　　front;
⁷at the moment of his rescue he wakes up,
　　and wonders that his fear came to nothing.
⁸With all flesh, both man and beast,
　　and upon sinners seven times more,
⁹are death and bloodshed and strife and sword,
　　calamities, famine and affliction and plague.
¹⁰All these were created for the wicked,
　　and on their account the flood came.
¹¹All things that are from the earth turn back to
　　the earth,
　　and what is from the waters returns to the
　　sea.

¹²All bribery and injustice will be blotted out,
　　but good faith will stand for ever.
¹³The wealth of the unjust will dry up like a
　　torrent,
　　and crash like a loud clap of thunder in a rain.
¹⁴A generous man will be made glad;
　　likewise transgressors will utterly fail.

39:28–30 Nine destructive forces of nature and human creation that God uses to punish the wicked.

39:32 Therefore: Begins the epilogue of the poem.

39:33 all good: Repeats the thesis in 39:16.

39:34 no one can say: Ben Sira has answered the skeptic's questions posed in 39:17, 21. No one should criticize any aspect of God's creation—even the destructive forces of 39:28–30—as lacking a purpose.

39:35 sing praise: Ben Sira ends his hymn as he started it with a call to praise (39:14–15).

40:1—41:13 Ben Sira reflects on the sufferings (40:1–11) and joys of life (40:18–27) as well as divine retribution (40:12–17) and death (41:1–13).

40:1 Much labor: Not ordinary work, but restless toil, lack of leisure, and weariness (Ps 90:9–10; Job 7:1–3; 14:1–2; Eccles 2:22–23). **sons of Adam:** All humans beings, who languish under the burdensome effects of Adam's fall (Gen 3:17–19). **the mother of all:** The earth, to which all return at death (16:30; 17:1–2; 25:24; Gen 3:19; Rom 5:12; CCC 402).

40:2 the day of death: The specter of death hovers behind every human anxiety and fear.

40:3–4 a splendid throne: All men are subject to the trials of human existence, from the rich and powerful to the poorest of the poor. **burlap:** A coarse cloth worn by the poor.

40:5–7 Seven human woes that affect everyone. The number seven, signifying completeness, suggests total misery.

40:5 confuses his mind: Restless sleep and nightmares appear to be in view (Job 7:4).

40:9 death ... plague: Eight woes in addition to the psychological distresses listed in 40:5 (Is 51:19; Ezek 5:17; 28:23).

40:10 created for the wicked: Ben Sira returns to the topic of retribution, (39:29–31; Deut 28:15–68; Prov 17:13). **the flood:** The biblical flood is an example of God's judgment of the wicked in history (Gen 6–8).

40:11 back to the earth: See 40:1; 41:10; Gen 3:19; Job 34:15. **what is from the waters returns to the sea:** See Eccles 1:7. The Hebrew and Syriac read: "What is from above returns above"—referring to the human spirit that returns to God at death (Eccles 12:7).

40:12 bribery: Often condemned in the OT (35:12; Ex 23:8; Deut 10:17; 16:19; Ps 15:5). **blotted out:** All gains achieved through dishonest means will come to naught.

40:13 dry up like a torrent: The wadis in the Judean desert carry rushing streams of water in the winter, but they are completely dry riverbeds in the summer (Job 6:15–18).

---

^rOther authorities read *are buried in.*

¹⁵The children of the ungodly will not put forth
many branches;
they are unhealthy roots upon sheer rock.
¹⁶The reeds by any water or river bank
will be plucked up before any grass.
¹⁷Kindness is like a garden of blessings,
and almsgiving endures for ever.

¹⁸Life is sweet for the self-reliant and the worker,^s
but he who finds treasure is better off than
both.
¹⁹Children and the building of a city establish a
man's name,
but a blameless wife is accounted better than
both.
²⁰Wine and music gladden the heart,
but the love of wisdom is better than both.
²¹The flute and the harp make pleasant melody,
but a pleasant voice is better than both.
²²The eye desires grace and beauty,
but the green shoots of grain more than both.
²³A friend or a companion never meets one amiss,
but a wife with her husband is better than
both.
²⁴Brothers and help are for a time of trouble,
but almsgiving rescues better than both.
²⁵Gold and silver make the foot stand sure,
but good counsel is esteemed more than both.

²⁶Riches and strength lift up the heart,
but the fear of the Lord is better than both.
There is no loss in the fear of the Lord,
and with it there is no need to seek for help.
²⁷The fear of the Lord is like a garden of blessing,
and covers a man^t better than any glory.

²⁸My son, do not lead the life of a beggar;
it is better to die than to beg.
²⁹When a man looks to the table of another,
his existence cannot be considered as life.
He pollutes himself with another man's food,
but a man who is intelligent and well
instructed guards against that.
³⁰In the mouth of the shameless begging is sweet,
but in his stomach a fire is kindled.

A Series of Contrasts

41 O death, how bitter is the reminder of you
to one who lives at peace among his
possessions,
to a man without distractions, who is prosperous
in everything,
and who still has the vigor to enjoy his food!
²O death, how welcome is your sentence
to one who is in need and is failing in strength,
very old and distracted over everything;
to one who is contrary, and has lost his
patience!

40:15 children of the ungodly: The Hebrew reads: "a branch sprung from violence". **not ... many branches:** The wicked will have no lasting posterity (23:25; Job 8:11–12; Wis 4:3–5). **upon sheer rock:** Roots growing on rock can never grow deep (cf. Mt 13:5, 21).

40:17 a garden of blessings: Or "a blessed Eden/paradise" (40:27). The Hebrew of this verse reads: "But goodness will never be cut off, and justice endures forever."

40:18–27 Ben Sira surveys life's joys and pleasures. He lists ten pairs of blessings, each followed by something that is "better than both". The list culminates in the greatest good in Ben Sira's eyes—the fear of the Lord.

40:18 treasure: Probably a reference to wisdom (1:25).

40:19 establish a man's name: A man is remembered either by his children who bear his name (Deut 25:5–6) or by a city named after him (2 Sam 5:9). The Hebrew text adds here: "But better than either is the one who finds wisdom. Cattle and orchards make one prosperous." **blameless wife ... better than both:** On the blessings of finding a good wife, see 7:19; 25:8; 26:1–4, 13–18.

40:20 the love of wisdom: The Hebrew reads: "the affection of friends" or "of lovers" (6:14–17; 7:18; 9:10).

40:21 a pleasant voice: Or "a pure tongue" (6:5; 19:6–17; 20:5–8, 13; 22:27).

40:22 green shoots of grain: The promise of a good harvest, and thus of a plentiful food supply, is worth more than what is aesthetically pleasing to the eye.

40:23 never meets one amiss: Or "is always welcome". **a wife with her husband:** The Hebrew reads: "a sensible wife" (Prov 19:14).

40:24 almsgiving rescues: On the redeeming power of almsgiving, see 3:30—4:6; 17:22; 29:8–13.

40:25 stand sure: Wealth provides security. **good counsel:** See 21:13; 22:16; 24:29; 25:4–5; 37:13, 16.

40:26 lift up the heart: Or "make one confident". **fear of the Lord:** The ultimate good of life, according to Ben Sira.

40:27 a garden of blessing: The Hebrew reads: "Eden of blessing" (40:17). The idea is that fear of the Lord leads back to a communion with God that the first couple enjoyed in paradise (1:11–30; 15:1; 19:20; 21:6; 23:27). • The Church, rich in graces and chaste delights, is rightly called paradise for the faithful who live in temperance, justice, and the love of God (St. Augustine, *Sermons* 12, 34). **better than any glory:** Perhaps in the sense that having the fear of the Lord protects a man better than any position of importance.

40:28–30 An appeal to avoid the humiliation of begging at all costs (29:24–28).

40:28 better to die: Exaggeration for rhetorical effect.

40:29 pollutes himself: He loses his self-respect.

40:30 the shameless: Those who are not embarrassed to depend on others for survival. **fire is kindled:** A burning shame that follows enjoying another's food.

41:1–13 A threefold reflection on death in general (41:1–4), on the death of the wicked (41:5–11), and on the death of the righteous (41:12–13).

41:1 O death: A personification of death (Hos 13:14; 1 Cor 15:55). **how bitter:** To the man who enjoys a good and peaceful life, the thought of death is bitter, threatening to bring his comfortable existence to an end. **without distractions:** Without anxieties, without worries.

41:2 your sentence: Death is personified as a judge passing out sentences (of death) to each person. This can come as a relief to the person who is needy, weak, ill, or burdened with many worries (Job 21:23–26; Eccles 12:1–7).

---

^s Cn: Gk *self-reliant worker.*
^t Gk *him.*

³Do not fear the sentence of death;
  remember your former days and the end of
    life;
this is the decree from the Lord for all flesh,
⁴ and how can you reject the good pleasure of
    the Most High?
  Whether life is for ten or a hundred or a thousand
    years,
    there is no inquiry about it in Hades.

⁵The children of sinners are abominable children,
  and they frequent the haunts of the ungodly.
⁶The inheritance of the children of sinners will
    perish,
  and on their posterity will be a perpetual
    reproach.
⁷Children will blame an ungodly father,
  for they suffer reproach because of him.
⁸Woe to you, ungodly men,
  who have forsaken the law of the Most High
    God!
⁹When you are born, you are born to a curse;
  and when you die, a curse is your lot.
¹⁰Whatever is from the dust returns to dust;
  so the ungodly go from curse to destruction.

¹¹The mourning of men is about their bodies,
  but the evil name of sinners will be blotted out.
¹²Have regard for your name, since it will remain
    for you
  longer than a thousand great stores of gold.
¹³The days of a good life are numbered,
  but a good name endures for ever.

¹⁴My children, observe instruction and be at peace;
  hidden wisdom and unseen treasure,
    what advantage is there in either of them?
¹⁵Better is the man who hides his folly
  than the man who hides his wisdom.
¹⁶Therefore show respect for my words:
  For it is not good to retain every kind of shame,
    and not everything is confidently esteemed by
      every one.

¹⁷Be ashamed of immorality, before your father or
    mother;
  and of a lie, before a prince or a ruler;
¹⁸of a transgression, before a judge or magistrate;
  and of iniquity, before a congregation or the
    people;
  of unjust dealing, before your partner or friend;
¹⁹ and of theft, in the place where you live.
  Be ashamed before the truth of God and his
    covenant.
  Be ashamed of selfish behavior at meals,ᵘ
  of surliness in receiving and giving,
²⁰ and of silence, before those who greet you;
  of looking at a woman who is a harlot,
²¹ and of rejecting the appeal of a kinsman;
  of taking away some one's portion or gift,
    and of gazing at another man's wife;
²²of meddling with his maidservant—
  and do not approach her bed;
  of abusive words, before friends—
    and do not upbraid after making a gift;
²³of repeating and telling what you hear,
  and of revealing secrets.

41:3 Do not fear: Since death is the common lot of everyone. **remember your former days and the end of life:** Literally, "Remember the former and the latter", perhaps a reminder that death is also the lot of one's ancestors and descendants.

41:4 how can you reject: It is futile to argue against God's decrees. **Hades:** The realm of the dead, where no one will question God's designs (14:12, 16; 17:27; 21:10; 51:5–6).

✦ **41:5 abominable children:** The subject shifts to the death of the wicked. • The children of sinners are abominable to the Lord, not because they are born of wicked parents, but because they followed their evils ways (Rabanus Maurus, *On Ecclesiasticus* 9, 2). **the haunts of the ungodly:** They place themselves in ungodly surroundings.

41:6 a perpetual reproach: Grave sin can have a dishonoring legacy in families where it is allowed to flourish and even unleash intergenerational curses that are passed on from parents to children (Ex 20:5). Contrast with the lasting name and memory of the righteous (15:6; 37:26; 39:9–11; 41:13).

41:8 forsaken the law: Possibly the Hellenizing Jews of Ben Sira's time who neglected Torah observance in favor of Greek practices and customs (as in 1 Mac 3:5–8).

41:9 a curse: Hounds the ungodly and leads to their demise.

41:10 returns to dust: The Hebrew reads: "All that is from nothing returns to nothing, so the ungodly go from emptiness to emptiness" (Is 40:17).

41:11 blotted out: From the memory of the living and from God's Book of Life (cf. Ex 32:33; Rev 3:5)

41:12–13 Have regard for your name: I.e., protect your reputation in life, for it will outlive you. **endures for ever:** A good reputation will be a lasting memory (15:6; 37:26; 39:9–11).

41:14—42:8 Ben Sira distinguishes between proper shame, which leads away from sin (41:17–23), and improper or false shame, which wrongly follows good deeds (42:1–8; cf. 4:21).

41:14–15 These two verses also appear in 20:30–31.

41:17 immorality: The Greek is *porneia*, which refers to sexual immorality specifically (9:6; 18:30–31; 19:2–4; 23:16–21).

41:18 transgression: Some form of unlawful behavior. **iniquity:** Some sinful behavior or breach of the law.

41:19 theft: See 5:14. **before the truth of God and his covenant:** Or "to break an oath or a covenant". **selfish behavior at meals:** Literally, "bending the elbow over pieces of bread" (31:12–20). **surliness:** Refers to being unpleasant when receiving or giving gifts.

41:20 silence: On returning a greeting, see 4:8; Tob 5:9.

41:21 rejecting ... a kinsman: Turning away a relative who asks for help. **portion:** Perhaps the portion of a sacrifice reserved for priests (7:31; Ex 29:26–28) or what is owed to the poor. **gazing at ... wife:** Coveting another's wife is forbidden by the Decalogue (Ex 20:17; Deut 5:21); it can lead to adultery (9:7–8; Prov 6:25–29; Mt 5:28).

41:22 meddling with his maidservant: Implies sexual sins. **upbraid after making a gift:** Or follow up one's gift with an insult (18:15–18; 20:14–15).

41:23 revealing secrets: On gossip and betraying confidence, see 19:7; 22:22; 27:16–21. **proper shame:** The result of a well-formed conscience prompting the soul to turn away from evil (CCC 1777).

ᵘGk *of fixing the elbow on the bread.*

Then you will show proper shame,
and will find favor with every man.

42
Of the following things do not be ashamed,
and do not let partiality lead you to sin:
²of the law of the Most High and his covenant,
and of rendering judgment to acquit the
ungodly;
³of keeping accounts with a partner or with
traveling companions,
and of dividing the inheritance of friends;
⁴of accuracy with scales and weights,
and of acquiring much or little;
⁵of profit from dealing with merchants,
and of much discipline of children,
and of whipping a wicked servant severely.ᵛ
⁶Where there is an evil wife, a seal is a good thing;
and where there are many hands, lock things
up.
⁷Whatever you deal out, let it be by number and
weight,
and make a record of all that you give out or
take in.
⁸Do not be ashamed to instruct the stupid or
foolish
or the aged man who quarrels with the young.
Then you will be truly instructed,
and will be approved before all men.

⁹A daughter keeps her father secretly wakeful,
and worry over her robs him of sleep;
when she is young, lest she not marry,
or if married, lest she be hated;
¹⁰while a virgin, lest she be defiled
or become pregnant in her father's house;
or having a husband, lest she prove unfaithful,
or, though married, lest she be barren.
¹¹Keep strict watch over a headstrong daughter,
lest she make you a laughingstock to your
enemies,
a byword in the city and notoriousᵂ among the
people,
and put you to shame before the great multitude.

¹²Do not look upon any one for beauty,
and do not sit in the midst of women;
¹³for from garments comes the moth,
and from a woman comes woman's wickedness.
¹⁴Better is the wickedness of a man than a woman
who does good;
and it is a woman who brings shame and
disgrace.

¹⁵I will now call to mind the works of the Lord,
and will declare what I have seen.
By the words of the Lord his works are done,
and in his will, justice is carried out.

42:1 the following things: Several good things of which one should never be ashamed (42:2–5). **lead you to sin:** Being ashamed of doing the right thing because of peer or societal pressure appears to be in view.

42:2 of the law: One should not be ashamed of observing the Torah, even when many Jews find Hellenistic ways of life attractive (17:12; 24:23; 39:8; 45:5). **rendering judgment to acquit the ungodly:** One should be fair even toward the ungodly when they are not guilty of what they are accused of (Deut 1:17; 16:18–20).

42:3 dividing the inheritance: Includes accepting one's rightful share of an inheritance.

42:4 scales and weights: Honest business transactions (Lev 19:35–36; Prov 11:1; 16:11; 20:10, 23). **of acquiring much or little:** There is nothing wrong with making a profit in honest ways.

42:5 dealing with merchants: Bartering and bargaining with merchants is a common practice in the Middle East. There is no shame in getting a good deal out of negotiations. **discipline of children:** A moral obligation for parents, not a cause for shame (30:1–13). **whipping a wicked servant:** Ben Sira's counsel reflects the harshness of a time when slavery was common.

42:6 an evil wife: An untrustworthy wife (23:22–26; 25:13–20). **a seal:** A metaphor advising to keep her at home, as one should lock up valuables away from thieves.

42:7 number and weight: Honest business dealings require just measurements and careful accounting.

42:8 quarrels with the young: The Hebrew reads: "engaged in immorality". **approved before all men:** Far from being shameful, the things previously noted are praiseworthy.

42:9–14 In the Middle East, shame is a family affair, so that if a misdeed becomes public, shame attaches not only to the perpetrator but to his entire family. This is particularly the case with women, explaining in part why Ben Sira speaks so harshly in what follows.

42:9–10 A daughter can be a source of anxiety to her father, who worries if **(1)** she will find a husband, **(2)** she will be divorced, **(3)** she will become pregnant out of wedlock, **(4)** she will be an adulteress, or **(5)** she will be childless.

42:9 lest ... hated: A reference to divorce (Deut 24:1).

42:10 lest ... pregnant: By rape or fornication. Virginity was typically required of a new bride. **lest ... unfaithful:** Adultery was punishable by death (Deut 22:22). **lest ... barren:** A cause for disgrace and disappointment in biblical times (Gen 11:30; 25:21; 29:31; Judg 13:2; 1 Sam 1:2; Lk 1:7).

42:11 Keep strict watch: Also appears in 26:10. **laughingstock:** A daughter's misbehavior was a public embarrassment. The Hebrew adds: "See that there is no lattice in her room, no spot that overlooks the approaches to the house"—to prevent her from becoming a cause of temptation to passersby (Prov 7:6).

42:12–13 Do not look ... for beauty: The Greek is unclear. The Hebrew reads: "Let her not show her beauty to any man or spend her time among married women." **from garments:** As moths feed on clothing, so women learn evil from other women.

42:14 Better is the wickedness of a man: Overstated for rhetorical effect. Still, it is evidence that Ben Sira was the product of a culture that greatly undervalued women.

42:15—43:33 A hymn that praises God's works in the natural world. It alludes several times to the creation story in Genesis and acts as a prelude to what follows in 44:1–50:24.

42:15–25 Ben Sira praises God's omnipotence and omniscience.

42:15 call to mind the works of the Lord: Alludes to Ps 77:12. **the words of the Lord:** Created the universe (Gen 1; Ps 33:6; Wis 9:1; Jn 1:1–3).

ᵛGk m*aking the side of a wicked servant bleed.*
ᵂGk *called out.*

¹⁶The sun looks down on everything with its light,
  and the work of the Lord is full of his glory.
¹⁷The Lord has not enabled his holy ones
  to recount all his marvelous works,
which the Lord the Almighty has established
  that the universe may stand firm in his glory.
¹⁸He searches out the abyss, and the hearts of
  men,ˣ
  and considers their crafty devices.
For the Most High knows all that may be known,
  and he looks into the signsʸ of the age.
¹⁹He declares what has been and what is to be,
  and he reveals the tracks of hidden things.
²⁰No thought escapes him,
  and not one word is hidden from him.
²¹He has ordained the splendors of his wisdom,
  and he is from everlasting and to everlasting.
Nothing can be added or taken away,
  and he needs no one to be his counselor.
²²How greatly to be desired are all his works,
  and how sparkling they are to see!ᶻ
²³All these things live and remain for ever
  for every need, and are all obedient.
²⁴All things are twofold, one opposite the other,
  and he has made nothing incomplete.
²⁵One confirms the good things of the other,
  and who can have enough of beholding his
  glory?

God's Greatness in Creation

43 The pride of the heavenly heights is the clear
  firmament,

the appearance of heaven in a spectacle of
  glory.
²The sun, when it appears, making proclamation
  as it goes forth,
  is a marvelous instrument, the work of the
  Most High.
³At noon it parches the land;
  and who can withstand its burning heat?
⁴A man tendingᵃ a furnace works in burning heat,
  but the sun burns the mountains three times
  as much;
  it breathes out fiery vapors,
  and with bright beams it blinds the eyes.
⁵Great is the Lord who made it;
  and at his command it hastens on its course.

⁶He made the moon also, to serve in its seasonᵇ
  to mark the times and to be an everlasting
  sign.
⁷From the moon comes the sign for feast days,
  a light that wanes when it has reached the full.
⁸The month is named for the moon,
  increasing marvelously in its phases,
  an instrument of the hosts on high
  shining forth in the firmament of heaven.

⁹The glory of the stars is the beauty of heaven,
  a gleaming array in the heights of the Lord.
¹⁰At the command of the Holy One they stand as
  ordered,
  they never relax in their watches.

42:16 his glory: Likened to the radiance of the sun (Ps 19:1–6).

42:17 his holy ones: The angels (Job 5:1; 15:15; Ps 89:7; Dan 8:13). Even these are unable to recount all the Lord's wonderful deeds (18:4–7; 43:27–31).

42:18 knows all that may be known: An assertion of God's omniscience. He has complete knowledge of the watery "deep" (1:1–3; 24:5; Gen 1:2; Ps 33:7; 36:6) as well as the innermost thoughts of men (Ps 139; Prov 15:11; Jud 8:14; Heb 4:13). **he looks into the signs of the age:** The Hebrew reads: "He sees what is to come forever."

42:21 Nothing can be added or taken away: See 18:6; Eccles 3:14. **needs no ... counselor:** See Is 40:13–14; Rom 11:34.

42:23 remain for ever: Not that creation is eternal, but that its structures and laws are firmly established. **obedient:** All the works of creation serve God's purpose (39:21, 33–34).

42:24 one opposite the other: Probably refers to opposites such as day and night, light and darkness, good and evil (33:15).

42:25 the good things of the other: Every created thing confirms the goodness of the rest of creation. **who can have enough ...?:** The implied answer: "no one"—for God's glory is infinite and infinitely beautiful.

43:1–26 The second part of the hymn praises the firmament and sun (43:1–5), the moon (43:6–8), the stars and the

rainbow (43:9–12). The poem ends with a renewed invitation to praise the Lord (43:27–33).

43:1 firmament: The first witness to God's glory (Gen 1:6–8; Ps 19:1). See note on Gen 1:6.

43:2 proclamation: The sun announces each new day (Ps 19:4–6).

43:3 it parches the land: The Hebrew reads: "It causes the world to boil", emphasizing the intensity of the sun's heat.

43:5 its course: The sun's daily circuit (Ps 19:5–6).

43:6 the moon ... the times: Even more than the sun, the moon plays an essential role in Judaism to mark festivals and divisions of time (Gen 1:14–18; Ps 104:19). **everlasting sign:** A sign that endures as long as the world remains (Ps 72:5; 89:37; Jer 31:35–36).

43:7 feast days: The holy days of Israel's liturgical calendar (Lev 23).

43:8 named for the moon: A pun on the Hebrew word *hodesh*, which means both "month" and "new moon" (= the start of each new month). **increasing:** Waxing or growing fuller each night until it becomes a full moon. **an instrument:** A beacon or fire signal to lead an army during the night. The moon leads, as it were, the "army of stars". • He speaks of the moon after the sun because the Church follows Christ. And as the moon is illumined by the sun, so the Church is illumined by Christ. The Church is rightly compared to the moon, since she has no splendor of her own but receives her light from the sun (Rabanus Maurus, *On Ecclesiasticus* 9, 7).

43:10 they stand as ordered: Like all other created things, the stars exist to accomplish God's purposes (39:16–34; 42:23; Ps 119:91). **never relax in their watches:** The stars are compared to soldiers standing guard at their post (Bar 3:34).

ˣGk *and the heart.*
ʸGk *sign.*
ᶻThe Greek of this line is uncertain.
ᵃOther authorities read *blowing.*
ᵇThe Greek text of this line is uncertain.

[11]Look upon the rainbow, and praise him who
    made it,
      exceedingly beautiful in its brightness.
[12]It encircles the heaven with its glorious arc;
    the hands of the Most High have stretched it
      out.

[13]By his command he sends the driving snow
    and speeds the lightning of his judgment.
[14]Therefore the storehouses are opened,
    and the clouds fly forth like birds.
[15]In his majesty he amasses the clouds,
    and the hailstones are broken in pieces.
[16]At his appearing the mountains are shaken;
    at his will the south wind blows.
[17]The voice of his thunder rebukes the earth;
    so do the tempest from the north and the
      whirlwind.
    He scatters the snow like birds flying down,
    and its descent is like locusts alighting.
[18]The eye marvels at the beauty of its whiteness,
    and the mind is amazed at its falling.
[19]He pours the hoarfrost upon the earth like salt,
    and when it freezes, it becomes pointed
      thorns.
[20]The cold north wind blows,
    and ice freezes over the water;
    it rests upon every pool of water,
    and the water puts it on like a breastplate.
[21]He consumes the mountains and burns up the
    wilderness,
    and withers the tender grass like fire.

[22]A mist quickly heals all things;
    when the dew appears, it refreshes from the
      heat.

[23]By his counsel he stilled the great deep
    and planted islands in it.
[24]Those who sail the sea tell of its dangers,
    and we marvel at what we hear.
[25]For in it are strange and marvelous works,
    all kinds of living things, and huge creatures
      of the sea.
[26]Because of him his messenger finds the way,
    and by his word all things hold together.

[27]Though we speak much we cannot reach the end,
    and the sum of our words is: "He is the all."
[28]Where shall we find strength to praise him?
    For he is greater than all his works.
[29]Terrible is the Lord and very great,
    and marvelous is his power.
[30]When you praise the Lord, exalt him as much as
    you can;
    for he will surpass even that.
    When you exalt him, put forth all your strength,
    and do not grow weary, for you cannot praise
      him enough.
[31]Who has seen him and can describe him?
    Or who can extol him as he is?
[32]Many things greater than these lie hidden,
    for we have seen but few of his works.
[33]For the Lord has made all things,
    and to the godly he has granted wisdom.

43:11 the rainbow: Its extraordinary beauty prompts man to praise God (50:7; Ezek 1:28). It is also the sign of God's covenant with Noah after the flood (Gen 9:12–17).

43:13–26 Ben Sira turns from the astral bodies to meteorological phenomena, which also fulfill God's will. The image of the storm provides a foretaste and anticipation of God's future judgment upon the world (cf. Ps 29).

43:13 snow: Rare in Israel but not unheard of (Ps 147:16; 148:8; Is 55:10). **lightning:** A sign of God's judgment, see 2 Sam 22:15; Job 36:30–33; Ps 144:6; Zech 9:14; Wis 5:21; Mt 24:27.

43:14 storehouses: Pictured as a treasure-house of weather that God can open and release at will (Deut 28:12; Jer 10:13; 51:16; Job 38:22).

43:15 hailstones are broken: As if chipped from a massive piece of ice in the heavens.

43:16 mountains are shaken: The appearance of God is often described as a mighty earthquake (Ex 19:18; Judg 5:5; Ps 68:8; 77:18; Jer 10:10). **south wind:** See Ps 78:26.

43:17 thunder: A manifestation of God's power (cf. Ex 19:19; Is 29:6; Ps 29:3–4). **tempest ... whirlwind:** Powerful natural phenomena are often associated with divine judgment (Is 40:24; 41:16; Jer 23:19; 30:23). **birds ... locusts:** The imagery shifts from violent weather to calm and order.

43:20 wind ... ice: The cold of winter is another manifestation of God's power (Ps 147:16–18; Prov 25:13). **like a breastplate:** The water is personified as a soldier, putting on a layer of ice as protective armor.

43:21 burns up the wilderness: The focus shifts from the cold of winter to the heat of summer, which causes devastating droughts.

43:22 dew ... refreshes: Dew in the summer is compared to a doctor giving relief to a sick patient (Gen 27:28; Deut 33:28; Ps 133:3; Prov 19:12).

43:23 the great deep: The unsearchable depths of the sea (42:18; Gen 1:2; Ps 104:25–26; Job 28:14; 38:16, 30).

43:25 huge creatures: The mythical sea monster, called Rahab or Leviathan, that was believed to represent the forces of evil (Is 27:1; 51:9; Ps 89:10; Job 3:8; 26:12; Rev 13:1).

43:27 cannot reach the end: Ben Sira could go on, but no words can exhaust the greatness of God's power and wisdom. **He is the all:** Language reminiscent of Greek philosophy. God is present throughout the created world (CCC 300).

43:28 greater than all his works: Although God is present within creation, he also transcends it and is not to be confused with it in a pantheistic sense (Ps 145:3; Wis 13:1–5; Rom 1:20; CCC 300).

43:29 Terrible: In the sense of "awesome" or "fearsome" (Ps 96:4).

43:30 cannot praise him enough: The contemplation of God's power in creation should lead every wise person to break forth in an unending song of praise.

43:31 Who has seen ...? Or who can extol ...?: Both questions expect the answer: "no one", underlining the limited human capacity to know God (Ps 106:2).

43:32–33 Many things greater: Points to the unsearchable mysteries of God's creation still undiscovered (16:21; Job 26:14). **to the godly ... wisdom:** The path to discovering these mysteries lies in the acquisition of wisdom through the fear of the Lord.

Praise of Our Fathers

44 Let us now praise famous men,
and our fathers in their generations.

[2]The Lord apportioned to them[c] great glory,
his majesty from the beginning.

[3]There were those who ruled in their kingdoms,
and were men renowned for their power,
giving counsel by their understanding,
and proclaiming prophecies;

[4]leaders of the people in their deliberations
and in understanding of learning for the
people,
wise in their words of instruction;

[5]those who composed musical tunes,
and set forth verses in writing;

[6]rich men furnished with resources,
living peaceably in their habitations—

[7]all these were honored in their generations,
and were the glory of their times.

[8]There are some of them who have left a name,
so that men declare their praise.

[9]And there are some who have no memorial,
who have perished as though they had not
lived;
they have become as though they had not been
born,
and so have their children after them.

[10]But these were men of mercy,
whose righteous deeds have not been
forgotten;

[11]their prosperity will remain with their descendants,
and their inheritance to their children's
children.[d]

[12]Their descendants stand by the covenants;
their children also, for their sake.

[13]Their posterity will continue for ever,
and their glory will not be blotted out.

[14]Their bodies were buried in peace,
and their name lives to all generations.

[15]Peoples will declare their wisdom,
and the congregation proclaims their praise.

[16]E'noch pleased the Lord, and was taken up;
he was an example of repentance to all
generations.

[17]Noah was found perfect and righteous;
in the time of wrath he was taken in exchange;

44:1—50:24 Praise of Israel's famous ancestors. Ben Sira holds that divine wisdom is manifest not only in the natural world, but even more in the heroic figures of biblical history. Following an introduction (44:1–15), he surveys the early Patriarchs (44:16–23), Moses, Aaron, and Phinehas (45:1–26), Joshua, Caleb, the Judges, and Samuel (46:1–20), Nathan, David, and Solomon (47:1–22), the prophets Elijah and Elisha in the Northern Kingdom of Israel (48:1–15), Hezekiah and Isaiah in the Southern Kingdom of Judah (48:16–25), then King Josiah, the great prophets, and the postexilic heroes of Israel (49:1–16). This is the most extensive survey of salvation history found in Scripture (see also Ps 78; 105; 106; 135; 136; 1 Mac 2:51–60; Jud 5:5–21; Wis 10; Acts 7:2–53). The author draws attention to these pious men so that others can learn from their wisdom.

44:1–15 Ben Sira outlines the traits of those heroes of the faith who left a lasting memory.

44:1 famous men: The Hebrew reads: "men of mercy" or "devout men" (44:10). **in their generations:** Of generations past.

44:2 great glory: Ben Sira lists in 44:3–6 twelve categories of heroes to be praised because they shared in God's glory.

44:3 ruled in their kingdoms: E.g., David and Solomon (47:1–22). **men renowned:** E.g., Joshua, Caleb, the Judges, and Samuel (46:1–20). **giving counsel:** E.g., Nathan and Isaiah (47:1; 48:20–22). **proclaiming prophecies:** E.g., Elijah, Elisha, Isaiah, Jeremiah, Ezekiel, and the 12 Minor Prophets (48:1–16; 49:6–10).

44:4 leaders: E.g., Joseph, Zerubbabel, Nehemiah (49:11–15). **understanding of learning:** E.g., Moses (45:1–5). **wise in their words:** E.g., Solomon, Job (Hebrew text of 49:9). The Hebrew text adds a fourth clause: "and speakers of proverbs in their traditions", i.e., Solomon and Ben Sira himself.

44:5 composed musical tunes: E.g., David. **set forth verses:** E.g., Solomon, Hezekiah (Is 38:9–20).

44:6 rich men: E.g., Abraham, Isaac, Jacob (44:19–23). **living peaceably:** E.g., Job.

44:7 all these were honored: The glory of the 12 categories of heroes was both recognized in their own time and remembered in Ben Sira's days.

44:8 some ... left a name: Some of these godly men are still remembered; their good reputation has outlived them (39:9–11; 41:12–13).

44:9 some who have no memorial: It is not clear whether Ben Sira means holy men who have been forgotten (cf. Wis 3:1–3)—in which case 44:10–15 refers to these anonymous saints, or to godless men who are rightly forgotten—in which case 44:10–15 refers to the heroes named in the rest of the hymn. Ben Sira's view of memory in 10:17; 39:9–11; and 41:6–13 favors the latter interpretation. **as though ... not been born:** See Job 10:19; Obad 16.

44:10 men of mercy: See 44:1.

44:11 their children's children: The blessings of the righteous are also for their posterity (45:25–26; Job 21:8), provided they remain faithful to God's covenants with Israel (11:20; 17:12; 24:23; 28:7; 39:8; 44:18, 20; 45:15, 24–25).

44:14 Their bodies ... their name: The righteous receive both an honorable burial and a lasting reputation for ages to come (41:11–13).

44:15 Peoples will declare their wisdom: This verse is almost identical to 39:10.

44:16–23 Praise for the early Patriarchs of the Book of Genesis.

44:16 Enoch: Lived before the flood (Gen 5:21–24). **pleased the Lord:** The Hebrew reads: "walked with the Lord". **was taken up:** The reason why God "took" Enoch is not stated in Genesis. Ben Sira's view that **he was an example of repentance** represents a theological development, as there is no record in earlier texts of Enoch sinning and repenting. The Hebrew calls him "a miracle of knowledge to all generations". Other traditions state that God took him to preserve him from sin (49:14; Wis 4:10–14; Heb 11:5).

44:17 Noah was found perfect: Noah and his family were the only ones found righteous in their generation (Gen 6:9; 7:1; 2 Pet 2:5). **the time of wrath:** When God flooded the world because of the sins of mankind (Gen 6:11–13). **he was taken in exchange:** The Greek is unclear. The Hebrew

---

[c]Heb: Gk *created.*
[d]Heb Compare Vg Syr: The Greek of this verse is uncertain.

therefore a remnant was left to the earth
    when the flood came.
¹⁸Everlasting covenants were made with him
    that all flesh should not be blotted out by a
    flood.

¹⁹Abraham was the great father of a multitude of
    nations,
    and no one has been found like him in glory;
²⁰he kept the law of the Most High,
    and was taken into covenant with him;
he established the covenant in his flesh,
    and when he was tested he was found faithful.
²¹Therefore the Lord^e assured him by an oath
    that the nations would be blessed through his
    posterity;
that he would multiply him like the dust of the
    earth,
    and exalt his posterity like the stars,
and cause them to inherit from sea to sea
    and from the River to the ends of the earth.

²²To Isaac also he gave the same assurance
    for the sake of Abraham his father.

²³The blessing of all men and the covenant
    he made to rest upon the head of Jacob;

he acknowledged him with his blessings,
    and gave him his inheritance;^f
he determined his portions,
    and distributed them among twelve tribes.

45 From his descendants the Lord^g brought
    forth a man of mercy,
    who found favor in the sight of all flesh
and was beloved by God and man,
    Moses, whose memory is blessed.
²He made him equal in glory to the holy ones,
    and made him great in the fears of his
    enemies.
³By his words he caused signs to cease;
    the Lord^g glorified him in the presence of
    kings.
He gave him commands for his people,
    and showed him part of his glory.
⁴He sanctified him through faithfulness and
    meekness;
    he chose him out of all mankind.
⁵He made him hear his voice,
    and led him into the thick darkness,
and gave him the commandments face to face,
    the law of life and knowledge,
to teach Jacob the covenant,
    and Israel his judgments.

---

reads: "He was the one who continued", apparently meaning that Noah kept the human race from dying out. **a remnant:** Noah, his wife, their three sons, and their wives (Gen 7:13).

44:18 Everlasting covenants: The Hebrew reads: "A lasting sign sealed the assurance to him ... ", referring to the rainbow as a sign of God's pledge never to flood the earth again (Gen 9:12–17).

44:19 Abraham: The great-grandfather of the people of Israel. **father of a multitude:** As stated in Gen 17:4–5. **no one ... like him in glory:** The Hebrew reads: "He kept his glory without stain."

44:20 he kept the law: Seems like an anachronism, since the Torah was given centuries after Abraham. However, ancient Jewish commentaries hold on the basis of Gen 26:5 that Abraham kept the Law even before it had been revealed to Israel. **covenant in his flesh:** The covenant of circumcision (Gen 17:9–11, 26). **when he was tested:** When Abraham was found willing to sacrifice his son, Isaac (Gen 22:1–19; 1 Mac 2:52; Heb 11:17).

44:21 assured him by an oath: God's solemn oath to bless all nations through Abraham's descendants occurs in Gen 22:16–18. **inherit from sea to sea:** This combines God's promise of the land of Canaan to Abraham's offspring with the prayer of Ps 72:8 asking God to expand Solomon's dominion beyond the borders of Israel so that all kings bow before him (cf. Ex 23:31; Deut 11:24; Josh 1:4; Ps 72:8; Zech 9:10; Rom 4:13).

44:21 the River: The Euphrates (Gen 31:21). **the ends of the earth:** Possibly the shore of the Mediterranean Sea or even the Atlantic coast of Spain.

44:22 To Isaac: God confirmed and renewed the Abrahamic covenant and promises with his son, Isaac (Gen 26:3–6, 24).

44:23 the covenant: That God made with Abraham and Isaac. **of Jacob:** The son of Isaac, whom God renamed "Israel" (Gen 32:28; 35:10). The Hebrew reads: "of Israel". **his blessings:** The blessing of the first-born (Gen 27:1–29; 28:3–4, 13–15; Deut 21:17). **his inheritance:** The land of Israel. Jacob is the father of the twelve tribes of Israel (Gen 35:22–26; 49:1–28).

45:1–26 This chapter covers the figures of Moses (45:1–5), Aaron (45:6–22), and Phinehas (45:23–26). The fact that Aaron gets by far the most attention shows the importance of the priesthood and liturgy for Ben Sira.

45:1 From his descendants: Jacob's descendants. **a man of mercy:** Moses (cf. 44:10). **who found favor:** Before Pharaoh's daughter (Ex 2:5–10), Reuel and his daughters (Ex 2:16–22), and the Egyptians (Ex 11:3). **beloved by God:** On Moses' unique relationship with God, see Ex 33:11; Num 12:7–8. **whose memory is blessed:** On the blessed memory of a good man, see 35:7; 39:9; 44:10–15.

45:2 equal in glory: God made Moses as glorious as the angels. **holy ones:** See note on 42:17. **the fears of his enemies:** Alludes to the terrifying plagues that Moses unleashed upon Egypt (Ex 7–12; Deut 4:34; 26:8).

45:3 caused signs to cease: Or, following the Hebrew, "he brought signs swiftly to pass". **the presence of kings:** Moses stood before Pharaoh (Ex 7:1–7). **gave him commands:** See Ex 6:13. **part of his glory:** Moses was permitted to see God's "back" (Ex 33:18–23; 34:5–8).

45:4 He sanctified: Or "set him apart". **faithfulness and meekness:** See Num 12:3, 7; Heb 3:2, 5.

45:5 hear his voice: The voice of God at Mt. Sinai (Ex 33:11; Num 12:8; Deut 4:36). **thick darkness:** A manifestation of God's presence on Sinai (Ex 20:21; 24:18). **the commandments:** The Decalogue (Ex 20; 32:15; Deut 6:1). **the law of life:** The Torah is the source of life for Israel (17:11; Lev 18:5; Deut 30:15–16; Ezek 20:11). **to teach Jacob:** I.e., to teach the nation of Israel (Ps 147:19).

---

^e Gk *he.*
^f Heb: Gk *by inheritance.*
^g Gk *he.*

⁶He exalted Aaron, the brother of Moses, ʰ
a holy man like him, of the tribe of Levi.
⁷He made an everlasting covenant with him,
and gave him the priesthood of the people.
He blessed him with splendid vestments,
and put a glorious robe upon him.
⁸He clothed him with superb perfection,
and strengthened him with the symbols of
authority,
the linen breeches, the long robe, and the
ephod.
⁹And he encircled him with pomegranates,
with very many golden bells round about,
to send forth a sound as he walked,
to make their ringing heard in the temple
as a reminder to the sons of his people;
¹⁰with a holy garment, of gold and blue
and purple, the work of an embroiderer;
with the oracle of judgment, U'rim and Thummim;
¹¹ with twisted scarlet, the work of a craftsman;
with precious stones engraved like signets,
in a setting of gold, the work of a jeweler,
for a reminder, in engraved letters,
according to the number of the tribes of Israel;
¹²with a gold crown upon his turban,
inscribed like a signet with "Holiness,"
a distinction to be prized, the work of an expert,
the delight of the eyes, richly adorned.

¹³Before his time there never were such beautiful
things.
No outsider ever put them on,
but only his sons
and his descendants perpetually.
¹⁴His sacrifices shall be wholly burned
twice every day continually.
¹⁵Moses ordained him,
and anointed him with holy oil;
it was an everlasting covenant for him
and for his descendants all the days of
heaven,
to minister to the Lord ⁱ and serve as priest
and bless his people in his name.
¹⁶He chose him out of all the living
to offer sacrifice to the Lord,
incense and a pleasing odor as a memorial
portion,
to make atonement for the people. ʲ
¹⁷In his commandments he gave him
authority in statutes and ᵏ judgments,
to teach Jacob the testimonies,
and to enlighten Israel with his law.
¹⁸Outsiders conspired against him,
and envied him in the wilderness,
Da'than and Abi'ram and their men
and the company of Ko'rah, in wrath and
anger.

***

45:6 Aaron, the brother of Moses: The sons of Amram and Jochebed (Ex 4:14; 6:20). **a holy man:** Specially sanctified (set apart) by virtue of his priesthood (Ps 106:16). **Levi:** The fourth son of Jacob (Gen 29:34; Ex 2:1–2; 4:14).

45:7 everlasting covenant: The priesthood would always remain in Aaron's line (Ex 29:9; 40:15; Num 25:13; 1 Mac 2:54). **the priesthood:** Given to Aaron and his sons (Ex 29:44; 40:13–15). The Hebrew reads: "bestowed upon him his majesty" (Num 27:20; 1 Chron 29:25). **splendid vestments:** The priestly vestments that Ben Sira describes at length in 45:8–13 (Ex 28:1–4).

45:8 perfection: On the beauty of the high priest's garments, see 50:11; Ex 28:2, 40. **breeches:** The undergarments (Ex 28:42–43). **the long robe:** The blue ephod (Ex 28:31–35). **the ephod:** An apron of gold, blue, purple, and scarlet yarns that the high priest wore over the robe (Ex 28:6–14). The Hebrew reads: "the breeches, tunic, and robe". • The vestments of the high priest are the virtues and wise teaching that must adorn the priest of the Lord at all times (Rabanus Maurus, *On Ecclesiasticus* 10, 9).

45:9 pomegranates: Small decorations knitted of blue, purple, and scarlet stuff (Ex 28:33). **golden bells:** Sewn with the pomegranates on the lower hem of the robe (Ex 28:34). **heard in the temple:** The congregation could hear the high priest ministering inside the sanctuary, especially on the Day of Atonement when he entered the Holy of Holies (Ex 28:35; Lev 16).

45:10 a holy garment: Either the high priest's outfit as a whole (Ex 28:2–6) or the ephod in particular (Ex 28:6–14).

Urim and Thummim: Literally, "the decider of truth". These were small objects kept in the breastplate and used to determine God's will (33:3; Num 27:21; 1 Sam 14:41).

45:11 precious stones: Set in the breastplate and arranged in four rows of three stones. Each stone was engraved with the name of one of the Israelite tribes (Ex 28:17–21, 29).

45:12 gold crown: See Ex 28:36–38; 29:6. **with "Holiness":** Literally, "with a seal of holiness". According to Ex 39:30, the inscription read: "Holy to the Lᴏʀᴅ".

45:13 such beautiful things: Ben Sira marvels at the beauty of the high priest's garments, a symbol of his mediation between God and the people. **No outsider:** The garments were strictly reserved for the sons of Aaron (Ex 29:29).

45:14 His sacrifices: The high priest's liturgical functions are in view, including his daily offerings. **twice every day:** One lamb was sacrificed as a burnt offering in the morning, and one in the evening (Ex 29:38–42; Num 28:3–8).

45:15 Moses ordained him: Literally, "Moses filled his hands." Aaron's ordination also included anointing with oil (Lev 8:12). **everlasting covenant:** See note on 45:7. **all the days of heaven:** As long as creation endures (50:24; Deut 11:21; Ps 89:29). **bless his people:** The priestly blessing of Num 6:23–27.

45:16 to offer sacrifice: One of the most important tasks of the priests (Lev 1–7). **as a memorial portion:** The part of the grain offering that was consumed by fire (35:7; Lev 2:2, 9, 16). **make atonement:** To obtain forgiveness (Lev 4:20, 31; 16:32–34).

45:17 authority in statutes: The Levitical priests were the original teachers and judges of the Israelites (Lev 10:11; Deut 17:9–12; 21:5; 33:10).

45:18 Outsiders conspired: The wicked attempted to seize priestly authority in Num 16:1–35. **Dathan and Abiram:** From the tribe of Reuben. **Korah:** A Levite, but not a descendant of Aaron (Num 16:1).

***

ʰ Gk *him.*
ⁱ Gk *him.*
ʲ Other authorities read *your people.*
ᵏ Heb: Gk *in covenants of.*

¹⁹The Lord saw it and was not pleased,
  and in the wrath of his anger they were
    destroyed;
  he wrought wonders against them
    to consume them in flaming fire.
²⁰He added glory to Aaron
    and gave him a heritage;
  he allotted to him the first of the first fruits,
    he prepared bread of first fruits in abundance;
²¹for they eat the sacrifices to the Lord,
    which he gave to him and his descendants.
²²But in the land of the people he has no inheritance,
    and he has no portion among the people;
  for the Lord¹ himself is hisᵐ portion and
    inheritance.

²³Phin′ehas the son of Elea′zar is the third in glory,
    for he was zealous in the fear of the Lord,
  and stood fast, when the people turned away,
    in the ready goodness of his soul,
    and made atonement for Israel.
²⁴Therefore a covenant of peace was established
    with him,
  that he should be leader of the sanctuary and
    of his people,
  that he and his descendants should have
    the dignity of the priesthood for ever.
²⁵A covenant was also established with David,
    the son of Jesse, of the tribe of Judah:
  the heritage of the king is from son to son only;
    so the heritage of Aaron is for his descendants.

²⁶May the Lordⁿ grant you wisdom in your heart
    to judge his people in righteousness,
  so that their prosperity may not vanish,
    and that their glory may endure throughout
      their generations.°

46 Joshua the son of Nun was mighty in war,
    and was the successor of Moses in
      prophesying.
  He became, in accordance with his name,
    a great savior of God'sᵖ elect,
  to take vengeance on the enemies that rose
    against them,
    so that he might give Israel its inheritance.
²How glorious he was when he lifted his hands
    and stretched out his sword against the
      cities!
³Who before him ever stood so firm?
    For he waged the wars of the Lord.
⁴Was not the sun held back by his hand?
    And did not one day become as long as two?
⁵He called upon the Most High, the Mighty One,
    when enemies pressed him on every side,
⁶and the great Lord answered him
    with hailstones of mighty power.
  He hurled down war upon that nation,
    and at the descent of Beth-ho′ronᵠ he
      destroyed those who resisted,
  so that the nations might know his armament,
    that he was fighting in the sight of the Lord;
    for he wholly followed the Mighty One.

45:19 destroyed: The earth opened up and swallowed the rebels (Num 16:31–33). **flaming fire:** Consumed another 250 men who had joined the rebellion (Num 16:35).

45:20 added glory to Aaron: The rights, privileges, and responsibilities of the priests were increased after Korah's rebellion (Num 18:1–7). **first fruits:** The first part of the harvest was reserved for the priests (Num 18:11–13). **bread of first fruits:** An unusual expression, perhaps referring to the bread of the Presence that was kept in the sanctuary and was eaten by the priests (Lev 24:5–9).

45:21 eat the sacrifices: Priests were given sacrificial portions as food (Num 18:8–10).

45:22 no inheritance: Unlike the lay tribes, the Levitical tribe did not inherit any territory in the land of Israel. **the Lord himself is his portion:** Serving God in his sanctuary was a higher privilege than owning land (Num 18:20; Deut 18:1; Josh 13:14).

45:23 Phinehas the son of Eleazar: Aaron's grandson (Ex 6:25; Num 25:6–13). **third in glory:** After Moses and Aaron. **he was zealous:** In killing an Israelite idolater and fornicator, along with his concubine (Num 25:6–9). **in the fear of the Lord:** By identifying fear of the Lord as the driving force behind Phinehas' action, Ben Sira implies that he is a great wise man of Israel. **atonement for Israel:** Phinehas' action averted God's wrath and stopped a devastating plague (Num 25:8–11; Ps 106:30–31).

45:24 priesthood for ever: Because of his zeal, Phinehas and his descendants inherited a covenant of perpetual priesthood (45:7; Num 25:12–13).

45:25 David: The first king of Israel, from the tribe of Judah. **from son to son:** The royal covenant God made with David, like the priestly covenant he made with Aaron, is a hereditary covenant that passes down his genealogical line (2 Sam 7:11–16; 2 Chron 13:5; Ps 89:3–5).

45:26 May the Lord grant: A prayer for wisdom for the successors of Aaron and Phinehas, especially the high priest in Ben Sira's own day, Simon the son of Onias (50:1–24).

46:1–20 Praise for Israel's ancient heroes: Joshua, Caleb, the Judges, and Samuel.

46:1 Joshua the son of Nun: Successor of Moses as leader of Israel. He was from the tribe of Ephraim and originally named "Hoshea" (Ex 17:9–14; 24:13; 33:11; Num 13:8, 16). **prophesying:** Joshua is considered a prophet. The Book of Joshua is the first of the "former prophets" according to the Jewish canon of Scripture. **a great savior:** A pun on the Hebrew name Joshua, which means "the Lord saves". **God's elect:** Israel. **the enemies:** The Amorites (Josh 10:12–13). **inheritance:** The land of Canaan (Deut 1:34–38; Josh 11:23).

46:2 lifted his hands: As a signal for his army to attack the city of Ai (Josh 8:18–19, 26).

46:3 wars of the Lord: It was not really Joshua who led Israel into battle, but God himself (Josh 10:14).

46:4 the sun held back: When the sun stood still at Gibeon (Josh 10:12–13).

46:6 hailstones: Hurled by the Lord against the Amorites in Josh 10:6–11. **his armament:** The Lord gave protection and military strength to Joshua because of his obedience.

---

¹ Gk *he*.
ᵐ Other authorities read *your*.
ⁿ Gk *he*.
° The Greek of this line is obscure.
ᵖ Gk *his*.
ᵠ Compare Joshua 10:11: Greek lacks *of Beth-horon*.

⁷And in the days of Moses he did a loyal deed,
    he and Caleb the son of Jephun′neh:
    they withstood the congregation,ʳ
    restrained the people from sin,
    and stilled their wicked murmuring.
⁸And these two alone were preserved
    out of six hundred thousand people on foot,
    to bring them into their inheritance,
    into a land flowing with milk and honey.
⁹And the Lord gave Caleb strength,
    which remained with him to old age,
    so that he went up to the hill country,
    and his children obtained it for an inheritance;
¹⁰so that all the sons of Israel might see
    that it is good to follow the Lord.

¹¹The judges also, with their respective names,
    those whose hearts did not fall into idolatry
    and who did not turn away from the Lord—
    may their memory be blessed!
¹²May their bones revive from where they lie,
    and may the name of those who have been
      honored
    live again in their sons!

¹³Samuel, beloved by his Lord,
    a prophet of the Lord, established the kingdom
    and anointed rulers over his people.

¹⁴By the law of the Lord he judged the
      congregation,
    and the Lord watched over Jacob.
¹⁵By his faithfulness he was proved to be a
      prophet,
    and by his words he became known as a
      trustworthy seer.
¹⁶He called upon the Lord, the Mighty One,
    when his enemies pressed him on every
      side,
    and he offered in sacrifice a sucking lamb.
¹⁷Then the Lord thundered from heaven,
    and made his voice heard with a mighty
      sound;
¹⁸and he wiped out the leaders of the people of
      Tyre
    and all the rulers of the Philis′tines.
¹⁹Before the time of his eternal sleep,
    Samuelˢ called men to witness before the Lord
    and his anointed:
    "I have not taken any one's property,
    not so much as a pair of shoes."
    And no man accused him.
²⁰Even after he had fallen asleep he prophesied
    and revealed to the king his death,
    and lifted up his voice out of the earth in
      prophecy,
    to blot out the wickedness of the people.

46:7 the days of Moses: A reference to the wilderness period (Num 13–14). **Caleb:** One of the 12 spies that Moses sent to scout the land of Canaan. He was from the tribe of Judah (Num 13:6). **withstood the congregation:** Joshua and Caleb were the only two spies who supported Moses in the plan to conquer the Promised Land, while the people murmured, rebelled, and wished to go back to Egypt (Num 13:30—14:10).

46:8 six hundred thousand: See Ex 12:37. **inheritance:** See note on 46:1. **milk and honey:** Points to the abundance and prosperity of Canaan (Ex 3:8; Lev 20:24; Deut 6:3).

46:9 gave Caleb strength: Caleb remained vigorous even at the age of 85 (Josh 14:7, 10–11). **the hill country:** Populated by the Anakim whom Caleb conquered (Josh 14:12). **his children obtained it:** Caleb's inheritance of land remained the possession of his descendants long after his death (Num 14:24; Josh 14:9, 13–15).

46:11 The judges: The men and women who provided leadership for Israel from the death of Joshua until Samuel. Ben Sira provides only an overview of the Judges without naming them. The most important were Othniel, Ehud, Deborah, Barak, Gideon, Jephthah, and Samson. **did not fall into idolatry:** Perhaps stated tongue-in-cheek, since several of the Judges were far from exemplary models of faith (e.g., Judg 8:27; 16:16–20). **may their memory be blessed:** May they always be remembered and honored (35:7; 39:9; 45:1).

46:12 May their bones revive: Possibly a rare allusion to the resurrection of the dead in the OT (49:10; Ezek 37:1–14). **live again in their sons:** I.e., may their memory be preserved among their descendants (44:10–15; Tob 4:12).

46:13 Samuel: A transitional figure between the Judges and the founding of the kingdom. **a prophet:** Recognized as such both during his lifetime (1 Sam 3:19–20) and after his death (1 Sam 28:14–20; 2 Chron 35:18; Acts 3:24; 13:20). **established the kingdom:** By anointing Saul (1 Sam 9:15–17; 10:1) and David (1 Sam 16:13) as the first kings of Israel. The Hebrew of this verse is very different; it reads: "Honored by his people and beloved by his Maker, was he who was lent (unto the Lord) from his mother's womb, a Nazarite of the Lord in the prophetical office, Samuel, judge and officiating priest. By the word of God, he set up the kingdom, and anointed princes over the people."

46:14 By the law ... he judged: Samuel secured the Lord's protection over Israel by calling the people back to God and his commandments (1 Sam 7:3–6).

46:15 seer: An ancient term for a prophet (1 Sam 9:9, 11, 18–19).

46:16 called upon the Lord: On Samuel's role as intercessor, see 1 Sam 7:5–9. Almost the same words are used to describe Joshua's prayer (46:5). **his enemies:** The Philistines. **he offered ... a sucking lamb:** As a burnt offering (1 Sam 7:9).

46:17 the Lord thundered: After Samuel offered his sacrifice and as the Philistines were getting ready to attack Israel (1 Sam 7:10).

46:18 the leaders of the people of Tyre: The Hebrew reads, probably more accurately: "the leaders of the enemy" (the Hebrew words for "Tyre" and "enemy" are very close). Tyre is not mentioned in the story of 1 Sam 7:7–14, to which Ben Sira refers here.

46:19 Before ... his eternal sleep: Before his death. **Samuel called men:** A representative group of the people of Israel (1 Sam 12:1–4). **the Lord and his anointed:** God and King Saul, who were called as witnesses to his irreproachable life (1 Sam 12:5).

46:20 after ... he prophesied: When King Saul consulted him via the medium of Endor (1 Sam 28:7–19). **revealed ... his death:** The spirit of Samuel announced to Saul that he would die the following day (1 Sam 28:19). **to blot out the**

ʳOther authorities read *the enemy.*
ˢGk *he.*

47 And after him Nathan rose up
   to prophesy in the days of David.
²As the fat is selected from the peace offering,
   so David was selected from the sons of Israel.
³He played with lions as with young goats,
   and with bears as with lambs of the flock.
⁴In his youth did he not kill a giant,
   and take away reproach from the people,
when he lifted his hand with a stone in the sling
   and struck down the boasting of Goliath?
⁵For he appealed to the Lord, the Most High,
   and he gave him strength in his right hand
to slay a man mighty in war,
   to exalt the power ᵗ of his people.
⁶So they glorified him for his ten thousands,
   and praised him for the blessings of the Lord,
   when the glorious diadem was bestowed upon
   him.
⁷For he wiped out his enemies on every side,
   and annihilated his adversaries the Philis'tines;
   he crushed their power ᵗ even to this day.
⁸In all that he did he gave thanks
   to the Holy One, the Most High, with ascriptions
   of glory;

he sang praise with all his heart,
   and he loved his Maker.
⁹He placed singers before the altar,
   to make sweet melody with their voices.
¹⁰He gave beauty to the feasts,
   and arranged their times throughout the
   year, ᵘ
while they praised God's ᵛ holy name,
   and the sanctuary resounded from early
   morning.
¹¹The Lord took away his sins,
   and exalted his power ʷ for ever;
he gave him the covenant of kings
   and a throne of glory in Israel.

¹²After him rose up a wise son
   who fared amply ˣ because of him;
¹³Solomon reigned in days of peace,
   and God gave him rest on every side,
   that he might build a house for his name
   and prepare a sanctuary to stand for ever.
¹⁴How wise you became in your youth!
   You overflowed like a river with
   understanding.

---

wickedness: Ben Sira sees Saul's death as atoning for the sins of Israel.

47:1–22 Praise for key figures of the early monarchy: Nathan, David, and Solomon.

📖 **47:1 Nathan rose up:** By proceeding from Samuel to Nathan, Ben Sira emphasizes the line of succession of prophets in Israel. **the days of David:** Nathan announced God's covenant with David (2 Sam 7:2–3), rebuked him for his adultery with Bathsheba (2 Sam 12:1–15), and oversaw the succession of the throne from David to Solomon (1 Kings 1:8–45).

47:2 As the fat is selected: As the fat portions were separated from sacrificial animals to be burnt on the altar (Lev 3:3–5), so David was separated to be God's "choice portion" for royalty (1 Sam 16:4–13).

47:3 played with lions ... bears: David did not literally "play" with lions and bears but fought them off to protect his flock (1 Sam 17:34–36).

📖 **47:4 a giant:** The Philistine warrior Goliath of Gath (1 Sam 17:4–10). **reproach:** The shame that Goliath brought upon Israel when he defied their army (1 Sam 17:26). **a stone ... struck down:** David felled the giant by slinging a stone at his forehead (1 Sam 17:49–50).

47:5 appealed to the Lord: David defeated Goliath, not by his own strength, but by his faith in God (1 Sam 17:37, 45–47). **mighty in war:** See 1 Sam 17:33. **exalt the power:** Literally, to "raise up the horn" of his people (1 Sam 2:1; Ps 89:17).

47:6 So they glorified him for his ten thousands: The Hebrew reads: "Therefore the daughters sang of him and honored him with the name of [the slayer of] ten thousand" (1 Sam 18:6–7).

47:7 his enemies on every side: David won military victories against the Philistines (2 Sam 5:17–25; 8:1; 21:15–22), Moabites (2 Sam 8:2), Syrians (2 Sam 8:5–13), Edomites (2 Sam

8:14), and Ammonites (2 Sam 10:1–14). **annihilated his adversaries:** I.e., he permanently defeated them. **even to this day:** Up to Ben Sira's own time.

47:8 he gave thanks ... praise: Points to David's role as an author of numerous biblical psalms. **with all his heart:** David praised and loved God wholeheartedly, as commanded by the great *Shema* in Deut 6:4–5.

📖 **47:9 He placed singers:** The Hebrew reads: "music of stringed instruments"—the title of many psalms (Ps 4, 6, 54, 55, 61, 67, 76). Ben Sira refers to David's initiative in expanding Israel's liturgical worship by appointing the Levites as singers and musicians (1 Chron 15:16; 16:4–6; 23:5).

47:10 He gave beauty to the feasts: Through his liturgical reform and institution of liturgical praise (1 Chron 23:30–32). **from early morning:** See Ps 57:8.

📖 **47:11 took away his sins:** God forgave David's sin of adultery (2 Sam 12:13) with Bathsheba and the ensuing murder of her husband, Uriah (2 Sam 11:1–17). Beyond this, he **exalted his power for ever** by upholding the covenant with David and his descendants, so that his royal house and throne would endure forever (2 Sam 7:12–16; Ps 89:28–29).

📖 **47:12 a wise son:** Solomon is remembered as a great teacher of wisdom (1 Kings 2:3; 5:7). **who fared amply:** I.e., lived safely and well (1 Kings 4:21; 5:4). **because of him:** Solomon's prosperity (especially after he sinned) is attributed to the merits of his father, David, and his righteous reign (1 Kings 11:12–13, 32–36).

47:13 in days of peace: The name "Solomon" means "his peace". **God gave him rest:** Solomon's reign was an unprecedented time of peace, stability, and prosperity in Israel (1 Kings 5:4). **a house for his name:** The Jerusalem Temple (2 Sam 7:13; 1 Kings 5:5; 6:1–38). **a sanctuary:** Another name for the Temple (1 Chron 22:19). **to stand for ever:** The Temple was viewed as a microcosm that sustained the existence of the world (Ps 78:69).

47:14 How wise: Ben Sira addresses Solomon in the second person. **in your youth:** Solomon was wise in the early years of his reign, before he turned away from the Lord (1 Kings 3:9–12; 4:29–34; 10:1–8). **like a river:** Like wisdom and its blessings (24:27; 39:22).

ᵗ Gk *horn.*
ᵘ Gk *to completion.*
ᵛ Gk *his.*
ʷ Gk *horn.*
ˣ Gk *lived in a broad place.*

¹⁵Your soul covered the earth,
  and you filled it with parables and riddles.
¹⁶Your name reached to far-off islands,
  and you were loved for your peace.
¹⁷For your songs and proverbs and parables,
  and for your interpretations, the countries
    marveled at you.
¹⁸In the name of the Lord God,
  who is called the God of Israel,
you gathered gold like tin
  and amassed silver like lead.
¹⁹But you laid your loins beside women,
  and through your body you were brought into
    subjection.
²⁰You put stain upon your honor,
  and defiled your posterity,
so that you brought wrath upon your children
  and they were grieved[y] at your folly,
²¹so that the sovereignty was divided
  and a disobedient kingdom arose out of
    E'phraim.
²²But the Lord will never give up his mercy,
  nor cause any of his works to perish;
he will never blot out the descendants of his
  chosen one,
  nor destroy the posterity of him who loved him;
so he gave a remnant to Jacob,
  and to David a root of his stock.

²³Solomon rested with his fathers,
  and left behind him one of his sons,
ample in[z] folly and lacking in understanding,
  Rehobo'am, whose policy caused the people to
    revolt.
Also Jerobo'am the son of Ne'bat, who caused
  Israel to sin
  and gave to E'phraim a sinful way.
²⁴Their sins became exceedingly many,
  so as to remove them from their land.
²⁵For they sought out every sort of wickedness,
  till vengeance came upon them.

48 Then the prophet Eli'jah arose like a fire,
  and his word burned like a torch.
²He brought a famine upon them,
  and by his zeal he made them few in number.
³By the word of the Lord he shut up the heavens,
  and also three times brought down fire.
⁴How glorious you were, O Eli'jah, in your
  wondrous deeds!
  And who has the right to boast which you
    have?
⁵You who raised a corpse from death
  and from Hades, by the word of the Most High;
⁶who brought kings down to destruction,
  and famous men from their beds,
  and easily destroyed their dominion;

47:15 Your soul covered the earth: Solomon's wisdom spread throughout the world. **parables and riddles:** See 1 Kings 4:32.

47:16 far-off islands: Or "distant coasts" (1 Kings 5:14; 10:1–13). **your peace:** Solomon's peaceful reign. See note on 47:13.

47:17 songs . . . parables: On Solomon's literary output, see 1 Kings 4:32; Prov 1:6. **your interpretations:** Possibly an allusion to 1 Kings 10:1–3. **countries marveled:** See 1 Kings 4:34.

47:18 gold like tin . . . silver like lead: Solomon was so rich that he amassed precious metals as abundantly as cheap, ordinary ones (1 Kings 10:14–17; 27).

47:19 women: Solomon was notorious for having 700 wives and 300 concubines (1 Kings 11:1–8). **brought into subjection:** Solomon was controlled by his passions for women (Prov 31:3). • Even the extremely wise Solomon was deceived by giving himself to many women, who signify many teachings and philosophies. Desiring to investigate them, as one who is knowledgeable and wise, he was unable to stay within the bounds of divine law (Origen of Alexandria, *Homilies on Numbers* 20, 3, 3).

47:20 defiled your posterity: By violating the law of the king in Deut 17:17, Solomon dishonored not only himself but also his descendants, beginning a long decline that would end with the nation's exile.

47:21 divided: After Solomon's death, his kingdom was split in two (47:23; 1 Kings 12:16–20). **a disobedient kingdom:** The ten northern tribes, of which the most prominent was Ephraim, rebelled against Solomon's son Rehoboam, seceded from Judah, and formed the Kingdom of Israel.

47:22 nor destroy: The Lord pledged by covenant that David's line would endure forever (2 Sam 7:14–16; 1 Kings 11:13, 39; Ps 89:29–37).

47:23—48:15 Praise for the Northern Kingdom prophets Elijah and Elisha.

47:23 rested with his fathers: Solomon died (1 Kings 11:43). **caused the people to revolt:** Solomon's son Rehoboam acted foolishly by increasing the yoke of servitude upon the northern tribes. This led to their rebellion under **Jeroboam** (1 Kings 12:1–19), who led Israel into sin by erecting golden calf idols in Bethel and Dan (1 Kings 14:16).

47:24 from their land: The many sins of the Northern Kingdom eventually caused them to be deported by the Assyrians in 722 B.C. (2 Kings 17:20–23).

47:25 every sort of wickedness: On the evils of the Northern Kingdom, see 1 Kings 21:20, 25; 2 Kings 17:17.

48:1 Elijah: Prophesied in the Northern Kingdom of Israel during the reigns of Ahab and Ahaziah (1 Kings 17–21; 2 Kings 1–2). **like a fire:** An allusion to Elijah calling down fire from heaven (1 Kings 18:38; 2 Kings 1:10, 12). **like a torch:** The Hebrew reads: "like a burning furnace" (Mal 4:1).

48:2 a famine: Came upon King Ahab and the Northern Kingdom (1 Kings 17). **by his zeal:** Or "jealousy" (1 Kings 19:10, 14). **few in number:** Implies that many people died because of the famine.

48:3 shut up the heavens: Means that no rain fell on the land for three years (1 Kings 17:1; Jas 5:17). **brought down fire:** To consume a burnt offering (1 Kings 18:38) as well as King Ahaziah's troops (2 Kings 1:10, 12).

48:4 How glorious you were: Ben Sira addresses Elijah in the second person, as he did with Solomon (47:14).

48:5 raised a corpse: The son of the widow of Zarephath (1 Kings 17:17–22). **Hades:** The abode of the dead. See notes on 14:12; 17:27; 21:10.

48:6 kings . . . destruction: Elijah prophesied that all the descendants of King Ahab would be annihilated (1 Kings 19:17; 21:19–24). **famous men from their beds:** King Ahaziah died in his bed following an injury (2 Kings 1:1–17).

---

[y] Other authorities read *I was grieved*.
[z] Heb (with a play on the name Rehoboam) Syr: Gk *the people's*.

⁷who heard rebuke at Sinai
  and judgments of vengeance at Horeb;
⁸who anointed kings to inflict retribution,
  and prophets to succeed you.ᵃ
⁹You who were taken up by a whirlwind of fire,
  in a chariot with horses of fire;
¹⁰you who are readyᵇ at the appointed time, it is written,
  to calm the wrath of God before it breaks out in fury,
  to turn the heart of the father to the son,
  and to restore the tribes of Jacob.
¹¹Blessed are those who saw you,
  and those who have fallen asleepᶜ in your love;
  for we also shall surely live,
  but our name, after death, will not be such.ᵈ

¹²It was Eli′jah who was covered by the whirlwind,
  and Eli′sha was filled with his spirit;
  in all his days he did not tremble before any ruler,
  and no one brought him into subjection.
¹³Nothing was too hard for him,
  and when he was dead his body prophesied.
¹⁴As in his life he did wonders,
  so in death his deeds were marvelous.

¹⁵For all this the people did not repent,
  and they did not forsake their sins,
  till they were carried away captive from their land
  and were scattered over all the earth;
  the people were left very few in number,
  but with rulers from the house of David.
¹⁶Some of them did what was pleasing to God,ᵉ
  but others multiplied sins.

¹⁷Hezeki′ah fortified his city,
  and brought water into the midst of it;
  he tunneled the sheer rock with iron
  and built pools for water.
¹⁸In his days Sennach′erib came up,
  and sent the Rab′shakeh;ᶠ
  he lifted up his hand against Zion
  and made great boasts in his arrogance.
¹⁹Then their hearts were shaken and their hands trembled,
  and they were in anguish, like women with labor pains.
²⁰But they called upon the Lord who is merciful,
  spreading forth their hands toward him;
  and the Holy One quickly heard them from heaven,
  and delivered them by the hand of Isaiah.

48:7 Sinai ... Horeb: Elijah fled from Queen Jezebel to "the mountain of God", where God announced judgment upon the followers of Baal (1 Kings 19:8–18). See note on Ex 3:1.

48:8 to inflict retribution: Elijah anointed two kings, Hazael of Syria and Jehu of Israel, to destroy Ahab's line (1 Kings 19:15–17). **prophets to succeed you:** The Hebrew has "a prophet" in the singular, referring to Elisha (1 Kings 19:19–21).

48:9 taken up by ... fire: Elijah was taken to heaven in a fiery chariot after passing on the mantle of prophecy to Elisha (2 Kings 2:1, 11).

48:10 the appointed time: The "great and awesome day of the Lord" prophesied in Mal 4:5–6. **to calm the wrath of God:** Elijah became identified with the forerunner of the Messiah who would return before the Lord's great day of judgment. **turn the heart:** Malachi expected the Messiah's forerunner to bring reconciliation within the family (Mt 11:10, 14; 17:10–13; Lk 1:17). **restore the tribes of Jacob:** By regathering the exiles of Israel (Is 49:6).

48:12 Elisha: Elijah's successor (1 Kings 19:16–21). **filled with his spirit:** Elisha was given a "double share" of Elijah's spirit, making him an even more powerful miracle worker than his predecessor (2 Kings 2:9–12). See chart: *Elijah and Elisha* at 2 Kings 4. **he did not tremble:** Elisha prophesied during the reigns of Jehoram, Jehu, Jehoahaz, and Jehoash, often fearlessly opposing those godless monarchs (2 Kings 2–13).

48:13 Nothing was too hard: Ben Sira applies to Elisha language used for God in Gen 18:14.

48:14 in death ... marvelous: When a dead man was cast into the grave of Elisha, he came back to life (2 Kings 13:21).

48:15 did not repent: The Northern Kingdom of Israel continued on a path of spiritual and moral decline. **carried away captive:** The Assyrians conquered and deported the northern tribes of Israel in the eighth century B.C. (2 Kings 15:29; 17:22–23). **scattered over all the earth:** As foretold by the Law and the Prophets (Lev 26:33–35; Deut 4:25–27; 28:36, 63–68; Zech 7:9–14). **very few in number:** The Hebrew states more clearly that the surviving remnant was the Southern Kingdom: "And there were left to Judah but a few." **rulers from the house of David:** In contrast to the rival dynasties in the Northern Kingdom, the royal Davidic line was preserved in the Southern Kingdom of Judah. See chart: *Kings of the Divided Monarchy* at 1 Kings 13.

48:16–25 Praise for key figures of the Southern Kingdom of Judah: Hezekiah and Isaiah.

48:16 did what was pleasing: A few of the kings of Judah were evaluated positively by this formula, such as Asa (1 Kings 15:11), Jehoshaphat (1 Kings 22:43), Joash (2 Kings 12:2), Azariah (2 Kings 15:3), Hezekiah (2 Kings 18:3), Josiah (2 Kings 22:2). **others multiplied sins:** Most of the kings of Judah were as wicked as their northern counterparts.

48:17 Hezekiah: One of the best kings of Judah (reigned ca. 729–686 B.C.). He rebuilt and expanded the walls of the city to defend it from the Assyrian invaders (2 Chron 32:5, 30). **fortified his city:** A pun on Hezekiah's name, which in Hebrew means: "the Lord strengthened". **brought water:** By boring a tunnel from the Gihon spring to the Pool of Siloam—still known today as "Hezekiah's Tunnel" (2 Kings 20:20; 2 Chron 32:30). **built pools for water:** See Is 22:9–11.

48:18 Sennacherib: King of Assyria from ca. 705 to 681 B.C. **came up:** Sennacherib invaded Judah in 701 B.C., capturing 46 cities and besieging Jerusalem (2 Kings 18:13–37; 2 Chron 32:1–23; Is 36:1–22). **Rabshakeh:** Sennacherib's commander or high official (2 Kings 18:17, 19–35). **boasts in his arrogance:** The Rabshakeh blasphemed God when he brazenly defied Hezekiah's spokesmen (2 Kings 18:22, 28–35; Is 36:7, 14–20).

48:19 hearts were shaken: See 2 Kings 19:3; Is 37:3.

48:20 they called upon the Lord: Ben Sira extends Hezekiah's prayer for deliverance (2 Kings 19:14–19; Is 37:15–20) to the entire people. **by the hand of Isaiah:** God answered their prayers and protected Jerusalem, thanks to the prophetic ministry of Isaiah (2 Kings 19:20–34; Is 37:21–35).

ᵃ Heb: Gk *him.*
ᵇ Heb: Gk *are for reproofs.*
ᶜ Other authorities read *who have died.*
ᵈ The text and meaning of this verse are uncertain.
ᵉ Greek lacks *to God.*
ᶠ Other authorities add *and departed.*

²¹The Lord^g struck the camp of the Assyrians,
   and his angel wiped them out.
²²For Hezeki'ah did what was pleasing to the Lord,
   and he held strongly to the ways of David his
      father,
   which Isai'ah the prophet commanded,
      who was great and faithful in his vision.
²³In his days the sun went backward,
   and he lengthened the life of the king.
²⁴By the spirit of might he saw the last things,
   and comforted those who mourned in Zion.
²⁵He revealed what was to occur to the end of
      time,
   and the hidden things before they came to
      pass.

49 The memory of Josi'ah is like a blending of
   incense
   prepared by the art of the perfumer;
   it is sweet as honey to every mouth,
      and like music at a banquet of wine.
²He was led aright in converting the people,
   and took away the abominations of iniquity.
³He set his heart upon the Lord;
   in the days of wicked men he strengthened
      godliness.

⁴Except David and Hezeki'ah and Josi'ah
   they all sinned greatly,
   for they forsook the law of the Most High;
      the kings of Judah came to an end;
⁵for they gave their power to others,
   and their glory to a foreign nation,
⁶who set fire to the chosen city of the sanctuary,
   and made her streets desolate,
   according to the word^h of Jeremi'ah.
⁷For they had afflicted him;
   yet he had been consecrated in the womb as
      prophet,
   to pluck up and afflict and destroy,
      and likewise to build and to plant.

⁸It was Ezek'iel who saw the vision of glory
   which Godⁱ showed him above the chariot of
      the cherubim.
⁹For Godⁱ remembered his enemies with storm,
   and did good to those who directed their ways
      rightly.^j

¹⁰May the bones of the twelve prophets
   revive from where they lie,
   for they comforted the people of Jacob
      and delivered them with confident hope.

48:21 struck the camp: The angel of the Lord killed 185,000 Assyrians in their camp that night (2 Kings 19:35).

48:22 what was pleasing: Ben Sira views Hezekiah's piety as a decisive factor in the routing of the Assyrians. **he held strongly:** Another wordplay on the name of Hezekiah. See note on 48:17. **his vision:** Hezekiah's piety was guided by Isaiah's prophetic vision (2 Kings 19:1–7).

48:23 the sun went backward: A sign that the Lord would lengthen Hezekiah's life by 15 years (2 Kings 20:1–11; Is 38:1–8).

48:24 By the spirit: By a special inspiration. **he saw the last things:** Isaiah prophetically saw future events. **comforted those ... in Zion:** See Is 40:1–2.

📖 **48:25 what was to occur:** Isaiah foresaw Israel's ingathering from exile (Is 40:3–11), the name of Cyrus as the Lord's anointed one (Is 44:28; 45:1), and the rebuilt and glorified Jerusalem (Is 44:26–28; 62:6–7; 65:18–19; 66:10–13). **before they came to pass:** A claim that Isaiah foresaw events of the distant future. Ben Sira seems to have attributed the entire book of Isaiah to the eighth-century prophet. See introduction to Isaiah: *Author and Date*.

49:1–16 Praise for King Josiah and the writing Prophets (minus Daniel).

📖 **49:1 Josiah:** The best and last of the good kings of Judah, who reigned ca. 640–609 B.C. (2 Kings 22:2). **blending of incense:** Although Josiah was not a priest, his ministry in leading his people back to God is described in priestly terms. Ben Sira describes him with the same language he uses to describe wisdom. **incense:** See 24:15; 45:16. **honey:** See 24:20. **music ... wine:** See 40:20.

49:2 converting the people: The Hebrew reads: "He was grieved at our backsliding." After the book of the Law was found in the Temple, Josiah tore his clothes when he realized the extent of its neglect (2 Kings 22:11–13). **took away the abominations:** Josiah launched a religious reform ca. 622 B.C. to purify Judah of idolatry (2 Kings 23:1–20).

49:3 He set his heart: See 2 Kings 23:3, 25. **he strengthened godliness:** Although Josiah's reform turned out to be too little too late, God did postpone his judgment on Judah until after the king's death (2 Kings 22:18–20).

49:4 they all sinned greatly: Ben Sira's judgment on Judah's kings is severe, admitting of few exceptions. **kings of Judah came to an end:** Their sins brought an end to the line of Davidic kings in Jerusalem.

📖 **49:6 set fire to the chosen city:** The Babylonians destroyed Jerusalem and the Temple and exiled the people of Judah to Babylonia (2 Kings 25:8–10). **Jeremiah:** The last great prophet of preexilic Judah. He ministered in Jerusalem ca. 627 to 586 B.C. and tirelessly warned its last kings of impending destruction (Jer 36:2–4, 29–31; 37:8–10; 38:3).

49:7 afflicted him: The kings, nobles, and people of Judah persecuted Jeremiah (Jer 20:7–8, 10; 37:13–16; 38:4–6). **consecrated in the womb:** God chose Jeremiah for prophetic ministry even before he was born (Jer 1:5). **to pluck up ... plant:** See Jer 1:10.

📖 **49:8 Ezekiel:** The third major prophet of the OT canon. He ministered during the Babylonian Exile from 593 to 571 B.C. **vision of glory:** Ezekiel's inaugural vision of God enthroned on a glorious chariot (Ezek 1:4–28)—a moveable manifestation of the divine Presence that had rested in the Temple until its destruction (1 Chron 28:18).

📖 **49:9 God remembered his enemies:** Possibly Gog and Magog (Ezek 38–39). The Hebrew of this verse reads: "and also he made mention of Job, who maintained all the ways of righteousness"—a reference to Ezek 14:14, 20. The variation likely derives from the fact that the Hebrew words for "enemy" and "Job" are very similar.

📖 **49:10 the twelve prophets:** The 12 Minor Prophets (Hosea, Joel, Amos, Obadiah, Jonah, Micah, Nahum, Habakkuk, Zephaniah, Haggai, Zechariah, Malachi) are treated

---

^gGk *He.*
^hGk *by the hand.*
ⁱGk *he.*
^jThe text and meaning of this verse are uncertain.

¹¹How shall we magnify Zerub'babel?
 He was like a signet on the right hand,
¹² and so was Jesh'ua the son of Jo'zadak;
 in their days they built the house
 and raised a temple ᵏ holy to the Lord,
 prepared for everlasting glory.
¹³The memory of Nehemi'ah also is lasting;
 he raised for us the walls that had fallen,
 and set up the gates and bars
 and rebuilt our ruined houses.

¹⁴No one like E'noch has been created on earth,
 for he was taken up from the earth.

¹⁵And no man like Joseph¹ has been born,
 and his bones are cared for.
¹⁶Shem and Seth were honored among
 men,
 and Adam above every living being in
 the creation.

Simon Son of Onias; a Benediction, and an Epilogue

50 The leader of his brethren and the pride of his
 peopleᵐ
 was Simon the high priest, son of Oni'as,
 who in his life repaired the house,
 and in his time fortified the temple.

---

as a single book, as they came to be preserved in the Hebrew canon. **May the bones ... revive:** Perhaps expressing a hope for the resurrection of the dead (46:12; Ezek 37:1–14). **they comforted ... with confident hope:** A positive picture of the message of the Minor Prophets, although much of their writing warns of judgment and calls for repentance.

49:11 Zerubbabel: One of the leaders who returned from the Babylonian Exile and became the governor of Judah under Darius I of Persia (Ezra 2:2). **a signet on the right hand:** Refers to Hag 2:23, where God promises to restore to Zerubbabel the position that King Jeconiah (Jehoiachin) had lost before the Exile (cf. Jer 22:24).

49:12 Jeshua: The high priest in Jerusalem after the initial return from exile (Ezra 2:2). **they built the house:** I.e., they rebuilt the Temple. Zerubbabel and Jeshua oversaw the reconstruction of the Second Temple, prompted by the Prophets Haggai and Zechariah (Ezra 3:2; 5:1–2). **for everlasting glory:** Haggai had prophesied that the Second Temple would surpass Solomon's Temple in glory (Hag 2:6–9).

49:13 Nehemiah: Another major leader of the Jewish restoration after the Exile (Neh 2:1–11). **raised for us the walls:** Nehemiah led the effort to rebuild the walls of Jerusalem despite considerable opposition (Neh 2:17–7:3).

49:14–16 Ben Sira concludes his praise of Israel's ancestors by returning to a few of the oldest Patriarchs, working his way back to Adam.

49:14 No one like Enoch: The Hebrew reads: "few like Enoch"—probably to address the difficulty that Elijah was also taken up from the earth (44:16; Gen 5:24; Heb 11:5).

49:15 No man like Joseph: Ben Sira skipped over Joseph in his initial survey of the early Patriarchs. **his bones are cared for:** The Hebrew reads: "His body was visited"—an allusion to Joseph's request that his bones be brought back from Egypt to the land of Israel to be buried there (Gen 50:25; Ex 13:19; Josh 24:32).

49:16 Shem: Son of Noah (Gen 5:32; 6:10), survivor of the great flood (Gen 9:18), and father of Semitic peoples (Gen 10:22–31). **Seth:** Third son of Adam and Eve (Gen 4:25). The Hebrew adds "and Enosh"—the first-born son of Seth (Gen 4:26). **Adam above every:** The father of humanity is accorded special honor. The Hebrew reads: "but beyond that of any living being was the splendor (*tipheret*) of Adam".

50:1–24 Praise of Israel's ancestors gives way to praise of Israel's high priest, Simon II, son of Onias. The transition to this chapter following the praise of Adam in 49:16 suggests that Ben Sira wishes to compare the priestly "splendor" of Simon (Heb., *tipheret*) with the primeval "splendor" of the first man.

50:1 the pride of his people: The Hebrew reads: "the splendor of his people". **Simon:** High priest in Jerusalem from 219 to 196 B.C., thus making him a contemporary of Ben Sira. **son of Onias:** The Hebrew reads: "son of Jochanan". **in his life:** Suggests to many that Simon is no longer alive at the time of writing; however, the vivid description that follows also suggests that Ben Sira is recounting personal memories of his priestly ministry. **repaired the house:** Simon led an effort to fortify the city and sanctuary of Jerusalem to protect them better against enemy attack.

Word Study

High Priest (50:1)

Hiereus ho megas (Gk.): Literally, "the great priest", which was a common title for the high priest in biblical Israel (Heb., *hakkōhēn haggādôl*). The Levitical priesthood goes back to Aaron, the brother of Moses, whom God appointed to be Israel's first high priest (Ex 28:1). The high priest wore elaborate garments that represented the nation of Israel (Ex 28; 39:1–31). His primary role was to mediate between God and Israel by offering sacrifices on behalf of the people (Lev 1–7; Num 28). On Yom Kippur, the high priest entered the Holy of Holies to atone for the sins of the entire nation (Lev 16)—perhaps the events depicted in Sir 50. The priestly line was later restricted to the line of Phinehas (Num 25:13; Sir 45:23–24) and Zadok (1 Kings 2:35; 1 Chron 6:4–8). By the late Second Temple period, the high priest's garments had come to represent not only Israel but the whole world (Sir 45:6–13; Wis 18:24; Philo, *Life of Moses* 2, 109–35; Josephus, *Antiquities* 3, 180–87). Simon II, the son of Onias, was the high priest officiating in Jerusalem from 291 to 196 B.C., a short time before Ben Sira wrote his book. Ben Sira portrays him as an "incarnation" of wisdom, using much of the same language he used to describe Wisdom in chap. 24, such as roses, lilies, green shoots, Lebanon, olive trees, cedar and cypress, palm trees, and incense (50:8–12). This implies that Wisdom not only dwells in the sanctuary, but that she is present in a special way in the liturgical ministry of the high priest.

ᵏ Other authorities read *people*.
¹ Heb Syr: Greek adds *the leader of his brothers, the support of the people*.
ᵐ Heb Syr: Greek lacks this line. Compare 49:15.

[2]He laid the foundations for the high double walls,[n]
  the high retaining walls for the temple enclosure.
[3]In his days a cistern for water was quarried out,[o]
  a reservoir like the sea in circumference.
[4]He considered how to save his people from ruin,
  and fortified the city to withstand a siege.
[5]How glorious he was when the people gathered
    round him
  as he came out of the inner sanctuary![p]
[6]Like the morning star among the clouds,
  like the moon when it is full;
[7]like the sun shining upon the temple of the Most
    High,
  and like the rainbow gleaming in glorious
    clouds;
[8]like roses in the days of the first fruits,
  like lilies by a spring of water,
  like a green shoot on Lebanon[q] on a summer day;
[9]like fire and incense in the censer,
  like a vessel of hammered gold
  adorned with all kinds of precious stones;
[10]like an olive tree putting forth its fruit,
  and like a cypress towering in the clouds.
[11]When he put on his glorious robe
  and clothed himself with superb perfection
    and went up to the holy altar,
  he made the court of the sanctuary glorious.
[12]And when he received the portions from the
    hands of the priests,
  as he stood by the hearth of the altar

with a garland of brethren around him,
  he was like a young cedar on Lebanon;
  and they surrounded him like the trunks of palm
    trees,
[13] all the sons of Aaron in their splendor
with the Lord's offering in their hands,
  before the whole congregation of Israel.
[14]Finishing the service at the altars,
  and arranging the offering to the Most High,
    the Almighty,
[15]he reached out his hand to the cup
  and poured a libation of the blood of the
    grape;
he poured it out at the foot of the altar,
  a pleasing odor to the Most High, the King of
    all.
[16]Then the sons of Aaron shouted,
  they sounded the trumpets of hammered work,
they made a great noise to be heard
  for remembrance before the Most High.
[17]Then all the people together made haste
  and fell to the ground upon their faces
to worship their Lord,
  the Almighty, God Most High.
[18]And the singers praised him with their voices
  in sweet and full-toned melody.[r]
[19]And the people besought the Lord Most High
  in prayer before him who is merciful,
  till the order of worship of the Lord was ended;
  so they completed his service.

50:3 cistern: To supply water to the Temple precincts in the event of a siege. **reservoir:** The "molten sea" in the courtyard of the Temple, used for the ritual washings of the priests (1 Kings 7:23–26).

50:5–21 Possibly a description of Yom Kippur, the Day of Atonement, when the high priest went into the Holy of Holies with the blood of sacrificial animals to atone for the sins of Israel (Lev 16:1–34). Others contend that the liturgy of the daily burnt offering is in view (Ex 29:38–42). Either way, Ben Sira's reuse of language from the poem on wisdom in chap. 24 suggests he viewed the high priest as an incarnation of wisdom.

50:5 How glorious: The high priest is glorious like wisdom (6:31; 24:16–17). **the inner sanctuary:** Literally, "the house of the veil"—either the inner veil (meaning he exited the Holy of Holies on Yom Kippur) or the outer veil (meaning he exited the Temple building, which occurred daily).

50:6–7 morning star ... moon ... sun: Simon's glorious appearance recalls the celestial elements of the cosmos (43:1–12; Gen 1:14–18; Ps 19:4–5; 148:3). **the rainbow gleaming:** Echoes Ezekiel's description of the divine glory (Ezek 1:28).

50:8 like roses ... lilies ... green shoot: Ben Sira uses the imagery of lush flowers and vegetation to describe the fruitful, life-giving ministry of the high priest. He used the same imagery to describe wisdom in 24:13–17, 30–31; 39:13–14.

50:9 fire and incense: Recalls the portrayal of wisdom as an offering of incense (24:15; 39:14; 45:16). **gold ... precious stones:** See 45:11. Wisdom is described in terms of gold and precious stones in Job 28:16–19.

50:10 like an olive tree ... cypress: Like wisdom (24:13–14; Ps 52:8; Is 41:19).

50:11 his glorious robe: The splendor of the priestly vestments was renowned in the days of the Second Temple (45:6–12; Ex 28:2–43). **the holy altar:** The bronze altar used for burning animal sacrifices (Ex 27:1–2; 2 Chron 4:1). **the court:** The outer court surrounding the bronze altar, made glorious by the presence of the high priest.

50:12 the portions: The portions of the sacrificial animals (Ex 29:17; Lev 1:6, 8; 8:20; 9:13). **a garland of brethren:** His fellow priests. **cedar on Lebanon ... palm trees:** Again, the high priest and his assistants are portrayed in the same terms as wisdom (24:13–14).

50:13 all the sons of Aaron: All the priests.

50:14 the service: The daily Temple liturgy.

50:15 libation: A drink offering of wine (39:26) to be poured at the base of the altar (Num 15:5–7; 28:7). **a pleasing odor:** Indicating that God had favorably received the offering.

50:16 the sons of Aaron: The priests. **trumpets:** Metal trumpets were sounded for solemn occasions, whether for military summoning or liturgical commemorations (Num 10:9–10).

50:17–18 fell to the ground: The entire assembly of Israel prostrated themselves to join the high priest in worshiping the Lord. **singers:** The Temple choir and orchestra (47:9; 2 Chron 29:28).

50:19 the order of worship: The sacrificial liturgy, either of the Day of Atonement or of the daily burnt offering. See note on 50:5–21.

---

[n] The meaning of this phrase is obscure.
[o] Cn Compare Heb: Gk *was diminished.*
[p] Gk *the house of the veil.*
[q] Or *a sprig of frankincense.*
[r] Other authorities read *in sweet melody throughout the house.*

[20]Then Simon[s] came down, and lifted up his hands
over the whole congregation of the sons of
Israel,
to pronounce the blessing of the Lord with his
lips,
and to glory in his name;
[21]and they bowed down in worship a second time,
to receive the blessing from the Most High.

[22]And now bless the God of all,
who in every way does great things;
who exalts our days from birth,
and deals with us according to his mercy.
[23]May he give us[t] gladness of heart,
and grant that peace may be in our days in
Israel,
as in the days of old,
[24]that Israel may believe that the God of mercy is
with us
to deliver us in our[u] days!

[25]With two nations my soul is vexed,
and the third is no nation:
[26]Those who live on Mount Se'ir,[v] and the Philis'tines,
and the foolish people that dwell in She'chem.

[27]Instruction in understanding and knowledge
I have written in this book,
Jesus the son of Si'rach, son of Elea'zar,[w] of
Jerusalem,
who out of his heart poured forth wisdom.
[28]Blessed is he who concerns himself with these
things,
and he who lays them to heart will become wise.
[29]For if he does them, he will be strong for all
things,
for the light of the Lord is his path.

The Search for Wisdom

51 I will give thanks to you, O Lord and King,
and will praise you as God my Savior.
I give thanks to your name,
[2] for you have been my protector and helper
and have delivered my body from destruction
and from the snare of a slanderous tongue,
from lips that utter lies.
Before those who stood by
you were my helper, [3]and delivered me,
in the greatness of your mercy and of your name,
from the gnashings of teeth about to devour me,[x]
from the hand of those who sought my life,
from the many afflictions that I endured,

50:20 Simon came down: From the bronze altar of sacrifice. **lifted up his hands:** To give a blessing, as in Lev 9:22–23. **blessing of the Lord:** The priestly blessing (Num 6:22–27). **to glory in his name:** In this blessing, the high priest would pronounce the "Ineffable Name" of God: YHWH.

50:21 they bowed down in worship: According to an ancient description of Yom Kippur, when the priests and people in the Temple heard the high priest utter the ineffable name of the Lord (= YHWH), they would fall on their faces and bless the divine name (Mishnah, *Yoma* 6, 2).

50:23 May he give us gladness of heart: The Hebrew reads: "May He grant you wisdom of heart" (45:26). **peace ... days of old:** Ben Sira is presumably thinking of the "golden age" of Solomon's reign, when Israel was a strong, independent nation, free of foreign occupation.

50:24 that the God of mercy is with us to deliver us in our days: The Hebrew reads: "May his mercy be established with Simon, and may he establish for him the covenant of Phinehas, that one may never be cut off from him, and from his seed as the days of heaven." The reason for the difference is easily explained: after Ben Sira wrote his Hebrew text, the "covenant of Phinehas" (45:24) and Simon's line came to an end when his son Onias III was assassinated. When Ben Sira's grandson translated the text into Greek, he adapted it to reflect the situation of his own day better.

50:25 two nations: The Edomites, longtime rivals of Israel who descended from Esau and lived in the highlands of Seir, south of the Dead Sea (Obad 10–14; Ps 137:7; Ezek 25:12–14), and the Philistines, whom David had subdued long ago but who symbolized the pagan Hellenizers that threatened Israel's faith in Ben Sira's day. From their name came the term "Palestine".

50:26 foolish people: The Samaritans, whose origins trace back to the Assyrian conquest of northern Israel in 2 Kings 17:24–41. They had opposed the rebuilding of the Jerusalem Temple and established a rival temple on Mt. Gerizim, overlooking Shechem, which the Jews considered illegitimate. They later allied themselves with the Seleucids against the Jews. It may be that Ben Sira inserts these two verses to dismiss the Samaritan cult as a counterfeit to Simon's ministry.

50:27 Instruction: The aim of Ben Sira's work. **Jesus the son of Sirach, son of Eleazar:** Serves as an author's signature for the book. The Hebrew reads: "Simon the son of Jesus the son of Eleazar the son of Sira". **poured forth wisdom:** From his own pursuit of wisdom, Ben Sira has become a source of wisdom for others (16:25; 18:29; Prov 1:1–3).

50:28 Blessed is he: A benediction upon those who contemplate the wisdom of the book.

50:29 the light of the Lord is his path: The Hebrew reads: "for the fear of the Lord is life". Many scholars believe that the book originally ended here and that the last chapter was added later.

51:1–30 Possibly an addition to the original text of Sirach. It consists of **(1)** a prayer of thanksgiving, which draws heavily from the Psalms (51:1–12) and **(2)** an autobiographical poem on Ben Sira's search for wisdom (51:13–30). The Hebrew version also includes between these two sections a psalm of praise that is not included in the RSV2CE.

51:1 God my savior: See Lk 1:47. The Hebrew reads: "God of my salvation". **I give thanks to your name:** Or "I confess your name." The Hebrew adds: "strength of my life" (Ps 27:1).

51:2 you ... delivered my body: See Ps 56:13; 116:8. The Hebrew reads: "For you have redeemed me from death; you have kept my flesh from the pit and my foot from the power of Sheol" (Ps 49:15). **a slanderous tongue:** Ben Sira warns against slander elsewhere in 5:14; 28:13–26 (cf. Ps 109:2–3).

51:3 greatness of your mercy: See Ps 5:7; 106:7, 45. **gnashings of teeth:** The author compares his enemies to wild animals (Ps 17:12; 22:20–21; 35:16). **those who sought my life:** See Ps 35:4; 40:14; 63:9; 70:2.

---

[s] Gk *he*.
[t] Other authorities read *you*.
[u] Other authorities read *his*.
[v] Heb Vg: Gk *on the mountain of Samaria*.
[w] The text of this line is uncertain.
[x] Cn Compare Vg: Gk *when I was about to be devoured*.

⁴from choking fire on every side
    and from the midst of fire which I did not
      kindle,
⁵from the depths of the belly of Hades,
    from an unclean tongue and lying words—
6   the slander of an unrighteous tongue to the
      king.
My soul drew near to death,
    and my life was very near to Hades beneath.
⁷They surrounded me on every side,
    and there was no one to help me;
I looked for the assistance of men,
    and there was none.
⁸Then I remembered your mercy, O Lord,
    and your work from of old,
that you deliver those who wait for you
    and save them from the hand of their enemies.
⁹And I sent up my supplication from the earth,
    and prayed for deliverance from death.
¹⁰I appealed to the Lord, the Father of my lord,
    not to forsake me in the days of affliction,
at the time when there is no help against the
      proud.
¹¹I will praise your name continually,
    and will sing praise with thanksgiving.
My prayer was heard,
12   for you saved me from destruction
    and rescued me from an evil plight.

Therefore I will give thanks to you and praise
    you,
    and I will bless the name of the Lord.

¹³While I was still young, before I went on my
    travels,
    I sought wisdom openly in my prayer.
¹⁴Before the temple I asked for her,
    and I will search for her to the last.
¹⁵From blossom toʸ ripening grape
    my heart delighted in her;
my foot entered upon the straight path;
    from my youth I followed her steps.
¹⁶I inclined my ear a little and received her,
    and I found for myself much instruction.
¹⁷I made progress therein;
    to him who gives wisdom I will give glory.
¹⁸For I resolved to live according to wisdom,ᶻ
    and I was zealous for the good;
    and I shall never be put to shame.
¹⁹My soul grappled with wisdom,ᶻ
    and in my conduct I was strict;ᵃ
I spread out my hands to the heavens,
    and lamented my ignorance of her.
²⁰I directed my soul to her,
    and through purification I found her.
I gained understandingᵇ with her from the first,
    therefore I will not be forsaken.

51:4 choking fire: Ben Sira compares his troubles to a consuming fire that engulfed him, with no possibility of escape.

51:5 the belly of Hades: The author was very close to death and the underworld because of lies that were said about him (Ps 119:69).

51:7 They surrounded me: The author's enemies. **no one to help me:** The author was utterly alone in his troubles; he could not find any human help (Ps 107:12; Is 63:5).

51:8 I remembered your mercy: Having despaired of finding human assistance, Ben Sira turned to the Lord for help, recalling how he had helped his people in the past (Ps 25:6).

51:9 prayed for deliverance from death: The Hebrew reads: "cried out for help from the gates of Sheol" (Jon 2:2).

51:10 I appealed to the Lord, the Father of my lord: This clause has been interpreted in a messianic sense (cf. Ps 110:1). The Hebrew reads: "I cried out, 'Lord, you are my Father', for you are the hero of my salvation" (Ps 89:26; 140:7).

51:11 I will praise: Because the Lord answered his prayer.

51:12 you saved me: From death. **from an evil plight:** Or "from a time of trouble". **bless the name of the Lord:** See 39:35.

51:13–30 Ben Sira's search for wisdom. Like 24:30–34 and 33:16–18, this final section is autobiographical, providing a glimpse of Ben Sira's own journey toward wisdom.

51:13 still young: One key to becoming wise is to begin searching for wisdom early in life (6:18; Wis 8:2). **before … my travels:** Ben Sira was evidently a well-traveled man, and his experiences abroad played a key role in his cultivation of wisdom (34:10–13; 39:4). **I sought wisdom … prayer:** A reminder that wisdom is a gift from God for which one must ask (1:19; 1 Kings 3:9; Prov 8:17; Wis 9:1–4, 9–10).

51:14 Before the temple: Wisdom can be found everywhere, and yet her "home" is in the sanctuary (24:10). **to the last:** I.e., until the end of my life.

51:15 blossom … ripening grape: Means either "from the first blossoming of wisdom in me to its mature fruit", or "from my blossoming youth to my ripe old age". **I followed her steps:** Wisdom is personified, not just as a body of teachings to be learned, but as a teacher to follow (4:17; 6:26–27; Prov 8:20; Ps 25:5; 26:3; 27:11).

51:16 my ear: Listening to the voice of wisdom, along with receiving and obeying it, is another condition to grow in her (6:23, 33, 35; 16:24). **much instruction:** The cost-benefit ratio of seeking wisdom is always advantageous: One can gain *much* instruction by listening to her even a *little* (6:19; 51:27).

51:17 I made progress therein: The Hebrew reads: "And her yoke was glorious to me" (6:24, 30; 51:26). **I will give glory:** Either to God or to human teachers of wisdom. The Hebrew reads: "And to my teacher I offer thanks."

51:18 to live … wisdom: By putting her teachings into practice. **I shall never be put to shame:** The theme of seeking the good and being shielded from shame echoes the story of the Garden of Eden (15:4; 24:22; Gen 2:25; 3:6–7).

51:19 I spread out my hands: A typical posture for prayer (1 Kings 8:22; 2 Chron 6:12–13). The Hebrew reads: "My soul longed for her [= wisdom]. And I turned not my face away from her. I gave my soul to follow her, and for ever and ever I will not turn aside (from her). My hand opened her gates, and I entered in [?] and gazed upon her."

51:20 purification: By avoidance of sin. **gained understanding:** Literally, "acquired a heart" (Prov 15:32; 19:8). **I will not be forsaken:** By wisdom (2:10; 4:19; Prov 4:6).

ʸ Other authorities read *As from.*
ᶻ Gk *her.*
ᵃ The Greek text of this line is uncertain.
ᵇ Gk *heart.*

²¹My heart was stirred to seek her,
  therefore I have gained a good possession.
²²The Lord gave me a tongue as my reward,
  and I will praise him with it.

²³Draw near to me, you who are untaught,
  and lodge in my school.
²⁴Why do you say you are lacking in these
    things,ᶜ
  and why are your souls very thirsty?
²⁵I opened my mouth and said,
  Get these thingsᵈ for yourselves without
    money.

²⁶Put your neck under the yoke,
  and let your souls receive instruction;
  it is to be found close by.
²⁷See with your eyes that I have labored little
  and found for myself much rest.
²⁸Get instruction with a large sum of silver,
  and you will gain by it much gold.
²⁹May your soul rejoice in his mercy,
  and may you not be put to shame when you
    praise him.
³⁰Do your work before the appointed time,
  and in God'sᵉ time he will give you your
    reward.

51:22 a tongue: An ability to speak eloquently (Is 50:4) and utter words of praise.

51:23 Draw near to me: A final invitation for readers to learn from Ben Sira's wisdom (Prov 9:4, 16). **lodge in my school:** Literally, "make your home in my house of instruction" (Heb., *bet midrash*—the traditional Jewish term for the "house" where students gather to study the Torah) (14:23–27; 24:7–8, 19). • The Church of Christ is the house of instruction, where one learns from Christ to live well and thus live forever (St. Augustine, *Sermons* 399, 1).

51:24 thirsty: On "thirsting for" and "drinking" wisdom, see 15:3; Prov 9:5; Amos 8:11.

51:25 without money: Wisdom is a free gift (Is 55:1); Ben Sira apparently offers his own instruction without asking for a fee.

51:26 Put your neck ... yoke: Submit to the teachings and discipline of wisdom (6:23–31; Mt 11:29). **receive instruction:** The Hebrew reads: "Bear her burden."

51:27 labored little ... much rest: Ben Sira testifies that the effort required to seek wisdom is trivial compared to the reward of obtaining her (6:19; 51:16).

51:28 much gold: Seems to contradict 51:25, but the point is the same as 51:27: whatever one invests in seeking wisdom, one will obtain a significant return on one's investment.

51:29 not be put to shame: On shame as incompatible with wisdom, see notes on 24:22; 51:18.

51:30 Do your work: Of seeking wisdom. **before the appointed time:** I.e., before death. **your reward:** Wisdom herself, along with all the benefits that she brings. The Hebrew text adds a subscription: "Blessed be the Lord forever and praised be his name from generation to generation. Thus far the words of Simeon, the son of Yeshua, who is called Ben Sira. The Wisdom of Simeon, the son of Yeshua, the son of Eleazar, the son of Sira. May the name of the Lord be blessed from now to eternity."

ᶜCn Compare Heb Syr: The Greek text of this line is uncertain.
ᵈGreek lacks *these things*.
ᵉGk *his*.

STUDY QUESTIONS
Sirach

Chapter 1

For understanding
1. **1:11–30.** What virtue gives men and women access to wisdom? What place does the relationship between wisdom and fear of the Lord have in the author's thought? What is the importance of this theme in the Old Testament?
2. **1:14.** How important is fear of the Lord in the quest for wisdom? According to St. Augustine, how do the seven spiritual gifts presented by Isaiah teach us to ascend through fear of the Lord to wisdom?
3. **1:20.** How is wisdom pictured here, and what identification does this picture imply? Eating from what tree is equivalent to gaining wisdom, and how does this contrast with eating from the tree of the knowledge of good and evil?
4. **1:28.** How does one disobey the fear of the Lord? What does it mean to have a divided mind? According to Isaac of Nineveh, what is the conflict between the body and the will when one is attached to things of the world?

For application
1. **1:1–10.** In v. 10, the author says that wisdom can dwell with all flesh. Is there a difference between the wisdom that comes through normal growth in age and experience and that which comes from God? If so, how would you describe both types?
2. **1:11–20.** According to Ben Sira, what are some of the benefits of fear of the Lord? How does his description accord with your own experience?
3. **1:26–28.** How can keeping the commandments lead to the acquisition of wisdom? How does a divided mind undermine it?
4. **1:29–30.** How does an honest fear of the Lord improve one's relationships, especially with other Christians? How does a dishonest or hypocritical religiosity, in the words of v. 30, "bring dishonor upon" oneself? How does Sirach's admonition compare with Jesus' warnings regarding doing religious acts for public approval (see Mt 6:1–8, 16–18)?

Chapter 2

For Understanding
1. **2:6.** At what point in life does trust in God amidst severe tribulations reap rewards? Although it is our duty to seek God's straight way, what does God himself do for us?
2. **2:10.** On what considerations are readers invited to reflect regarding the past? Although it is tempting to answer "yes" when suffering presses hard, why does Ben Sira insist that the answer is "no"?
3. **2:15–18.** What virtues and what confidence do those who fear the Lord display? While God's majesty places high expectations on those who follow him, what does his mercy make up for?

For application
1. **2:1.** Why should a person who wishes to serve the Lord need to prepare himself for trials? Should this desire not make life easier? Of what kinds of trials might the author be thinking?
2. **2:2.** Why does Ben Sira counsel against being impetuous or hasty in times of calamity? Why should one be cautious about making decisions when adversity strikes?
3. **2:10–11.** Read the note for v. 10. Have you ever felt that the Lord has forsaken you or that his silence has shaken your trust? How was your trust in God's compassion and forgiveness restored? How deeply convinced are you that persevering in the fear of the Lord will increase your trust in his compassion and mercy?
4. **2:12–14.** Of the four cardinal virtues (prudence, justice, fortitude, temperance), which one is primarily threatened by timidity and despair in the face of adversity? Which is more difficult, physical or moral courage? Given the hostility that the modern world shows toward Christian morality, where do you think moral courage is most needed for Christians to lead a righteous life today?

Chapter 3

For understanding
1. **3:1–16.** On what are these verses a commentary? Why should children who aspire to be wise be particularly careful to show honor and respect toward their parents? How important is this commandment to relating well with all figures of authority for the right ordering of society?
2. **3:2.** Whereas in Catholic tradition the fourth commandment to honor one's father and mother begins the second tablet of the Decalogue, which pertains to love of neighbor, where does Jewish tradition place this commandment? If honoring one's parents is directly related to honoring God, what does disrespect of parents amount to?
3. **3:8.** In the Bible, what does the father's blessing mean? Would the father's blessing be gratuitous or based on whether it was deserved?
4. **3:15.** In times of distress, how will the Lord remember a son's kindness to his father? What is Sirach *not* teaching about kindness to parents? In what context is the ability to merit spiritual blessings given by God? According to St. Augustine, to what do our merits amount?
5. **3:21–24.** By turning to the dangers of intellectual pride, against what is Ben Sira likely reacting? What does he contend about what his fellow Jews need to know?

For application
1. **3:1–9.** What benefits does Ben Sira say will accrue to adult children who honor their parents? How do you as an adult show honor to your father? Your mother? What kind of honor would you expect from your adult children?

2. **3:10–16.** Ben Sira writes in the context of intact families, where the father for good or ill determines the direction and reputation of the family. In today's society, what is the influence of the father on his children in an intact family? In a dysfunctional one? When a father is absent, is abusive, has abandoned the family, or is even unknown to his children, how can the adult child obey the commandment to honor his father?

3. **3:21–24.** Modern technological and scientific advances can lead even experts to believe that there are no limits to what human beings should know. How does this attitude compare with the one against which Ben Sira cautions? What are some ethical limits that researchers in the physical and biological sciences should observe, and why?

Chapter 4

For understanding

1. **4:1.** If almsgiving is not as an optional work of mercy left to the discretion of the giver, what does Ben Sira take it to be?

2. **4:17.** Why does wisdom at first act harshly toward those who seek her? Once the wise man passes the test, how does wisdom behave? In what way does this process describe well the spiritual life?

3. **4:21.** How does "a shame which brings sin" appear to reverse the causal relationship between sin and shame? What is perhaps the meaning here? How might the text about shame bringing glory and favor be understood? According to St. Gregory the Great, when is shame praiseworthy, and when is it reproachful?

4. **4:23.** What are the wise called to share with others? When is the wisdom of the wise of most use?

For application

1. **4:1–6.** What is your own practice of almsgiving? How seriously do you take the practice as an obligation? Where do you choose to contribute alms, and where do you avoid contributing? What moves you to give alms or to refrain from giving?

2. **4:7–10.** Have you ever volunteered to serve the poor at a homeless shelter or the imprisoned in a county jail or prison? If so, how did you see the face of Jesus in those you served, and what impression did they make on you? If not, what prevents you from doing some active service for the poor?

3. **4:17–19.** Read the note for v. 17. Why would someone who is starting out in the spiritual life encounter difficulty at first rather than consolation? How does a beginner learn discipline in the practice of prayer? What can one expect from perseverance in prayer? What happens if the beginner gives up because of the difficulties?

4. **4:26.** How often do you go to confession? Have you ever avoided confessing a sin because you were ashamed of it? If you hid a sin because of shame, how did you feel about hiding it, and did you eventually repent and actually confess it?

Chapter 5

For understanding

1. **5:4.** What does the wicked man think he can do? Although God is slow to anger, what will he do?

2. **5:5.** How did Jews seek forgiveness of sins? Against what does Jewish oral law warn?

3. **5:7.** Why is it a mark of wisdom to repent quickly? According to St. Fulgentius, what is the danger of putting off repentance?

4. **5:9.** How do farmers winnow grain? What happens if winnowing continues when the winds change direction? Similarly, what happens when the double-tongued sinner speaks dishonestly in order to accommodate everyone?

For application

1. **5:6.** Critics of the Catholic Sacrament of Reconciliation sometimes allege that it encourages a casual attitude toward sinning, since one can always go to confession afterward. Why is a firm purpose of amendment required of the penitent? Why must the penitent even avoid the "near occasions of sin"?

2. **5:7.** When you commit serious sin, what do you think God's attitude is toward you? How does that idea affect your willingness to turn to him?

3. **5:11–12.** How would you apply these verses to the use of social media, especially in regard to controversial issues? While you may not be able to avoid receiving inflammatory communications, how should you handle your responses to them?

4. **5:14.** Why is gossiping considered a sin? When does gossip become slander? How easy is it for you to fall into gossip, and how hard is it for you to refrain when others want you to participate? Have you ever confessed gossip?

Chapter 6

For understanding

1. **6:7.** How will a friend prove his loyalty to you? How soon can you trust him? How does Lady Wisdom trust the faithfulness of her followers?

2. **6:16.** What does "elixir of life" mean? How does the Hebrew read, and what does it imply? For those who fear the Lord, what is a faithful friend?

3. **6:25.** To what is wisdom compared? Paradoxically, what will the one who bears her load find? According to Jewish tradition, of what will one who accepts the yoke of the Torah be relieved?

4. **6:30.** To what does the expression "a cord of blue" refer? What do wisdom's "bonds" thus serve as a reminder to do?

For application

1. **6:5–7.** What is the difference between an acquaintance and a friend? How many close friends do you have? How do you choose them, and how do you test their friendship?

2. **6:14–17.** How do those you consider close friends measure up to the description of a faithful friend in these verses? How many of your friends would you consider companions in the spiritual life? With how many can you share spiritual concerns and insights?

3. **6:19–31.** As you learn a new skill, when do attempts to practice the skill seem to be hardest, and when do they become easier? Why does growth in the spiritual life seem so difficult at first? How does it become easier over time?

4. **6:34–37.** Why is it important for one who is serious about the spiritual life to have a spiritual director? What qualities should one look for in a spiritual director? Although a good spiritual director can teach the principles of spiritual development, where does actual growth come from?

Chapter 7

For understanding

1. **7:6–7.** What virtues should one possess who sets his heart on becoming a judge? Why does he need them?
2. **7:10.** What does it mean to be fainthearted in prayer? On the contrary, how should one pray? In the present context, what kind of prayer is presumably meant? Why should the one who prays not neglect to give alms?
3. **7:15.** What kind of work is held in high esteem in rabbinic writings? According to one Jewish tradition, what does the father who fails to teach his son to work actually teach him? If farm work is created by the Most High, to what passages in Genesis might Ben Sira be alluding?
4. **7:19.** Why is a wise and good wife not to be lightly dismissed? What charm in her is better than her external beauty? What does the Hebrew text say instead?
5. **7:25.** How does the Hebrew text for this verse read? Since Jewish fathers typically arranged marriages for their daughters, how important was finding a wise husband? What would succeeding in that task bring the father?

For application

1. **7:13.** The *Catechism* defines a lie as "speaking a falsehood with the intention of deceiving" (CCC 2482); subsequent paragraphs explain the seriousness of lying. What is the purpose of speech? Aside from the violence a lie does to another, what harm does the liar do to himself?
2. **7:23–24.** How did your parents discipline you as you were growing up? If you have children, how do you discipline them, and how different is your method of applying discipline from that of your parents? Since chastity is important for both sons and daughters, how can you teach them that virtue in an age that seems to abhor it?
3. **7:31.** What motive does this verse give for honoring priests? How do you show honor to the priests with whom you are acquainted or those you meet? How can you criticize a priest without dishonoring him?
4. **7:36.** Read the note for this verse. What is the Christian tradition regarding remembrance of the "four last things"? Since the end of your life is in the future, what does "remembrance" mean?

Chapter 8

For understanding

1. **8:1–19.** What advice do these verses provide? Since life provides only limited time and resources to do good, how do we "choose our battles"? How are all injunctions in this section expressed? Against what does the first part also warn readers?
2. **8:8.** What does "Do not slight the discourse of the sages" mean? What are maxims? With what do people of the Middle East typically sprinkle their speech? What does it mean to "gain instruction"? For what purpose, according to the Hebrew?
3. **8:9.** How is wisdom passed down? Otherwise, if wisdom is not passed down that way, what would every new generation need to do? What does one avoid by listening to the wise advice and lessons of the more experienced? By learning from your elders, what will you be able to do?
4. **8:19.** To what does Ben Sira now extend the need for prudence and discretion? Why is it not a good idea to "think aloud" unless surrounded with close, trustworthy friends? To what does "your good luck" refer here?

For application

1. **8:3.** How might this verse apply to the temptation to refute controversial posts on social media? How might any response "heap wood on [their] fire"?
2. **8:10.** Read the note for this verse. How can it apply to your conduct with friends or associates, for example, at a party or in a competition?
3. **8:13.** Why should you be careful about co-signing on a loan? What will happen if the person for whom you are co-signing defaults?
4. **8:17–19.** Have you ever revealed a secret to others that was entrusted to you in confidence, or entrusted a secret to another only to learn that it was subsequently spread abroad? If so, what lessons did you learn from that experience?

Chapter 9

For understanding

1. **9:3.** What does the expression "a loose woman" mean? What is the danger of going to meet her? What is the contrast with wisdom here?
2. **9:8.** How does the Hebrew for this verse read? Whose beauty is referred to here? What is the problem with a woman's beauty? According to St. John Chrysostom, if beauty is a work of God's wisdom, and God's work could never be a cause of wickedness, what is the problem with looking on it?
3. **9:9.** What warning is being given here? To what can putting oneself in compromising circumstances lead? According to the Torah, what was the penalty for adultery? To what else, perhaps, can the "destruction" refer?
4. **9:10–18.** With what practical exhortations do these verses deal? For the author, to what do they apply? But in a modern context, to what can his counsel be extended?

For application

1. **9:2–8.** Compare these verses with what Jesus says about looking at women (Mt 5:28). What is the difference between seeing and looking? Is all looking sinful? If not, at what point does it become sinful?
2. **9:10b.** What is the analogy between a new friend and new wine intended to communicate? How do you "age" a friendship? Who are some of your lifelong friends, and what attracts you to their friendship?
3. **9:11.** Why does the *Catechism* define envy as a capital sin (CCC 2539)? When can envy become a mortal sin?
4. **9:15.** Do you have any friends with whom you can discuss spiritual things? What do you gain from conversations about matters pertaining to God?

Chapter 10

For understanding

1. **10:8.** How does Ben Sira view political regime changes? If "pride goes before destruction, and a haughty spirit before a fall", how does he view the situation of rich and powerful states? What event does Ben Sira perhaps have in mind?
2. **10:13.** What does this verse seem to say? How does the Vulgate reverse it? How is the idea of a vicious circle of causality where sin engenders pride, which in turns causes more sin, plausible and compatible with the rest of the verse? How does the Hebrew read? To what topic does Ben Sira return? What explains why God's judgment on prideful rulers and nations is so harsh?
3. **10:19—11:9.** What does this section cover? If prideful people seek honor but are unworthy of it, then who is worthy of it? What act is discouraged here?
4. **10:30.** About what is this verse not a claim? Rather, what is the point?

For application

1. **10:4.** As you survey the history of your country, how would you regard Ben Sira's contention that God raises up the right leader for the time? Who would some of these people be, and why? How would you apply this verse to the history of the Church?
2. **10:13.** Read the note for this verse. Pride is considered one of the seven capital, or deadly, sins. Verse 18 below says that "pride was not created for men"; how, then, does it originate in the human heart? What makes it so deadly?
3. **10:19–24.** By what standards does the world honor certain individuals? By what standards does Ben Sira say they should be honored? As you examine your own life, by what standards would you like to be honored?
4. **10:28.** Jesus invites his disciples to learn from him because he is meek and humble of heart (Mt 11:29). What does he mean by meekness and humility? Is humility contrary to proper self-esteem or its very definition? How does one acquire it?

Chapter 11

For understanding

1. **11:10.** In this new section, against what does Ben Sira caution? What does the warning about not going unpunished imply? Possibly what is one pursuing, and what is he fleeing?
2. **11:18.** Normally, diligence and self-denial are praised as virtues, but what is Ben Sira describing here? Although it is wise to prepare for one's financial future, how are life and wealth to be used? Since no one knows the day of his death, what does the miser who hoards riches not know about them?
3. **11:26.** Of what are past fortunes or misfortunes unreliable indicators? While the Lord may allow temporary chastisements upon the righteous or prosperity upon the wicked, when will he render to each one according to his conduct? What does Ben Sira perhaps have in mind?
4. **11:28.** Although everyone experiences pleasurable moments during his lifetime, of what are such moments poor indicators? According to St. John Cassian, as long as one continues the struggle of this life, what is he never without? What does Cassian warn about the acquisition of virtue? According to Ben Sira, how will people know a deceased man's true worth?

For application

1. **11:2–4.** What impresses you or puts you off when you first meet someone? How do you prepare to make a good impression on those you will meet for the first time? How do you judge others' character more reliably, and how do you want them to judge yours?
2. **11:7.** If you are not acquainted with the facts, what should you do when someone you know is said to have done something wrong? What does charity demand? At what point would it be appropriate to conclude blame or innocence? Even if the person is guilty, what does charity continue to demand?
3. **11:25.** This verse applies also to the ups and downs of the spiritual life: when prayer is good, one forgets feelings of desolation; and when one is in the doldrums, one forgets that consolation will come. When you are feeling good about your prayer, how can you prepare for the times when it seems flat? And when prayer feels unfruitful, how do you prepare for it to improve?
4. **11:28.** Aside from physical descendants, what "children" does a person leave behind when he dies? According to St. Paul (1 Cor 3:11–15), upon what foundation should one build his life? How will his accomplishments—his children—be tested?

Chapter 12

For understanding

1. **12:1.** What should you know about the beneficiary of a deed that you do? What is the literal translation of the second half of the verse, and what does it mean?
2. **12:5.** Although Ben Sira's adamant stance not to help the wicked seems harsh, what is his rationale? An ancient Jewish saying claims that doing good to an evil person is what sort of act?

3.   **12:10.** To what does the copper refer? How were mirrors made of bronze treated to give a distinct reflection? How does the analogy apply to the ever-shifting wickedness of an enemy?

4.   **12:13.** What kind of person does Ben Sira think a snake charmer is? Why should he not expect sympathy if he is bitten? How does this apply to one who cavorts with a sinner?

For application

1.   **12:5.** Read the note for this verse. Why would the ancient Jewish saying maintain that doing good to an evil person is an evil act? What is the Christian answer to Ben Sira (Lk 6:27–36)?

2.   **12:8–9.** Gilbert K. Chesterton was able to maintain strong friendships with people who fundamentally disagreed with him on almost everything, such as George Bernard Shaw. What enabled him to accomplish that? How do you relate to persons whose moral or political beliefs are directly contrary to yours? How do you hold them close as friends and keep them from becoming enemies?

3.   **12:14.** How might friendship with someone whose conduct is consciously immoral become a "near occasion of sin" for you? While you may need to associate with persons known to live immoral lives, how might you protect yourself from their influence?

Chapter 13

For understanding

1.   **13:1.** What is pitch? Just as pitch defiles and is difficult to clean off, how is it comparable with associating with a proud man?

2.   **13:11.** Even if a powerful person speaks in a friendly way toward you, how should you conduct yourself? What might his friendly demeanor be masking?

3.   **13:17.** Why do lambs avoid wolves? Likewise, why should godly men avoid sinners?

4.   **13:24.** Under what condition is wealth not intrinsically evil? While poverty is undesirable, what behaviors are not always its cause?

For application

1.   **13:1–7.** How would you apply Ben Sira's advice to relationships between executives of competing businesses, between employees and employers, between sales people and potential customers, or between yourself and competitive neighbors? Why is caution in such relationships always necessary?

2.   **13:10.** How experienced are you at networking when looking for a job? What are some strategies you use so as to see and be seen by prospective employers?

3.   **13:22–23.** Have you ever tried to communicate moral or ethical concerns to an authority figure such as a politician or an executive in your company? If so, what reception did you receive? If you were ignored or put off, what did you do? If you have not tried to address concerns to authorities, what keeps you from doing so?

4.   **13:25.** Read the note for this verse. Does the term "heart" here refer simply to mood changes or to something else? Why would a positive change in your circumstances, such as a new love or a windfall in your finances, change the way you appear?

Chapter 14

For understanding

1.   **14:6.** In what sense is a miser even worse than a selfish person who does not give to others for the sake of self-indulgence? To what punishment does "retribution" refer in this verse?

2.   **14:11.** Why does Ben Sira address readers in a fatherly way? What does the commandment "you shall love your neighbor as yourself" presuppose?

3.   **14:21.** To what are the "ways" of wisdom equivalent? What is one able to do only after learning obedience?

4.   **14:24.** What does the pursuer of wisdom become, so to speak? Why does he live next to her? How does one learn the deeper teachings of wisdom?

For application

1.   **14:5–10.** How does a literary character like Ebenezer Scrooge exemplify these verses? According to the story, how does he learn the virtue of magnanimity? How do you think the Lord would like you to use your financial resources?

2.   **14:11.** Read the note for this verse, particularly the comment about avoiding "harsh forms of asceticism". Is it acceptable for the prudent Christian to avoid all asceticism? In contrast, is the devout Christian supposed to imitate saints who practiced extreme forms of asceticism? If not, what sorts of asceticism does Christian spirituality require, and why?

3.   **14:14–16.** In the same vein as above, what should be the Christian attitude toward the pursuit of luxury? How does poverty of spirit call the Christian to live?

4.   **14:20–27.** What is the difference in attitude between one who is open to wisdom and one who seeks it? Why is openness not sufficient for acquiring wisdom? How long should the active pursuit of wisdom last?

Chapter 15

For understanding

1.   **15:9.** Why are songs of praise to God the natural response of the righteous? What form of prayer is praise? Why is praise unfitting on the lips of a sinner?

2.   **15:11–20.** What topics does Ben Sira address in these verses? What claim does he refute? What must people do with respect to their own sins?

3. **15:14.** What extra clause does the Hebrew add to the middle of this verse? What idea does this verse refute? If God created man good, where did sin come from? Thus, where does evil originate? According to the Church, why does God permit evil?

4. **15:15.** Of what is this verse a strong affirmation? How will the commandments save you? What does the Hebrew text add here?

For application

1. **15:1–6.** According to Ben Sira, what benefits can the seeker of wisdom expect? How do these compare to the blessings of the Beatitudes (Mt 5:3–12)?

2. **15:9–10.** Spiritual writers say that the prayer of praise does not benefit God, who does not need it, but it does benefit the one who prays. How so?

3. **15:11–12.** It seems to be a human trait to shift blame for sin from oneself to others. Have you ever directly or implicitly blamed others for the ways you were raised or for how you react to injury or for a wrong you have done? How might shifting blame resolve such issues for you? What is your responsibility for your own behavior?

4. **15:15.** When a temptation to commit sin seems overwhelming, how might it seem to limit the choices you think you have? If you give in to it, what should you do to recover? How might you prepare for the next time that temptation occurs?

Chapter 16

For understanding

1. **16:4.** How does the Hebrew text for this verse read? To whom is it probably alluding? To which "tribe of lawless men" is the verse probably alluding?

2. **16:11.** With whom is the expression "a stiffnecked person" usually associated? To whom is it employed to refer here? If the wilderness generation did not escape punishment, what of those who repeat their mistake? What are two facets of God's character?

3. **16:17.** What does the speaker in this verse foolishly suppose? What does he downplay?

4. **16:27.** To which works does Ben Sira specifically refer here? To what does "their dominion" refer, and how long will it last? What point about the stability of the created order is the author making?

For application

1. **16:1–3.** In ancient Israel, why would childlessness be a problem for a married couple? Why would some modern couples choose not to have children? Why does the Church require that couples be open to having children for their marriage to be considered valid?

2. **16:11.** Read the note for this verse. In your view, which facet of God's character is more dominant: his mercy or his wrath? Why? If, according to the New Testament, God is love (1 Jn 4:8), how do you understand what his wrath is? Why are the two not incompatible?

3. **16:17.** According to Ps 139, how well does God know you? How likely are you to escape his notice? How well do you want God to know you? How would such knowledge help you to know yourself?

Chapter 17

For understanding

1. **17:1.** What does the "earth" made into God's image indicate? According to the Church, of what is the human person composed? As the only one of God's visible creatures willed for its own sake, to what is he called?

2. **17:22.** What is a signet? How is a person's almsgiving like a signet? What does it mean that God keeps a person's deeds "like the apple of his eye"?

3. **17:23.** How does Ben Sira respond to the skeptics who think that God does not act? For what is "on their heads" a metaphor?

4. **17:28.** What is the state of the dead of the OT like? How does this perspective change in the NT?

For application

1. **17:4.** What does dominion over beasts and birds entail for human beings? Even though we use them for food and clothing, what respect do we owe these animals?

2. **17:11–14.** What makes human beings human? How consistent through the ages are the moral standards of the natural law? If historical circumstances change, do moral standards change with them? Why or why not?

3. **17:14.** This verse mentions the commandments of the Decalogue that refer to one's neighbor. What is their purpose? Even though most are phrased in the negative, what are their positive meanings?

4. **17:27–28.** At what point in life is one's choice for or against God finalized? Why cannot that choice be changed after death?

Chapter 18

For understanding

1. **18:8.** To whom does Ben Sira now shift attention? Compared to his Maker, how significant is man? What does this verse not deny but rather strongly affirm? To what does this perhaps refer?

2. **18:20.** What preparation is even more important than preparing for speaking or falling ill? What is the hour of visitation? What does self-examination reveal?

3. **18:23.** Before you make a vow to the Lord, what should you do? Why is it unwise to make a rash vow that you are unlikely to keep?

4. **18:25.** What is this verse possibly an appeal to do in times of wealth or poverty? More likely, since hunger and poverty are often viewed as punishments for sin, of what is this a reminder?

For application

1. **18:5–7.** St. Thomas Aquinas says that the human mind cannot *comprehend*—that is, understand—God, but that it can *apprehend*, or perceive, him as he chooses to reveal himself. How do you perceive the presence of God in your life? How can perceiving him change your understanding of your relationship with him?
2. **18:20.** Spiritual writers recommend examining one's conscience daily. How often do you do it? When is a good time to do it? In addition to reminding yourself of your faults, what other purposes can self-examination have?
3. **18:22–23.** What promises have you made to the Lord out of personal devotion? Have you been able to keep them? What does keeping a promise indicate about your relationship with God? (On the subject of promises and vows, see CCC 2101–3.)
4. **18:32–33.** What is your position on whether or not to buy on credit? What sorts of things, such as luxuries or entertainments, do you buy with credit cards? How deeply in debt are you, and how quickly do you repay the charges?

Chapter 19

For understanding

1. **19:1.** How does the Hebrew for this verse read, and to what does it refer? To what does neglect of small matters lead?
2. **19:10.** What should you do with a rumor? What does Ben Sira's sarcastic remark imply about fools?
3. **19:11.** How are fools' inability to control their speech like a newborn coming from his mother's womb? How does restraining themselves resemble a woman's labor pains?
4. **19:25.** How can one be scrupulous in his affairs but unjust? How does one distort kindness?

For application

1. **19:4.** How does sin injure the sinner? What kinds of injury does sin cause him? If it takes a long time for a good character to develop through the practice of virtue, how quickly does a bad character develop?
2. **19:16.** What is the purpose of speech? St. James compares the tongue to a rudder that turns a ship or to a spark that ignites a forest fire (Jas 3:4–5). What are some of the ways we can do great damage with our tongues? How can we control the rudder or stamp out the fire once it starts? When we cause damage through what we say, how do we undo the damage?
3. **19:24.** There is a popular belief that evil people are more interesting than good ones; yet the saints maintain that evil people are actually *less* interesting than good ones. Why do worldly people believe that goodness is boring? Why are they wrong? In contrast, why do the saints believe that holy people are some of the most interesting you will ever meet?
4. **19:29–30.** Ben Sira says that a "sensible" person can judge another's character by how he looks, dresses, laughs, and even walks. How often do you use these or similar criteria to determine whether you like or dislike those you meet? How often are your first impressions borne out? How do you think you appear to others?

Chapter 20

For understanding

1. **20:1.** If it is appropriate to rebuke someone who has done wrong, what can happen when the timing is wrong? What is sometimes wiser than speaking?
2. **20:18–26.** What do these verses provide? With what consequences do they deal?
3. **20:29.** To what do "presents and gifts" refer here? Why are they forbidden? What do they inhibit authorities from doing?
4. **20:30–31.** How is hidden wisdom like hidden treasure? How is wisdom to be beneficial? What is it better for a fool to hide and for the wise to reveal? According to St. Gregory the Great, why should persons who can preach the gospel but shrink back out of excessive humility be admonished? If they do not supply the bread of grace when souls are perishing from a famine of the word of God, what are they liable to receive?

For application

1. **20:1–2.** The note for v. 1 refers to Mt 18:15–17, on fraternal correction. What does Jesus say is the Christian's duty in this regard? What kinds of offenses does Jesus have in mind that would involve taking corrections to the Church as a last resort? If, then, you see a parishioner doing something that is objectively wrong, what is your duty? What would be the desired benefit for the parishioner whom you are admonishing?
2. **20:10.** When you invite a friend or acquaintance to dinner, what do you expect in return? When you are invited, what do you expect to do in return? Do you feel that some form of reciprocation is in order? What would Jesus recommend for you (see Lk 14:12–14)?
3. **20:24.** How do lies distort a person's character? How does lying violate the cardinal virtues (prudence, justice, fortitude, temperance)? How does telling the truth, even when inconvenient or dangerous, strengthen them in one's character?
4. **20:29.** Why do most societies forbid bribery? Have you ever been offered a payment or a favor, either to squelch a wrong or to promote some purpose? What was in it for you? Why would conscience be bothered at such offers?

Chapter 21

For understanding

1. **21:3.** What is the danger in "a two-edged sword"? What does the analogy emphasize?
2. **21:9.** Of what does tow consist, and what is its danger? Why is "a flame of fire" not necessarily a form of punishment in the afterlife?

3.   **21:21.** In contrast to the fool's view of education, in what does submitting to the education of wisdom result? To what is wisdom thus likened?
4.   **21:26.** When do fools speak, and when do the wise? According to Hilary of Poitiers, why is the heart of a fool in his mouth? By contrast, where does the tongue of the wise come from? To what does the tongue of the wise subject itself?

For application
1.   **21:3.** If lawlessness is like a two-edged sword, what are some of its benefits? What are some of its dangers? St. John regards sin as lawlessness (1 Jn 3:4). How does it kill? What does it kill?
2.   **21:6.** Why should one who fears the Lord invite his correction? What benefit is there in praying that the Lord will reveal your faults to you?
3.   **21:10.** Compare this verse with what Jesus says about the wide and narrow doors (Mt 7:13–14). Why is the door to heaven so narrow and hard and that to hell so wide and easy? Some theologians believe that no one goes to hell. What do you think? Why is the existence of hell not an indictment of God's goodness?
4.   **21:23–24.** What is a voyeur? Why is voyeurism more than mere boorishness or lack of manners? Why did medieval society regard curiosity as a serious sin, and why do modern people dismiss it as such? How can it lead to sin?

Chapter 22

For understanding
1.   **22:4.** How does the Latin for this verse read? What is the sense of the verse? What kind of daughter will attract a good husband who will cherish her?
2.   **22:11.** While one naturally mourns the dead, why should one mourn the fool even more?
3.   **22:18.** Instead of "fences", how do some manuscripts read? Where were they placed, and why? Just as small rocks easily fall off the wall, what happens to a cowardly, unresolved person with foolish thoughts?
4.   **22:19.** What are two of the most sensitive parts of the human body? Though both are quickly wounded, how quickly do they heal?

For application
1.   **22:3–5.** Much attention is given in our culture to raising girls to be strong, independent women. If you are or desire to be a parent, how would you raise a girl to be a strong Christian woman? What virtues would you emphasize? How would you prepare her for her vocation in life, whether as a married or a single woman?
2.   **22:7–15.** What are some of the marks of a fool in these verses? What is Ben Sira's view of the fool's future? What word would Scripture use for an intelligent person who has been taught the way to eternal life but ignores it?
3.   **22:16.** Compare this verse with Jesus' parable about a house built on rock versus one built on sand (Lk 6:47–49). Whereas Ben Sira focuses on a mind built on good principles, on what does Jesus focus? How compatible are the two points of view?

Chapter 23

For understanding
1.   **23:2.** To what does the expression "discipline of wisdom" allude? To what does wisdom's discipline over the mind really amount? What does Ben Sira pray might correct his sins?
2.   **23:9.** What are oaths? When only should oaths be sworn?
3.   **23:16.** To what does this numerical proverb refer? To what two acts might "fornication with his near of kin" refer?
4.   **23:18.** What does the adulterer wrongly think is hidden? According to St. Cyril of Jerusalem, why must we take care of our body as our own? Just as a scar remains after a wound in the body has healed, what does sin do?

For application
1.   **23:2.** If you wish to progress in prayer, how do you discipline your thoughts? Why is silence before God important? How difficult is it for you to silence your imagination when you are at prayer? Why is it important not to give up because of the difficulty?
2.   **23:9.** Why does Ben Sira advise not habitually uttering the name of God? How might doing so risk violating the second commandment of the Decalogue? What is your response when you hear companions thoughtlessly utter God's or Jesus' name? If you do not respond, at least mentally, why not?
3.   **23:17.** How is fornication actively promoted in our society? Why do most people in our culture see little wrong with it? Despite that, how does the practice of fornication injure the Christian community? What does the New Testament say that fornicators can expect (e.g., Eph 5:3–5)?
4.   **23:25.** Read the note for this verse. Why would the Jewish law take such a harsh position toward the children of an adulterous union? How does the Church regard children whom society considers illegitimate?

Chapter 24

For understanding
1.   **24:10.** Where did personified Wisdom dwell? What kind of ministry did Wisdom perform before the Lord? Of what was the Tabernacle an earthly representation? What did Solomon's Temple in Jerusalem replace? Thus, how long was Wisdom present with Israel?
2.   **Topical Essay: Nuptial Union with Lady Wisdom through Salvation History.** How does the Bible often portray the pursuit of Wisdom as a romantic courtship and nuptial mystery? How should wise men court her? How is the nuptial nature of this union with Wisdom underscored in Sirach? In the following four ways, how does the imagery of Sirach 24 evoke specific

moments in salvation history: Wisdom's initial presence at creation and in the Garden of Eden, her restoration in the Torah, her indwelling in the Temple's liturgy, and her final revelation to the world at the end of times?
3. **24:13.** What is the cedar of Lebanon? What is the cypress? With what does Ezekiel associate both trees? Where were both types of wood used, and of what are both characteristic? Where is Hermon?
4. **24:15.** What are cassia and camel's thorn? What were both used to make for the Tabernacle? What are galbanum, onycha, and stacte used to make, together with frankincense? What role does Wisdom thus play?

For application
1. **24:3-9.** Compare these verses with the opening of John's Gospel (Jn 1:1-5, 10-14). How is Wisdom like the Word, who was with God in the beginning? How is she as a created being different from the Word? Where do both make their dwelling?
2. **24:15.** What is the liturgical purpose of incense? Why does the celebrant cause smoke to rise before the altar, the crucifix, and the Gospel book at Mass? Why does he incense the remains of the deceased at funerals? How does incense serve as a reminder of prayer?
3. **24:19-21.** Compare these verses with Jesus' invitation for all who labor and are weary to come to him (Mt 11:28-30). What is the yoke that Jesus invites all to take up? How does it give rest? What does Lady Wisdom offer?

Chapter 25

For understanding
1. **25:3.** To what does "you have gathered nothing" refer? When should wisdom be acquired? What happens if a man neglects to pursue wisdom throughout his life? According to St. John Cassian, how should the wealth of the old be measured?
2. **25:8.** What find is closely related to finding wisdom? What do the Hebrew and Syriac versions add here, and to what does the analogy refer? What situation was an embarrassment in the ancient world?
3. **25:13—26:27.** With what counsel does this section deal? If this controversial section can appear misogynistic to modern readers, what considerations can offset the author's harsh critique of "bad wives"?
4. **25:24.** According to Ben Sira, to what did Eve's fall in the Garden of Eden lead? For what is Eve declared responsible, although other texts of Scripture underscore Adam's culpability?

For application
1. **25:4-5.** Some cultures prize the wisdom of the aged. What is the attitude of our culture toward the elderly? How many old people do you know? Which of them has the sort of wisdom you would want to learn from? What sort of wisdom do they offer (e.g., technical expertise, social savvy, insight into life)?
2. **25:10-11.** What kinds of spiritual reading do you do? When it comes to the saints, do you prefer biographies or works that they have written? Either way, what do you hope to learn from them?
3. **25:16-20.** What Ben Sira says of wicked wives can just as easily be said of wicked husbands. What seems to be the principal marital issue he cites in these verses? What problems in communication characterize your family of origin, and how have they carried over into the ways you communicate?
4. **25:24.** Read Rom 5:12-19. What does St. Paul say about the origin of sin among mankind? What was the result of the sin of that first man? What is the result of the grace brought about by the second Adam?

Chapter 26

For understanding
1. **26:1.** How is Ben Sira's hyperbole about being married to a good wife confirmed by modern studies?
2. **26:13.** In the ancient world, of what was being fat a sign? What does a good wife do for her husband?
3. **26:16.** What time of day is it when the sun is at its zenith? What is the Greek word for "ordered", and what does it mean? How, then, could the verse be rendered? To what does Ben Sira liken the good wife's home?
4. **26:18.** To what do the "pillars of gold" probably refer? What role does the sensible wife play? How does Jewish tradition also hold that the world is supported?

For application
1. **26:1-4.** What to you is the mark of a good marriage? In your experience, what are the roles of the husband and of the wife that make for a good marriage? According to the vows spoken in the wedding liturgy, what are the spouses to be for each other? What are they to do for each other?
2. **26:8.** Alcoholism is a scourge for many families and may affect them for generations. Do you have any experience with alcoholism in current or previous generations of your family? If so, how have you or other members of your family dealt with it? What kinds of external support have you or your family received (e.g., from organizations like Alcoholics Anonymous)?
3. **26:15.** How would you describe the virtue of chastity? Given that married couples have sexual relationships, how is chastity demonstrated within a marriage? How can chastity within marriage be violated, apart from an adulterous relationship?
4. **26:29.** Read the note for this verse. What are the challenges in running an honest business? What business ethics policies are in place at your place of employment? Which of these are written down, and which are merely assumed? What are the consequences of violating company ethics policies?

Chapter 27

For understanding
1. **27:4.** For what is a sieve used? What passes through the mesh, and what is filtered out? How does the analogy apply to the faults of a bad man? How do his faults become evident?

2. **27:5.** What happens to a potter's vessel when it is improperly made and is baked in a furnace? How is the quality of just men manifested? Rather than "in tribulation", how does the Greek text read?
3. **27:23.** How does the deceptive man appear, and how does he speak? What does he pretend to do? When will he speak very differently? What will he do with your words?
4. **27:28.** What is the literal translation of this verse? In what sense can it also mean that "mockery and abuse are the lot of the proud"?

For application
1. **27:1-3.** These verses continue the thought of 26:29. What is a scam? How do you think people who perpetrate such frauds rationalize their behavior? Which of the commandments do con artists violate?
2. **27:4-7.** Jesus says that from the heart the mouth speaks (Mt 12:34) and that what comes from the mouth defiles a person (Mt 15:18-20). What things did he have in mind? As you analyze your own speech habits, what comes from your mouth that glorifies God, and what comes out that can defile you?
3. **27:13-14.** How often do you spend time with friends who tell off-color jokes or pepper their speech with vulgar or scato-logical language? Why does St. Paul advise Christians to avoid such speech themselves (Eph 4:29, 5:4)?
4. **27:16-21.** As you read these verses carefully, does Ben Sira seem to have in mind a single betrayal of secrets or multiple ones? Accidental or deliberate? If the betrayal is a single occurrence, or accidental, what hope for restoring the friendship might there be? How does one restore trust?

Chapter 28

For understanding
1. **28:9.** How does a sinful man disturb friends? According to Rabanus Maurus, why are the contentious wicked? Why are heretics and schismatics chief among them?
2. **28:14.** What is the literal meaning for the word translated as "slander"? To what two things may it refer? What does Ben Sira's poetic exaggeration illustrate about slander?
3. **28:19.** From what does God shield the man who is protected? Whom does slander enslave?
4. **28:23.** What will those who slander suffer? What does the burning quality of slander illustrate? What do the comparisons of slander to lions and leopards underline?

For application
1. **28:1-6.** How are these verses similar to Jesus' admonitions about forgiving others (Mt 6:14-15; 18:21-35)? Although forgiving others is necessary for us if we wish to receive God's forgiveness, why is it usually so difficult to do? Since unfor-giveness has consequences in the next life, what consequences can it have in this life?
2. **28:17.** "Sticks and stones may break my bones", but how much injury can words cause? Are written insults less injurious than spoken ones? Why do social media users freely level insults online that they would never think of doing face-to-face?
3. **28:21.** Read the note for this verse. What is calumny? When a reputation is ruined through calumny, which of the Ten Commandments is violated? How grave a sin is this?
4. **28:25.** What does it mean to "make balances and scales for your words"? What does a child learn who frequently hears negative speech such as sarcasm, criticism, barbed humor, or derogatory nicknames coming from you? If your conversations are marked by negative speech patterns, what can you do to correct these habits?

Chapter 29

For understanding
1. **29:3.** How do you as the borrower confirm your word? What will happen if you repay your loans faithfully?
2. **29:12.** To what is giving alms likened? What will God do for a generous person? According to St. Augustine, why will people who show mercy to others be saved?
3. **29:14-20.** Of what does the practice of "giving surety" consist? Although Proverbs is wary of this practice, what does Ben Sira think of it?
4. **29:21-28.** What counsel do these verses offer? In the ancient world, how could one seek a better life, but at what cost? What kind of life does Ben Sira prefer?

For application
1. **29:4-7.** Many financial counselors advise against lending money to relatives for many of the reasons Ben Sira gives here. Do you have any experience of asking relatives for a loan or of being asked for one? If you borrowed from a relative, how quickly did you repay the loan? If you lend a relative money, how will you ensure that you will be repaid?
2. **29:14-20.** If you cannot afford to finance a child's education with your own resources, what alternatives do you have for helping him financially? What financial programs are available to you? Which of you, yourself or the student, will be responsible for repaying the student's loans? If you, how will the student learn financial responsibility?
3. **29:23.** How satisfied are you with what you have? How often do you want to upgrade your possessions? How would you feel about a downturn in the economy that would restrict your ability to spend? What was St. Paul's motive for being content with plenty or scarcity (Phil 4:11-13)?

Chapter 30

For understanding
1. **30:1-13.** What counsel do these verses offer? What kind of disciplinarian is it assumed that a father should be? How should these guidelines be taken in a modern context?
2. **30:9.** What is the meaning behind "he will frighten you"? What is Ben Sira concerned that a father may lose?

3. **30:12.** In what sense should a father bow down his son's neck? What analogy is Ben Sira using here? What penalty did the Torah prescribe for a stubborn and rebellious son? What record is there that the sentence was ever carried out?

4. **30:17.** Although even the righteous sometimes express a desire to die, what do they always do? What do they recognize, in other words? What does eternal rest mean here? For whom does the Church call for special respect to be given? What does she deem about euthanasia?

For application

1. **30:1.** What is your philosophy of how to discipline children? What part does corporal punishment play in it? How do you expect your methods of discipline to change as your children get older?

2. **30:7-13.** How do you discipline a child so as to teach respect for your authority without alienating him? What is the danger in making your child your "best friend"? By the same token, how do you encourage your child to confide in you during times of trouble?

3. **30:16-17.** What becomes of your relationship with the Lord when you contract a serious and incurable illness such as cancer? What does it mean to die with dignity? What is "redemptive suffering", and how do you transform your suffering accordingly?

4. **30:21-25.** What kind of life do you think the Lord is giving you? If physical comfort is not his will for you, what is? What role do penitential disciplines such as physical mortification play? From a spiritual perspective, what attention should you be giving to the food you eat?

Chapter 31

For understanding

1. **31:8.** Why is the rich man blessed? Who is Ben Sira praising?

2. **31:11.** Ultimately, what is wealth? If it is not money that is evil, what is? What does the person who has acquired wealth honestly deserve? What does the verse assume?

3. **31:17-18.** What should the well-mannered person not be the first to do? What virtue should he display, and what should he be the first to do?

4. **31:28-30.** What contrast do these verses draw? According to St. Ambrose, when God gave wine, what did he know about it? To human freedom, what choice did he give in that regard? Of what did the Lord make it a means?

For application

1. **31:5-7.** What are your concerns about management of your wealth? In terms of investment, where do you think you should put your money? If you are married, in what ways do you and your spouse agree about the use of money?

2. **31:12-14.** What is a reasonable Christian approach toward food? In response to the Corinthian axiom that "food is made for the stomach, and the stomach for food", what did St. Paul answer about the purpose of the body (1 Cor 6:13)?

3. **31:21.** Read the note for this verse. Does the Christian approach to food approve of Ben Sira's solution to feeling overstuffed? What are some of the causes behind eating disorders such as bulimia or anorexia? How can they be treated?

4. **31:27-30.** How does the *Catechism* define the virtue of temperance (CCC 1809)? What about the consumption of alcohol does temperance forbid (CCC 2290)? How might these principles apply to the abuse of drugs (CCC 2291)?

Chapter 32

For understanding

1. **32:1.** Who is the "master of the feast"? In that capacity, how should he act?

2. **32:12.** Where and when should the banqueter presumably amuse himself? What does the pleasant atmosphere at banquets make people prone to do? What does Ben Sira remind banqueters to do?

3. **32:17.** What does the sinful man reject? How does the Hebrew for this verse read? Instead of following the Torah, what does the sinful man do with it?

4. **32:24.** How does the Hebrew for this verse read? What actions constitute a path to flourishing?

For application

1. **32:1-2.** When you give a party, what is your role before your guests? When is it appropriate for you to join the fun? Until that time, what should you be doing?

2. **32:11.** How do you decide when is a good time to leave an enjoyable party? What message do you send by leaving too soon or lingering too long?

3. **32:14-17.** Do you believe that traditional moral teachings apply to current cultural situations or that they should be amended to reflect changing cultural norms? How does your position align with Ben Sira's? Why does Scripture generally hold that doing what each person thinks is right leads to moral chaos?

4. **32:19.** What kind of decision-maker are you: bold and confident or irresolute and uncertain? If you are the first, how do you respond when you realize your judgment is mistaken? If you are the second, how can you overcome the fear that any decision you make could be wrong?

Chapter 33

For understanding

1. **33:3.** What were the Urim and the Thummim? For what were they used?

2. **33:16.** What does Ben Sira consider himself to be? What is one who gleans? From what has Ben Sira gleaned? How has he "filled [his] wine press"?

3. **33:24–33.** With what do the instructions in these verses deal? For whom does Ben Sira advocate severity, and for whom kindness? What sort of time does his counsel reflect?
4. **33:26.** To what is the slave compared? What are some instruments for disciplining disobedient servants? What did Israelite law limit, and what did it protect? On the basis of the seventh commandment, why does Catholic teaching denounce the enslavement of human beings?

For application
1. **33:3.** When you seek God's will for your life, how do you go about it? For example, if you face two alternatives, both of which appear equally good, how do you decide which one (if either) the Lord is leading you toward? What trust do you have that the Lord is leading you when you decide?
2. **33:7–9.** Why does the Church establish certain days as Holy Days of Obligation? Which day of the week is the most important? What does it celebrate? What is Ordinary Time, and why is it called that?
3. **33:17.** Since there is very little money to be gained from it, why do spiritual writers pen spiritual books? What spiritual works have you read, and what have you learned from them?
4. **33:27.** How does meaningful labor enhance one's life? How do you teach children the value of work? What purpose does periodic leisure serve? What is the difference between rest and idleness?

Chapter 34

For understanding
1. **34:5.** What do the occult practices of divinations and omens attempt to know? Just as these are strictly forbidden by the Torah, what occult practices does the Church continue to forbid, and why?
2. **34:7.** According to St. Gregory the Great, what faith should one have in dreams? Who can best distinguish illusions from revelations and discover the meaning of their words and images? If a soul is not prudent in the matter of dreams, what can happen and by what spirit?
3. **34:18–26.** Whom does Ben Sira, like many before him, criticize, and for what? Because these sacrifices are empty rituals, what does the Lord do?
4. **34:20.** What does the shocking comparison (alluding to 2 Kings 25:6–7) illustrate? Why is such a sacrifice offensive to the Lord?

For application
1. **34:6.** According to Matthew's Gospel, St. Joseph was four times directed by the Lord through dreams, mainly in critical situations (1:20–21; 2:13, 19–20, 22). Described as a "just man" (Mt 1:19), what may have protected him from misinterpreting his dreams? Given Ben Sira's cautions against dreams, what qualities of a dream might lead one to test and see if it is from the Lord?
2. **34:9.** How does travel enhance a person's education? If one cannot afford to travel abroad, how else can he gain the experience that travel provides?
3. **34:14.** According to St. Paul (2 Tim 1:7), what spirit have Christians been given? How does that spirit manifest itself in your spiritual and emotional life?
4. **34:23–26.** When you recite an Act of Contrition, what promises are you making to God? If you have no real intention to reform your behavior, is the priest's prayer of absolution valid? If not, why confess the sin?

Chapter 35

For understanding
1. **35:1.** In what two ways can the making of many offerings be interpreted? What is a peace offering?
2. **35:4.** What does it mean to appear before the Lord empty-handed? Of what does Ben Sira underscore the spiritual significance? At the same time, what obligation of his fellow Jews does he not lessen?
3. **35:12.** What can sacrifices not do with God? What does it mean that God is perfectly just?
4. **35:16–17.** Whose sacrifices does the Lord find pleasing? What does Ben Sira mean by saying that prayer "pierces the clouds"? How long does Israel persist in prayer, and who is perhaps referred to here? According to St. Fulgentius, when is the only time that victory over the adversary is won?

For application
1. **35:4.** What do you have to offer the Lord? What do you think he wants from you? How many of your goods, both internal and external, have you placed at his disposal?
2. **35:8.** How do you feel about requests for money from the pulpit? If you believe that "the Church is always asking for money", when was the last time you actually heard a homily about money? How generously do you respond to diocesan or parish money requests?
3. **35:9.** Do you tithe? If not, why not? Based on your adjusted gross income, what percentage of your income do you actually contribute to the Church? If you contribute one percent or less, what prevents you from increasing your contribution?

Chapter 36

For understanding
1. **36:11.** Even though many Jews had returned to Judea from exile in Babylon, what was the fate of many more Israelites? For what does Ben Sira pray, and to what does in "the beginning" refer? What is the most frequently attested prophecy in the Bible?
2. **36:15.** What does Ben Sira ask God to acknowledge? What prophecies does he want God to fulfill?

3. **36:19.** What parallel between types of discernment does Ben Sira draw? As a well-trained palate can discern good food from bad, what can an intelligent man discern?
4. **36:25.** What does the Hebrew for this verse say? Whose pathetic saying does it echo? What does Ben Sira, speaking in an OT context, imply about unmarried men? In a NT context, what is celibacy elevated by Jesus to become?

For application
1. **36:1–5.** How did God use the Israelites to show the nations his mighty deeds? How does Ben Sira want him to use the nations to show Israel his glory? What goal does he hope to achieve?
2. **36:6.** In announcing the Second Vatican Council, Pope John XXIII invited the faithful to ask the Holy Spirit to show new signs and work new wonders in the Church. Why are signs and wonders important in our day? What new signs and wonders would you like to see the Holy Spirit pour out on the Church?
3. **36:19.** How should a lie be constructed so as to convince the unwitting to accept it? How can a theologian convince the faithful to believe that an act that the word of God forbids is acceptable and may even be virtuous? How does one recognize the lie there?
4. **36:25.** Read the note for this verse. In what ways is a wife a "fence" or "hedge" for a man? How does marriage encourage a holy life? Why are both marriages and celibate vocations declining in our culture? How can they be encouraged?

Chapter 37

For understanding
1. **37:5.** How is the Hebrew text different from the Greek, and how does it better fit the second half of the verse? What does a real friend not hesitate to do?
2. **37:11.** Why should one not seek counsel from the nine types of people listed? To whom does a woman's rival perhaps refer?
3. **37:12.** To whom should one turn for reliable advice? Why will he likely be faithful to you? What does "one who is in accord with your soul" mean?
4. **37:13.** If you fear the Lord, what may your own deliberations constitute, and why? Why may a person's own conscience be more reliable than several counselors?

For application
1. **37:7–8.** To whom do you go to seek advice? What are this person's qualifications for giving advice? How reliable do you find it? If you detect a bias of some sort, how does it influence the advice you are given and your willingness to follow it?
2. **37:12.** How do you select a spiritual director? What do you look for in a spiritual director? Assuming your director is trustworthy, how willing are you to obey his direction when it goes counter to your own sensibility?
3. **37:23.** In school, who was your favorite teacher? What attracted you to this person? How lasting an influence has this teacher had on you? How willing are you to pass the teacher's wisdom on to those whom you teach?
4. **37:30.** How do you know when you have had too much of a good thing? Whether it be food, drink, entertainment, sports, leisure time, even enjoyable conversation, how do you know when it is time to quit? Before involving yourself in such activities, how do you prepare to avoid going to excess?

Chapter 38

For understanding
1. **38:1.** How does the OT usually see illness, and what does it suggest to many? How is Ben Sira's positive view of physicians consonant with the practical wisdom he exhibits throughout the book? Indeed, from whom does the physician's skill come?
2. **38:10.** What correlation does cleansing one's heart from sin imply? For what can sickness be a punishment that God inflicts? What can be an important step toward recovering health?
3. **38:11.** What was "a sweet-smelling sacrifice", and what did it include? What does this passage imply about prayer, repentance, and fulfilling religious obligations?
4. **38:17.** In Middle Eastern cultures, what do people not suppress at the death of a loved one? How is it appropriate to express it? What does every person who dies deserve? What would anything less bring against the mourner? How long does the formal period of mourning in Judaism last? What should the mourner do after that?
5. **38:24.** In what did the scribe, as a professional religious scholar, specialize? What is the Greek term for leisure? What point does the etymology confirm in this section?

For application
1. **38:1–3.** What is your attitude toward medical doctors (whether or not you are one)? How often have you needed to make use of their services? As a patient, how compliant are you with following the doctor's directions?
2. **38:9–14.** What part does prayer play when you need medical attention? In cases of serious illness or danger of death, have you ever made use of the Sacrament of the Anointing of the Sick?
3. **38:16–20.** How do you express grief over the death of a loved one? What do you think is an appropriate way to grieve? What is the purpose of a Christian funeral? What sort of funeral would you like for yourself?
4. **38:25–33.** Ben Sira questions the wisdom of those engaged in manual labor, valuable as their work is. What sort of education have you had to date (e.g., in liberal arts, the law, technical pursuits, business)? If you chose a particular course of studies, why did you choose it? What kind of wisdom has it given you?

Chapter 39

For understanding
1. **39:1.** What is the scribe's object of study? What is the foundation of all wisdom and the focus of the scribe's attention? For what does it provide the foundation?

2. **39:4.** Because of his wisdom, what influence does the scholar have? Ideally, about what should the well-traveled sage acquire experience?
3. **39:13-15.** To what does Ben Sira, speaking in a fatherly tone, invite readers, and how? What do these parallels imply when the wise praise and thank the Lord?
4. **39:16.** What is the theme of the hymn? What brought the universe into existence? How does God continue his work in the history of the world?

For application
1. **39:1-3.** What is your approach to studying Scripture? What do you hope to gain from it? If you are not familiar with Scripture study, where would you go to learn some tools and techniques?
2. **39:5.** What is your favorite time for prayer? Your favorite place? What pattern of prayer do you tend to follow? What part does Scripture play in your daily prayer?
3. **39:14-15.** Since God does not need our praise, what is the purpose of praising him? In these two verses, how does Ben Sira suggest one should praise the Lord? How else might you do it?
4. **39:24.** Has your life taken a direction different from what you expected? If so, how confident are you that the change of direction was the Lord's doing? Has the direction of your life influenced your growth in holiness? If so, in what way?

Chapter 40

For understanding
1. **40:13.** When do the wadis of the Judean desert carry rushing streams of water, and when do they dry completely?
2. **40:18-27.** What does Ben Sira survey in these verses? How does he list life's blessings? In what does the list culminate?
3. **40:19.** How is a man remembered? What does the Hebrew text add here?
4. **40:27.** How does the Hebrew of this verse read? To what idea does the fear of the Lord lead back? According to St. Augustine, what is the Church, rich in graces and chaste delights, rightly called, and for whom? What is perhaps the sense behind saying that fear of the Lord covers a man better than any glory?

For application
1. **40:2-4.** How often do you think about death? What aspects of it occupy your thoughts? What do you most fear about it? How do you try to allay these fears?
2. **40:13.** Ben Sira compares the wealth of the unjust to a flash flood in the desert that dries up quickly or to a thunderclap whose roar rumbles away into silence. How would you put his meaning into your own words? In an era when the rich seem to get richer while the poor get poorer, how do you reconcile Ben Sira's thought with your experience? What brings an end to the unjust man's wealth?
3. **40:22.** What things do you find most beautiful? Which do you prefer: the beauty of nature or beautiful objects made by artists? Why has God blessed mankind with the ability to appreciate beauty for its own sake and even create it?
4. **40:28-30.** How familiar are you with homelessness where you live? What is your opinion of homeless people, and on what is this opinion based? How many homeless people actually choose that life? Assuming you are not homeless yourself, what can you do to help those who are?

Chapter 41

For understanding
1. **41:2.** As what is Death personified? For whom can it come as a relief?
2. **41:5.** To what does the subject shift? According to Rabanus Maurus, why are the children of sinners abominable to the Lord? Where do sinners place themselves?
3. **41:6.** What sort of legacy can grave sin have in families where it is allowed to flourish? Who has the contrasting legacy in name and memory?
4. **41:14—42:8.** What is the distinction Ben Sira makes between proper and improper shame?

For application
1. **41:2.** Have you ever known anyone who took his own life? According to the *Catechism* (CCC 2281-83), why is suicide objectively and gravely evil? What can diminish the moral responsibility of the one committing suicide? Why, then, should we not despair of the eternal salvation of those who take their own lives?
2. **41:5-6.** What types of sins practiced or tolerated within families can you think of that tend to perpetuate themselves across generations? How can the children of "inherited sins" free themselves from their influences?
3. **41:12-13.** In these days of mass media, what dangers can threaten one's reputation? Why is the destruction of someone's good name likened to murder? Since a good name is so important, how do you protect it?
4. **41:20-22.** What is "custody of the eyes"? How is it possible to be around physically beautiful people and not look lustfully at them? How does custody of the eyes help with custody of the imagination?

Chapter 42

For understanding
1. **42:5.** What is a common practice in the Middle East in relation to dealing with merchants? How should one feel in getting a good deal out of negotiations with them? What is a moral obligation, not a cause for shame, for parents?
2. **42:9-14.** In the Middle East, since shame is a family affair, what happens if a misdeed becomes public? What explains in part why Ben Sira speaks so harshly in what follows?

3. **42:9–10.** What are five ways in which a daughter can be a source of anxiety for her father?
4. **42:11.** What did a daughter's misbehavior become for the family? What does the Hebrew add, and for what reason?

For application
1. **42:9–10.** Read the note for this verse. In connection with the examples given, how have our cultural standards changed? How have they remained the same?
2. **42:11.** Read the note for this verse. Which modern religious groups impose such stringent controls over women's behavior? What criticisms do men in these groups have of the behavior and dress of Western women? To what extent might controversies over these issues result from the clash between a society where behavior is a family concern and one where it is the business only of the individual? Which is right?
3. **42:18–19.** Why does God's knowledge of what people will do not determine how they will act? If man has free will, what control does God have over his future?

Chapter 43

For understanding
1. **43:6.** Even more than the sun, what role does the moon play in Judaism? How long will the moon endure as a sign?
2. **43:8.** What does the pun on the Hebrew word *ḥodesh* mean? How does the moon increase? As what sort of instrument does it serve for the hosts on high? According to Rabanus Maurus, why does Ben Sira speak of the moon after the sun? And as the moon is illumined by the sun, how is the Church illumined? How is the Church rightly compared to the moon?
3. **43:13–26.** From the astral bodies, to what does Ben Sira turn, and what do they do? What foretaste and anticipation does the image of the storm provide?
4. **43:28.** Although God is present within creation, what is his relation to it?

For application
1. **43:2–5.** Read Ps 19, which speaks of the sun in similar terms. In the psalm, what benefits does the Law give that compare to those given by the sun?
2. **43:6–8.** How is the Blessed Virgin, like the Church, compared to the moon? What light does she reflect? Who benefits from it?
3. **43:21.** How can forest fires, which cause enormous damage to humans, benefit nature? When should such fires be fought, and when should they be allowed to burn themselves out?
4. **43:30.** Of what strength in praising God might Ben Sira be thinking? What purpose does liturgy serve? Of all liturgical functions, which most directly and powerfully exalts the Lord?

Chapter 44

For understanding
1. **44:1—50:24.** With what do these chapters deal? What does Ben Sira say is manifested not only in the natural world but even more in the heroic figures of biblical history? Following an introduction, how does his survey proceed? Why does the author draw attention to these pious men?
2. **44:11.** Under what conditions are the blessings of the righteous also for their posterity?
3. **44:16.** When did Enoch live? How does the Hebrew read in his regard? Is anything stated in Genesis about the reason why God "took" Enoch? How does Ben Sira's view that he was an example of repentance represent a theological development? What does the Hebrew call him? What do other traditions state about why God took him?
4. **44:20.** Why does the statement that Abraham "kept the law" seem like an anachronism? However, on what basis do ancient Jewish commentaries hold that Abraham kept the Law even before it had been revealed to Israel? What is the "covenant in his flesh"? When was Abraham tested?

For application
1. **44:1.** Why do we honor the saints? What examples do they give us? Although it is not always wise to imitate some of the things the saints did, such as extreme penances, what is there about even these actions that is commendable?
2. **44:8–14.** Whom does the Church celebrate on the feasts of All Saints and All Souls? How often do you remember the souls in Purgatory, especially deceased relatives and friends? How appropriate is it to pray to deceased persons whose virtue you admire for their intercession?
3. **44:19–21.** From Abraham's story in Genesis, what do you most admire about his fidelity? How does it speak to you in your own struggles with trust in the Lord?
4. **44:23.** According to Genesis, Jacob tricked Esau out of his birthright; yet, as Ben Sira says, God acknowledged him in place of the first-born anyway. How has God regarded you despite your faults? How has he fulfilled his plan for your life to date?

Chapter 45

For understanding
1. **45:8.** What part of the high priest's garments were the breeches? What was the "long robe"? What was the ephod? According to Rabanus Maurus, what do the vestments of the high priest signify?
2. **45:9.** On the vestments, what were the pomegranates? Where were the golden bells sewn? On what day could the congregation especially hear the high priest ministering inside the sanctuary?
3. **45:20.** When were the rights, privileges, and responsibilities of the priests increased? What part of the harvest was reserved for the priests? To what does the unusual expression "bread of first fruits" perhaps refer?

4.   **45:23.** Who was Phinehas? After whom was he third in glory? How did he prove himself zealous? By identifying fear of the Lord as the driving force behind Phinehas' action, what does Ben Sira imply? What did Phinehas' action avert?

For application

1.   **45:4.** Moses was known for his meekness, despite being a strict and uncompromising leader of Israel; likewise, Jesus called himself meek and praised meekness in his disciples (Mt 5:5; 11:29). What is meekness? What vice does it oppose? In what way is meekness necessary for persons who exercise authority?
2.   **45:8–12.** What kinds of vestments do priests and bishops wear? Why should their vestments look beautiful and imposing? How does the bishop's miter compare with the high priest's headdress (v. 12)?
3.   **45:15–17.** These verses allude to three of Aaron's priestly roles: to sanctify through sacrifice, to govern with authority, and to teach the commandments. How do Christian bishops and priests exercise these same roles? How do they receive the authority to exercise these roles (see the first part of v. 15)?
4.   **45:25.** The priesthood of Aaron is passed on through lineal descent, from son to son. How is the priesthood of Jesus Christ passed on? How does a candidate for the Christian priesthood discern a vocation?

Chapter 46

For understanding

1.   **46:1.** Who was Joshua the son of Nun? What tribe did he come from, and what was his original name? Because Joshua was considered a prophet, how is the Book of Joshua classified? What does the Hebrew name Joshua mean?
2.   **46:7.** To what period do the days of Moses refer? Who was Caleb, and to what tribe did he belong? When the people murmured, rebelled, and wished to go back to Egypt, who were the only two who supported Moses?
3.   **46:11.** Who were the Judges? Although Ben Sira does not name them, who were the most important? Though Ben Sira says that the hearts of the Judges did not fall into idolatry, why is his comment perhaps stated tongue-in-cheek?
4.   **46:13.** Who was Samuel? As what was he recognized both during his life and after his death? How did Samuel establish the kingdom? How differently does the Hebrew read?

For application

1.   **46:1.** Look up the passage in Luke's Gospel where the angel Gabriel announces to Mary the birth of her son (Lk 1:30–35). How does the pun mentioned in the note for this verse also appear in Gabriel's message? In contrast to the inheritance into which Joshua led the Israelites, into what inheritance does Jesus lead us?
2.   **46:11.** A refrain that runs through parts of the OT, particularly in Judges, is that "doing what is right in [one's] own eyes" is not a good thing (Deut 12:8; Judg 17:6, 21:25; Prov 12:15, 21:2). Why not? In Judges, what were the consequences of doing what each person thought was right? What are the consequences now? Whose eyes determine what it is better to do?
3.   **46:13.** How did the young Samuel learn that the Lord was calling him as a prophet (1 Sam 3:9ff.)? How valuable is this advice in the spiritual life? How does one invite the Lord to speak, and how does one know when the Lord answers?

Chapter 47

For understanding

1.   **47:9.** How does the Hebrew for this verse read? To what initiative of David's in liturgical worship does Ben Sira refer?
2.   **47:11.** What sins of David did God forgive? How did God exalt David's power, and with what expectation for his royal house and his throne?
3.   **47:19.** For what was Solomon notorious? By what was he controlled? According to Origen of Alexandria, what do the many women to whom Solomon gave himself signify? Desiring to investigate them, as one who is knowledgeable and wise, what was he unable to do?
4.   **47:23.** How did Solomon's son Rehoboam cause the people to revolt? To what did this lead, and what did Jeroboam do?

For application

1.   **47:9.** What should music contribute to the liturgy? When Pope Pius X reformed Church music, he placed special emphasis on Gregorian chant. How often have you either heard or sung chant melodies in your parish? At your parish, what is the balance between having a choir perform versus everyone being encouraged to sing?
2.   **47:12–17.** According to v. 13, what seems to have been the God-intended purpose of Solomon's reign? How well did he fulfill it? These verses describe the encyclopedic nature of Solomon's knowledge; however, is knowledge the same as wisdom? If not, what is the difference?
3.   **47:18–19.** Why do peace and prosperity often pose dangers to the faith? During the era of economic prosperity that has followed World War II, how has the Church fared? If this prosperity continues, what do you think the future of the Church will be?
4.   **47:22.** What sort of root from David's stock do you think Ben Sira had in mind? In the Christian understanding, who was that root?

Chapter 48

For understanding

1.   **48:10.** To what does "the appointed time" refer here? With whom did Elijah become identified? What did the prophet Malachi expect the Messiah's forerunner to bring? How would God restore the tribes of Jacob?
2.   **48:12.** What was Elisha's relationship to Elijah? Because Elisha was given a "double share" of Elijah's spirit, what did that make him? During whose reigns did Elisha prophesy, and what position did he take regarding them?

3. **48:15.** Despite Elisha's miracle-working power, on what path did the Northern Kingdom of Israel continue? Who conquered and deported the northern tribes of Israel in the eighth century B.C.? What does the Hebrew state more clearly was the identity of the surviving remnant? In contrast to the rival dynasties in the Northern Kingdom, what happened to the royal Davidic line in the Southern Kingdom?

4. **48:17.** Who was Hezekiah, and what did he accomplish? What is the pun on Hezekiah's name? How did he bring water to Jerusalem?

For application

1. **48:7.** Read the note for this verse. When Elijah came to Sinai, God asked him, "What are you doing here?" (1 Kings 19:9). What happened at Sinai that made Elijah want to go there? Why do Christians go to places where significant events happened? What pilgrimages have you made, and what effects did they have on your faith?

2. **48:12–15.** Periodically, God raises up saints and charismatic leaders to bring about renewal in the Church. What renewal movements are you aware of that either have taken place in the past or are now ongoing? What have been their effects on the Church? When such movements seem to peak and then die out, what long-term legacy do they leave behind?

3. **48:25.** What is the purpose of prophecy? If it is not primarily for the sake of foretelling the future, what does it intend to communicate (see 1 Cor 12–14)? Assuming prophecy still occurs as private revelation, how should Christians judge whether it is genuine?

Chapter 49

For understanding

1. **49:2.** What does the Hebrew for this verse read about Josiah? After the book of the Law was found in the Temple, what was Josiah's reaction? In response, what did he launch?

2. **49:6.** When the Babylonians destroyed Jerusalem and the Temple, what did they do to the people of Judah? Who was Jeremiah? When did he minister in Jerusalem? Of what did he tirelessly warn its last kings?

3. **49:10.** Who were the 12 Minor Prophets? How have they come to be preserved in the Hebrew canon? For what does Ben Sira's prayer that their bones might be revived perhaps express a hope? Although much of their writing warns of judgment and calls for repentance, what picture does Ben Sira present of these Prophets?

4. **49:16.** Who was Shem, and what was his importance? Who was Seth? What name does the Hebrew add? What is said of Adam, the father of humanity?

For application

1. **49:3.** How would you describe the behavior of a person who "sets his heart" upon the Lord? How might his behavior be construed as a threat to some people? Would you like to live with such a person?

2. **49:7.** As recounted in the autobiographical sections of the Book of Jeremiah, what similarities do you notice between his life and that of Jesus? For example, when did God give Jeremiah his mission, and what was it? Why did God call him to remain celibate in a culture when men were expected to marry? How was he treated by the religious authorities?

3. **49:8.** What influence did the Book of Ezekiel have on New Testament writings, particularly on the Revelation to John? How do both works envision heaven and its inhabitants? How are those intended for God identified with a brand or mark in both? What form does that same brand still take in today's Church (hint: at the beginning of the baptismal liturgy)?

4. **49:14.** Catholics believe that the Blessed Virgin Mary was assumed body and soul into heaven. How might the assumptions of Enoch and Elijah validate this dogma?

Chapter 50

For understanding

1. **50:1–24.** To what does praise of Israel's ancestors give way? What does the transition to this chapter following the praise of Adam in 49:16 suggest that Ben Sira wishes to do?

2. **Word Study: High Priest (50:1).** What does the Greek title *hiereus ho megas* mean literally? What did the elaborate garments that the high priest wore represent? What was his primary role, especially on Yom Kippur? By the late Second Temple period, what had the high priest's garments come to represent? Who was the high priest officiating in Jerusalem from 291 to 196 B.C., a short time before Ben Sira wrote his book? In what kind of language does Ben Sira portray him as an "incarnation" of wisdom? What does this language imply?

3. **50:5–21.** Of what are these verses possibly a description? What do others contend is in view? Either way, what does Ben Sira's reuse of language from the poem on wisdom in chap. 24 suggest?

4. **50:24.** How does the Hebrew for this verse read? What easily explains the reason for the difference in textual variations? When Ben Sira's grandson translated the text into Greek, how did he adapt it?

For application

1. **50:1.** The note for this verse says that the high priest Simon fortified the city and the Temple to protect them from enemy attack. How can Christian churches protect themselves from attacks such as bombings and shootings? What if any safety precautions does your church have in place?

2. **50:5–11.** In the Roman Catholic Church, certain vestments, such as the pallium, are reserved for specific members of the clergy, and then only at certain times. When worn, what do such vestments signify? How might Ben Sira's description of the high priest's vestments and the impression they made help us understand the significance of these modern vestments?

3. **50:15.** The expression "blood of the grape" has eucharistic overtones. In Christian art and church decoration, what does the image of a bunch of grapes symbolize? What does the wine consecrated at Mass actually become?

Study Questions

Chapter 51

For understanding
1. **51:1–30.** As possibly an addition to the original text of Sirach, of what does this chapter consist? What does the Hebrew version also include between these two sections?
2. **51:13.** What is one key to becoming wise that Ben Sira offers? What role did Ben Sira's experiences as a well-traveled man abroad play? What reminder does Ben Sira give about wisdom?
3. **51:23.** What does Ben Sira offer here? What literally is his invitation? What does *bet midrash* mean? According to St. Augustine, what does one learn in the Church, the house of instruction?
4. **51:30.** What work is one to do? When? What is your reward? What subscription does the Hebrew text add?

For application
1. **51:13.** When did you begin to sense a desire for a relationship with God? How did you pursue it? What conversion events have you been through, and how have they matured that relationship?
2. **51:19–20.** Have you ever pursued a goal, such as a skill in sports, following a strict regimen? Why is strictness of self-control necessary for that? How does this apply to the practice of virtue? How often and how long should you pray for the grace to be perfect as your Heavenly Father is perfect?
3. **51:23.** St. Paul invites Christians to "be imitators of me, as I am of Christ" (1 Cor 11:1). What aspects of Paul's imitation of Christ should we imitate? How do the lives of other saints encourage this imitation? When would you be able to ask others to imitate you as you imitate Christ?
4. **51:30.** When should you be seeking holiness? How long will it take to achieve it? How does God grant it to you? When will you know that you have received it?

BOOKS OF THE BIBLE

THE OLD TESTAMENT (OT)

Gen	Genesis
Ex	Exodus
Lev	Leviticus
Num	Numbers
Deut	Deuteronomy
Josh	Joshua
Judg	Judges
Ruth	Ruth
1 Sam	1 Samuel
2 Sam	2 Samuel
1 Kings	1 Kings
2 Kings	2 Kings
1 Chron	1 Chronicles
2 Chron	2 Chronicles
Ezra	Ezra
Neh	Nehemiah
Tob	Tobit
Jud	Judith
Esther	Esther
Job	Job
Ps	Psalms
Prov	Proverbs
Eccles	Ecclesiastes
Song	Song of Solomon
Wis	Wisdom
Sir	Sirach (Ecclesiasticus)
Is	Isaiah
Jer	Jeremiah
Lam	Lamentations
Bar	Baruch
Ezek	Ezekiel
Dan	Daniel
Hos	Hosea
Joel °	Joel
Amos	Amos
Obad	Obadiah
Jon	Jonah
Mic	Micah
Nahum	Nahum
Hab	Habakkuk
Zeph	Zephaniah
Hag	Haggai
Zech	Zechariah
Mal	Malachi
1 Mac	1 Maccabees
2 Mac	2 Maccabees

THE NEW TESTAMENT (NT)

Mt	Matthew
Mk	Mark
Lk	Luke
Jn	John
Acts	Acts of the Apostles
Rom	Romans
1 Cor	1 Corinthians
2 Cor	2 Corinthians
Gal	Galatians
Eph	Ephesians
Phil	Philippians
Col	Colossians
1 Thess	1 Thessalonians
2 Thess	2 Thessalonians
1 Tim	1 Timothy
2 Tim	2 Timothy
Tit	Titus
Philem	Philemon
Heb	Hebrews
Jas	James
1 Pet	1 Peter
2 Pet	2 Peter
1 Jn	1 John
2 Jn	2 John
3 Jn	3 John
Jude	Jude
Rev	Revelation (Apocalypse)